A Culture
of Deference

PETER LANG
New York • Washington, D.C./Baltimore • Bern
Frankfurt am Main • Berlin • Brussels • Vienna • Oxford

F. Ugboaja Ohaegbulam

A Culture
of Deference

Congress, the President,
and the Course of the U.S.-Led Invasion
and Occupation of Iraq

PETER LANG
New York • Washington, D.C./Baltimore • Bern
Frankfurt am Main • Berlin • Brussels • Vienna • Oxford

Library of Congress Cataloging-in-Publication Data
Ohaegbulam, Festus Ugboaja.
A culture of deference: Congress, the President, and the course
of the U.S.-led invasion and occupation of Iraq / F. Ugboaja Ohaegbulam.
p. cm.
Includes bibliographical references and index.
1. War and emergency powers—United States. 2. United States. President.
3. United States. Congress. 4. Executive-legislative relations—United States.
5. Iraq War, 2003– 6. United States—Politics and government—2001– I. Title.
JK558.O53   956.7044'31—dc22   2006101473
ISBN 978-0-8204-9544-6 (hardcover)
ISBN 978-0-8204-9538-5 (paperback)

Bibliographic information published by **Die Deutsche Bibliothek**.
Die Deutsche Bibliothek lists this publication in the "Deutsche
Nationalbibliografie"; detailed bibliographic data is available
on the Internet at http://dnb.ddb.de/.

Map on cover courtesy of www.theodora.com/maps.

The paper in this book meets the guidelines for permanence and durability
of the Committee on Production Guidelines for Book Longevity
of the Council of Library Resources.

Printed in the United States of America

To my wife Emma B. and our daughter Adanna Ogechi

Table of Contents

Chapter 1
Introduction

The United States has gone down a road in which the use of force has become a chronic feature of US foreign policy and the country's security has been weakened rather than bolstered as a consequence.[1]

Today [in 2005] a transportation bill [receives] more deliberation [in the US Congress] than a decision to send American troops to war. It seems safe to assume that this is not what the Framers [of the US Constitution] intended. They worked hard to ensure that the power to spend American lives and treasure be exercised collectively and wisely. Their solution is written in the Constitution itself.[2]

This [war in Iraq] is President [George W.] Bush's war, and America's failure will be his legacy.[3]

The central thesis of this study is that the resolution by the 107th Congress of the United States in October 2002 authorizing President George W. Bush, *as he determines to be necessary and appropriate*, to go to war in Iraq was constitutionally an aberration. The Constitution designates the president as the commander in chief of the armed forces only in wars declared by Congress and in wars to "repel sudden aggression." To refer loosely to the president as the commander in chief, as the George W. Bush administration and, indeed, the American public generally are doing is to make an expansive use of the specifically limited designation. The president is not commander in chief of civilians. He is not even commander in chief of National Guard troops unless and until they are called into actual service of the United States or federalized. The Constitution is very clear on its allocation of the power to declare war. It vests in Congress the power to decide the ultimate question as to whether the nation shall or shall not go to war. This required the 107th Congress, at least, to do the following: hold hearings of officials and non-governmental experts; independently examine and establish credible evidence of any alleged threats or rationale for war; and assess the objectives, costs, strategies, and ramifications and probable consequences of the contemplated war. Deliberate action along these lines would ultimately inform the votes of its members after a full-floor, sustained debate.

In passing the Iraq Resolution, the 107th Congress ignored these requirements. It abdicated its own critical part of the shared responsibility and thus doubled that of the presidency without attaching any conditions. Historically, it became the first to do so. Hearings and debates on the Bush administration's draft resolution were rushed. They did not deliberately require of President Bush any certifications to Congress of any credible evidence of his justification to go to war. The 107th Congress did not independently examine and establish such evidence or the costs and aftermath of the war. Nor did its resolution, in keeping with the American tradition, require the president to exhaust all other options before embarking on war as a last resort. Therefore, the resolution was both unwarranted and an excessive, unguided, and uncontrollable delegation of its authority to President Bush. By such delegation, the 107th Congress fundamentally shifted its constitutional role from one of ultimate authority to one of subordinate supporter of the executive branch.

As the George W. Bush administration waged the authorized war, the succeeding 108th and 109th Congresses also, like their immediate predecessor, abdicated one of the key roles of Congress: oversight of the Bush administration to make sure that as it waged the war the administration was faithfully executing relevant provisions of the Constitution. So far, over the four-year course of the war, congressional oversight of the administration's conduct of the war and other foreign and national security policy virtually collapsed.[4] Very seldom did the lawmakers ask tough questions of the administration and the military or challenge wartime decisions of the Bush administration, or investigate allegations of torture of prisoners at Abu Ghraib, Iraq, and detainees at Guantanamo Bay, Cuba.

This pattern of behavior represented a clear manifestation of what in recent years has become a consistent pattern of abdication of its constitutional responsibility by the Congress as well as its culture of deference to the executive branch on foreign policy issues. The pattern contributed to the trend towards an imperial presidency and a move away from the idea of a republic. Also, it demonstrates how easily, at considerable cost in human and material resources, the United States has gone to war over the past forty years.[5]

It is important to explore how this pattern and culture of deference to the executive on war making developed and to assess its impact not only on the United States as a republic and global leader but also on US relations with the rest of the world. Apparently, the resolution echoed a previous fateful resolution by Congress: the 1964 Gulf of Tonkin Resolution which gave President Lyndon B. Johnson the authority "to take all necessary steps, including armed forces, to assist any member or protocol state of the Southeast Asia Collective Defense Treaty (SEATO) requesting assistance." At that time, members of Congress thought that passage of the resolution was not an endorsement of war but rather a bipartisan support of President Johnson that could avoid war with North Vietnam.[6] Senator J. William Fulbright, at that time chairman of the Senate Foreign Relations Committee and floor manager of the resolution, believed that the resolution was "calculated to prevent the spread of...war, rather than to spread it."[7]

In seeking and obtaining the authorization to use military force against another country, President Johnson, like President George W. Bush after him, enjoyed the trust of Congress as well as that of a docile press that accommodated both the request for the authorization and the story of the incident that precipitated the request. It did not matter that there was much doubt about the circumstances of the alleged attacks by North Vietnamese torpedo boats on two American destroyers—the *Maddox* and the *C. Turner Joy*—on patrol in the Gulf of Tonkin or indeed whether any attack on them that provoked the resolution had occurred.[8] Later, investigations by the staff of the Senate Foreign Relations Committee concluded that the executive branch had either fabricated or exaggerated the attacks. Tapes he made in the White House in the early days of the Vietnam War show that, only weeks after Congress had authorized him to wage the war in 1964, President Johnson privately acknowledged that the incident that inspired the resolution probably never happened. "When we got through with all the firing" [on the two American destroyers], Johnson said ruefully to his secretary of defense, Robert S. McNamara, "we concluded maybe [the North Vietnamese] hadn't fired at all."[9] Nevertheless, President Johnson used the resolution prompted by the alleged attacks on the destroyers to escalate US intervention in Vietnam. Eventually, the resolution was symbolically repealed in 1970 after the Richard M. Nixon administration had secretly expanded the Vietnam War to Cambodia in May 1970.

The Bush administration's justification for the Iraq Resolution—the threat of Iraq armed with weapons of mass destruction—proved to be a fabrication more so than a failure of US intelligence. The US media demonstrated no curiosity regarding the veracity of the case the Bush administration made for the war while, at the same time, it was masquerading at the UN for a diplomatic solution. Rather, they became more chauvinistic and patriotic in their language on the need to disarm Iraq of its alleged weapons of mass destruction.[10] In particular, Judith Miller of the *New York Times,* relying on a small circle of highly interested official sources (often anonymous), became the leading journalistic purveyor of dubious allegations that Saddam Hussein had weapons of mass destruction and was tied to al-Qaeda terrorist groups.[11] Even more incredibly, the media displayed an unusual silence on two major developments regarding the Bush administration's invasion of Iraq.

The first development was an opinion editorial in the *New York Times* (6 July 2003) by former US Ambassador Joseph Wilson IV asking whether the Bush administration had manipulated intelligence about Saddam Hussein's weapons programs to justify an invasion of Iraq. The ambassador went on to assert that, based on his experience with the administration in the months leading up to the war in Iraq, he had "little choice but to conclude that some of the intelligence related to Iraq's nuclear weapons program was twisted to exaggerate the Iraqi threat."[12] The former ambassador had been sent on a mission by the Central Intelligence Agency (CIA) to Niger to verify a report about a memorandum of agreement that documented the sale of uranium yellowcake by Niger to Iraq. His findings led him to conclude that there had been no such sale and that news accounts pointed out that the documents had glaring errors and were probably forged. The findings of the US ambassador to Niger at the time of the mission, who was briefed by Wilson, were consistent with those findings and conclusions. Accordingly, Wilson reported them to the CIA and to the Africa Bureau of the Department of State. It was after the Bush administration repeated the charges, especially in the January 2003 State of the Union address, about Iraq's efforts to purchase uranium from Africa that Wilson wrote his opinion editorial. He suggested that at "a minimum Congress, which authorized the use of military force" in Iraq at the president's behest, "should want to know if the assertions about Iraq were warranted." Congress expressed no such interest or desire to know. Instead, the lawmakers put their parochial short-term politics ahead of the national interest and their need to know.

For their part, instead of pursuing the serious question raised in Wilson's opinion editorial, certain members of the media allowed themselves to be used by high officials of the Bush administration in efforts to discredit and victimize the former ambassador by revealing that his wife was a CIA agent.[13] Thus, the administration effectively subverted the free press in its efforts to misinform the public. This leads one to conclude that what used to be known as investigative journalism became, under the manipulations of the George W. Bush administration, "a glittering and carefully choreographed waltz in which all the dancers shared the unspoken agreement that the one unpardonable faux pas is to ask who is calling the tune."[14]

The other major development to which the media remained incredibly silent was a leaked memo—the Downing Street Memo—published in the *Sunday Times* of London in May 2005. Actually, the memo was the minutes of British Prime Minister Tony Blair's meeting with his cabinet colleagues in July 2002.

During that meeting, the chief of British overseas intelligence briefed his colleagues about his recent visit with officials of the Bush administration in Washington. Among other things, he informed them that President Bush had decided "to remove Saddam Hussein [from power in Iraq] through military action justified by the conjunction of terrorism and WMD [weapons of mass destruction]." For five weeks after the release of this information, the US media ignored this revelation, which meant that President Bush had decided on waging war to remove Saddam Hussein of Iraq from office months before he sought authorization from the US Congress to do so and for a reason other than what he had told the American people. The media assent to the administration through silence definitely contributed in no small way to lubricate its march to the war against Iraq.

For their part, members of Congress, in spite of their large staff, ignored the avalanche of other information that was publicly available casting doubt on the Bush administration's case for war. Rather, they allowed themselves to be persuaded by unsubstantiated claims by a hawkish Bush administration about threats from a nuclear-armed Iraq to grant the administration the authority to make a decision that was constitutionally and traditionally theirs. Apparently, given the obvious passion and hawkish disposition of the Bush administration for war, they were naive to hope that their resolution would make the use of military force against Iraq unnecessary. What the resolution accomplished, instead, was to embolden an ideologically driven and secretive administration to enhance its power in its drive towards an imperial presidency. As such, the resolution appeared to be a more serious threat to American democracy and its constitutional system than the Bush administration's perceived threat from Iraq.

For the United States, the consequences of the earlier Vietnam War were enormous. They included, among other things, an estimated cost of $167 billion, an inflation that dislocated the US economy, "internal division and rioting in American streets, a drug plague that infected several US troops and returned to America with them, and over 58,000 American casualties."[15] The Vietnam intervention also bitterly demonstrated the limits of doctrines—the domino theory in this case—the impotence of force in certain situations, and America's internal fragility. There are echoes of that experience in the Iraq War. Did Congress indicate it had learned any lessons from the resolution that culminated in the Vietnam intervention and its aftermath when it passed a similar resolution at the request of President George W. Bush? Had it forgotten so soon the aura of imperial presidency associated with the Vietnam War? Had it forgotten that the Vietnam experience made it far less costly for its members to challenge a president pursuing a belligerent policy? Or was it no longer cognizant and appreciative of the use of its power of the purse to make its preferences felt by the executive branch?

The Bush administration's war of choice in Iraq has been the focus of many scholarly works.[16] No study has similarly focused on the action of the US Congress in authorizing President Bush to wage war in Iraq at his own discretion. This study attempts to provide that focus. It explores the culture of deference by Congress to the executive on foreign policy issues, particularly with respect to the George W. Bush administration's war in Iraq. Contextually, it summarizes the constitutional provisions for the conduct and management of American foreign policy: specifically, how and why the Constitution shares foreign policy powers among the three branches of the US government. It identifies the war powers as constitutionally those of Congress and demonstrates how, historically, in spite of that fact, presidents have engaged in war making and how Congress has attempted without much success to curb such war making. Providing a historical background to President George W. Bush's war in Iraq, the book documents how doggedly his administration made the case for war. The author argues that by authorizing Bush to go to war in Iraq at his own discretion, the 107th Congress abdicated its constitutional responsibility and its members failed to uphold their oath to uphold the Constitution of the United States. The book traces how this culture of deference to the chief executive on foreign policy and war making evolved and how, especially in the case of the war in Iraq, it has adversely affected the interests of the nation, its constitutional framework, and its position in the world.

Chapter 2
Terrorism and the
Foreign Policy of
President George W. Bush

Prior to the terrorist attacks of 11 September 2001 on US territory, President George W. Bush had no real foreign policy.

When George W. Bush became president in January 2001, the United States confronted several continuing and emerging foreign policy issues. These included such prominent foreign policy issues as the proliferation of weapons of mass destruction, global environmental degradation, the creation of the International Criminal Court, global migration, military and defense spending, the Israeli-Palestinian peace process, and the threat of terrorism. About eight months after Bush's inauguration, terrorism emerged as the most dominant foreign policy issue of his presidency. Suddenly and unexpectedly on 11 September 2001, about 19 members of Osama bin Laden's al-Qaeda terrorist network audaciously bombed the World Trade Center towers in New York and the west section of the Pentagon in Washington, D.C.—two powerful symbols of America's economic and political might. Their plan to attack another US target was foiled by passengers in the fourth of the hijacked American airplanes that the terrorists used as their weapons.

The magnitude of those terrorist attacks was huge. The attacks leveled both the north and south towers of the World Trade Center and the west section of the Pentagon and killed about 3,000 people. The events left an indelible mark on the United States of America. They served abrupt notice of a challenge to US global dominance, indicating at the same time that the United States' defense of its post–cold war status and global stability would not be cheap. Thus, they aroused great fear and emotions among American nationals about the security and economic well-being of their nation. Indeed, to most leaders of both the Democratic and Republican Parties, 11 September was the defining event of the new millennium, after which nothing could ever again be the same. Also very significantly, the events provided President George W. Bush a critical lever first for domestic mobilization and consensus just as the cold war had done and, second, for diversion from controversial domestic issues. Furthermore, the events would soon seriously affect public liberties and the rule of law in the United States. Witness the USA PATRIOT Act (see below) which was hurriedly enacted by Congress in the wake of those criminal events. But also, they generated great sympathy around the world for America and families of the victims and changed the way American leaders see and approach the world.

Perhaps more importantly, the catalytic tragic events of 11 September 2001 transformed the Bush presidency, although they did not transform the president's unilateralist proclivity and view of the world. The attacks

> produced immediate and striking changes within the White House. [Vice President] Cheney snapped into action on 9/11 and immediately went from being a very influential conservative vice president into the hub of the ideologically driven policy formation process his colleagues described. [Defense Secretary] Rumsfeld... the most-likely cabinet member to depart early, was redeemed that day, and the primacy of his department for the foreseeable future was insured. The importance of [National Security Advisor] Rice to a president for whom national security was now the central issue grew geometrically, and she was drawn inexorably to his side and away from the process and the institution she might otherwise have managed. The neocons [in the administration] saw the opportunity to assert their case that diplomatic balancing acts in the Middle East had created danger for the United States and that the time had come for stronger measures whatever the cost.[17]

It is no wonder that, given these changes in the wake of the 11 September attacks, Bush chose to interpret the facts of the tragedy to suit his world view and sense of mission. Hence, "precisely, the war on terrorism [and how to wage it], became the defining mission of his presidency."[18] Indeed, to him, terrorism came to resemble the cold war as the central organizing idea around which he sought to restructure American foreign policy. The exception was that he abjured the multilateral strategies of US containment policy during the cold war. Critical constraints on decisions were muted, if not entirely removed, by the end of the cold war and the collapse of the Soviet Union. Thereafter, there was no more calculating of what the Soviet reaction might be to policy decisions. Unburdened by such considerations, the Bush administration showed little if any concern with the consequences of its actions beyond how the American people would respond. The national mind-set developed and instilled in the wake of the 11 September 2001 terrorist attacks ensured that such a response would be a relatively diminished one. Because Bush was someone who knew what he wanted to do and only wanted to hear how to get it done, that response eventually suited Bush very well.

It was in this manner that, immediately after the surprise attacks, an appropriate American response began to preoccupy and dominate the Bush administration's approach to all other foreign policy issues. The attacks provided the administration a much-needed political capital. President Bush deliberately exaggerated their significance and gave them a global and undifferentiated meaning. Further, he exploited their trauma. By playing with virtuosity on the fears of the American public, he used the occasion of the attacks as a propitious lever to increase his administration's power and grip on the nation. Consequently, the terrorist assault changed the political and strategic priorities of American foreign policy and opened for the US administration a new era of international politics and an opportunity to alter the overall US strategic conception of global security. As elaborated in chapter 7, it allowed the administration to carry out preexisting policy goals under the banner of a war on terror and regime change in Iraq.

Leading neoconservative ideologues, such as Paul Wolfowitz, Dick Cheney, Donald Rumsfeld, and Richard Perle, who earlier had served in the Ronald Reagan and George H. W. Bush administrations came to office in the George W. Bush administration nursing disappointment and anger against the former presidents for not implementing their plans and neoconservative dreams. They assumed office in the George W. Bush administration with a preconceived notion that American foreign policy in the twenty-first century should be guided by the need to establish US dominance over virtually all of Eurasia and that the aim of US foreign policy should be to remake the world and to use America's overwhelming military power preemptively to remove threats and promote democracy worldwide. These dreams had been articulated in the Defense Planning Guidance of 1992, nicknamed "the masterpiece of Dick Cheney" but co-authored by Paul Wolfowitz and Lewis "Scooter" Libby. Among other things, the Defense Planning Guidance explicitly introduced the necessity of US unilateral action, imposing constraints on US allies, and intervention anywhere and stressed the use of America's unrivaled military power to preempt the proliferation of weapons of mass destruction.[19]

These neoconservatives in the Bush administration saw the occasion of the tragic attacks on 11 September 2001 as an opportunity to implement their ideology. Immediately after the attacks, without any credible evidence, Iraq, ruled by a widely known brutal dictator and already believed by many within and outside the United States to possess weapons of mass destruction, was linked by President Bush's top neoconservative advisers to Osama bin Laden and the al-Qaeda terrorists who had perpetrated the attacks. The advisers exploited the terrorist attacks, as well as George W. Bush's lack of both foreign policy experience and clearly visible priorities, to make a strong case for "regime change" in the Persian Gulf nation. They were concerned that, unless

Saddam was preemptively removed from office, he would provide the terrorists weapons of mass destruction with which to attack the United States and its allies. They believed that such a change would democratize the Middle East and ensure the security of Israel. These were tasks, they insisted, that the United States with its unprecedented power had to accomplish regardless of the existing international order as represented by the United Nations.

Meanwhile, President Bush himself found a grandiose purpose in the presidency: making the United States and the world "safer and better." He told his political strategist Karl Rove that, just as his father's generation had been called in World War II, his own generation was being called. "'I am here for a reason,' he claimed, 'and this is going to be how we're going to be judged.... We have an opportunity to restructure the world toward freedom, and we have to get it right.'"[20] As part of his efforts to restructure the world and to get it right, Bush declared war on terrorism and proclaimed himself "a war president." In his address on 20 September 2001 before a joint session of Congress, Bush declared,

> I will not forget this wound to our country or those who inflicted it. I will not yield; I will not rest; I will not relent in waging this struggle for freedom and security for the American people.[21]

On the same occasion, Bush announced the creation of a cabinet-level Homeland Security Office (now Homeland Security Department), amalgamating twenty-two agencies into one. The new agency was charged with the responsibility of devising measures to identify, prevent, and, if necessary, respond to an attack on the United States. It immediately took several measures to protect American airports and cities and to curtail terrorists' flow of funds. Bush also outlined a multipronged global approach, including military, diplomatic, intelligence, law enforcement, and financial means and every necessary weapon of war, to foil global terrorist activities.[22] In keeping with the approach, any state struck by terrorists, regardless of whether its own acts had nurtured terrorism and its methods were similar to those of terrorists, could count on American support. Such support was one of the means of legitimizing America's attempt to suppress terrorism. Bush went further to issue Executive Order 13224 on 24 September 2001, freezing terrorist assets and denying access to US markets to all foreign banks that refused to cooperate in seizing terrorists' assets. In launching these activities against terror, Bush paid no comparable attention to addressing simultaneously the deeper causes of global instability and terrorism: poverty and political and social injustice, especially as a consequence of some US foreign policy tradeoffs in the Middle East and around the world.

In addition to these measures, the Bush administration introduced sweeping legislative proposals entitled Uniting and Strengthening America by Providing Appropriate Tools Required to Intercept and Obstruct Terrorism Act of 2001 (USA PATRIOT Act), which the Attorney General John Ashcroft asked Congress to pass without changes within a week. Without providing the traditional system of checks and balances to safeguard civil liberties, the proposed bill introduced a superabundance of legislative changes that increased enormously the surveillance and investigative powers of US law enforcement officials.[23] For example, it authorizes agents of the Federal Bureau of Investigation (FBI) to conduct secret searches of homes of people suspected of being terrorists, to increase wiretaps, and to examine the files of banks, universities, libraries, airlines, and other entities without warning. Congress, many of whose members did not even read the bill, hastily passed it (357 to 66 in the House and only one dissenting voice [Senator Russ Feingold] in the Senate) with little debate and without a House-Senate Conference report. The events of 11 September 2001 had so convinced the vast majorities in Congress that law enforcement and national security officials needed vastly increased authority to fight terrorism that no deliberate effort was made to debate the proposed changes. Indeed, Attorney General Ashcroft had warned Congress that further terrorists acts were imminent and that it could be blamed for such attacks if it failed to pass the bill immediately.[24] Congress obliged. President Bush signed the bill (USA PATRIOT Act) into law on 26 October 2001, forty-five days after the 11 September attacks.

Among other things, the USA PATRIOT Act

- Expands terrorism laws to include "domestic terrorism," which could subject political organizations to surveillance, wiretapping, harassment, and criminal action for political advocacy.
- Expands the ability of law enforcement to conduct secret searches and gives them wide powers of phone and Internet surveillance and access to highly personal medical, financial, mental health, and student records with minimal judicial oversight.
- Allows FBI agents to investigate American citizens for criminal matters without probable cause of crime if they say it is for "intelligence purposes."
- Permits noncitizens to be jailed based on mere suspicion and to be denied readmission to the United States for engaging in free speech. Suspects

convicted of no crime may be detained indefinitely in six-month increments without meaningful judicial review.[25]

These expanded powers granted to law enforcement officials provoked widespread criticism against the USA PATRIOT Act at home and abroad. Critics denounced it as threatening the civil liberties of American citizens as well as those of resident foreign nationals.[26]

While some critics denounced what they perceived as the administration's threat to civil liberties, others regarded the response of its top neoconservative advisers to the terrorist attacks of 11 September 2001 as counterproductive to US national security interests broadly defined. These advisers tended to silence opposing views. As noted above, they vigorously advocated a unilateral preemptive war to remove perceived threats, such as those they believed were represented by Saddam Hussein in Iraq, and to promote freedom and democracy worldwide. Their critics believed that, for a more pragmatic response, President Bush needed a very effective, shrewd but honest broker. Such a broker would make sure that he heard from all sides of a foreign policy debate and considered the consequences before acting. His national security adviser at the time, Condoleezza Rice, did not effectively perform this function. Although inexperienced, she was very close to the president and had his ear. "But she seemed to use [the privileged position] to tell him only what he wanted to hear. Her staff knew the evidence that Saddam Hussein was actively pursuing nuclear weapons was dubious at best, yet [she] fanned those fears to promote her boss's ill-advised [quest for the invasion of Iraq]."[27]

Unlike her onetime mentor Brent Scowcroft, who believed that the United States could not succeed in the world without working with and through friends, allies, and international organizations, Rice accepted the doctrine of a unilateral preemptive war advocated by the Bush administration's neoconservatives without deliberately considering the consequences of the doctrine. "She [allowed] herself to be pushed around by [Defense Secretary] Donald Rumsfeld and [Vice President] Dick Cheney. Rice saw herself more as a personal adviser to the president than as a referee of bureaucratic battles. But by narrowly defining her role, she [allowed] Rumsfeld's Defense Department to become…a 'thumb on the scales' of debate, and permitted Dick Cheney's shadow national security staff to end-run the regular foreign policy-making process."[28]

As Bush's national security adviser, Rice was also weak in coordinating the foreign policy-making system.[29] Deputy Secretary of State Richard Armitage, during Bush's first term, believed that the foreign policy-making system that she was supposed to coordinate was essentially dysfunctional. He bluntly told her so and added that foreign policy was not sufficiently debated and then settled.[30] It is therefore not surprising that, in hindsight, she herself "candidly predicted...that it would take 30 or 40 years before we know whether [the foreign policy] initiatives of the Bush administration were 'really creative responses' to 9/11 or 'disastrous' ones."[31]

The George W. Bush Approach to Foreign Policy

It was in this manner that Bush began his presidency with a propensity to demolish the caution and "assertive multilateralism" policies of his immediate predecessor, Bill Clinton. The Clinton administration conducted foreign policy on the premise that the United States could not resolve the world's many problems solely by itself and that many of the nation's most important objectives could not be achieved without the cooperation of other members of the international community. Hence its policy of assertive multilateralism: collective action through the building of international institutions and through multilateral diplomacy.

Immediately after the end of the cold war, Clinton's predecessor, George H. W. Bush, had similarly espoused the need to eschew unilateralism and promote a new world order in which the United States would lead the world community in addressing its needs and problems under UN auspices with the cooperation of its member states. Essentially, his new world order strategy sought to convince potential competitors that they did not need to fear the United States or aspire to a greater role. Also, the elder Bush sought to uphold the policy of his predecessors towards the Middle East, which was to maintain stability in the region.

But George W. Bush, Clinton's successor and the son of George H. W. Bush, guided by neoconservatives—such as Dick Cheney, Donald Rumsfeld, and Paul Wolfowitz—rejected the approach of his two immediate predecessors. His belief was that the United States did not need to reach out to traditional friends and allies or rely on the international institutions to promote and protect America's interests, since it had an unrivaled military might to do so. He also believed that his predecessors had mistakenly stressed stability over democracy in the Middle East.

Bush described his approach to foreign policy as "new realism," which would shift the focus of American efforts away from the Clinton administration's multilateralism, "preoccupation with nation building, international social work, and the promiscuous use of force, toward cultivating great-power relations and rebuilding the nation's military."[32] He shared the view of his neoconservative advisers that the multilateral policy adopted by Clinton and his predecessors since the end of World War II was threatening the nation's sovereignty and weakening its capacity to use its vast power and influence to maximum advantage. America, therefore, had to chart a new course in its foreign policy.

From the perspective of the administration's neoconservative advisers, Bush's immediate predecessors had dangerously reduced military expenditures. Bill Clinton especially, whose policy Bush himself believed had been risk averse, had allowed threats to US national security, such as terrorism and the pursuit of weapons of mass destruction by Iran, Iraq, and North Korea, among others, to gather by relying on multilateral institutions and by not confronting the threats aggressively enough. Clinton was particularly accused of lacking "moral clarity" and the conviction to pursue unilaterally US strategic interests abroad. When the country was challenged or attacked, Clinton's response, Donald Rumsfeld asserted, was "reflexive pullback."[33]

According to Richard Perle, one of the most high-profile neoconservatives, an aggressive policy against these threats called for a departure from the Clinton administration approach. It required the United States to shed all of the norms of international law and reliance on multilateral institutions that constrain its power but are incapable of defending its national security interests. Therefore, he insisted that the United States cannot abdicate responsibility for its own security. "Multilateralism," he said, "is preferable...but if the only way you can get consensus is by abandoning your most fundamental interests, then it is not helpful."[34] The critical and rational choice then becomes unilateralism.

Richard Perle went on to argue that the Clinton administration had gone so overboard with multilateralism that it "created the impression that the United States was just another country," that it "would be bound in the same way that every little dictatorship in Africa would be bound...and would behave the way everyone else would behave."[35] This reasoning was part of the core of neoconservative ideology that brought about the George W. Bush administration's rejection of the Kyoto Protocol on Climate Change and the International Criminal Court, withdrawal from the Anti-Ballistic Missile (ABM) Treaty, and scuttling of the Land Mine Treaty and the Comprehensive Test Ban Treaty. Such rejection of diplomatic and multilateral efforts to deal with global security and other issues antagonized much of the world, including America's European allies.

Besides the unilateralist approach, the administration's new realism also refocused emphasis in the Middle East from stability to democratization of the entire region. Bush disparaged the Clinton administration's efforts towards resolving the interminable Israeli-Palestinian conflict—perhaps, the greatest emotional issue and most potent cause of instability in the entire Middle East. At the beginning of the administration, Bush's Secretary of State Colin Powell maintained that, in the Israel-Palestine peace process, the United States would "assist but not insist" on any modality of a resolution of the conflict. Barring that, the administration was extremely slow to declare publicly its policy. It was mainly in response to pressures from Saudi Arabia, Europe, and the British Prime Minister Tony Blair, as he waged the war in Iraq, that Bush declared his administration's support for a future independent Palestinian state.[36] But even so, his administration made no appreciable determined effort to bring that about by serving as an honest broker between Israel and the Palestinians. A diplomatic blueprint named the "road map" which the administration backed and which laid down a step-by-step path to an independent Palestinian state alongside Israel languished from the date it was unveiled in 2003 because neither government of Israel nor the Palestinian authority had fulfilled initial commitments. On 19 February 2007, the administration's first peace talks convened in six years between Israeli and Palestinian leaders by the Secretary of State Condoleezza Rice ended without any apparent concrete progress beyond an agreement to meet again. Rice expressed her intention to keep pursuing the process for the rest of her tenure in office.[37]

It was in this manner that the administration's "revolutionary" policy moved away from those of his predecessors. Bush's moves through existing international institutions immediately after the terrorist attacks of 11 September 2001 were seen by observers as tactical responses to those attacks instead of a fundamental conversion from his unilateralist and revolutionary preferences to the multilateralist creed.[38]

As the Republican Party presidential candidate in 2000, Bush flatly rejected any participation of US armed forces in nation building. US soldiers, he said, should be engaged mainly in fighting wars in order to conserve military strength. Similarly, he was opposed to multilateral humanitarian intervention in such places as Somalia, Rwanda, and Kosovo. Initially, as president, Bush remained committed to these beliefs. Soon, however, the war he declared on terrorism would cause him to engage in nation building in Afghanistan and Iraq.

In its National Security Strategy of the United States of America, the Bush administration emphasized the obvious: The United States "possessed unprecedented—and unequaled—strength and influence in the world." The administration assumed that global peace and stability required the use of such strength and maintenance of this primacy. Hence, Bush decided on increasing US defense spending as not only an insurance policy that allows the United States to take risks but also one that enables it "to dissuade potential adversaries from pursuing a military build-up in hopes of surpassing, or equaling, the power of the United States."[39]

Besides increasing defense spending, the Bush administration said it would restructure and transform America's national security institutions, so that they can meet the challenges and opportunities of the twenty-first century. He would ensure US access to bases and stations within and beyond Western Europe and Northeast Asia, as well as arrangements for long-distance deployment of forces. Thus, the United States was to maintain its "defenses beyond challenge." Collectively, these measures would meet the nation's requirements to contend with uncertainty and security challenges. However, American power would be deployed only to encourage "free and open societies," not to seek "unilateral advantage." But one observer asserted that the administration's militarization of foreign policy left it increasingly dependent on the armed forces to carry out its foreign affairs.[40]

President Bush also decided on deploying a national missile defense system even before research proved the capabilities of the system[41] and while scientists were almost unanimous in arguing against the efficacy of the system. In pursuit of the unproven system, Bush unilaterally abrogated the Anti-Ballistic Missile (ABM) Treaty with Russia in spite of strong opposition by Russia and other countries. He argued that the treaty was a cold war relic that had been overtaken by post–cold war realities of rogue states and international terrorism and so was no longer relevant to America's necessary strategic framework. The new realities, President Bush stressed, demanded a fundamental change in US strategy, response to emerging threats, and its counter-proliferation efforts. The United States, he said, would no longer rely on counter-proliferation treaties and promises, because they had failed. It would preemptively strike against states and terrorist groups it perceived as being "close to acquiring weapons of mass destruction or the long range missiles capable of delivering them." The United States would also "stop transfers of weapons components in or out of the borders" of such states.[42]

Critics claimed that Bush rushed to deploy the missile defense system in his attempt to boost his reelection chances, but his reelection was followed by more embarrassing test failures of the system. A Pentagon panel of outside rocketry experts described the system as "pie in the sky" and offered the president two pieces of advice: "Manage quality first and then schedule; reorient the program and actually make testing success, not the political calendar, the primary objective."[43] Also, several retired admirals urged him "to cut taxpayer losses and shift money to the more imminent threat of low-tech terrorism at the nation's vulnerable ports, borders and nuclear weapon depots."[44] President Bush ignored each piece of advice and cited North Korea's plan to develop nuclear missiles as a worthy justification for his persistence on the deployment of a national missile defense system.

President Bush focused a great deal of attention on combating terrorism, which he regarded as the underlying and most serious source of global instability. As part of the war he declared on terrorism, he demanded that the Taliban government of Afghanistan, which had provided a safe haven for Osama bin Laden and al-Qaeda's terrorist training camps, should hand bin Laden over to the United States. When the Taliban government refused to do so, Bush ordered military actions against it and all al-Qaeda targets. Military strikes began in October 2001. By the end of 2001, the military actions had succeeded in overthrowing the Taliban. However, they failed to capture bin Laden and his deputy, although several of his lieutenants were either captured or killed.

After the successful military action in Afghanistan, terrorism and the war against it continued. Although Africa does not rank with the Middle East or Southeast Asia as a top priority in the war against terrorism, the Bush administration extended the war to the continent. For example, it designated the Greater Horn of Africa—an area that includes the Sudan, Eritrea, Djibouti, Ethiopia, Somalia, Kenya, Uganda, and Tanzania—as a front-line region in the global war on terrorism. The region had been the scene of massive bombings outside US embassies in August 1998, as well as other subsequent terrorist activities. In 2002, the administration initiated a program—the Combined Joint Task Force—Horn of Africa (CJTF-HOA)—to dismantle al-Qaeda terrorist infrastructure in the region. Based in Djibouti, CJTF-HOA involves about 1,800 US soldiers. It is backed by the US Central Command and assisted by a multinational naval interdiction force. Specifically, its mission is to deter, preempt, and disable terrorist threats originating mainly from Somalia, Kenya, and Yemen in the Persian Gulf.[45] In addition to initiating this mission in the Greater Horn of Africa, the Bush administration engaged with Senegal, Mali, Niger, and Chad—in west Africa—in the Pan-Sahel Initiative, a program designed to bolster security and intelligence along the Sahara's southern border. In December 2006, Pentagon officials announced that the Bush administration planned to create a new military command for Africa–The US African Command or AFRICOM–which would focus on anti-terrorist operations, border security and humanitarian aid. In addition, said the officials, the command would oversee strategic developments and military operations across the entire continent. The plan is indicative of Africa's growing strategic importance to the United States as well as the Bush administration's concerns with the problems of political instability in such places as Somalia and the Darfur region of Sudan which create havens for Islamic militants allied with al-Qaeda terrorists.[46]

Meanwhile, before the focus on Africa, the administration's top officials had articulated a need for regime change in Iraq. President Bush had identified Iraq as part of an "axis of evil" harboring terrorists and defying the UN Security Council's resolution that it disarm itself of its weapons of mass destruction. The administration became preoccupied with forcibly disarming the nation preemptively to prevent its supplying weapons of mass destruction to terrorists. The preoccupation culminated in the invasion of Iraq in March 2003 by a US-led "coalition of the willing." The administration hoped that political change in Iraq would help to democratize the Middle East and contribute positively to the global war on terrorism.

The administration's preoccupation with the war on terrorism and in Iraq preempted its attention to other challenges. It forced the administration to ignore other challenges to US primacy in the world, such as the process of economic globalization and its close association with the United States and the difficulties faced by past world powers in preserving their advantages.[47] The eventual war in Iraq provided the Taliban an opportunity to regroup and fight the Afghanistan government and its American and other allies.

A significant aspect of the Bush administration's approach to foreign policy which should not be ignored is the role of religion on that approach. Like many of his predecessors in office President Bush frequently invoked his religious beliefs to justify or explain his foreign policy as dedicated to end evil and to promote the spread of freedom and democracy—God's gift to all humanity. This Protestant millennialist mentality has been part of the Bush administration's foreign policy approach, designed in part to ensure the support of Bush's political base, the Christian religious right. According to Bush, the United States has a unique role in human events. He and all other Americans "are here for a mission"—to transform the world in the face of evil. In a speech at West Point in May 2003 President Bush asserted: "We are in a conflict between good and evil, and America will call evil by its name."[48] Before and after the speech Bush and members of his administration continually referred to Saddam Hussein as evil. Saddam's regime and those of Iran and North Korea were described by Bush as comprising "an axis of evil" that had to be dealt with in order to usher in the millennium. The administration's belief that regime change in Iraq would set off a chain reaction that would transform the entire Middle East reflected this millennialist mentality. Thus, regime change in Iraq, President Bush and his top national security officials insisted, would lead to democratic governments in "Syria, Iran and Saudi Arabia; the marginalization of Palestinian militants; and the end of the Organization of Petroleum Exporting Countries."[49] This viewpoint spawned by Protestant millennialism detracted the administration from a clear understanding of the challenges that confronted the United States and "laid the basis for the greatest American foreign policy disaster since the war in Vietnam."[50]

The George W. Bush Administration's Statement on
National Security Strategy of the United States of America

In his first State of the Union address on 29 January 2002, President Bush declared that the United States would extend the war on terrorism to states that aided and harbored terrorists. In the course of the address, he provoked international concern when he identified Iran, Iraq, and North Korea as comprising an "axis of evil" that had to be confronted. He promised that the United States would not allow "the world's most dangerous regimes to threaten us with the world's most destructive weapons." Later on, he espoused the need for "regime change" in Iraq.

On 20 September 2002, about a year after those horrific 11 September 2001 attacks on the World Trade Centers and the Pentagon, President Bush, in keeping with the requirement of the National Security Act of 1947 that presidents should periodically submit to Congress and the American people a national security strategy statement, released a comprehensive statement to that effect. Forthwith, his statement on the National Security Strategy of the United States of America boldly stated that the United States possesses unprecedented—and unequaled—strength and influence in the world and unveiled plans to maintain that strength and influence beyond challenge. The statement further proclaimed that America, as the dominant global power, would meet its challenges.

To many a nation, what stood out most significantly from the comprehensive statement was not Bush's emphasis on the obviously unprecedented US military power and economic strength. Rather, first, it was the idea that the United States possesses and plans to maintain strengths perpetually beyond challenge—an unnecessarily arrogant language that flaunted US power without explaining its purpose.[51] Secondly, it was the statement's doctrine of unilateral preemptive war against rogue states and terrorists: Because of contemporary realities, the statement declared "the United States can no longer solely rely on a reactive posture as we have in the past.... We cannot let our enemies strike first.... As a matter of common sense and self-defense, America will act against emerging threats *before they are fully formed*,"[52] (emphasis added). The statement added,

> While the United States will constantly strive to enlist the support of the international
> community, we will not hesitate to act alone, if necessary, to exercise our right of self
> defense by acting preemptively against such terrorists, to prevent them from doing
> harm against our people and our country.... The greater the threat, the greater is the
> risk of inaction—and the more compelling the case for taking anticipatory action to
> defend ourselves, even if uncertainty remains as to the time and place of the enemy's
> attack. To forestall or prevent such hostile acts by our adversaries, the United States
> will, if necessary, act preemptively.[53]

In an earlier address at the 2002 graduation exercises of US Military
Academy at West Point, New York, Bush hinted at the doctrine as he sought,
among other things, to convince the nation that both its security interests and
ideals were in jeopardy. On that occasion, Bush had proclaimed, "The war on
terror will not be won on the defensive; we must take the battle to the enemy,
disrupt his plans, and confront the worst threats *before they emerge* (emphasis
added). In the world we have entered, the only path to safety is the path of
action. And this nation will act."[54] In this manner, Bush moved preemption
"from the classic, internationally recognized 'anticipatory self-defense' in the
face of imminent danger to a flat assertion that the United States can even
change regimes in order to obviate dangers not yet operational."[55] This was later
exemplified by the war he launched against Saddam Hussein's regime in Iraq
in March 2003.

Clearly, Bush's national security strategy statement was a calculated
response to the 11 September terrorist bombings. The statement was a major
definition of his administration's approach to the war he had proclaimed on
terrorism in its full dimension. But the statement went further to assert that the
United States would remain powerful enough to prevent potential rivals and
adversaries from engaging in a military buildup that would surpass or equal the
power of the United States. It can thus be surmised that the origins of the Bush
doctrine of preemption predated those terrorist bombings of 11 September 2001.
Bush had already embraced the basic principles of the doctrine: US primacy and
the virtues and benefits of unilateral action but, with few exceptions—the
rejection of both the Kyoto Protocol on Climate Change and the International
Criminal Court, for example—had not vigorously promoted them before that
date. In fact, the principles of the doctrine and most of the tenets of his National
Security Strategy of the United States of America are a resurrection of the
dreams of the Defense Planning Guidance that Vice President Dick Cheney and
other neoconservatives in the Bush administration had drafted in 1992, which
his father as president at that time had rejected.

Bush's national security strategy statement made unilateral preemption a doctrine rather than an option. Bush placed at the center of the strategy a combination of America's unprecedented and unrivaled military strength, its political and economic influence, and his assumption that the United States of America is the embodiment of freedom and democracy that should be extended to undemocratic regions of the world. His national security strategy was thus designed, in keeping with Bush's disposition to moralizing and messianic language and his perception of America's "special destiny," to "make the world not just safe but better" and to deploy American power only to secure the world, to encourage "free and open societies," and not to seek America's "unilateral advantage." This reflected a moral agenda reminiscent of Wilsonian idealism during World War I when President Woodrow Wilson's ostensible rationale for US entry into that war was "to make the world safe for democracy," not the defeat of Germany to ensure that American creditors to Britain and financiers of the war would be repaid.

In his address at West Point, New York, on 1 June 2001, President Bush had stressed, "Our Nation's cause has always been larger than our Nation's defense. We fight, as we always fight, for a just peace—a peace that favors liberty. We will defend the peace against the threats from terrorists and tyrants. We will preserve the peace by building good relations among the great powers. And we will extend the peace by encouraging free and open societies on every continent."[56] Evangelical in tone, the Bush statement clearly extolled the benefits of US primacy not only for the United States, but also for international security.

Not only did Bush make the case for his new doctrine of preemption in principle, but he also made the case in public. In doing so, he rattled more targets than he had intended, unsettled US allies abroad, and sparked critics at home as well as overseas. Furthermore, Bush rejected the cold war doctrine of containment and deterrence as no longer a sufficient basis for defending the security of the United States against perceived imminent danger from rogue states and terrorists. "After September 11," he declared, "the doctrine of containment just doesn't hold any water.... My vision shifted dramatically after September 11 because I now realize the stakes, I realize the world has changed."[57] Therefore, the United States, he asserted, "must adapt the concept of imminent threat to the capabilities and objectives of today's adversaries." It must act preemptively by "taking anticipatory action to defend [itself] even if uncertainty remains as to the time and place of the enemy's attack."[58]

In view of the terrorist assault of 11 September 2001, supporters of the Bush doctrine of unilateral preemptive war praised it as a necessary response to the threats that terrorism and rogue states posed to the United States and the international community. They agreed with Bush on the need to adapt the idea of imminent threat as a precondition for preemptive action to the newer tactics of terrorists and rogue states that risk and gamble with the lives of their people. But according to Sir Michael Howard, an eminent British historian, the Bush doctrine of preemptive war "seemed to be demolishing the whole structure of international law as it had developed since the seventeenth century."[59]

Other critics of the doctrine insisted that preemptive war is a justifiable measure only in instances of a clear, imminent, and present threat; otherwise, it is inherently wrongheaded and dangerous. They expressed their apprehension about the precedent the doctrine might set: Other countries might invoke preemptive war for their own purposes. Perceptions and suspicions rather than credible and verifiable evidence might become the basis of foreign policy. These might lead to a rejection of the standard American practice of due process of the law: The accused is innocent until proven guilty. In addition, critics believed that the doctrine of unilateral preemptive war undermines the concept of sovereignty and international law—the defining feature of the international system within which each state must operate—and would lead to a more dangerous world, as it would only encourage other states to seek a nuclear arsenal in order to protect themselves against their alleged enemies. Critics insist that, in accordance with the Golden Rule, "if preventive war is moral for America, everybody has America's right to preventive self-defense (just as everybody else has America's right to self-government and democracy). Or, if America denies others that right, its own resort to prevention cannot be morally justified."[60] As such, it betrays and negates President Bush's sermons on "moral clarity."

Undoubtedly, in his special doctrine of preemption, Bush departed radically from both the conventions of US strategic doctrine and actual warfare and from the posture and practice of all his predecessors in office. Although these never repudiated the nation's right to preemption and to act alone, they reserved that right as an option—a last resort—but did not declare it a doctrine. Nor did they confuse preemptive with preventive action. But, in either case, war was to be waged only to protect vital national security interests and only after diplomacy and moral suasion had failed. For example, President Franklin D. Roosevelt was well aware of Japan's growing bellicose challenge in the Pacific Ocean, yet he did not anticipate an immediate threat that would require the United States to strike first. Also, although the circumstances of the eventual Japanese surprise attack on Pearl Harbor on 7 December 1941 were different from those of 11 September 2001, and both prevention and preemption were already too late,

President Roosevelt did not rely on unilateralism and overt hegemony in his response. He believed, and acted in the belief, that "security was a seamless web: if it came apart anywhere, the fabric could unravel everywhere. The international community must therefore prevent such threats to peace from developing, and if necessary retaliate against whoever had broken the peace."[61] Therefore, he strategically cooperated with the other great powers, including the Soviet Union—in that case, he joined hands with the devil, as he said, in order to cross the bridge.

President Harry Truman, who faced an expansive and ideologically hostile Soviet Union, said that he did not "believe in aggressive or preventive war." To him, "such war is the weapon of dictators, not of free democratic societies."[62] Thus, despite the Soviet Union's rapidly growing nuclear arsenal, declared hostility towards the United States and its capitalist/free market democracy, and a credible capacity to influence the outcome of several regional conflicts, Truman refrained from initiating a military confrontation against it as America's formidable cold war rival.[63]

Similarly, in the explosive Cuban Missile Crisis in October 1962, President John F. Kennedy refused to launch a preemptive strike against Cuba. Rather, prudently, he chose compromise and multilateral diplomacy over preemption and succeeded in disarming Cuba of its Soviet missiles without war. Thus, in general, Bush's predecessors, from F. D. Roosevelt to Bill Clinton, exercised self-restraint by seriously considering the possibilities of something worse and by caring for what the rest of the world thought and so sought to frame their policies accordingly. In that manner, they inspired the world to embrace their cause.

Virtually throughout his first administration, President George W. Bush ignored this foreign policy management style of his predecessors. In direct contrast to the Nixon Doctrine that the United States had neither the desire nor the resources to serve as a policeman of the world, the Bush approach and doctrine asserted that the United States had a need to become unilaterally the policeman of the world as well as the judge, the jury, and the executioner, unrestrained by international law and the voices of its allies. He insisted that the United States did not need anybody's "permission slip" in order to defend its national security interests. Bush subordinated diplomacy to the use of force. As a presidential candidate in 2000, he had criticized the "assertive multilateralism" of the Clinton administration and preferred instead unilateral action based on narrow US self-interests. Accordingly, as president, Bush promulgated a modern doctrine of the Nicolaitans—a deliberate determination to intimidate and dominate other nations in the name of US national security. He chose Iraq for the initial implementation of this doctrine. Although the jury is still out as to whether the strategy as applied to Iraq will advance or degrade US national security, it appears at the moment to be undermining the ends the Bush administration is seeking for the United States as a global leader.

Conclusion

Collectively, the approach and national security strategy of the Bush administration to US foreign policy, which has been discussed above, introduced three major changes in US security strategy. First, it reduced Washington's post–World War II reliance on permanent alliances and international institutions. Secondly, it expanded US traditional right of preemption into a new doctrine of preventive war. And thirdly, it advocated coercive democratization in Iraq as a solution to political instability and terrorism in the Middle East. But realistically, in spite of these changes in strategy, the United States still needs allies and the cooperation of international institutions. Apparently, coercive democratization in Iraq so far has not resolved the problem of political instability and terrorism in the country and the entire Middle East.

The approach demonstrated the administration's propensity during its first term to isolate itself on matters of global security. The administration's go-it-alone tough talk after 11 September 2001, contempt for the Kyoto Protocol, rejection of the International Criminal Court, war and then chaos in Iraq, secret prisons in Europe, and alleged use of torture at Guantanamo Bay, Cuba, brought about a precipitous decline of America's moral standing in the world. The approach created a widespread perception that (i) the administration placed narrow domestic short-term interests over and above maintaining a US leadership role for global peace, security, and well-being; (ii) for Bush, America's narrow interests, not global laws, determine the relevance of all rules; (iii) America's security requires violating the sovereignty of any selected state whenever a US president chooses to do so, thus making all other states tense and nervous; (iv) the United States had become a global policeman, unrestrained by international law and unaccountable to any higher authority. In addition, the approach contributed to an apparent alienation of the friends and allies of the United States and to lingering distrust and hostility towards the United States, not only throughout the Middle East, but also in practically every other region of the world. This widespread hostility is demonstrated by, among other things, the series of travel warnings issued to American nationals by the US Department of State every week of the month throughout the year. And it certainly undermines the ability of the United States to advance its global interests in important ways.

These consequences of Bush's approach to, and management of, foreign policy should seriously concern Congress, among other reasons, because it is, by Constitutional designation, a coequal manager of American foreign policy. As such, it has a major responsibility to know and check President Bush's foreign policy actions and initiatives, especially those that are likely to be counterproductive to America's national security interests broadly defined. So far, Congress has not demonstrated such a concern.

On the eve of the inauguration of his second administration, Bush appeared to have recognized these negative consequences of his administration's foreign policy.[64] Shortly after his second inauguration in January 2005, Bush decided to seek assistance and cooperation from America's European allies in his ambitious vision of remaking the broader Middle East, curbing the growth of terrorism, and addressing other global security issues. His new secretary of state, Condoleezza Rice, was dispatched to Europe early in February 2005 to mend fences, to seek such cooperation, and to prepare the ground for a Bush visit later in the month. President Bush began that visit on 20 February 2005 for a four-day campaign for a thaw in US-European relations. During that occasion, as well as the weeks preceding it, European governments were warily optimistic. They had accentuated the positive after Bush's reelection as they realized that they would have to deal with him for four more years.

Although the visit marked the beginning of a thaw in the relations, there remained lingering disagreements between the Bush administration and Western European allies to the United States over the following issues:[65]

1. The environment—the Bush administration's continued rejection of the Kyoto Protocol on Climate Change, which the administration argues is not in the best interest of US economy. According to the Bush administration, the Kyoto Protocol would damage American economic growth.
2. The role of the International Criminal Court. After unsigning the treaty creating the Court, the Bush administration continued to insist that the court violates US sovereignty and to reject its jurisdiction over US soldiers accused or suspected of war crimes against humanity. In April 2005, it opposed the recommendation of the International Commission of Inquiry on Darfur (western Sudan) to hand over to the International Criminal Court for immediate trial fifty-one individuals identified by the Commission as responsible for the violation of human rights and humanitarian law amounting to crimes against humanity. It suggested instead the setting up

of a tribunal in Tanzania that eventually would be able to put the identified individuals on trial. Furthermore, the administration sought to undermine the court by signing bilateral agreements with 100 countries (as of January 2007) exempting US citizens from being rendered to the court's jurisdiction and threatening to eliminate military assistance to others that had not signed such bilateral agreements.[66]

3. Approaches to dealing with nuclear weapons development by Iran. Initially, the Bush administration distrusted the approach of Britain, France, and Germany to persuade Iran to abandon its uranium enrichment activities in exchange for economic and political rewards. It preferred possible UN censure, even sanctions, against Iran or even regime change in the country. When that approach appeared unlikely because of likely vetoes of Russia and China, the administration relented and tolerated the approach of its major European allies. By 2006, the administration began to work with other members of the UN Security Council to address the Iranian nuclear weapons development program.

4. The European community's plans to lift the arms embargo it imposed on China in 1989 after the massacre resulting from democracy demonstrations in Tiananmen Square. The European Union saw lifting the embargo as part of an attempt to fully reintegrate China into the international community. But the Bush administration remained apprehensive that lifting the embargo might help China modernize its military for use against Taiwan. The European Union decided to maintain the embargo not because of pressure from the Bush administration but because China had passed a legislation to use force against Taiwan if the island attempted to declare itself an independent state.

5. Europe's, especially France's, conviction that a "multipolar world" with multiple centers of power is a fact not a desire or aspiration for world peace and stability. The Bush administration rejects this conviction, because it challenges the idea of a unipolar world and envisions powers that compete with American interests and influence.

6. America's belief and insistence that globalization should occur only in the orthodox form of America's free market and probusiness policies. Several European nations reject this belief as a denial of the responsibility of the state to provide public services, social justice, and safety nets for the poor, the unemployed, and workers.

These disagreements plagued the relations between the United States and its European allies especially. Political observers who had expected that fences would be mended after Bush was reelected to a second term in November 2004 welcomed the publication of his second statement on the National Security Strategy of the United States of America.[67] Released in March 2006, the new strategy statement echoed its September 2002 predecessor by reaffirming the doctrine of preemption as a key part of the strategy. It shifted the target of the doctrine to Iran but failed to devote sufficient attention to the dangers posed by North Korea and global warming. However, the statement was essentially a return to a foreign policy strategy that was much more akin to the foreign policies pursued by the administration's predecessors than by the one the administration itself pursued in its first term. The twin pillars of the new strategy stressed the traditional pillars of American foreign policy: promoting human rights, freedom, and democracy and working together with America's friends and allies. It shifted the balance from emphasizing force to emphasizing diplomacy, from relying on America's unilateral power to relying on multilateral alliances and institutions, and from stressing the need to ensure America's preeminence to stressing the importance of enhancing the nation's power by working with others.

The roots of the course reversal lay "in the fact that reality [had] demonstrated the limits of revolutionary foreign policy. One key reality is that most of the threats [the United States] faces…cannot be effectively defeated by America's (military) power alone; it requires a multifaceted use of power and the active cooperation of willing and able allies. Another is that America's actions must enjoy international legitimacy if they are to be effective in solving global problems."[68] Thus, President Bush was forced to change course by necessity rather than out of conviction. To date, the theoretical course correction is not evident in his Iraq policy of staying the course. In addition, the Europeans complained that the signs of political overtures to the world in general, and Europe in particular, which Bush had demonstrated after his reelection, had quickly reached their limits. They pointed to the nominations of two of the administration's leading neoconservatives—Paul Wolfowitz as president of the World Bank and John R. Bolton as US ambassador to the United Nations—as demonstrating that the Bush administration was moving more towards the unilateralism of its first term than the willingness to engage in dialogue displayed at the beginning of its second. The two nominations, they added, looked like nothing more than another display of American arrogance and a new proof of the administration's indifference, perhaps even cynicism, towards poor countries.[69]

In the meantime, the war on terror became another source of dissension between the Bush administration and America's European allies. The allies were dismayed by the administration's unwillingness to grant due process to terror suspects and to provide assurances that the suspects' human rights were not violated. The allies became even more outraged following media reports in November 2005 that the administration had detained top al-Qaeda and other terrorism suspects in secret prisons in eight European countries and that the CIA was at the same time violating the airspace of European states in transporting such detainees to countries in the Middle East that regularly torture detainees. The allegations provoked a lot of public outrage and reinvigorated already strong antiwar and anti-Bush administration sentiment in Europe. Secretary of State Condoleezza Rice undertook a diplomatic mission to four European nations to assuage the dismay of the allies. She strongly defended the legality of the Bush administration's tactics against the global threat of terrorism, and added that the administration "does not permit, tolerate, or condone torture under any circumstances."[70] Rice's assurances, however, were undermined by the instances of prisoner abuse scandals at Abu Ghraib, Guantanamo Bay, and Afghanistan and by the administration's opposition at the time to congressional anti-torture legislation sponsored by Senator John McCain. Later, in September 2006, President Bush announced that his administration had transferred fourteen individuals it had held in secret prisons overseas to Guantanamo Bay.

Chapter 3
The US Constitution and
American Foreign Policy

One of the major concerns of the founders of the American republic was to ensure that its government would be responsive to its citizens, that its decisions and behavior in domestic as well as foreign affairs would be subject to the influence of the citizens directly and indirectly through their representatives in Congress. This concern derived from the historical experience of British colonial rule. In addition, the founders especially disdained and despised political practices in the Old World of European monarchies, such as

1. *Concentration of power in the executive*, a practice that tended to corrupt the executive and to tempt him to go to war without sufficient consultation or counting the cost.
2. *Calculations of power and political expediency* as represented in the European doctrine and practice of statecraft. The doctrine held "that statecraft constituted an autonomous realm governed by its own rules, that the vital interests of the state were supreme over the interests of civil society, and that the restraints of legality must give way before necessity."[71]
3. *Oppressive restrictions on human freedom.*
4. *Debt and taxes as a crushing burden inherent in war as an instrument of national policy*—used by European monarchies in the eighteenth century.

Another concern of the founders was to establish "a more perfect Union," which, relative to foreign affairs, would be better able to conduct relations with other nations than it had been under the Articles of Confederation.

To address these concerns and other needs of the desired "more perfect Union," the founders created a federal Constitution, based on the rule of law and a system of power sharing and checks and balances. The Constitution was made the supreme law of the resultant republic in domestic as well as foreign affairs. In it, the framers articulated not only the principles of the rule of law, limited government, power sharing, and official accountability, but also their projection of the new republic's conduct of foreign affairs. These principles remain in force despite the transformation of the United States and the entire world during the period of more than 215 years since the Constitution was created. However, they have encountered challenges and have been interpreted and used by individuals within the American political system in a manner undreamed of by the founders. Today, they confront new changes and issues in the international system, including contemporary international laws and practices far different from those of the last quarter of the eighteenth century when the Constitution was crafted.

Constitutional Provisions for the Conduct of American Foreign Relations

It is appropriate to review the constitutional provisions for foreign relations, even though the expression "foreign affairs" is not found in the Constitution. Under the Constitution, the new American republic, the United States of America, began as a federation of thirteen states. The federal system contemplated a small superstructure of central or national government with a few specifically delegated or enumerated powers. The Constitution, in accordance with international practice, granted to the national government virtually full authority in foreign affairs, to the exclusion of the component states. James Madison argued in *The Federalist:* "If we are to be one nation in any respect it clearly ought to be in respect of other nations."[72] In the interest of a unified and coherent foreign policy, a nation speaks with only one voice: that of the national government. That voice, effectively, is what the chief executive—the US president—communicates to other nations. Today, Congress, even some bold state governor, may be heard around the world, but such voice "is diffuse and restrained by historic limitations, by the custom of international life, and by the reluctance to have the United States speak uncertainly and in a confusion of different voices."[73]

That the national government has exclusive jurisdiction over the making and conduct of foreign policy in no way excludes the interests of the various component states from the decision-making process, which involves the collective good of the organic political entity. It does, however, create some problems, including consultation and coordination, for a federation such as the United States. In recent years, we have witnessed a growing diplomacy and participation in foreign affairs by the component units of the United States—states and even local governments.[74] Among other reasons, this may be attributed to the realities of a changing world in which the national government has become larger and more remote, and the line between national and state or local concerns has become blurred. Thus, it was reported in 1987 that more than one thousand US state and local governments were participating in foreign affairs activities: negotiating international trade and investment pacts, participating in cultural exchanges with foreign nations, supporting divestment as a measure against apartheid in the Republic of South Africa, making resolutions about freezing nuclear weapons, protesting against waves of illegal aliens, and demanding stricter border management and control.[75] For instance, in 1989, Illinois provided Poland with $100 million in aid, Kentucky obtained a direct loan from Japan, and, by the same date, Atlanta had established twenty-four overseas offices.

California, with an estimated population of thirty-two million people in 1996, best illustrates this situation. Believing that the US Department of Commerce was no longer adequate to meet its trading needs, it set up the California World Trade Commission in 1985. The commission established offices in Tokyo, Hong Kong, Mexico City, London, and Frankfurt. In January 1993, the state replaced the commission with the California Trade and Commerce Agency, to deal with trade with foreign nations and the other forty-nine states. In creating the agency, the legislature explained that "the expansion of international trade is vital to the overall growth of California's economy."[76] Also, collaborating with Texas, California actively supported the North American Free Trade Association (NAFTA) negotiations as well as the relevant debates in Congress.

In assigning functions or powers, the framers of the Constitution were reluctant to assign unrestrained foreign policy powers to either the Congress or the executive branch because of their concern with human nature, especially the tendency of individuals to act on their own, free of restraint from others. Therefore, the Constitution they framed provided for institutional structures to be more important in both domestic and foreign affairs than any one person. It gave first place to Congress to which it allocated considerable foreign policy powers in contrast to a limited grant of specific authority to the president. It vested all or general legislative powers on the bicameral legislature. The president—whose powers, though significant, were circumscribed—was to exercise the executive powers, to take care that all the laws were faithfully executed. Congress was to ensure that the president was faithfully doing so. In practice, however, in keeping with the American political system of separate institutions sharing powers, the president recommends to Congress measures he deems necessary to enact into law. The judiciary, including the Supreme Court and the lower courts, was assigned a specific and less elaborate jurisdiction.

The Constitution also has provisions to ensure that officials of the executive and legislative branches of the national government are responsive to the wishes of the American people in their conduct of the nation's domestic and foreign affairs. Furthermore, the First Amendment to the Constitution enjoins the Congress from abridging the freedom of speech or the press, of the right of the people to assemble peaceably, and of the right to petition the government for a redress of grievances. This provision, in addition to the requirement for periodic election of national leaders, makes it possible for the American people to influence the conduct of foreign policy as the government responds to their views and activities. Similarly, it enables state and local governments to express and publicize views about foreign policy and international relations. During the first half of the 1990s, the governors of California and Florida, for example, expressed their views on the issue of influx of Mexican, Cuban, and Haitian migrants into their states. They exerted pressure on the national government to take urgent measures to deal with this problem, and they sought relief from the federal government for the burdens they had borne in dealing with illegal aliens. Documents 3.1 and 3.2 outline, respectively, the specific constitutional powers of the Congress and the presidency in the task of making and managing foreign policy.

Constitutional Division of Foreign Affairs Authority

Documents 3.1 and 3.2 show that the Constitution principally divides authority for the conduct and management of foreign relations between the legislative and executive branches. The two branches were made co-determinants of the role and behavior of the United States in foreign policy and have remained the principal actors in the making and conduct of American foreign policy. In a number of areas, the constitutional division of authority in foreign affairs between Congress and the president is ambiguous, not completely clear, incomplete, or silent (see below). Some analysts assert that the tension arising from this constitutional allocation of powers was deliberately designed by the framers of the Constitution as a means of forestalling absolutism and the corruption of power, of checking ambition with ambition, and of proceeding in both domestic and foreign affairs deliberately rather than precipitously.[77] But Arthur Restor believes that the conflict between these two branches of government was not intentional. He argues that "far from establishing two centers of power at war with one another over the conduct of international relations, the Framers of the Constitution believed they were designing a continuously deliberative and collaborative relationship between President and Senate, one that would guarantee the nation a unified and consistent policy beyond the water's edge."[78]

Others believe that, besides the system of separation of powers and checks and balances, the struggle between the two branches over foreign policy derives from the fact that the Constitution works by interpretation. Frequently, the executive branch, on the basis of its interpretation of the flexible Constitution, takes some action regarding foreign policy that Congress considers an encroachment on its own powers. Over the years, Congress and the executive appear to have come to realize that the Constitution, as well as the international norms, customs, and rules it absorbed, is an organic, evolving body of law. However, this knowledge, added to national experience, periods of emergency, and negotiations, has only moderated—but not completely eliminated—the friction. Congress and the president continue to contend over the privilege of controlling and directing American foreign policy. Still, the history of the making and management of American foreign policy is a history of presidential dominance.

Besides Congress and the presidency, the Constitution, in Article III, Section 2, Paragraph 1, extends the jurisdiction of the Supreme Court and the lower courts from the laws of the nation to treaties made, or to be made, by the United States; all cases affecting ambassadors, other public ministers, and consuls; cases of admiralty and maritime jurisdiction; and controversies between a state and foreign states, citizens, or subjects. Paragraph 2 vests in the Supreme Court original jurisdiction in all cases affecting ambassadors, other public ministers, and consuls and in cases in which a state is a party. In other cases, the Supreme Court is given appellate Jurisdiction, as to both Law and Fact.

Also, Article VI, Paragraph 2, provides that the Constitution and laws of the United States, and treaties made and to be made under the nation's authority, are the *supreme law of the land.* They prevail over, or preempt, state law. Executive agreements that are within the president's constitutional authority have similar force. Despite this provision and those of Article I, Paragraphs 1 through 3, however, states and local governments, except as preempted by Congress or the executive, may conclude certain kinds of agreements with foreign governments and their subordinate units. They have engaged and do engage in cultural and educational exchanges with other nations and have participated in missions abroad promoting trade or investment.

Document 3.1
Constitutional Powers of Congress in Foreign Affairs

1. Article I, Section 1 vests all legislative powers affecting domestic and foreign affairs in Congress, consisting of a Senate and House of Representatives.
2. Article I, Section 7, Paragraph 1 requires all bills raising revenue to originate from the House of Representatives.

3. Article I, Section 8, Paragraphs 1, 2, 3, 10, 11, 12, 13, 14, and 15, respectively, empower the Congress to
    i. Raise revenue through taxes, excise, and customs duties for the provision of the common defense of the United States. Later, in 1913, Congress was authorized by the Sixteenth Amendment to raise additional revenue through levying and collecting personal income taxes.
    ii. Borrow money on the credit of the United States.
    iii. Regulate Commerce with foreign nations.
    iv. Define and punish Piracies and Felonies committed on the high seas and Offenses against the Law of Nations.
    v. Declare War, grant Letters of Marque and Reprisal, and make Rules concerning Captures on Land and Water.
    vi. Raise and support Armies, but no Appropriation of Money for that Use shall be for a Term longer than two years.
    vii. Provide and maintain a Navy.
    viii. Make Rules for the Government and Regulation of land and naval forces.
    ix. Provide for calling forth the Militia to execute the Laws of the nation, suppress Insurrections, and repel Invasions.
4. Article I, Section 9, Paragraphs 7 and 8, respectively, require that
    i. No money shall be drawn from the Treasury, but in Consequence of appropriations made by Law; and a regular Statement and Account of the Receipts and Expenditures of all public Money shall be published from time to time.
    ii. No Title of Nobility shall be granted by the United States; and no Person holding any Office of Profit or Trust under them, shall, without the Consent of the Congress, accept of any present, Emolument, Office, or Title, of any kind whatever, from any King, Prince, or foreign State.
5. Article I, Section 10, Paragraphs 1, 2, and 3, respectively, require that
    i. No State shall enter into any Treaty, Alliance, or Confederation; grant any Letters of Marque and Reprisal; coin Money; emit Bills of Credit;... or grant any title of Nobility.
    ii. No State shall, without the Consent of the Congress, lay any Imposts or Duties on Imports or Exports, except what may be bsolutely necessary for executing its inspection Laws; and the net Produce of all Duties and Imposts, laid by any State on Imports or Exports, shall be

for the Use of the Treasury of the United States; and all such Laws shall be subject to the Revision and Control of the Congress.

iii. No State shall, without the Consent of the Congress, lay any Duty of Tonnage, keep Troops, or Ships of War in time of Peace, enter into any Agreement or Compact with another State, or with a foreign Power or engage in War, unless actually invaded.

Source: F. Ugboaja Ohaegbulam, *A Concise Introduction to American Foreign Policy* (NY: Peter Lang, 1999), pp. 168–169.

Document 3.2
Constitutional Powers of the Presidency in Foreign Affairs

1. Article II, Section 1, Paragraph 1 vests executive power in the president of the United States, duly elected, with a vice president, as stipulated by the Constitution. Paragraph 8 requires that, before he assumes his executive office, the president should swear or affirm that he will faithfully execute the office of the president of the United States and preserve and defend the Constitution of the United States.

2. Article II, Section 2, Paragraph 1 designates the president as commander in chief of the armed forces and authorizes him to grant reprieve and pardons for offenses against the United States, except in cases of Impeachment. Paragraph 2 vests him with the power to make treaties, by and with the *advice and consent of the Senate*, provided two-thirds of the senators present concur, and to appoint, by and with the *advice and consent of the Senate*, ambassadors and other public ministers and consuls.

3. Article II, Section 3 requires the president, from time to time, to provide the Congress Information regarding the state of the union and to recommend to their consideration such measures as he shall judge necessary and expedient, to receive ambassadors and other public ministers, and to take care that the laws are faithfully executed.

4. Article II, Section 4 requires that the president, vice president, and all civil officers of the United States, shall be removed from office on impeachment for, and conviction of, treason, bribery, or other high crimes and misdemeanors.

Source: F. Ugboaja Ohaegbulam, *A Concise Introduction to American Foreign Policy* (NY: Peter Lang, 1999), pp. 169–170.

Constitutional Powers of Congress in
Foreign Affairs: A Summary

The Constitution delegates to Congress seven groups of powers in foreign affairs:

1. *General legislative powers.* These include amendments to legislation and adoption of resolutions.
2. *General budgetary powers of the House and the Senate.* This is the power of the purse—the power to raise and appropriate funds and to determine how those funds are spent.
3. *War powers of the House and the Senate.* This includes the power to "provide for the common defense," to declare war, to raise and support armies (including the navy), and to make rules for the governance and regulation of the armed forces.
4. *Commerce powers of the House and Senate.* This includes the power to regulate interstate and foreign commerce and to impose tariffs on imports. Congress shares this power with the president.
5. *Powers of oversight of the House and Senate.* This includes the authority to supervise the executive branch, to ensure the president faithfully executes all the laws of the United States. In this regard, Congress may carry out investigations of the executive branch.
6. *Treaty powers of the Senate.* The Senate advises in treaties and must approve by two-thirds of its voting members all treaties negotiated by the president with other nations.
7. *Confirming powers of the Senate.* The Senate is vested with the authority to confirm major appointments of the president, such as cabinet members, undersecretaries, and ambassadors.

Constitutional Powers of the Presidency in
Foreign Affairs: A Summary

The president has both formal and informal powers in foreign affairs. In summary, the *formal powers* of the presidency include the following:

1. *Chief executive.* The president is the senior servant of the United States in both domestic and foreign affairs. He is sworn to execute faithfully all the laws of the land and to "preserve and defend the Constitution of the United States." According to John Marshall, who later became chief justice of the United States, the president is the "sole organ of the nation in its external relations, and its sole representative with foreign nations."[79] In this capacity,

the president presides over all agencies that carry out the functions and business of the national government. He is assisted in the supervision of the agencies by the Executive Office of the President (the presidential bureaucracy) and by a sprawling federal bureaucracy. In foreign affairs, particularly, the president is assisted by other national agencies, such as the Department of State, the National Security Council, the Office of Management and Budget, the Department of Defense, the Central Intelligence Agency, and the Office of the US Trade Representative.

2. *Chief of state*. The president is America's ceremonial head of state and the "symbolic personification of the American nation."[80] The president's family is the first family. The nation looks to the president for moral, economic, and political leadership in all spheres, domestic as well as foreign. He speaks for the nation and transacts the nation's business with other heads of state. The president's role as chief of state gives him an advantage, when he deals with Congress, over the conduct of both domestic and foreign affairs.

3. *Power to nominate key members of the executive branch*. The president is constitutionally required to appoint key members of the executive branch by and with the advice and consent of the Senate. The Senate has occasionally used this requirement to veto the president's nominations or to delay and frustrate the process of confirmation, for a variety of reasons—for example, the nominees' suitability or their political views. In 1981, the Senate rejected Ernest W. Lefever, nominated by President Reagan as assistant secretary of state for human rights. In 1989, it rejected President Bush's nomination of former Senator John Tower of Texas as secretary of defense. During the Reagan administration, Senator Jesse Helms (Republican, North Carolina), for personal ideological reasons, unsuccessfully sought to veto the appointment of Chester A. Crocker as assistant secretary of state for African affairs and the appointment of an ambassador to Mozambique. In 1997, again for personal reasons, Helms, as chairman of the Senate Foreign Relations Committee, killed President Clinton's nomination of William F. Weld (former governor of Massachusetts) as ambassador to Mexico by flatly refusing to schedule confirmation hearings. In most cases, however, presidents have had wide latitude in selecting their foreign affairs advisers and officers. Some nominees have been confirmed as ambassadors on the basis of party patronage or campaign contributions. At times presidents make recess appointments after their nominee for one reason or another had been rejected by the Senate or its committee. John R. Bolton was so appointed

by President George W. Bush in 2005 as US Ambassador to the United Nations. Eventually, he was denied confirmation when Bush renominated him at the end of the 109th Congress in 2006.

4. *Commander in chief of the armed forces.* This constitutionally designated role has, through practice and precedent over the years, increased the power of presidents in foreign affairs, especially in making war, beyond the original intent of the framers of the Constitution. Successive presidents have used their expansive interpretation of the designation, and the precedent set by their predecessors, to assert the authority to determine where, why, and when to commit American armed forces to combat overseas without a formal declaration of war by Congress. This practice has been one source of tension between Congress and the president over the conduct of American foreign policy. (For details see Chapter 4.)

5. *Treaty-making powers* The president has the constitutional authority to initiate negotiation of international agreements, but he is required to carry out the process by and with the advice and consent of the Senate and to obtain the concurrence of two-thirds of the senators present before such an agreement becomes a legally binding commitment and part of the supreme law of the land. Failure to obtain such concurrence—especially Woodrow Wilson's failure to gain it on the Treaty of Versailles (1919) and American membership in the League of Nations—has caused succeeding presidents to rely heavily on *executive agreements* rather than on the treaty process. Their reliance on such a strategy, which circumvents the treaty process, became another source of conflict between Congress and the executive branch on the management of foreign policy. (More on this later in this chapter.)

6. *Power to recognize foreign governments and to receive ambassadors and other foreign public officials.* This power is a major instrument of foreign policy. It includes the authority to terminate diplomatic relations with other nations, to expel foreign diplomats, and to recall American ambassadors accredited to other nations. Presidents exercise the authority to enhance national interests judiciously. The United States did not recognize the Communist government of the Soviet Union until 1933, during the F. D. Roosevelt administration, when it had already been in existence for fifteen years. The Marxist government of Angola was not recognized until 1993, during the Clinton administration—by then, Angola had been independent of Portugal for eighteen years. In both cases, the issue was ideological incompatibility with the foreign government. In the case of the People's Republic of China, with which the United States had no diplomatic

relations from 1949 to 1978, the reason was more than ideological incompatibility with a Communist government: US administrators had made a political decision to support the defeated Nationalist government in Taiwan as the representative of China. In 1972, President Nixon visited China, having decided to alter the policy. Full diplomatic relations were established in 1979, during the Carter administration.

Usually, US administrations apply the following criteria in recognizing emergent governments: whether the government is stable, has established de facto control throughout its territory, enjoys popular support and is based on the will of the people, respects the rights of its citizens, behaves in accordance with international law, and is fulfilling its international obligations. However, in all cases, American national security interests are the most decisive factor in granting or withholding diplomatic recognition, whether or not these conditions are present.

7. *Power to repel sudden attacks.* It is the responsibility of the president to defend the nation. To repel a sudden attack is one of the more dramatic ways of doing this. The nature of Congress as a deliberative body, comprising many members (currently 535) scattered throughout the fifty states of the Union, made this responsibility incumbent on the president. Besides, the task is inherent in the president's designation as commander in chief of the armed forces.

8. *Commerce powers.* Constitutionally, the power to regulate foreign commerce is delegated to Congress, but Congress shares this power with the president, who negotiates commercial treaties that Congress may approve, amend, or reject.

Informal Powers of the Presidency in Foreign Affairs: A Summary

The formal powers of the presidency are relatively modest compared with those of Congress. Yet, historically, as noted above, presidents have dominated the American foreign policy process. The explanation is that, among other reasons, presidents have been able to resort to the informal powers of their office in the conduct of the nation's foreign relations. Generally, these informal powers derive from the nature of the presidency and the incumbent's ability to exploit it. Among the informal powers of the presidency is what Donald M. Snow and Eugene Brown have identified as *presidential singularity*.[81]

While the Congress comprises 535 members (currently), the presidency is occupied by a single individual. The president is assisted, it is true, by several people. But, as Harry Truman said of the presidency, "The buck stops here."

Furthermore, the presidency, based in Washington, is always in session. In contrast, Congress meets during fixed sessions, and, at other times, its members are dispersed. Most politically informed people in and outside the United States know the president as the leader of the nation. Much is expected of such a leader, and the president—wanting to leave a memorable legacy—must therefore not disappoint national and international expectations. The office makes the man. It also defines the scope of the incumbent's role and activities. Presidential singularity makes it easier for the president to act more swiftly and decisively in crises and emergencies than the more deliberative Congress. In addition, it enhances his ability to act informally, often discreetly or secretly. Again, in contrast, Congress can only act formally, by statute or resolution, and publicly, except in sessions of the Executive Committee.

The presidency gives incumbents another informal power through a variety of opportunities to shape public opinion and to mobilize the American public around domestic as well as foreign policy issues. Presidents use their skills and such tools as the constitutionally required annual State of the Union address, press conferences, radio and television addresses, and tours of the nation to accomplish several goals. Skillful presidents have used the State of the Union address to define domestic and foreign policy agendas, enunciate unilateral doctrines, and arouse the public to support their programs. James Monroe, Theodore Roosevelt, Harry S. Truman, Dwight Eisenhower, Richard Nixon, Jimmy Carter, and Ronald Reagan are examples of presidents who have used unilateral declarations to put their distinctive stamp on American foreign policy. Although his aim was not achieved, Woodrow Wilson toured the nation in 1919 to appeal for support for his proposed League of Nations. Franklin D. Roosevelt used his "fireside chats" to create a bond between himself as president and the American public. Since his administration, virtually every president has used not only radio and television but also press conferences to define specific foreign policy objectives and to mobilize the public for such objectives. Press conferences, which John F. Kennedy used very effectively to appeal directly to the people, provide an opportunity for the president to respond directly and without rehearsal to questions and concerns of the national and international press corps. As discussed in chapter 2, President George W. Bush, given the background of the events of 11 September 2001, espoused the doctrine of preemption when he complied with the congressional requirement that the executive branch should periodically provide the nation a statement on the national security strategy of the United States. Skillful use of such occasions enhances public support for a president's foreign policy.

International diplomacy is another component of the informal powers of the presidency. Whether through personal summit conferences, which may be bilateral or multilateral, or through personal telephone calls or personal emissaries and US diplomats, or through mobilizing congressional support for diplomacy, the conduct of international diplomacy enhances the influence of the president as the one in charge of promoting American national security interests overseas. Promoting national interests is the essence of American foreign policy, which encompasses formulation, as well as execution, of policies. In this sense, then, the president has the primary responsibility to determine not only the objectives of American foreign policy but also the operational techniques—means and mechanisms—of achieving those objectives.

Uncertainties in the Constitutional Distribution of Foreign Affairs Powers

As has been noted, the US national government is one of delegated powers. Using the system of separate institutions sharing overlapping powers, the framers of the Constitution delegated separate responsibilities to each branch of the national government. They went further in using a system of shared power and checks and balances to keep the powers of each branch in check. The president is the chief executive of the nation, but Congress determines or legislates the laws he enforces. The president negotiates treaties with other governments and appoints key personnel of the national government, but he must do so by and with the advice and consent of the Senate. As President Reagan learned in 1987, when he reinterpreted the Antiballistic Missile Treaty with the Soviet Union in order to facilitate his Strategic Defense Initiative, a president could not substantially reinterpret a treaty without the advise and consent of the Senate. The president is the commander in chief of the armed forces, but Congress has the authority to initiate wars. In practice, these responsibilities overlap. Presidents do initiate legislations and have, on many occasions, sent American armed forces into combat without a formal declaration of war by Congress.

But there are areas of foreign affairs where the constitutional distribution of powers is silent, uncertain, or ambiguous. In most cases, presidents assume authority in such areas. The power to terminate a treaty with another nation is one such area of ambiguity. In 1978, against substantial congressional opposition, President Carter terminated a mutual defense treaty with Taiwan in order to facilitate full diplomatic relations with the People's Republic of China. Several senators, led by Barry Goldwater, challenged the president's constitutional authority to do this without the advice and consent of the Senate, and the matter went all the way to the Supreme Court. The Supreme Court ruled in favor of the president. It asserted, among other things, that the challenged action rested "upon the President's well-established authority to recognize, and withdraw recognition from, foreign governments."[82] Other uncertain areas include the power to declare neutrality in wars, to establish or break diplomatic relations with foreign governments, to conclude agreements about military bases with various foreign governments, and to withhold information on foreign policy from Congress. By practice and precedent, presidents have historically exercised authority in these areas—but usually not without straining relations between them and Congress.

The uncertainty in constitutional delegation of powers in foreign affairs extends to the role of state and local governments despite the exclusionary clause in the Constitution. Michael H. Shuman provides elaborate evidence to illustrate how, this clause notwithstanding, many state and local governments have become engaged in foreign affairs. He argues that "very little of [their] activism falls into any of [the] forbidden categories"— establishing armies or navies, violating national treaty commitments, and levying duties on exports and imports—and that "attorneys and courts have found that countervailing constitutional principles render the general legal wisdom against participation by state and local governments in foreign affairs almost meaningless."[83]

These uncertainties have been among several sources of controversy between the presidency and Congress in the making and conduct of American foreign policy. Contention between the president and Congress over the conduct of American foreign relations is historically a constant feature of the American political system. The intensity of this contention varies from time to time and tends to pose a threat to the unity and effectiveness of American diplomacy. On the one hand, presidents, starting with George Washington, have viewed Congress—especially the Senate—as obstructing their conduct of the nation's foreign affairs by limiting their freedom of action. On the other hand, Congress has tended to regard some chief executives, notably George Washington, F. D. Roosevelt, Lyndon Johnson, Richard Nixon, and Ronald Reagan, as acting in a high-handed way to subvert the Constitution by excluding the legislature from meaningful participation in the conduct of foreign affairs. In 1920, the Senate's opposition to Woodrow Wilson's conduct of foreign relations led to the defeat of the Treaty of Versailles and of US membership in the League of Nations. In recent years, presidents Nixon, Ford, Carter, and Reagan, for example, were each challenged by the Senate or certain of its members in the law courts over particular foreign policy actions. In a number of cases, the Senate conducted investigations of specific foreign policy initiatives of the executive branch. In

1975, it investigated alleged plots by the CIA to assassinate foreign leaders. In 1987, during Reagan's second administration, it investigated the Iran-Contra affair. This involved the administration's arms trade with Iran in exchange for hostages and its use of profits from the trade to finance forbidden covert activities in Nicaragua.

In the context of this study, the most salient areas of controversy between the president and Congress in foreign affairs include the following:

1. The war powers of Congress versus the role of the president as the commander in chief of the armed forces.
2. Advice and consent role of the Senate in treaty making versus efforts of presidents to circumvent that role, especially through failure to consult the senators and frequent resort to executive agreements.
3. General budgetary powers of Congress versus measures by the executive branch to impede the exercise of those powers.
4. Sharing of information on foreign policy issues, especially strategic intelligence.

In this chapter, the last three of the identified sources of conflict are discussed. The most relevant source of conflict (for this study), the first source listed above, is discussed in Chapter 4.

Treaty-Making Powers

The power of war and peace, including treaty making, was one of the thorny issues upon which the Constitutional framers deliberated at length. Some delegates at the Constitutional Convention stated that, barring only the Senate's participation, the conduct of foreign relations, including the power of war and peace, was "the absolute and uncontrollable" responsibility of the chief executive. Other delegates rejected the notion of granting that authority to the chief executive but were prepared to grant the executive branch some share in that power.[84] Because he thought that the president "would necessarily derive so much power and importance from a state of war that he might be tempted, if authorized, to impede a treaty of peace," James Madison proposed that two-thirds of the Senate should be empowered to make treaties without the concurrence of the President.[85] After debating the issue at length, the Convention assigned it to its Committee on Postponed Parts. The eventual Constitutional provision on the issue was based on the recommendations of that committee:

The President, by and with the advice and consent of the Senate, shall have power to make treaties; and he shall nominate by and with the advice and consent of the Senate and shall appoint Ambassadors and other public Ministers, Judges of the supreme Court, and all other officers of the U.S. whose appointments are not otherwise herein provided for. But no Treaty shall be made without the consent of two thirds of the Members present.[86]

It followed from this that, by constitutional provision, the president was made a full participant both in treaty making and in the appointment of diplomatic envoys and other high-ranking officials of the United States government. Therefore, treaty making became a joint responsibility of the presidency and the Senate. The president makes treaties with foreign governments by and with the *advice* and *consent* of the Senate, provided that *two-thirds of the Senators present concur*. The Senate's authority to grant or withhold concurrence, especially by two-thirds of its members voting, gives it the last word in the treaty-making process and in the appointment of high-ranking executive branch officials. The president has no constitutional authority to override or veto the Senate's last word such as Congress has in the case of a presidential veto of an ordinary legislative measure. In addition, the prerogative of the Senate to advise the President on treaties "is nowhere limited as to the stage at which the advice may properly be offered."[87]

Dexter Perkins and other scholars believe that this provision of concurrence by two-thirds majority of the Senate reflected the founders' "congenital distrust of Europe" and their determination to ensure that the nation's involvement in international politics would remain limited.[88] In "Federalist No. 75," Alexander Hamilton provided a detailed rationale for treaty making as a joint responsibility of the executive and the Senate: It was to ensure cooperation between the president and the Senate and to assure the nation of a "greater security against an improper use of the power of making treaties," especially those that might have the potential of leading to war.[89]

Constitutionally, the relationship between Congress and the president and the procedures appropriate to the task of making and conducting American foreign policy are fundamentally different from those governing the procedures and the relationship between them when domestic measures are involved. In domestic matters, the president recommends to Congress measures he deems necessary and expedient. Committees of both chambers of Congress study, debate, and amplify as necessary such recommendations. Both chambers iron out any differences between them on the measures. From the procedure, a piece of legislation emerges and is signed or vetoed by the president without any alteration. The president's veto may be sustained or overridden by Congress.

In foreign affairs, the central role of the executive in the treaty-making process is unmistakable. The president initiates the treaty-making process. He appoints the negotiators, monitors the negotiation process, modifies and approves the provisions of the treaty, submits it to the Senate, and, upon the required concurrence by two-thirds majority of that body, proclaims the treaty as law. He may withdraw the treaty from further consideration, as President Jimmy Carter did in 1979 relative to the second Strategic Arms Limitation Talks (SALT II) Treaty immediately after the Soviets invaded Afghanistan. He can also terminate an existing treaty, as Carter again did in 1978 when he allowed the mutual security pact with Taiwan to lapse in order to reestablish diplomatic relations with the People's Republic of China, or as George W. Bush did when he terminated the Anti-Ballistic Missile (ABM) Treaty.

The vital role of the president in treaty making, therefore, has not been a major source of controversy between the presidency and the Senate. But, in recent years, the constant competition between the presidency and Congress for power and prestige has also become evident in the struggles between the two branches over treaties. Key senators tend to hold up treaties whose provisions they dislike in order to obtain changes. In this manner, for one reason or another, the Senate has obstructed about forty-eight treaties already negotiated and signed by presidents.[90] Many senators stalled the Law of the Sea Treaty, concluded in 1982 and signed by more than 170 nations. They believed that its provisions dealing with seabed mining were unfair to American companies, and they were also opposed to the provision of an international mechanism for resolving disputes. Other examples of treaties stalled in the Senate include the Convention on the Elimination of All Forms of Discrimination Against Women (1979) and the Rio Treaty on Biodiversity (1992). The Chemical Weapons Convention, a worldwide ban on the production and possession of poison gas stocks, was approved only after it had been holed up in the Senate by key Republican senators, led by Jesse Helms.

There are three traditional sources of contention between the presidency and Congress in treaty making: input by the Senate into the treaty-making process, measures by the executive branch to bypass senatorial advice and consent, and the role of the House of Representatives. Each of these is discussed below.

Input by the Senate into the Treaty-Making Process
Arthur Bestor writes that, at the time the Constitution was adopted in the eighteenth century, the phrase "by and with the advice and consent of the Senate," "described the close and continuous consultation that was expected to go on, usually face to face, between a ruler and a council of state or privy

council."[91] In his view, therefore, the Senate was originally intended to be a kind of advisory council, making recommendations to the president throughout the treaty-making process. It was understood, he adds, that

> negotiations with foreign powers are necessarily under the direction of the President, this being the Executive component of treaty making. It is therefore he who must decide (subject to further advice as needed) when and what to yield in the give-and-take of bargaining.[92]

In practice, this is not exactly how the process has been carried out. For a variety of reasons—including timing, differences between the executive and the Senate in their perspectives on world affairs and on national interests, and the requirements of confidentiality and secrecy in the diplomatic negotiations—presidents tended to fail to consult the Senate and to exclude its members from the treaty-negotiating team. Although he presented to a joint session of Congress the essence of his plans to end World War I, President Wilson failed to consult the Senate in the development of those plans, which became the basis of the armistice that ended World War I on 11 November 1918 and the Versailles Treaty of 1919. He also failed to include any senators in the delegation he led to the Paris Peace Conference. The result, as we have already seen, was that the Senate failed to approve the resulting treaty. Before the United States entered World War II, President Roosevelt entered into a lend-lease agreement with Britain without prior consultation with the Senate. The agreement provided Germany with a justification for a possible declaration of war against the United States. Timing and Britain's critical need accounted for Roosevelt's action, but his behavior became a precedent for future similar agreements and commitments.

Following Wilson's experience with the Senate after World War I, presidents developed some informal means for obtaining senatorial input in the treaty-making process. For one thing, they include key members of the Senate in the negotiation delegation. Another method is bipartisanship in foreign policy: The president consults key members of Congress on issues of foreign policy, generally during the process of formulation and implementation, and obtains input from them.

The Senate accepted these strategies and has cooperated fairly with the executive in the treaty-making process, rejecting some (nineteen) of the treaties submitted between 1789 and 1982 but consenting on the vast majority (1,400).[93] It never voted on some. Some, for example the Kyoto Protocol on Climate Change, were never submitted, in the face of strong Senate opposition. Others were withdrawn, such as SALT II by President Carter in 1979.

A related issue in the controversy over the role of the Senate in the treaty-making process emerged in 1987. This was the question of authority to reinterpret the meaning of a treaty between the United States and other nations. In that year, the Reagan administration claimed that it had the authority to reinterpret the ABM Treaty with the Soviet Union (1972). The administration sought to use this reinterpretation to test technology essential to the development of Reagan's Strategic Defense Initiative. In the Senate, opponents disputed the reinterpretation because they believed that it constituted a significant revision of a prior agreement as well as a major amendment that called for senatorial advice and consent. Furthermore, they argued that reinterpretation of the treaty would weaken the confidence of foreign governments in treaties they negotiated with the United States. Senator Sam Nunn led the successful opposition to the reinterpretation. Eventually, the Reagan administration promised that it would not adopt a different meaning for the treaty without the approval of the Senate, but the struggle further strained the constitutional relationship between the Senate and the executive.

Resort by the Executive Branch to Executive Agreements
Presidents have resorted to *executive agreements* as a principal means of bonds with other nations and thus have bypassed the constitutionally required senatorial advice and consent on treaty making. To do so, they claimed a constitutional authority to engage in agreements (known as *executive agreements*[94]) with the governments of other nations by means other than treaties. Presidents have favored such agreements over treaties made with the advice and consent of the Senate as a better method of entering into understandings with other nations. In doing so, they enhanced their ability to make and conduct foreign policy by executive action only and consequently eroded the advice and consent treaty power of the Senate. Thus, their making binding international commitments through executive agreements became one of the major sources of constitutional dispute between Congress and the presidency in the 1950s and beyond.

The continuing dispute over such agreements was rooted in a series of Supreme Court rulings in the 1930s and 1940s that accorded executive agreements the same legal force and constitutional status as treaties and therefore made them part of the supreme law of the United States. The dispute was exacerbated by the extensive use Franklin D. Roosevelt had made of executive agreements during World War II. For example, Roosevelt concluded such agreements with Britain in August 1940, whereby he gave fifty old US warships to the British in exchange for bases in the Atlantic, and at Yalta in

February 1945 with Stalin. Many more were concluded after 1945 either in writing or orally by the president or his representatives.[95] Congress objected to the fact that the agreements were as binding as treaties but did not require the approval of two-thirds of the Senate membership required of treaties. Their use, they argued, therefore diminished the authority of Congress over international commitments by the United States.

According to calculations by James M. McCormick, 16,074 executive agreements were made between 1789 and 1999, compared with 1,745 treaties during the same period.[96] During the ten-year period between 1980 and 1990, the executive branch concluded 3,851 executive agreements but only 170 treaties.[97] Between 1990 and 1999, it concluded 2,857 executive agreements but only 247 treaties.[98] These agreements committed the nation militarily especially and to assistance to other nations to an extent to which Congress was either not fully aware or was completely in the dark.[99] They appeared to undermine congressional oversight of the executive and to threaten US security through overcommitment abroad. Therefore, they provoked congressional attempts at remedial measures.

Attempts by Congress to Curb Executive Branch Resort to Executive Agreements

The first effort to curb presidential use of executive agreements was the Bricker Amendment.[100] In 1953, Senator John Bricker (Republican, Ohio) proposed a constitutional amendment to require executive agreements to receive the same two-thirds majority vote of approval from the Senate as treaties. The senator was especially concerned that impending human rights treaties and other agreements in the United Nations might commit the United States to undertakings or measures that might infringe on the constitutional rights of US citizens as well as congressional and state prerogatives. He believed that putting a stop to self-executing treaties that require no congressional implementing legislation and that strengthening the role of Congress in implementing all treaties and executive agreements would prevent such likely infringements. Hence, his resolution. In 1954, his proposed amendment failed by one vote to receive the necessary two-thirds majority in the Senate needed to initiate the ratification process at the state level. It failed because it was impossible to distinguish between agreements that require senatorial consent and those the president ought to be able to make on his own authority.

The second effort was a National Commitments Resolution adopted in 1969 by the Senate. The resolution was prompted by the Senate's displeasure and frustration at the secret executive branch commitments to countries in southeast

Asia during the 1950s and 1960s, which had gradually led to extensive US involvement in Vietnam. The resolution declared that it was the sense of the Senate that no future national commitments should be made without affirmative action by Congress. It defined national commitments as the use of US armed forces on foreign territory, the promise to use them, or the granting of financial aid.

Because the measure of 1969 failed to produce the desired curb, Congress enacted a significant legislation in 1972, which it believed would end executive branch commitment making. This was the Case-Zablocki Act (after its sponsors, Senator Clifford Case, Republican, New Jersey, and Congressman Clement Zablocki, Democrat, Wisconsin). This legislation required that Congress should be informed of all executive agreements entered into by the executive branch within sixty days of their execution. The goal was to give Congress an opportunity to take the action of blocking an agreement if it saw fit to do so. Senator Case said that the act was needed because there were at least four thousand executive agreements in effect in the early 1970s about which Congress knew nothing. The act was amended and strengthened in 1977. From that time, it required that all agreements made by all agencies within the executive branch should be reported to the Department of State within twenty days of execution for eventual transmittal to Congress, as provided by the original act.[101]

Congress took further action to strengthen Case-Zablocki in October 1978, when it added specific provisions to the Foreign Relations Authorization Act for the fiscal year 1979. The relevant provisions of that act require that the president report annually each executive agreement not reported within the sixty-day reporting period, that oral agreements with other governments should be put in writing, and that the secretary of state should determine specifically what arrangements constitute an international agreement.

The Role of the House of Representatives in Treaty Making and Implementation

The House of Representatives has no formal constitutionally assigned role in treaty making. A proposal to include the House in treaty making was debated at length during the Convention of 1787 but was rejected. There was widespread feeling among the delegates to the convention that "diplomatic negotiations required a degree of secrecy and dispatch possible only in a small body comparable to a privy council, with members chosen for comparatively long terms and insulated from the heats and ferments of direct popular election."[102] This feeling also derived from experience with the Articles of

Confederation. Under the Confederation, the entire Congress had handled foreign policy and had woefully mismanaged it. Hence, it seemed to the delegates to the convention that the smaller and more mature Senate, which was to be elected indirectly (as it turned out, until 1913), should serve this role "as a kind of council of state to advise the president on foreign relations."[103]

The Constitution, however, does give the House an indirect but very highly significant role in treaty making. This is the general budgetary powers: to initiate the raising of revenue and the appropriation of funds. In "Federalist No. 58," James Madison underscored the significance of this role. He argued that the "power of the purse represented the 'most compleat [*sic*] and effectual weapon with which any constitution can arm the immediate representatives of the people, for obtaining a redress of every grievance, and carrying into effect every just and salutary measure.'"[104]

It was in keeping with this that, after many years of simply observing the treaty-making process, the House began to assert its role by using its budgetary powers. It has been able to do so because treaties "are not always self-executing" but "typically require enabling legislation and the expenditure of funds" before their provisions go into force.[105] The House thus may exercise its power of the purse and legislation to nullify a treaty negotiated by the president and approved by the Senate. It sought to do this with the Panama Canal Treaties in 1977, NAFTA in 1993, and the General Agreement on Tariffs and Trade (GATT) in 1994. It nearly derailed the Panama Canal Treaties, rejecting the Carter administration's implementation of legislation and proposing its own. The Senate approved a version more in line with the administration's bill. After hard bargaining, a conference committee was able to reach a compromise acceptable to the House about four days before the treaty was to take effect.

General Budgetary Powers versus Budget Impoundment

General budgetary powers—to raise and appropriate funds to defray national expenditures, including the common defense and the general welfare of the American people—are expressly constitutional powers of the House and the Senate. Congress uses these powers, which it believes to be exclusive, to influence the direction of American foreign policy and to reduce the executive's discretion in foreign affairs. Occasionally, presidents have found the congressional exercise of these powers constricting, restrictive, and frustrating. They have occasionally needed funds for foreign policy projects that Congress, for one reason or another, flatly refused to appropriate. In 1994, Congress denied President Clinton's request for funds to help Mexico resuscitate its collapsed peso and economy. Clinton had to use an alternative source to provide the loan to Mexico.

Before the Clinton administration, chief executives had devised some alternative means of funding foreign policy projects that Congress had refused to finance. One means is secret spending. In this case, an administration buries the fund in appropriations for the CIA and other intelligence units whose funds are handled under secrecy. It may also include the funds in the Defense Department's annual budget under secrecy provisions with the cooperation of the leaders of the Armed Services Committees of both the House and the Senate. At other times, it may divert funds away from one foreign policy account to another without legislative approval or knowledge. This happened during the military intervention in Vietnam, when the Department of Defense transferred to Vietnam funds that had been earmarked for military assistance to Taiwan. In 1981, President Reagan used his defense "drawdown" authority to transfer funds specifically earmarked for military emergencies to increase military aid to El Salvador from $5.5 million (the amount appropriated by Congress) to $30.5 million. Similarly, in 1982, he increased the amount from $26 million to $81 million and used military exercise funds to build bases in Honduras.

Administrations have also used foreign military arms sales to replace congressionally initiated cuts in foreign aid, for example. The most egregious use of this kind of alternative funding, when Congress shuts off funds for a particular program, was made by the Reagan administration in the 1980s.[106] During the period from 1982 to 1987, Congress banned (by the Boland Amendments) direct or indirect assistance to the Contra guerillas fighting against the Sandinista government of Nicaragua. The Reagan administration, frustrated by this ban, sought and obtained money from private American citizens and foreign governments, such as Saudi Arabia. In addition, using senior officials in the National Security Council and the CIA, it traded arms with Iran in 1985 and 1986 in exchange for its influence over the release of Americans held hostage by terrorists in the Middle East. It then secretly used the profits from the sales, about $4 million, and the fund obtained from private parties and foreign governments to finance the Contras' guerilla war in Nicaragua. Congress called these activities an attempt to privatize American foreign policy and to subvert and thwart its will and its constitutional powers. After consequent investigations by Congress in November 1986, the Reagan administration officials involved—Admiral John Poindexter, Robert McFarlane, and Colonel Oliver North—were prosecuted, convicted, and punished. North, however, eventually managed to win an appeal of his conviction.

Although Congress has occasionally refused to appropriate funds for foreign policy projects requested by presidents, the executive branch, for its part, has capitalized on its constitutional duty to take care that the laws are faithfully executed to arrogate to itself a role in overseeing how funds raised and appropriated by Congress are spent. Careful management of the nation's financial resources by its stewards, as presidents see themselves, surely enjoins such a role. The exercise of this role caused the spending power to become an additional source of tension between the executive and Congress, which frequently embarks on a pork-barrel spending binge to satisfy pet projects, political constituencies, lobbyists, and defense and other contractors.

Because of this congressional tendency, and for a number of other reasons, including excessive costs and changed circumstances, presidents have found occasion to *impound*, or freeze in the federal treasury, funds already appropriated by Congress. Another measure the executive has employed to circumvent full exercise of the general budgetary powers by Congress is the veto of an entire appropriations bill when it believed a portion of it was not in the national interest. To eliminate this strategy, the 104th Congress granted the executive a line-item veto that it could use to rescind specific parts of an appropriations bill that, in the national interest, it finds unacceptable. President Clinton, the first chief executive to have that authority, used it eighty-two times in 1997. But on 25 June 1998, the Supreme Court ruled, in favor of lawmakers who had challenged the authority, that the grant was unconstitutional.[107] Therefore, the traditional practice of vetoing an entire appropriations bill because of one or more unacceptable items is likely to continue.

Lastly, presidents have rejected at other times weapons systems recommended and funded by Congress in favor of a shopping list preferred by the Department of Defense. In 1971, the Nixon administration refused to spend $700 million that Congress had appropriated for a manned bomber because the administration was opposed to the project. Similarly, upon the insistence of the navy, the Bush administration refused to purchase four fast sea lift vessels for which Congress had appropriated $600 million in 1989. The defense secretary, Dick Cheney, diverted part of the fund to other projects and froze the rest in the federal treasury.

To remedy its own defects over the handling and control of the budget and to tighten control over executive use of budget impoundment, Congress passed the Budget and Impoundment Control Act of 1974. Among other things, the act required the president to give Congress a justification of his intention to impound any appropriated funds so as to enable the legislators to review, accept, or dismiss the rationale.[108] Thus, subject to congressional review, the act allowed the president to defer authorized spending temporarily, up to twelve months, and to rescind authorized spending permanently.

Sharing of Strategic Information on Foreign Policy Issues

The collection, analysis, and dissemination of information essential to the conduct of foreign policy are essentially functions of the executive. Congress plays a role in that responsibility, using, for example, expert staff assistants and expert witnesses during legislative hearings. Also, its members occasionally travel abroad to obtain directly information needed for their role in the conduct of foreign affairs. However, these congressional resources do not approach either the range or the magnitude of those used by the executive branch. Congress therefore is compelled to rely on briefings by executive branch officials and agencies. Tension occurs between the two when, for a variety of reasons, the executive branch refuses to share information on foreign policy with Congress.

The most frequent areas of controversy in this respect include covert operations by strategic intelligence units, foreign arms sales and transfers, and general misbehavior by the executive branch. In such cases, the executive branch advances specific reasons for monopolizing information. For example, this is said to

1. Avoid interruptions of foreign policy initiatives.
2. Protect the nation's security interests.
3. Prevent endangering the lives of individuals engaged in the nation's intelligence service. Release of information may impair the confidentiality of advice given to the president.
4. Prevent revelation of secrets that may embarrass or bring about the fall of a foreign government and thereby undermine the credibility of the US government with its friends and allies.

President Reagan's national security adviser during congressional investigations into the Iran-Contra affair, Admiral Poindexter, testified that the Reagan administration could withhold information from Congress because the Contras were being assisted with nonappropriated funds.

It has become obvious to Congress that the executive branch attempts to monopolize information on foreign policy in order to maximize its own power, to avoid legislative criticism, or to hide its mistakes and thereby keep embarrassing policy errors from becoming public knowledge. In spite of this argument, however, rulings by the Supreme Court have upheld, at times, the refusal of the executive branch to share strategic information with Congress. At other times, the court has found reason to compel a president to share such information with Congress and the news media. In the case of *Chicago and S. Airlines v. Waterman S.S. Corp.* (1948), Justice Robert Jackson wrote,

> The President both as Commander-in-Chief and as the Nation's organ for foreign affairs, has available intelligence services whose reports are not and ought not to be published to the world. It would be intolerable that courts, without the relevant information, should review and perhaps nullify actions of the Executive taken on information properly held secret.[109]

The executive branch has devised ways to deny or attempt to deny the legislature strategic information on foreign policy issues. During the Watergate investigations in 1973, the Nixon administration invoked *executive privilege*. This privilege, it asserted, conferred on the president the constitutional authority to withhold information from Congress and the law courts whenever he determined that the disclosure of such information would damage the performance of his constitutional duties. In 1973, when that contention was taken to the Supreme Court, (*United States v. Nixon*), the Court agreed that the administration could claim executive privilege if foreign policy or military secrets were involved, but it rejected the administration's assertion of absolute executive privilege. Earlier, in 1971, the administration had invoked a similar rationale for its court injunction to prevent the *New York Times* from publishing excerpts from the findings of an in-house study of the Vietnam War by the Department of Defense, known as the Pentagon Papers. In this instance of *prior restraint*, the Supreme Court, in *New York Times Co. v. United States* (1971), ruled against the administration. The use of prior restraint impedes congressional access to information and also undermines American citizens' ability to evaluate the nation's foreign policy.

When revelations of the Iran-Contra affair surfaced in November 1986, President Reagan denied them. Earlier, in 1985, he and his adviser on national security affairs, McFarlane, had assured the Congress that the "letter and spirit" of the Boland Amendments banning assistance to Nicaraguan Contras was being observed. In June 1986, when Reagan approved the shipment of arms to Iran, he ordered the CIA director, William Casey, not to report the arms shipment to the intelligence committees of the legislature. As more and more details of the secret activities began to unfold, Reagan persisted in his denial. In the midst of intensive media coverage of the scandal, he began to contemplate invoking executive privilege to prevent relevant officials of his administration from testifying before the Tower Commission appointed to investigate the covert activities. After he relented, abandoning his *delay and deceit strategy*,[110] and allowed those officials to testify, the officials still hid behind a wall of secrecy, as they argued, in order not to damage national security.

At times, the executive branch shares or provides requested information subject to an injunction of secrecy. Finally, it uses *contractual secrecy* as one means of withholding information from Congress and the public generally. It requires officials to commit themselves to a contract not to divulge classified material or any sensitive information of which they became aware during their tenure of office. This is an additional procedure to safeguard classified information. Contractual secrecy also requires individuals, once they leave office, to allow the government to review their subsequent public speeches and writings so as to forestall unintentional inclusion of classified information.

Summary

This chapter has examined the constitutional provisions for the conduct and management of American foreign relations. Aspects of those provisions have been a source of struggles and controversy between the president and Congress over the direction of American foreign policy. Whether or not that was the intent of the founders, those provisions have stood the test of time. They have worked relatively well in spite of changes in the internal and external environments of American foreign policy that the founders may not have anticipated. Executive misbehavior and differing pressures exerted by constituencies on both the president and the legislators have become additional sources of tension between the two branches over the conduct of foreign policy.

For most of the period prior to American military intervention in Vietnam and the end of the cold war, Congress acquiesced in the executive branch's usurpation of its constitutional prerogatives in foreign policy. It did so for a variety of reasons:[111]

- Congressional preoccupation with the cold war made that war a centripetal force in Washington relative to the making and conduct of American foreign policy.
- Preceding the cold war, the Depression and World War II had already had the effect of centralizing power in the executive branch.
- The ghost of the Versailles Treaty (1919), rejected by the Senate under the leadership of Henry Cabot Lodge, and the consequent failure of the United States to become a member of the League of Nations were also factors. Right or wrong, many minds in the United States saw a causal link between

the Senate's refusal to approve the Treaty of Versailles and the high incidence of totalitarian aggression during the 1930s, culminating in World War II. In effect, this link inhibited some members of Congress from aggressively opposing executive usurpation of congressional powers in foreign policy.

• Some legislators believed in the merit of bipartisanship and national concord in foreign affairs, especially in the so-called dangerous post-World War II period. It was thus deemed essential by most legislators to eschew partisanship and rally behind the president. After World War II, chief executives themselves frequently used bipartisanship to pressure and lull latent congressional opposition into supporting their foreign policy agenda.

• Finally, legislators were reluctant to question the executive branch on matters of foreign policy for fear that such questioning might be construed as a lack of patriotism or a lack of proper support for the nation in an age of continuous crisis.

The task for this post–cold war generation of American leaders is to eschew any ambitions, misbehavior, or ideological constructs that may tend to subvert the constitutional system that has worked so well for so long. Tinkering with the system most likely will create more problems. Rather, Congress and the executive need to develop greater faith in consultation and cooperation for a unified voice in world affairs. Contemporary world leadership demands no less. Congress and the executive must therefore come to realize that, while the framers of the Constitution established a system of shared powers and checks and balances to avoid a concentration of power, they also understood that those powers were inseparable from the standpoint of national security. Finally, they have to accept what the founders understood: "If governmental powers and responsibilities were actually set apart, each branch would exercise its powers in isolation from the other coordinate branches, to the detriment of cooperation and accommodation among them."[112] They should thus accept and implement the system they have inherited as one of separated institutions sharing overlapping powers that call for accommodation and cooperation. In the conduct of American foreign policy, the simple truth is that the president and Congress need each other.

Chapter 4
Presidential War Making

America's founders knew all too well how war appeals to the vanity of rulers and their thirst for glory. That's why they took care to deny presidents the kingly privilege of making war at their own discretion.[113]

Generally, war or peace is regarded as the paramount decision in foreign policy. Conscious of both the awesomeness and weight of such a decision as well as taxes and debt burdens—not to mention other horrors that result from war—the framers of the US Constitution provided specific measures against war making by one man or one branch of government. First, the written Constitution, which they created, guaranteed the rule of law and the principle that the US government is one of delegated powers. The ruler must rule or act in accordance with the authority or stipulations of the supreme law of the Republic. Officials who conduct the affairs of the state with other nations derive their authority to do so from the Constitution. They perform such functions in a framework of institutions and processes determined by it. They not only carry out their duties according to constitutional prescriptions and restrictions, they also act under oath to abide by those prescriptions and restrictions and to support and uphold the Constitution.

To ensure that the decision to use overt military force was made in a deliberate, reflective manner, the framers of the Constitution specifically delegated to Congress the war powers: First is the power *to declare war* against hostile nations. "This system," wrote James Wilson, one of the most penetrating political thinkers at the Philadelphia Constitutional Convention, "will not hurry us to war; it is calculated to guard against it. It will not be in the power of a single man, or a single body of men, to involve us in such distress."[114] It is thus clear that the framers of the US Constitution reserved the "sole and exclusive right and power of determining on peace and war" to Congress. Had they intended otherwise, "they might have said, in language they used elsewhere in the Constitution, that war could be declared by the President with the advice and consent of Congress, or by Congress on the recommendation of the President. They did not, but chose not to mention the President at all in connection with the war-making power."[115] James Madison emphasized this choice in a letter to Thomas Jefferson in 1798. He wrote, "The constitution supposes, what the

History of all Governments demonstrates, that the Exec[utive] is the branch of power most interested in war, and most prone to it. It has accordingly vested the question of war in the Legis[lature]."[116]

Additional war powers that framers of the Constitution vested exclusively in Congress include the powers to raise and support armies, to provide and maintain a navy, and to make rules for the governance and regulation of the armed forces. They also delegated to Congress general budgetary powers: to raise and appropriate funds for the common defense and to determine how the funds are to be spent.

The Constitution *designated* the president as *commander in chief* of the armed forces. This designation meant that the president is commander in chief of the armed forces only in wars declared by Congress, that once Congress had declared war, the president as commander in chief had full authority to prosecute the war and conduct all military operations. There is no evidence that any of the authors of the Constitution supposed that, as commander in chief, the president was endowed with an independent source of authority to initiate war except in repelling sudden aggression, an authority vested in him by the Constitution.

The framers of the Constitution designated the president as commander in chief of the armed forces in order to avoid fragmented direction of military operations and to assure civilian supremacy over the military. They saw the designation "simply as an office [to perform this function] and not an independent source of decision-making authority."[117] Here is how Alexander Hamilton specifically explained this designation of the president as commander in chief of the armed forces in the "Federalist No. 69." The president's power as commander in chief of the armed forces

> would be nominally the same with that of the king of Great Britain, but in substance much inferior to it. It would amount to nothing more than the supreme command and direction of the military and naval forces... while that of the British king extends to the *declaring* of war and to the *raising* and *regulating* of fleets and armies—all which, by the Constitution under consideration, would appertain to the legislature.[118]

Because the constitutional framers recognized how international agreements and "entangling alliances" could drag the signatories into war as they seek to enforce their formal and informal obligations under the treaty, the Constitution they crafted delegated to the executive branch the power to negotiate international agreements. But in doing so, it definitely withheld from the presidency the exclusive authority enjoyed by contemporary European monarchs to make treaties. Thus, the president is required to carry out the process by and with the advice and consent of the Senate, the upper chamber, comprising seasoned and more elderly statesmen. Specifically stipulated in the Constitution also is that such consent must be demonstrated by the concurrence of two-thirds of the senators present before the agreement becomes a legally binding commitment and part of the supreme law of the United States. In effect, the treaty powers of the Senate were designed to keep the United States free of foreign entanglements and in part also to preserve remnants of states' rights.

While the Constitution delegates the war powers in the manner delineated above and delegates to Congress the competence to initiate full resort to war, it speaks only of "war" but does not mention "the range of lesser coercion involving the symbolic or actual use of armed force."[119] Does the commander in chief have an independent competence to symbolic uses of force, such as conspicuously changing the levels of alert, sending a wing of fighter bombers to a beleaguered country, and conducting joint or separate maneuvers or war games as protest or warning, deterrence, or expansion of power? Or must Congress authorize such symbolic uses of force? The Constitution is silent. In practice, therefore, because of this apparent silence, US presidents have tended to initiate and engage in coercion short of overt war.

Besides delegating the war powers to Congress, the Constitution provides for tight civilian control of the military, making the armed forces strictly accountable to civilian officials. In 1951, President Harry S. Truman abruptly dismissed General Douglas MacArthur from his Far Eastern command during the Korean War. The general had flagrantly disobeyed a presidential order against pronouncements on foreign policy by government officials without prior clearance from the Department of State.

Finally, to ensure accountability of all public officials, especially the president and all members of Congress, the Constitution provides for their periodic election and guarantees the people—the electorate—as well freedom of expression and assembly. They may peaceably assemble and demonstrate to seek redress of any grievances. In addition, the national government has delegated and limited powers, and each of its branches has defined and explicit powers in order to safeguard the people's liberties.

It was collectively and philosophically from these concerns that the first president, George Washington, and his immediate successors sought to safeguard the new nation by shunning foreign entanglements. In his Farewell address, Washington admonished the nation to "steer clear of permanent alliances," and Thomas Jefferson warned against "entangling alliances." It was for the same concerns that, although the position of the United States had radically changed from what it had been in its earlier years as a nation, the

Senate rejected its membership in the Woodrow Wilson-proposed League of Nations. Article X of the League Covenant imposed on member nations the "obligation" to "preserve against external aggression the territorial integrity and existing political independence of all members of the League." This was an obligation in conflict with the provision of the US Constitution regarding the commitment of American armed forces into combat. The Senate and most Americans were unwilling to delegate to the League, a collective security organization, the exclusive constitutional power of Congress to declare war with the dispatch of American troops into hostilities.

It was not until after the devastations of World War II and the postwar blueprints for international organization meticulously devised by President Franklin D. Roosevelt before the war ended that the United States would become a member of a new collective security organization, the United Nations. Permanent membership with a veto power in the UN Security Council made that membership possible. Washington's veto in the Security Council and the UN Participation Act of 1945 ensured the membership. The UN Participation Act ensured that US soldiers would not be sent into combat over a president's objection. The act "authorized the United States to commit limited force [in defense of world order and the peace system] through congressionally approved special arrangement as provided for in Article 43 of the UN Charter. Presidents could not enter into such agreements on their own."[120] If more force was required than the agreement specified, the president was obligated to return to Congress for further authorization.

The Creep towards Presidential War Making

Resort to symbolic uses of force and departures from the Constitutionally stipulated measures began when presidents steadily expanded their legal powers and began to send US armed forces into combat overseas at will. Louis Henkin, a constitutional scholar, investigated the original constitutional concept of the president as commander in chief of the armed forces. He believes that the designation derived from the experience of the Revolutionary War. Having learned their lesson in that war—that "too many cooks spoil the broth"—the framers "determined that there should be a single, civilian commander-in-chief, rather than command by Congress or a congressional committee." According to Henkin, the

> evidence is that in the contemplation of the framers the armed forces would be under the command of the president but at the disposition of Congress. Principally, the president would command the forces in wars declared by Congress. As an exception, the framers agreed to leave to "the executive the power to repel sudden aggression."[121]

Henkin concludes that there is no evidence that the framers of the Constitution contemplated any independent role or authority for the president as commander in chief when there was no war.

However, presidents began to assert independent authority in response to events, challenges, and perceived threats to US national security. Jefferson ordered the navy to defend US commercial vessels in the Mediterranean against Barbary pirates, who were endangering American maritime commerce, and he informed Congress of his action only afterward. Later, though, he did seek and obtain Congress's permission for offensive action against the pirates. In 1846, President James K. Polk ordered the army to occupy a territory disputed by the United States and Mexico, thereby provoking a Mexican attack that he then had to repel by obtaining a congressional declaration of war. During the Civil War, Abraham Lincoln used both his designation as commander in chief and the constitutional requirement that he "take care that the laws are faithfully executed" to assume war-making powers. Among other actions, he blockaded southern ports, suspended the writ of habeas corpus in several places, and caused the arrest and military detention of individuals suspected of actual or likely treasonable offenses. In the context of the Civil War, Congress approved his actions. Similarly, Congress acquiesced during the late 1800s when presidents carried out "hot pursuit" of criminals across international borders and undertook operations against piracy and the international slave trade.

Slowly, precedents accumulated, increasing the confidence and the inclination of future presidents to act more independently. Thus, in several instances, presidents in the twentieth century deployed armed forces abroad for purposes determined on their own authority.[122] After the Russo-Japanese War of 1905, Theodore Roosevelt sent the navy around the world to impress the Japanese with America's naval might. In addition, Roosevelt and his immediate successors, William Howard Taft and Woodrow Wilson, repeatedly intervened militarily in the domestic affairs of Mexico and the Caribbean and Central American states.

Before the United States became a belligerent in World War II, Franklin D. Roosevelt ordered the navy to shoot on sight any German or Italian war vessels that entered the Western Hemisphere "security zone." In 1950, Truman unilaterally, without congressional joint resolution, ordered US armed forces in the Pacific to repel North Korea's thrust into South Korea. His secretary of state, Dean Acheson, argued that the president had the authority to use the armed forces to implement foreign policy, including treaties duly concluded and ratified by the national government. Indeed, on that occasion, the Senate majority leader and other senior members counseled against a suggestion that had been offered to President Truman that he should strengthen his political hands by asking Congress to pass a resolution endorsing his decision to defend South Korea. The senators argued, instead, "that such a resolution was unnecessary and might prompt a damaging and divisive debate."[123] In 1961, President John F. Kennedy authorized an abortive Bay of Pigs invasion by a CIA-backed Cuban force of 1,500 exiles attempting to overthrow Fidel Castro's Communist regime. Planned and organized during the Eisenhower administration, the invasion was justified, after the fact, to Congress and the American people as an attempt to halt the spread of communism and to reassert the Monroe Doctrine against European political intervention in the Western Hemisphere. Furthermore, when he imposed a naval quarantine on Cuba during the missile crisis in October 1962, Kennedy did so on his own authority as commander in chief and without any congressional approval or consultation. Believing the situation was an imminent threat to US security, no member of Congress complained publicly that he had exceeded his powers, since the imposition of a naval quarantine was essentially an act of war.

The pattern continued when President Lyndon Baines Johnson dispatched twenty-four thousand marines to the Dominican Republic in 1965 to prevent what was perceived to be an imminent Communist takeover. In May 1970, Nixon extended the Vietnam War into Cambodia, claiming that he was meeting his responsibility as commander in chief to protect men in the US armed forces. Presidents Ronald Reagan and George H. W. Bush launched their own military actions between 1982 and 1990, beginning with the dispatch of troops to Lebanon. In 1983, Reagan invaded Grenada to remove a radical Grenadan government that had aligned itself with Castro's Cuba, an ally of America's antagonist, the Soviet Union. During the period from 1982 to 1987, Congress, by the Boland Amendments, banned direct or indirect assistance to the Contra guerillas—President Reagan's "freedom fighters"—fighting against the Sandinista government of Nicaragua. The result, as discussed above, was that a frustrated President Reagan embarked upon measures that culminated in the Iran-Contra scandal and further violation of national law.

Furthermore, in 1985, Reagan persuaded Congress to repeal the Clark Amendment, which, in 1975, in the wake of America's Vietnam experience, had forbidden further US covert support for any of the factions involved in the Angolan war of political succession. Reagan had convinced the Congress that the amendment obstructed his efforts to conduct foreign policy, specifically, to provide political support for insurgents whom he regarded as "freedom fighters" seeking to overthrow Soviet- and Communist-supported regimes. Thus, following the repeal of the amendment, Reagan resumed US covert military and diplomatic support for the insurgency of the Jonas Savimbi-led National Union for the Total Independence of Angola against the Angolan government. The renewed covert support, at the expense of the American taxpayer, reescalated the Angolan conflict, increasing the scale of devastation and human suffering in the African country.

In April 1986, Reagan ordered bombing raids on the residence of the Libyan leader Muammar Khaddafi for his alleged sponsorship of a terrorist attack on Americans in a discotheque in what was then West Germany. Congress never questioned that attack, which may have triggered the bombing of Pan Am Flight 103 over Lockerbie in December 1988 by Libyan agents. That tragic bombing took 270 lives, most of them American citizens.

Like his predecessor, without congressional authorization, President George H. W. Bush invaded Panama in 1989 and brought its leader, Manuel Noriega, to Miami, Florida, to be tried, as he eventually was, for his alleged role in drug trafficking and money laundering. In 1990, Bush told congressional opponents of his planned war in the Persian Gulf that he had sufficient authority to dispatch US armed forces to the region against Saddam Hussein who had invaded, conquered, and annexed oil-rich Kuwait. After losing the presidential election in November 1992, Bush went to the United Nations rather than to Congress for authorization for Operation Restore Hope, a humanitarian intervention in Somalia during which thirty thousand US troops were dispatched to the war- and famine-ravaged African state. Later, President William Jefferson Clinton bombed Iraqi intelligence headquarters because of an alleged attempt by Saddam Hussein to assassinate former President George H. W. Bush. In 1995, he committed two-hundred thousand American troops to Bosnia-Herzegovina as part of the Dayton Accords and enforcement of the UN-authorized no-fly zone over Bosnia. In 1997, he bombed suspected Osama bin Laden's terrorist facilities in Afghanistan and the Sudan, even as he faced the prospect of an impeachment trial at home. Later, in early 1999, Clinton deployed American forces again to former Yugoslavia in a bombing campaign against Bosnia in reaction to its actions against ethnic Albanians in Kosovo. Although Congress definitely opposed these actions, it took no substantive measures to foil them.

Besides precedents, world conditions and the US position in the world, which had changed drastically from those that prevailed in 1789, have aggrandized the power of the executive and encouraged presidential war making. This is what, in the 1840s, Alexis de Tocqueville had predicted. In *Democracy in America*, he wrote, "if the existence of the United States were constantly menaced, and if its great interests were continually interwoven with those of other powerful nations, one would see the prestige of the executive growing, because of what was expected from it and of what it did."[124] Generally, the complexities and challenges of the post–World War II world and America's global and security interests have undoubtedly increased the power of the US presidency in foreign affairs at the expense of those of Congress. Especially during the period from 1945 to the late 1960s, Congress deferred to the president maximum discretion in foreign affairs because of the perceived great threat that the United States faced from communism and expansionist Soviet bloc. Its members believed that US interests would best be served if the president were granted such discretion. US membership in the UN further expanded the president's power in foreign affairs. As a function of that membership and as a permanent member of the Security Council, the president can and does deploy US armed forces in war, in order to enforce UN Security Council resolutions, without explicit congressional authorization. President Truman did so in Korea in 1950 to enforce the Uniting for Peace Resolution.

The National Security Act of 1947, for example, was a response to changed world conditions and the position of the United States as a global superpower. The act created the National Security Council (NSC) and the Intelligence Community, including the Central Intelligence Agency (CIA). In addition to its advisory and strategic intelligence functions, the CIA was mandated by the act to perform such other functions related to intelligence affecting national security as the National Security Council may direct from time to time. Given the national security challenges and perplexities of the post-war world, the CIA was frequently assigned clandestine missions and operations, some of which required the use of force. Furthermore, the National Security Act of 1947 renamed the War Department as the Department of Defense. These new agencies established by the 1947 National Security Act became institutionalized in an unprecedented way. They planned and positioned themselves on a global scale and operated in a high degree of secrecy. As part of the executive branch, they have tactical options, such as the use of proxies, not easily available to Congress and tend to involve themselves in the regular planning for and use of force in international politics in a manner not entirely foreseen by the constitutional framers and that, also, Congress has been unable to prevent. In cultivating a symbiotic relationship with the national media, they shape popular perceptions in order to advance their plans.

Historically, of more than 127 wars fought by the United States, Congress has declared only five: the War of 1812, the Mexican War, the Spanish War, World War I, and World War II. Why were the rest of the wars and other skirmishes initiated by presidents? Although Congress has never accepted the enlarged concept of presidential war making, it has itself contributed to the steady growth of that power. It did not seriously challenge presidential war making until the disastrous military intervention in Vietnam, when it felt a compelling need to reassert its power by adopting three measures: the National Commitments Resolution (1969), the symbolic repeal of the 1964 Gulf of Tonkin Resolution (1970), and the War Powers Resolution (1973). Before these actions, it had generally acquiesced in and funded the presidents' deployment of the armed forces. Presidents often disarmed members of Congress by informal consultation. Thus, the reality is that, when its ground rules were violated, Congress, as a body, notably failed to defend either its rules or prerogatives. As Thomas M. Franck has put it,

> Even when [the law] courts ... hinted that they might feel compelled to umpire a direct conflict between [the] President and Congress over the use of the armed forces in the absence of a declaration of a war, the legislature ...shied away from occasioning such a confrontation. Instead, it... acquiesced, specifically or tacitly, in unilateral presidential initiatives.[125]

Although some of its members criticized Truman's failure to consult it before dispatching troops to Korea in 1950,[126] Congress did not take the president to task for doing so. Rather, it endorsed what he had done. In 1965, President Johnson used a congressional resolution (Gulf of Tonkin) to escalate American military intervention in Vietnam. At his request for congressional authorization to protect an American naval vessel that had been attacked off the coast of Vietnam, Congress passed the Gulf of Tonkin Resolution. By the resolution, Congress gave its approval and support to Johnson, as commander in chief of the American armed forces, "to take all necessary measures to repel any armed attack against the forces of the United States and to prevent further aggression." Even before the passage of the resolution, Johnson's predecessors had already dispatched US military advisers to South Vietnam. Indeed, American military involvement in Southeast Asia began progressively, starting surreptitiously when President Truman subsidized the French colonial war against Vietnamese nationalists led by Ho Chi Minh. It was formalized in 1954, after the defeat of the French at Dien Bien Phu and the French decision, against American suggestion, not to continue the war. Upon that French decision, President Eisenhower began to provide Ngo Dinh Diem of South Vietnam US military and economic support as an instrument of the struggle between communism and the so-called free world. Eisenhower's successor, John F. Kennedy, increased the US assistance to South Vietnam in 1962. President Johnson escalated the military assistance incrementally after his electoral victory against Barry Goldwater in the November 1964 presidential election. After the military intervention in Vietnam had increased enormously, Congress asserted that Johnson had misused the Gulf of Tonkin Resolution as a blank check to commit the nation to a vastly different war in Southeast Asia.

Congress had passed similar resolutions earlier, when President Eisenhower asked for authorization to use military force in Formosa (Formosa Resolution, 1955) and in the Middle East (Middle East Resolution, 1957). The Formosa Resolution authorized Eisenhower to use the armed forces, if necessary, to ensure the security of Formosa and the Pescadores against Chinese Communists. The Middle East Resolution granted him the authority to use American armed forces in the Middle East to assist any nation requesting support against Communist-led aggression. Before passing the 1957 Middle East Resolution, Congress deleted from the Eisenhower administration's draft resolution language explicitly authorizing the use of force. Members were apprehensive that "the country might be harmed if presidents came to believe they could use force only if they first obtained approval of Congress."[127] Eisenhower used the authority of the resolution to intervene in Lebanon in 1958. Reagan followed that precedent in 1982 with a disastrous intervention in Lebanon; he used the Middle East Resolution as a basis, although he did not explicitly invoke it.

Another factor contributing to presidential war making is the problem of defining when a state of war exists. No state can wait until a war has broken out or has been declared before mobilizing its armed forces. There is always a definite advantage in a preemptive strike against a clear and imminent danger and a very determined enemy. Furthermore, the American people tend to applaud aggressive leadership. Kennedy's approval ratings rose significantly after his naval quarantine of Cuba in October 1962, even though he had been reluctant to apply force short of war, as Congress had urged. So did Reagan's approval ratings soar after the bombing raids he ordered on Libya in 1986; Ford's after the Mayaguez rescue attempt, in spite of American losses in men; and Bush's after Operations Desert Shield and Desert Storm in 1991. Thus, the evidence is that decisive military actions by presidents tend to be politically popular and disarming of Congress. It is when they are protracted and especially costly in human lives and so unpopular that Congress shows some will to act. Finally, during the cold war, presidents capitalized on these factors, as well as on the perceived Communist and Soviet threat to American values and institutions, to amplify their role as commander in chief of the armed forces and their duty to protect national security interests overseas. Ultimately, in the process, they have led America into undeclared wars—so far, all conventional.

Congressional Measures to Curb Presidential War Making

Chapter 3 discussed the initial measures by which Congress had attempted to curb presidential resort to executive agreements and war making without the express authorization by Congress. The first attempt, the Bricker Amendment, as noted, failed by one vote to receive the required two-thirds majority in the Senate. The second attempt, the National Commitments Resolution (1969) failed to curb both presidential war making and use of executive agreements to circumvent the advice and consent role of the Senate in treaty making. The symbolic repeal of the Gulf of Tonkin Resolution in 1970 was intended to demonstrate Congress's frustrations and anger over President Nixon's extension of the Vietnam War into Cambodia in May 1970 more so than to prevent its future use by presidents, especially since it was space and location specific.

After the repeal of the Gulf of Tonkin Resolution, the Senate adopted a more audacious measure when it passed the Cooper-Church Amendment requiring the withdrawal of American armed forces from Cambodia. The amendment stipulated that all funding for support of US forces in Cambodia would be cut off if President Nixon failed to withdraw them by 1 July 1970. Nixon withdrew the troops but stated that it had in fact been his intention to do so all along.

The Case-Zablocki Act of 1972 went beyond the scope of the earlier attempts, except the Cooper-Church Amendment, by including provisions that required annual reporting of executive agreements not reported within the original sixty-day period, as well as a determination by the secretary of state of what specifically constituted an international agreement.

The War Powers Resolution of 1973

So far, the War Powers Resolution (1973) is the most serious attempt by Congress to curb presidential war making and to recapture and protect its own power. Specifically, the resolution sought to prohibit, discourage, and contain presidential war making. It was provoked by the national malaise caused by the Vietnam War. Its passage was facilitated by the Watergate scandal, which politically weakened President Richard M. Nixon. Contextually, the resolution sought to prevent future wars like the Vietnam War, to reduce future presidential commitment of American troops to conflicts in regions where there was no clear and imminent threat to American national security interest, and to redress the balance between Congress and the presidency in the use of armed forces abroad. The resolution requires the president to

1. Consult Congress, in every possible instance, before committing troops "into hostilities or into situations where imminent involvement in hostilities" is likely. [128]
2. Inform Congress within forty-eight hours after the introduction of troops if there has been no declaration of war.
3. Remove troops within sixty days (or ninety days in certain special circumstances) if Congress does not either declare war or adopt a joint resolution approving the action.

By the resolution, Congress may also terminate military involvement before the sixty-day limit by passing a concurrent resolution. (Such a resolution does not require a president's signature, and so cannot be vetoed by him). In addition, Congress stipulated in the resolution that

> nothing in this resolution…shall be construed as granting any authority to the President with respect to the introduction of United States Armed Forces into hostilities or into situations wherein involvement in hostilities is clearly indicated by the circumstances which authority he would not have had in the absence of this joint [resolution].[129]

It is unmistakable that, above everything else, the agony, frustrations, and tragedy of the war in Vietnam and Nixon's military incursions into Cambodia triggered the passage of the War Powers Resolution. In explaining the rationale for the resolution, Senator Spark Matsunaga (Democrat, Hawaii) wrote, "If we have learned but one lesson from the tragedy of Vietnam, I believe it is that we need definite, unmistakable procedures to prevent future undeclared wars. 'No more Vietnams' should be our objective in setting up procedures."[130]

President Nixon and his successors challenged the constitutionality of the resolution. In fact, Nixon, who maintained that the resolution would seriously undermine the nation's ability to act decisively and convincingly in times of international crisis, vetoed it. But Congress overrode his veto.[131] Despite this, in reality, the resolution has not achieved its objectives.

Thomas Franck argues that the resolution authorized executive use of the armed forces "in unlimited circumstances for a fixed period,"[132] thereby giving the president even wider powers in war making than he had with the constitutional designation as commander in chief. Others note that the resolution's procedure has not worked as intended. Rather, it has not inhibited presidents from deploying force on their sole authority. Although it has caused the presidents to be more cautious in their deployment of the armed forces, it has promoted neither genuine prior consultation nor cooperative sharing of responsibility between the legislative and executive branches.

Presidents have reluctantly complied with the reporting aspects of the resolution and have become more cautious in their war making. But, in general, they have rejected the applicability of the resolution to their perceived responsibilities and have creatively evaded it whenever they believed that their duty warranted unilateral deployment of force abroad. This is illustrated by Reagan's deployment of US troops in Lebanon in 1982 and his invasion of Granada in 1983 and George H. W. Bush's invasion of Panama in 1989. Furthermore, in 1987 and 1988, the Reagan administration deployed US war ships in the Persian Gulf to protect, as it claimed, US-flagged Kuwaiti oil tankers without reporting to Congress under the War Powers Resolution. In 1993, Senator Dole called for a repeal of the resolution. Such a repeal would tilt the balance further in favor of the executive.

The National Security Revitalization Act
One of the most recent attempts by Congress to curb presidential war making is the National Security Revitalization Act enacted by the House of Representatives in 1995. Backed by the Republican Speaker of the House Newt Gingrich, the bill reflected the determination of conservative Republican members of Congress and neoisolationists to reduce US participation in UN peacekeeping operations. What immediately provoked the passage of the bill was the sequel to Operation Restore Hope—a humanitarian mission under UN auspices—in Somalia during which eighteen American soldiers were killed in a failed state that Congress believed was peripheral to US national security.

President Clinton's attempt to conciliate congressional critics of US participation in the mission by issuing his Presidential Decision Directive 25 (PDD-25) failed to prevent the House passage of the bill. His PDD-25 had stipulated very stringent conditions under which American armed forces would participate in UN peacekeeping missions. For example, the mission would have to be one in which a vital US security interest was at stake, the mission would have clear objectives, there would have to be adequate resources to undertake the mission, and there would have to be an exit strategy.

Critics of US participation in UN peacekeeping operations were not satisfied with Clinton's stipulations. The consequent National Security Revitalization Act passed by the House sought to increase congressional control over peacekeeping deployments under UN auspices. The bill had three proposals for attaining this objective: It would reduce US financial support for ongoing UN peacekeeping operations by more than $1 billion, it would limit the president's ability to approve new UN peacekeeping missions, and it would prevent him from placing US forces under foreign command as part of a UN peacekeeping operation.

The Peace Powers Act

In the Senate, Senator Robert Dole, who argued that there was a need "to rein in the blank check for UN peacekeeping,"[133] introduced the Peace Powers Act in 1995. His proposed bill, which was not enacted, sought, among other things, to

1. Strengthen the consultation provisions of the War Powers Act.
2. Strengthen congressional oversight of UN-sponsored peacekeeping missions by amending the UN Participation Act of 1945 to give Congress a statutory role in the relationship between the United States and the United Nations.
3. Impose "significant new limits" on UN-sponsored peacekeeping missions, which Senator Dole charged was jeopardizing American interests and squandering American human and material resources.[134]
4. Forbid US troops participating in UN-sponsored peacekeeping missions to serve under foreign commanders.

Collectively, the measures identified above have not prevented presidents from waging wars on their own initiative. While America's second war in the Persian Gulf against Iraq since 1990 was authorized by the 107th Congress, the initiative was completely that of President George W. Bush. That war, as discussed in subsequent chapters 7, 8, 9, and 10, has vindicated most of the arguments of the framers of the US political system against entrusting the nation's war powers to the chief executive. It is true that time is not static and that as times and circumstances change so do people in them also change, adapting their institutions to changing times and realities. But human nature has not changed, and presidential war making has not appreciably advanced the national security interest of the United States. Given this claim, it is not pragmatic to tinker unnecessarily with the provisions of the Constitution, especially regarding the war powers, which were carefully devised by the framers.

Chapter 5
A Culture of Deference in Congress to the Presidency on Foreign Affairs in Recent Historical Perspective

The operation of a free government requires constant vigilance and housecleaning whenever necessary. In the US political system, this requirement is a central function and purpose of congressional oversight and investigations of the executive branch. This key role requires Congress to make sure that the provisions of the Constitution as well as the laws that it writes are faithfully executed by the executive branch in domestic, diplomatic, and military activities of the nation. The purpose is to prevent mistakes from happening or becoming uncontrollable or recurring. Congress, as a corporate body, has largely lost its will to carry out this function and to co-determine American foreign policy with the president. Since the beginning of the continuing crisis in world affairs, it has progressively and substantially ceded its fundamental constitutional role in foreign policy to the executive branch. For most of the time, from the late 1930s to the present, it acquiesced or merely reacted to the president's foreign policy initiatives. Why? [Author, FUO]

Greater participation by elected representatives in [foreign policy] decision making cannot...guarantee a sound foreign policy. But in principle at least, an indifferent Congress makes it harder to achieve good decisions.[135]

For the effective management of the domestic and foreign affairs of the federation they formed, the framers of the American Constitution and political system created separate institutions, with both sharing powers and checking and balancing each other. The system of power sharing and balancing, the framers believed, was crucial to democratic control of government. To them, the system was a solution to the concentration of powers in one branch of the government that leads to tyranny. James Madison, one of the framers of the Constitution, wrote in "Federalist No. 51,"

the great security against a gradual concentration of the several powers in the same department consists in giving to those who administer each department, the necessary constitutional means, and personal motives, to resist encroachments of the others.... Ambition must be made to counteract ambition. The interest of the man, must be connected with the constitutional rights of the place. It may be a reflection of human nature that such devices should be necessary to control the abuses of government. But what is government itself, but the greatest of all reflections on human nature? If men were angels, no government would be necessary. If angels were to govern men, neither external nor internal controls on government would be necessary.[136]

Furthermore, the framers of the Constitution believed in the notion that politics stops at the water's edge, that American foreign policy should be subservient to domestic policy and values, and that Congress and the presidency should play a coequal role in its making and management. The president was to conduct the day-to-day business of foreign policy. To perform its own part of this function competently in the interest of the nation, Congress was granted more specific powers, especially those of war, the purse, oversight of the executive, and advice and consent in treaty making with other nations and in the confirmation of executive appointment of high-ranking members of the president's national security team. By exercising these powers—reviewing the conduct of foreign policy by the president and his national security team, rendering advice whether it is solicited or not, and granting or withholding its consent to any major proposed acts of foreign policy—Congress would restrain the president. But acting together, the two would provide a unified front for the advancement of the nation's foreign policy goals.

In "Federalist No. 75," Alexander Hamilton, regarded as the architect of the American Constitution, articulated the rationale for requiring the two branches of the government to act together:

> The history of human conduct does not warrant that exalted opinion of human virtue which would make it wise in a nation to commit interests of so delicate and momentous a kind, as those which concern its intercourse with the rest of the world, to the sole disposal of a magistrate created and circumscribed as would be a President of the United States.[137]

In practice, in spite of these constitutional provisions and the intent of the creators of the US political system, presidents have played a more dominant role in the making and management of US foreign policy, even when some, like William Jefferson Clinton and George W. Bush, assumed the presidency with little or no experience in foreign affairs.

Historically, especially since the beginning and the end of World War II, several forces contributed to this presidential dominance in foreign affairs. Prominent among the forces include the following: the international custom and practice of a nation speaking with one voice in foreign affairs, usually that of the nation's chief executive who serves as the nation's channel of communication to foreign countries; the growth in the executive powers of the presidency in response to changing times and increasing needs and challenges but especially as incumbents of the office make expansive use of their interpretation of these powers, often for political purposes; the frequent resort to executive agreements in place of treaties;[138] legislative delegation of authority to the executive; judicial rulings and interpretation of the Constitution;[139] and emergencies and other situations that arise in the external environment.

Throughout the history of the nation, beginning with George Washington, presidents have used the necessity to act in response to external developments they perceived to be threatening US national security as a means of acquiring additional power and dominating the foreign policy process. Routinely, Congress acquiesced in such actions as Washington's 1793 proclamation of US neutrality in the Napoleonic Wars, the Monroe Doctrine of 1823, the Truman Doctrine of 1947 regarding Greece and Turkey, and the Carter Doctrine of 1980 regarding the oil-rich Persian Gulf after the Soviet invasion of Afghanistan. Such acquiescence to presidential initiation of foreign policy contributed to the erosion of the power of Congress in foreign policy and enhanced the power of the presidency.

In addition to these examples, presidents have enormous foreign policy resources compared to what is available to members of Congress. Presidential singularity is an advantage in that the president is the one individual American leader and chief executive universally known as such, while Congress is a corporate body of 535 members. The incumbent of the office is the one that deals with leaders of other nations and the one to whom the American people look in both domestic and international crises and emergencies. Among other advantages, presidents have unrivaled access to information and several means and resources for dispensing patronage. The office has structural advantages to decide and act in secrecy with dispatch and stability of purpose. These advantages over members of Congress are enhanced by the availability to the president of the expertise and longevity in government of the established foreign policy bureaucracies that shape and implement foreign policy. Added to these advantages is the president's constitutionally based weapon—the veto power—which enables the incumbent of the office to terminate congressional initiatives that counter or infringe on the president's preferences. Members of Congress find it difficult to muster a two-thirds majority in both of their chambers to override a president's veto.

Furthermore, incumbents of the presidency have developed hidden but effective strategic means of increasing their influence in foreign affairs and diminishing that of Congress. Privately, they brief, importune, or publicly pressure leaders of congressional committees and other key lawmakers to support their policy. They tend to use the bully pulpit in a variety of ways: For example, to undermine the effectiveness or perspective of those members of Congress who oppose their policy or present options different from theirs, they use creative language such as "manifest destiny," "a dangerous world," "evil

empire," "rogue states," "axis of evil," and images of global threats, such as
terrorism, and domestic ideals to mobilize public support for their policy and
to deflate opposition by members of Congress. President George W. Bush used
this strategy effectively in making his case for the US invasion of Iraq. For his
top officials, Vice President Cheney and Defense Secretary Rumsfeld, who had
the ambition to reduce to the barest minimum congressional limits on the
president's power to conduct foreign policy, the terrorist acts of 11 September
2001 became a golden opportunity to unfetter the imperial presidency, cut the
Congress down to size, and embark on a war to disarm Iraq of its alleged
weapons of mass destruction. Hence, the administration adroitly exploited post-
11 September 2001 fear of terrorism in the country and invoked frightening
images of the "axis of evil," "mushroom clouds," buried caches of germ
warfare, and drones poised to deliver germ-laden death in America's major
cities.[140] Consequently, apprehensive of being perceived as unpatriotic by the
electorate, several members of Congress who did not favor US invasion became
docile and voted for the draft resolution Bush had submitted to Congress to
authorize military action against Iraq.

The executive branch prefers to keep lawmakers and the public in the dark
about the specifics of its conduct and management of foreign affairs by a variety
of measures: Frequently, it invokes *executive privilege* by which it asserts that
the president has constitutional authority to withhold information whose
disclosure he has determined would damage the performance of his
constitutional duties. Sometimes, it *stonewalls*. At other times, it resorts to *prior
restraint*, preventing publication or disclosure of information pertaining to some
specific foreign policy issue. Resort to these practices prevents Congress from
participating optimally in the selection of foreign policy options or the
supervision of the management of selected policy. This was how the George W.
Bush administration resisted cooperation with members of a special
Congressional Joint Committee in establishing the facts about events that
preceded the terrorist attacks of 11 September 2001.

Presidents also resort to recess appointments to overcome blocked
confirmation of their appointments. Clinton did so in 1997 to send James
Hormel as US ambassador to Luxembourg, and Bush subsequently did so in
August 2005 to send John R. Bolton as US ambassador to the United Nations.
At times, presidents co-opt key members of Congress into the early phase of the
foreign policy process through consultation and the practice of bipartisanship
in foreign policy. They sign executive orders and presidential decision
directives that do not require congressional approval for their execution. In
addition to these strategies, there are individuals who support the idea of

presidential supremacy in foreign policy. Individuals, such as Vice President Dick Cheney, suggest that, in the current world of weapons of mass destruction and terrorism, the United States cannot afford to have a decentralized foreign policy process in which power is rigidly shared between the president and Congress. Rather, they advocate that, in our contemporary complex world, global decisions should be left to the presidency.[141]

These forces and strategies worked collectively with others inherent in the vagaries of domestic politics to enhance the role of presidents in foreign affairs and to diminish that of Congress. Particularly after the end of World War II, the need for a foreign policy consensus during the cold war and the US emergence as a global hegemon concentrated foreign policy powers in the presidency. The exigencies of the period, such as the conflicts in Korea and Vietnam and the Cuban Missile Crisis, not only made it seem necessary for Congress to defer to the chief executive in the making and management of foreign policy, but also contributed to erode constitutional constraints on the president. Incumbents of the office exploited these developments to transform themselves virtually into imperial presidents with unchecked authority in the international arena. The growth of the imperial presidency became the greatest challenge to the role of Congress in the foreign policy process. Concomitantly, because of frequent misperceptions of reality, the imperial policies of presidents often led to foreign policy blunders and seldom promoted America's national security interests both narrowly and broadly defined. Frequently, the policies tended to alienate America's friends and allies, enraged potential foes, created enemies, and tarnished America's image and credibility overseas. At the same time, the imperial policies, as in Southeast Asia in the 1960s and early 1970s, in the Philippines after the Spanish-American War, and in Iraq in the first decade of the twenty-first century, cost the nation enormous human and material resources.

Presidents John F. Kennedy and Lyndon B. Johnson, with no public debate, committed the United States militarily to Southeast Asian countries. Slowly, they embroiled the nation in a war that was intended to prevent other "dominoes" from falling to communism. This they did in a manner that tore the nation apart. Their successor, Richard M. Nixon, stealthily continued their policy by secretly expanding the war to Cambodia in spite of his 1968 election campaign promises that he had a plan to extricate the nation from Vietnam. Ultimately, the policies of the three administrations ended in virtual defeat. But the Nixon administration attempted "systematically and, until the Watergate affair, successfully to restrict" the congressional powers of oversight and investigation.[142]

In 1982, less than ten years after US withdrawal from Vietnam, President Ronald Reagan dispatched eight hundred US marines to Lebanon to ensure stability in the region that he believed was a "vital interest" of the United States. Later, he reported this action to Congress as required by the War Powers Resolution (1973) (see chapter 4). After a period of one month, President Reagan deployed 1,200 troops back into Lebanon, this time without reporting to Congress. In October 1983, 241 US marines were killed in a suicide truck bombing of their headquarters. Anger of Congress at this development forced Reagan to withdraw US forces in February 1984. This development did not prevent Presidents Reagan and George H. W. Bush from waging unilateral wars in Grenada and Panama, respectively, in 1983 and 1989, nor did it prevent President William J. Clinton from waging unilateral wars in Bosnia and Kosovo. Earlier in the 1980s, the nation witnessed a disconcerting case of presidential aggrandizement in foreign policy by the Reagan administration that threatened the rule of law and US democratic institutions. In deception and disdain for the law, the administration conducted secret diplomacy by which it traded arms with Iran for hostages held in Lebanon and aided Contra rebels in Nicaragua with the profit.

Several claims and actions of the George W. Bush administration further illustrate the manifestation and tenacity of imperial presidency in US foreign policy. Following the terrorist attacks on US territory in September 2001, the administration and its lawyers insisted that, as commander in chief, President Bush had the authority to act unilaterally on several foreign policy issues, including the authority to

- Launch a major preemptive invasion without congressional approval.
- Order the indefinite detention of any and all people he alleges to be "enemy combatants" (including Americans seized on American soil) without due process or access to lawyers or courts.
- Authorize indiscriminate torture to make such detainees talk, in defiance of international treaty obligations and a 1994 law making torture a crime.
- Prosecute non-American detainees in "military commissions" devised by his administration, which offer defendants limited protections, no appeals outside the chain of command, and the prospect of execution.
- Order eavesdropping on Americans' international telephone conversations with suspected al-Qaeda agents, without court warrants.[143]

The administration's claim that it had unilateral power to launch a preemptive war without congressional approval began at the same time that it started making its case for such a war against Iraq. In a speech on 26 August 2002 at the Veterans of Foreign Wars Convention in Nashville, Tennessee, Vice President Dick Cheney, who was a driving force behind the eventual war, made the following declaration: "The Bush Administration is fully committed to launching a war against Iraq with the aim of removing Saddam Hussein, regardless of UN efforts to insert weapons inspectors.... The Administration *will brook no dissent on this matter from Congress or senior figures in the Republican Party....* At bottom, those who favor caution and delay in removing Saddam are advocating a dangerous path that could have devastating consequences for many countries, including our own" (emphasis added).[144] Note that, at the time Cheney made his speech, there was no national emergency or transcendent crisis. There was neither imminent threat to the US national security nor a popular demand or a public necessity to act.

President Bush himself did not repudiate his vice president's imperial posture on Iraq. Rather, he reinforced it and vowed that he would allow no bounds to his exercise of national power relative to dethroning Saddam Hussein. On the same 26 August 2002, when Cheney made his speech, White House lawyers asserted that Bush required no congressional approval for an attack on Iraq. The administration, they said, did not want to be in the legal position of asking Congress to authorize the use of force in Iraq when the president already had that authority.

To those who expressed qualms about the administration's imperial policy and intolerance of dissent, typified by the reinforced Cheney statement on Iraq, Bush responded that, while he was aware that some very intelligent people were expressing their opinion about Saddam Hussein and Iraq and he would listen carefully to them, Americans needed to know that his decision would be based on the latest intelligence and how best to protect America and its allies. But there were indications at the time that his administration was manipulating intelligence to suit its policy and that he himself was misleading the public on his Iraq policy.

Conscious of the fact that the founders of the US political system deliberately rejected executive absolutism in foreign affairs, members of Congress have occasionally taken measures to redress the balance and to curb the growth of imperial presidency (see chapter 4).The claims of the Bush administration to unilateral authority were challenged by Congress, as were those of its predecessors in office. In 2004, the Supreme Court curbed the administration's claimed power to detain suspected enemies (whom it described as "enemy combatants") at Guantanamo Bay. The Court required that Americans detained at Guantanamo Bay should be granted access to counsel and hearings and that foreign detainees were to have access to federal courts. At the persistence of Senator John McCain, Congress attached an amendment named after the senator to a 2005 Pentagon funding bill limiting brutal methods of interrogating detainees.

However, in signing the McCain Amendment, President Bush asserted that he has the right to set aside any statute passed by Congress when it conflicts with *his interpretation* of the Constitution. Hence, he avowed that he would construe the McCain Amendment in a manner consistent with his authority as president. The implications of the signing statement are far reaching: The US constitutional system is abrogated, finished, if a president can decide that a law passed by Congress is inconvenient and simply proceeds to circumvent or ignore it.

In the wake of the Vietnam War, members of Congress strove to restrain the executive's ability to conduct foreign policy without congressional authorization and oversight. In the 1980s, they enacted the Boland Amendments to prevent President Ronald Reagan from making proxy war in Nicaragua. But, so far, such measures as they have taken have not made any appreciable dent on the increasing growth of presidential pretensions, power, and authority over US foreign policy. Instead, there exists within the Congress a culture of deference to the president that contributes to the growth of those pretensions and cedes even more power to the presidency. Therefore, American leaders, such as the late Senator J. William Fulbright and the historian Arthur M. Schlesinger Jr., who believe in the democratic process and the preservation of constitutional limitations on the power of the executive, expressed genuine concerns about the future in view of the contemporary trends.[145] Concerned about the trend towards what he believed was presidential dictatorship, Senator Fulbright protested,

> I believe that the Presidency has become a dangerously powerful office, more urgently in need of reform than any other institution in American government.... Whatever may be said of Congress—that it is slow, obstreperous, inefficient or behind the times—there is one thing that can be said for it: It poses no threat to the liberty of the American people.[146]

Furthermore, Fulbright called for wiser use of national power and a balanced approach to foreign policy between Congress and the executive branch in which the two jointly chart the desired approach. This done, the president, he advocated, would take the lead to implement the approach, making necessary periodic adjustments in consultation with more experienced and leading members of Congress. As chair of the Senate Foreign Relations Committee,

Fulbright openly and vigorously criticized President Lyndon B. Johnson's policy on Vietnam.

For his part, Schlesinger argued in *The Imperial Presidency* that the American Constitution envisaged a strong presidency with an equally strong system of accountability, that upsetting the constitutional balance in favor of presidential power at the expense of presidential accountability transforms the presidency into an imperial authority. Doing so is destructive of the American constitutional system. "For," Schlesinger went on, "history had shown that neither the Presidency nor the Congress was infallible, and that each needed the other—which may well be what the Founding Fathers were trying to tell us."[147]

More recent opponents of imperial presidency agree with the earlier critics that American freedom and democracy cannot coexist with an imperial presidency regardless of its justification. To surrender foreign policy powers to the executive branch, they argue, "is to risk making decisions that are contrary to the will of the people and thereby undermining, in the name of national security, the very essence of democracy and the American form of government."[148] They emphasize that consolidating power in one person is dangerous not only because power is a corrupting influence, but also because it tends to shape truth. "Power, in the end," they assert, can determine reality, or at least the reality that most people accept."[149] Furthermore, these critics warn that the loss of the American political system of power sharing and balancing is more of a security danger than the 11 September 2001 terrorist attacks that President Bush exploited in his quest for imperial power. Others argue that vital national resources ought not to be sacrificed to promote the personal ambition, ideology, and world view of an imperial president at the expense of national security and the well-being of the American people.

One of the most recent expressions of concern about the continuing departure from the constitutional system and congressional statutes was by Lawrence Wilkerson. Based on his vast experience in the military and government and observations as former chief of staff of former Secretary of State Colin Powell in the first George W. Bush administration, Wilkerson recalled how, in the past, such departures from the constitutional process had led the United States into a host of disasters. He cited the embarrassments of the last years of the Vietnam intervention, the Iran-Contra scandal, and, more recently, the Bush administration's unilateral foreign policy. He argued that, given the multifaceted, complex, and fast-breaking crises, with their incredible potential for regional and global ripple effects, which confront the US government, to depart from the constitutional and systematic decision-making process as was laid out in the 1947 National Security Act invites disaster.[150]

This chapter focuses on the practices and patterns of behavior of members of Congress that tend to increase the role and influence of presidents in foreign affairs at the expense of that of Congress and, more importantly, to the detriment of the interests of the nation, the well-being of its people, and its constitutional system.

Practices and Patterns of Behavior in Congress Contributing to Growth in Presidential Power in Foreign Affairs

Congress defends freedom by asking rude questions; by stubbornly insisting that technology be discussed in terms of its human effects; by eliciting new ideas from old heads; by building a sympathetic bridge between the bewildered citizen and the bureaucracy; by acting as sensitive register for group interests whose fortunes are indistinguishable from the fortunes of vast numbers of citizens and who have a constitutional right to be heard.

Congress defends freedom by being a prudent provider; by carefully sifting and refining legislative proposals; by compromising and homogenizing raw forces in conflict; by humbling generals and admirals—and, on occasion, even Presidents.[151]

The statement above remains a critical function of the US Congress, which is generally regarded as the strongest legislative branch of government in the modern world. To perform the function and to influence the foreign policy process, Congress uses a variety of legislative and nonlegislative measures, including investigations, hearings by standing or select committees, and lawsuits by its individual members, derived from its constitutional powers. It imposes foreign policy reporting requirements on the executive branch as part of the oversight responsibility of congressional committees. But, over the years, Congress has faced an uphill battle in challenging and overseeing the executive branch in the making and conduct of foreign policy.

Apart from its structure, certain of its practices and patterns of behavior have tended to undermine its performance of this critical function. Thus, since World War II, members of Congress have contributed to the growth and influence of the incumbents of the presidency at the expense of their own constitutional powers in foreign policy in a variety of ways. They have not always lived up to their *constitutional* responsibilities. Rather, too often, their tendency has been either to engage in foreign policy in a lackadaisical manner or to defer to the executive branch. This tendency became most manifest early in the period of a persisting permanent crisis that can be traced to World War II in the late 1930s and the early 1940s when Congress began increasingly to defer to the president in the making and conduct of foreign policy. It allowed the president a free hand to act in the national security interest. Members believed that, in emergencies and certain situations, the chief executive had the information, and needed the requisite authority and resources, to make decisions and act decisively and appropriately. It was therefore necessary for Congress to restrain itself and allow the chief executive to manage the nation's foreign policy on a daily basis. However, the executive branch was obligated to consult and inform Congress as it was doing so.

Consequently, under this unwritten compact, foreign policy making essentially became the domain of a few powerful executive officials and congressional leaders, while the average member of Congress began to have little if any say in foreign policy development.[152] This especially was the practice during the administrations of Franklin D. Roosevelt, Harry Truman, Dwight Eisenhower, John F. Kennedy, and Lyndon B. Johnson, who were in office during World War II and the beginning and the height of the cold war.[153] Of special significance is President Roosevelt's two executive agreements—the Lend-Lease Agreement with Great Britain in August 1940 and the February 1945 Yalta Agreement with the Soviet Union.[154] As France fell to Germany in the summer of 1940 and Britain faced an imminent German invasion, Roosevelt used executive order to provide the British fifty old American destroyers in exchange for bases in strategic locations on the Atlantic. This single act moved the United States closer to the war, as it provided Germany legal grounds to declare war on the United States. Consequently, the act became a source of controversy between the president and Congress. Later, in March 1941, as the war raged, Congress formally approved the Lend-Lease Program. It authorized President Roosevelt to sell, exchange, lease, and lend defense materials to "any country whose defense" he deemed necessary to the defense of the United States. Roosevelt's motives in the Lend-Lease Agreement were proper. The timing of his action was of essence as it avoided debate that might have benefitted Germany instead of Britain. However, his incursion into the Senate's constitutional power set a precedent for future incursions by presidents who would ignore the special emergency under which Roosevelt acted.

President Ronald Reagan acted in this wise when he incorporated the Director of Central Intelligence William Casey into his cabinet, thus politicizing the office. The intent of Congress when it established the office was otherwise: that its incumbent should be an independent and objective interpreter of foreign events. President Reagan further ignored Congress when he sent US marines to Lebanon and used the National Security Council to implement his policy of defying Congress, which resulted in the Iran-Contra scandal.

After the terrorist attacks on the New York World Trade Center and the Pentagon in 2001, George W. Bush successfully replicated in a more subtle way the practice of increasing the powers of the executive. He sought and obtained from Congress, through the USA PATRIOT Act, more powers for national security. Furthermore, he bypassed the Foreign Intelligence Surveillance Court that approves national security wiretaps to order the National Security Agency to eavesdrop on the communications of Americans and others inside the United States with suspected foreign terrorists. When the practice was made public in December 2005,[155] President Bush asserted that he had done so under his constitutional powers and those granted to him by the USA PATRIOT Act in order to protect American national security. Thus, by an expansive interpretation of an act of Congress by a president, American democratic principles began to be undermined in the name of national security. It is in this manner that legislative delegation of authority to the executive branch in the service of national security interest became one outstanding example of the ways by which Congress reduced its role and enhanced that of the president in the making and conduct of foreign policy. From that practice, what had begun "as emergency powers temporarily confided to presidents soon hardened into authority claimed by presidents as constitutionally inherent in the presidential office; thus the Imperial Presidency."[156]

Given the composition of Congress as a corporate body of 535 members of competing political parties and interests vis-à-vis the institutional and political unity of the presidency, certain foreign policy powers are best exercised by the executive and so are either shared with or delegated to it. Because it believed that American security demanded a level of secrecy, efficiency, and unity of action that makes prolonged debate and legislative checks obstructive, Congress found it proper to allow presidents to act not only in crises but also in other sensitive situations while they share with its key members the major elements of their policies. Occasionally, it granted presidents discretionary power through legislative acts and resolutions to use some of its authority in foreign affairs to assist, defend, protect, or promote American national security interests. The Reciprocal Trade Agreements Act of 1934 granted the executive branch wide freedom in negotiating tariff reductions with other nations. Similarly, the Foreign Assistance Act of 1961 gave the executive wide latitude in implementing foreign aid legislation. The Formosa Resolution (1955), the Middle East Resolution (1957), and the Gulf of Tonkin Resolution (1964) granted presidents the discretion to use US armed forces in the promotion of US foreign policy goals and objectives. The 1964 Gulf of Tonkin Resolution was abused by both Presidents Lyndon B. Johnson and Richard M. Nixon. Johnson used it to wage and escalate a war in Vietnam, while Nixon imperiously expanded the war to Cambodia. George W. Bush used a resolution that authorized him to defend US security, at his discretion, by military force to wage in Iraq a war that a powerful faction in his national security team had advocated even before he took office.

Another rationale for legislative delegation of authority to the presidency is the belief that that office is better equipped to deal more effectively with those problems of national security that require compromises between competing domestic interests or trade-offs between regional or factional considerations and the overall national security interest. The commerce powers are one example. By the authority of Congress, the executive branch negotiates and implements commercial treaties and trade policy, though not with an entirely free hand. The executive branch undertakes this task under congressional oversight. In 1962, Congress established the Office of the US Trade Representative but located it in the Executive Office of the President. The Office was created as part of the Trade Expansion Act of 1962 to counteract what Congress believed was an insensitivity on the part of the Department of State to the threat that cheap imports posed to American business and economic interests. The Office develops and administers all US trade policy and serves as chief negotiator for virtually all US trade activities. Later, in 1988, Congress passed the Omnibus Trade and Competitiveness Act, which required the president to take aggressive action against states that take advantage of US open markets but deny US firms access to their own markets. Occasionally, Congress grants the executive branch so-called fast track authority to negotiate trade treaties with other governments.

Legislative delegation of authority to the executive, while increasing the influence of presidents over foreign policy, has not been as detrimental to the constitutional designation of Congress and the president as coequal managers of American foreign policy as other practices and patterns of behavior in Congress. Discussed below are typical examples of such practices and patterns of behavior.

Unwarranted Support for Presidential Behavior in Foreign Policy
Members of Congress have a common practice of supporting indiscriminately presumed presidential prerogative in the making and management of foreign policy. It is not uncommon that presidents demand that they rubber-stamp their policies. Lacking strategic intelligence but inspired by patriotism and importuned by presidents, they tend to concede, as if it were a given, the chief executive's motives and authority to freely manage every aspect of foreign policy on a daily basis. One result is that "the Senate's constitutional powers of advice and consent have atrophied into what is widely regarded as…a duty to give [the president] prompt consent with a minimum of advice."[157] Supporters

of such prompt action argue that the president (apparently not the nation) deserves his policy and nominees. But the intent of the framers of the Constitution is that, as representatives of the people, members of Congress have a duty to advise the president not merely on his day-to-day conduct of foreign policy but also on direction and philosophy, as these are shaped by major decisions. It is the members' constitutional responsibility to be both informed critics and constructive partners of the president. It is not necessary that they and the executive branch should always have identity of views. Rather, creative tension between them would produce policies that are more likely to advance the national security interest.

As members of Congress concede authority and motive to the president and grant him their support, they expect that the executive will duly and fully inform Congress on the foreign policy process. The reality often is that presidents tend not to reciprocate fully. They remain secretive and hide their true motives and intentions under the wall of executive privilege and what they insist are the dictates of national security. Furthermore, they insist that ensuring their administration's credibility to friends and allies whose secrets they claim might be divulged requires utmost secrecy. As the powerful chair of the Senate Foreign Relations Committee in 1964, Senator J. William Fulbright helped President Lyndon B. Johnson to shepherd through Congress the fateful Gulf of Tonkin Resolution. President Johnson had not fully disclosed to Senator Fulbright and other congressional leaders his motives and the lack of credible evidence justifying the resolution. Later, he used that resolution as a blank check to make war on Vietnam. The war escalated and splintered the nation, which it had cost enormous human and material resources, and virtually drove him from office.

Unwarranted support by members of Congress for presidential behavior in foreign policy is further illustrated by their silence on aspects of President George W. Bush's 20 September 2002 statement on the National Security Strategy of the United States of America, which frightened the leaders of other nations. The Bush administration made those aspects of the national security statement the basis of its foreign policy. The major tenets of those aspects were a radical departure from US strategic doctrine and its traditional approach to foreign policy. In spite of Bush's pledge during the 2000 presidential election campaigns that, under his administration, the United States would be humble in its approach to foreign policy and leadership of the world, his September 2002 National Security Strategy statement unnecessarily and arrogantly flaunted US "unparalleled military strength and great economic and political influence."[158] It insisted that the United States would maintain its primacy in the world. It would prevent potential rivals and adversaries from engaging in a military buildup that would surpass or equal its power. It would take "anticipatory action to defend" itself "even if uncertainty remained as to the time and place" of an adversary's attack. "To forestall or prevent such hostile acts by [its] adversaries, the United States will, if necessary, act preemptively." Finally, the statement reiterated the administration's rejection of the extension of the jurisdiction of the International Criminal Court to American citizens.[159]

Members of Congress raised no criticism or countervailing voice against these aspects of the Bush administration's National Security Strategy statement, which made leaders of other nations nervous. As president, George H. W. Bush had rejected this approach to protecting US national security, as it had alarmed the foreign policy elites within and outside the Congress. But, under his son, members of Congress chose to be silent. This was in spite of the fact that they were aware that, over the past years, other nations had become increasingly alarmed by the manner and ways US leaders had chosen to wield their nation's power and that, consequently, developing a strategy for dealing with American power had become an essential element of their statecraft. But there was no attempt on their part to assuage the alarm of other nations by reminding the Bush administration that, while uncontested US primacy gives the nation many advantages, what other nations do would impact the outcome of US policy, especially as to whether it succeeds or fails. Nor was the Bush administration challenged to devise a foreign policy strategy that would minimize foreign opposition and maximize global cooperation and support. In this manner, Congress became especially deferential to the Bush administration on national security. It even followed the administration's lead on domestic policy. It wrote bills so close to the administration's liking that up until March 2006 Bush had not cast a veto since he assumed the presidency in January 2001. Former Democratic Congressman Lee Hamilton of Indiana was so stunned by this deference by the legislators that he said that he could not remember a president who was less criticized than George W. Bush in his first term.[160]

This pattern of behavior by Congress had obvious consequences. It emboldened Bush by feeding his rapacity and quest for an imperial presidency. Thus, he totally avoided consultation with Congress for almost a period of one year on his plans to achieve regime change in Iraq by military force. He acted in his speeches and war plans and negotiations with the governments of other countries, especially that of Great Britain, as if he had sole authority to wage war, which Congress was obligated to support and fund. When he decided to seek authority from Congress to wage war in order to overthrow the Iraqi leader Saddam Hussein, he gave Congress barely a month to approve his draft resolution for that purpose. And, for political reasons, he demanded that Congress should grant him the authority well in advance of forthcoming November 2002 congressional elections. Congress cowardly obliged him even though some of its members believed that much of his evidence justifying the war was not credible.

Indulgence in Partisan Politics

Partisan political ambition—the determination to capture national power, to retain it, and to control the allocation of national resources and the perquisites of national office—divides members of Congress as members of political parties with competing political interests, ideologies, and visions. Defined in this manner, partisan political ambition tends to determine the behavior of members of political parties and, thus, of Congress. It colors, if it does not absolutely determine, their perception and definition of the national interest. It tends to work inescapably in conjunction with a subtle reluctance of politicians to put the country first, their professions to act in the national interest and not in pursuit of personal and partisan agenda to the contrary. It is in this manner that votes in Congress on foreign policy issues tend to be shaped by partisanship and "such hidden influences as private executive-branch briefings and phone calls, the competing priorities of members,... and the quiet personal intervention of political fund-raisers and lobbyists."[161] Frequently, because of political partisanship, Congress proves unable or unwilling to engage in serious oversight of the executive branch. It was at one time described by a seasoned observer "as, like a dinosaur, a large, slow-witted, thin-skinned, defensible composite that wants to stay out of trouble. Its real passion is reserved for its creature comforts: salaries, recesses, office space, allowances, ever more staff to help it reach its timid decisions."[162]

Collectively, these tendencies and partisan political ambition tend to sap members of Congress of their ability to serve the national interest in a truly disinterested manner and in conscientious and individual allegiance to their constitutional duties. As this happens, and as this has happened in recent American political history, it undermines the constitutional role of Congress as a coequal manager of foreign policy with the executive branch. The culture thus advances partisan politics and an imperial presidency at the expense of America's constitutional system as a vital national security interest.

The Republicans tend to regard Democrats as untrustworthy and weak on defense and national security. They consider themselves, their party, and a Republican president as more capable of advancing and protecting the national security interest. For their part, the Democrats in Congress support a

Democratic president who is the de facto leader of their party, which they believe has a more liberal and less parochial vision of the world as well as a more pragmatic approach to managing foreign affairs. With few exceptions—Nixon's Watergate and Reagan's Iran-Contra affair—Congressional Republicans replicate the behavior. They refuse to oppose a Republican president even when they are fully conscious of his policy blunders. This is part of a culture of intellectual accommodation to political expediency that, in recent years, has evolved in the US Congress. This pattern of partisanship is illustrated by the manner in which, after the terrorist acts of 11 September 2001 in New York City and the Pentagon, President Bush, dutifully supported by Republican members of Congress, news media experts, civilian and military contractors hawking technology, and grant-seeking academics and think tanks, has effectively exploited terrorism for political purposes.

Another aspect of that emergent culture is the degree to which members of Congress as politicians, acutely sensitive to campaign contributions and other forms of political pressure, are being constrained to sacrifice their independence of action. Relying on corporate America and their party and its leadership more than on their voting constituents to finance their reelection and to satisfy their ambition—assignment on committees for example—members of Congress feel compelled to remain loyal to their party leader and corporate supporters. Thus, they are losing much of their independence. They are becoming insensitive to public opinion, which their party strategists and opinion mobilizers manipulate. Simply and willfully, they cooperate with their leaders and corporate America. They lose the capacity to ask their "eminent" party leader critical questions on his policy or speak the truth to him. Instead, they become his cheerleaders and defenders. This is what happened, for example, on 2 October 2002, when President Bush made his case at the Rose Garden to persuade House and Senate leaders to pass his draft resolution to authorize him to wage war on Iraq (see chapter 9).

On that occasion, congressional Republicans, in spite of the cautionary mood of the nation, refused to challenge the hawkish approach of the administration to Iraq. Instead, Senator John Warner of the Armed Services Committee, for example, assured the president that Congress would grant him the authority as it had earlier granted his father and at his own time with a greater majority vote.[163] This assurance emboldened Bush on his imperial foreign policy. Similarly, congressional Republicans heaped accolades on the Director of Central Intelligence George Tenet in order to support the Bush administration's rationale for war in Iraq when they knew that the intelligence he was providing the administration on Iraq's weapons of mass destruction was not supported by any credible evidence. They also were aware that the Bush administration had politicized the intelligence and had manipulated it to suit its Iraq policy. For partisan purposes, the congressional Republicans chose to ignore that awareness. It was by these means that President Bush became cursed with a Republican Congress that indulged his worst tendencies in foreign policy.

Regarding their constitutional duties, congressional Democrats did not behave better on the issue of the war of choice in Iraq than their Republican Party counterparts. They were anxious about being seen as antiwar and obstructionist even though there was no evidence that the American public broadly supported war against Iraq. The House Minority Leader at the time, Dick Gephardt, who was interested in contesting the presidency in 2004, broke ranks with many in his party and declared his support for the Iraq Resolution. It was necessary, he said, to have a consensus that would lead the country in the right direction. Senators John Edwards, Joseph Lieberman, and John Kerry, all interested in a 2004 bid for the presidency, also supported the Iraq Resolution. Similarly, Senator Majority Leader Tom Daschle supported the resolution and urged others to support it in an enthusiastic bipartisan way.[164] It was thus obvious that, to these democratic members of the Congress, patriotism had become indiscriminate flag waving at an apparent war of choice by the Bush administration, rather than "a public duty to confront government officials who urged war without [substantially] justifying it."[165]

Later, the Bush administration blamed its misjudgments in going to war in Iraq on faulty CIA intelligence, notwithstanding its officials' deep disdain of the agency and their creation of the Office of Special Plans in the Department of Defense to counter the strategic intelligence analyses by the established CIA and the Department of State's Bureau of Intelligence and Analysis. Yet, not long after the Director George Tenet resigned from office, President Bush awarded him the nation's highest civilian honor—the Medal of Freedom. The Republican Party-controlled Congress raised no objections that such an honor should be bestowed on an intelligence director whose office had failed to prevent the terrorist attacks of 11 September 2001 on symbols of US power and who had also erroneously assured the president that his case for war against Saddam Hussein was a so-called slam dunk.

Similarly, for partisan purposes, congressional Republicans attacked and endeavored to discredit Richard Clarke when, testifying before the Senate Intelligence Committee, he provided evidence critical of George Bush's policy and inaction on terrorism prior to the 11 September terrorist attacks. At the insistence of the Bush administration, the committee that was investigating the failures of the CIA and other members of the Intelligence Community postponed a sequel to that investigation—the Bush administration's political use of intelligence—until after the November 2004 presidential elections. The committee quietly abandoned the investigation after Bush's reelection. Obviously, the intelligence process had been politicized. The Bush administration relied on the Republican Party control of Congress to do so. Furthermore, it stonewalled and blocked public hearings into other alleged misdeeds—treatment of prisoners at Abu Ghraib and Guantanamo Bay and the CIA secret prison system. The US political system of accountability had indeed been subjugated to the reelection of President George W. Bush. Consequently, the nation was denied critical information as to what went wrong, and for what reason, in the lead up to the war in Iraq and how to remedy what had happened prior to the US invasion and occupation of the country.

There are occasions when Congress either on its own volition or by force of public pressure abandoned partisan politics and its culture of deference to the president. Here are a few examples: In 1975, House and Senate Committees, chaired by Representative Otis Pike and Senator Frank Church, respectively, investigated alleged CIA abuses. The excesses included cases of spying on American citizens and plots to assassinate leaders of foreign governments, such as Patrice Lumumba of the Congo, Fidel Castro of Cuba, Ngo Dinh Diem and his brother of South Vietnam, and Salvador Allende of Chile. The Frank Church Committee reported that the agency's covert operations had become overused as an instrument of foreign policy and had damaged the reputation of the United States. In light of the evidence, both chambers of Congress created permanent intelligence oversight committees to watch more closely future activities of the CIA and other components of the Intelligence Community.

For his part, President Ford, and later Presidents Carter and Reagan, issued executive orders forbidding the assassination of leaders of foreign governments. Furthermore, the work of the Frank Church Committee resulted in several reforms: For example, passage of the Foreign Intelligence Surveillance Act of 1978, which required special intelligence courts to approve national security wiretaps. Recommendations of the committee also laid the groundwork for the 1982 Intelligence Identities Protection Act that prevents identification of CIA operatives.[166] The George W. Bush administration was suspected of violating the latter act. As a consequence, a criminal investigation was instituted to identify the leading officials in the White House and in Vice President Cheney's office who, in violation of the act, outed the name of the wife of Ambassador Joseph Wilson after the former ambassador had criticized the administration's use of intelligence on Iraq's possession of weapons of mass destruction.[167]

When President Ronald Reagan blocked the shipment of wheat to the Soviet Union during his second term as part of his cold war measures against "the evil empire," Midwest farmers and their representatives in Congress strongly objected to the measure. The lawmakers urged the administration to spend more time listening to the plight of the American farmers and less time waging the cold war. Reacting to the political unrest in the Midwest and the pressure from Republican leaders in Washington, President Reagan changed course and allowed the wheat exports to go forward.

Following the Vietnam experience, Congress asserted itself in a number of instances against the tendency towards an imperial presidency. In 1975, the Gerald Ford administration tried to revive the domino theory that had played a major role in convincing US officials to intervene in Vietnam as a rationale for its intervention in a political struggle for political succession in the southern African country of Angola. It argued that Communists—the Soviet Union and Cuba—who were supporting a faction (the Popular Movement for the Liberation of Angola) in the civil war would upset the balance of power in southern Africa. Furthermore, the administration insisted, the Soviets "will take over Angola and will thereby considerably control the oil shipping lanes from the Persian Gulf to Europe.... They will have a large chunk of Africa and the world will be different in the aftermath."[168]

Congress rejected this argument and passed the Clark Amendment to the Military Appropriations Act of 1976. The amendment forbade all US support to any of the factions in the Angolan war. However, ten years later, Congress reversed itself in deference to President Reagan when, at his behest, it repealed the Clark Amendment in 1985. The president had argued that the amendment had tied his hands in dealing with the Cuban- and Soviet-assisted government of Angola. After the repeal, Reagan, who however had been intervening covertly in the Angolan conflict, resumed US military and diplomatic intervention. George H. W. Bush continued the policy of intervention and thus prolonged the war that devastated Angola and squandered American money and military material for over a period of ten more years.

Congress rejected a similar rationale for President Reagan's intervention in Central America, especially Nicaragua. There, the Reagan administration was engaged in a proxy war, arming and supporting the Contras against the Soviet- and Cuban-supported Sandinista government. Congress acted to stop that intervention by passing the Boland Amendments. The administration enmeshed itself into trouble when it traded arms with Iran for hostages and used the profits from the sale to finance the Contras. Despite the administration's attempts to sabotage congressional investigation into the scandals, eleven top officials, including two national security advisers and an undersecretary of state, were finally convicted. Reagan's Vice President and successor, George H. W. Bush, rushed to pardon four of them, as well as Defense Secretary Casper Weinberger, even before Weinberger could be indicted.

The Comprehensive Anti-Apartheid Sanctions Act of 1986 represents another instance when Congress asserted itself against President Reagan. The Reagan administration was pursuing a policy it described as one of "constructive engagement" with the apartheid regime in the Republic of South Africa. The policy was used to rationalize the administration's support for the apartheid government and its legalized racism. Partly in response to public pressure and the damage the policy was doing to the US image and credibility in Africa, Congress passed the Comprehensive Anti-Apartheid Sanctions Act to reverse the administration's policy. Reagan vetoed the act, but both chambers of Congress overrode his veto with large majorities—313 to 83 in the House and 78 to 21 in the Senate. Consequently, he and his immediate successor George H. W. Bush were compelled to impose the sanctions as required by Congress. The congressional measure contributed to the release of political prisoners, including Nelson Mandela, from prison and to the eventual transition to multiracial democracy in the Republic of South Africa.

Insufficient Use of the Budgetary Powers of Congress
The budgetary powers of Congress constitute the greatest power in the US constitutional system. Carefully wielded, these powers enhance the influence of Congress in the foreign policy process, for, constitutionally, it is that body, not the president, that has the key to the US Treasury. The legislature's general budgetary powers—the powers to raise and appropriate monies for national operations, to determine how appropriated monies are to be spent, and to oversee and investigate the executive branch for any improprieties in the expenditure of appropriated funds—affect several areas of foreign policy. Therefore, they are a potent instrument Congress may use to shape, control, and influence American foreign policy especially if the legislators muster the political will to do so.

Congress funds and supports the armed forces and the intelligence communities critical to national defense and the conduct of foreign policy. It establishes conditions for development assistance, security support programs, and US participation in international organizations and programs. It may exclude particular countries from US assistance and may insist on help for others. It may attach conditions on the use of US foreign aid. It may withhold the release of funds already appropriated for specific foreign policy purposes, such as contributions to UN peacekeeping operations. It may also earmark or micromanage funds to be used for specific foreign policy purposes. Thus, it may require the executive branch to spend appropriated funds for specific purposes and prohibit their use for others. Additionally, Congress may establish specific levels of funds to be granted to particular countries, as it did in the cases of Egypt and Israel after the Camp David Accords of 1979. It may also cut off military aid to authoritarian regimes, such as those in Argentina and Chile that were oppressing their citizens in the 1970s. It may even attach amendments, such as the Byrd and Clark Amendments in 1969 and 1976, respectively, to defense or other appropriation bills in order to work its will on a foreign policy issue.[169] In the 1990s, it insisted that the nation would not pay its dues to the United Nations until that organization reformed itself.

In response to what it regarded as presidential imperial policies in Southeast Asia in the 1960s and early 1970s, Congress attempted to shape foreign policy and to reduce American military involvement overseas through funding levels and restrictions. At that period, it adopted a broad measure that halted funding for US military activities in Southeast Asia, specifically North and South Vietnam, Laos, and Cambodia. In 1974, over the objections of President Gerald Ford, and later President Jimmy Carter, it cut off all military and economic assistance to Turkey for three years for using US weapons to invade Cyprus in that year in violation of statutory requirements that the American-supplied weapons should not be used for offensive purposes. In the late 1970s, it made foreign assistance conditional on human rights practices of potential recipients, as well as on their cooperation in the global war against drug trafficking. It also used legislative funding provisions to cut off covert actions in the less industrialized countries of the global south, to require congressional review of the sale and transfer of weapons and nuclear fuels to other countries, and to specify the trading relations with other nations.[170] By passing the Boland Amendments in the 1980s, Congress cut off funds for President Ronald Reagan's assistance to the Contras of Nicaragua. After the death of eighteen US soldiers in October 1993 in the UN humanitarian mission in Somalia, it hastened the withdrawal of US troops from the mission by setting a deadline for cutting off funds for their support.

But, for a variety of reasons, Congress is especially reluctant or refuses to wield these powers in the war-making area. Budget decisions are made in different settings, at different times, and by individuals and committees responding to different pressures, including those from the executive branch, lobbyists, and interest groups. Furthermore, the president's policies raise expectations and place US prestige on the line or commit the nation to a course of action in the eyes of other nations and international organizations, the abandonment of which may create credibility problems for the nation. When this occurs, Congress tends to find that it has little choice but to support—that is, to fund—the policy enunciated by the president, even if cosmetically. In 1905, after the Russo-Japanese War, for example, Congress rejected President Theodore Roosevelt's plan to send the US Navy around the world to impress the Japanese with America's naval might. Roosevelt ignored the Congress. He sent the navy on the mission, arguing that Congress would find the money to do what was necessary if the navy ran out of funds. Similar situations and problems confront Congress when it seeks or contemplates to cut off funds for unpopular overseas military actions, such as the Bush administration's war in Iraq. There was disagreement among the lawmakers, after President Bush told the nation on 10 January 2007 that he had decided to send 21,500 additional US troops to Iraq, about the wisdom of using their budgetary powers to prevent him from doing so. While some wanted to do so, others argued against denying the forces the funds they needed to carry out their mission. In addition to such dilemmas it is not unusual that chief executives tend to devise a variety of measures to circumvent full exercise of the budgetary powers of Congress.[171]

Reluctance to Use the Impeachment Powers of the House of Representatives

Impeachment—a formal accusation by the House of Representatives that commits any civil official, including the president, for trial in the Senate—is an extreme measure and a rarely used tool. Members of Congress are reluctant to use their impeachment powers as a proper remedy for presidential or executive branch misbehavior. Among other reasons, the process can be traumatizing and may leave a major festering wound in the nation's body politic. Part of the reluctance, especially relative to the misbehavior of chief executives, is a function of a strong national predilection to rally around the presidency when it comes to foreign affairs. Hence, in international affairs, Congress and the American people in general tend to be willing to place excessive and unwarranted trust in presidents and their aides in the executive branch. This tendency has contributed to the casting aside of the robust role for lawmakers in foreign policy advocated by the constitutional framers and has elevated the constitutionally limited presidential authority in that process.

The most recent cases when the impeachment powers were used involved Presidents Richard Nixon and William Jefferson Clinton. The latter's political enemies had charged him with perjury regarding his philandering with a White House intern, but he was not convicted by the Senate. The former, President

Nixon, had secretly bombed Cambodia as part of the Vietnam War outside the military chain of command and had ordered a burglary break into the headquarters of the Democratic National Committee at the Watergate Complex in Washington. The Cambodia article of impeachment was defeated by the House Impeachment Committee by twenty-six to twelve votes. Nixon's national security adviser Henry Kissinger, one of the architects of the secret bombings, escaped indictment. However, the bombings led to a symbolic rearguard repeal of the Gulf of Tonkin Resolution and the passage of the 1973 War Powers Resolution. That law, which Nixon vetoed and Congress passed over his veto, has been ineffective in curbing presidential war making.

The Watergate break-in and the elaborate cover-up[172] that followed were thoroughly investigated by Congress on a nonpartisan basis. The findings of the investigation forced Nixon to resign the presidency, as the House of Representatives was preparing to begin impeachment proceedings. Nixon was quickly pardoned by his successor and former vice president, Gerald Ford, in an effort to heal the nation and close that chapter in America's political and constitutional history.

Presidents Ronald Reagan and George H. W. Bush escaped congressional chastisement after their wars, respectively, in Grenada in 1983 and in Panama in 1989. In the Iran-Contra scandal in which the executive branch violated laws—the Boland Amendments and the restriction on negotiating with hostage takers or making concessions to their demands—only President Reagan's auxiliaries were punished. Reagan himself escaped scot-free without any call for his impeachment. Instead, for partisan purposes, conservative Republican members of Congress argued that Reagan should be allowed wide leeway to implement whatever policies were necessary to stop and prevent Communist aggression in Central America, even if doing so placed him above the Boland Amendments. Reagan himself was wiser than the congressional Republicans who defended him. After his initial attempts to sabotage the John Tower Commission, which had been appointed to investigate the covert activities, he went on national television and candidly and graciously admitted his error. Thereafter, he made documents and aides available to the congressional commission and skillfully rebuilt his presidency with new appointees.

There is overwhelming evidence of the George W. Bush administration's manipulation of intelligence, fear, and the events of 11 September 2001 to advance its march to war in Iraq. Its handling of prewar intelligence and diplomacy systematically distorted reality. In January 2004, three separate reports by the Carnegie Endowment for International Peace, the US Army War College, and the *Washington Post*, as well as statements from the former

Treasury Secretary Paul O'Neal, independently asserted that the administration overstated and misinterpreted prewar claims about the "gathering threat" posed by Iraq's biological, chemical, and nuclear weapons programs to the United States and Iraq's neighbors. The Carnegie report added (as was later confirmed by David Kay, head of the Bush administration's Iraq Survey Group) that a substantial amount of Iraq's chemical warfare agents, precursors, munitions, and production equipment had been destroyed between 1991 and 1998 as a result of Operations Desert Storm and Desert Fox and UN weapons inspections.[173] The Director of Central Intelligence, George Tenet, himself told an audience at Georgetown University that the CIA "never said there was an imminent danger."[174]

Also, members of Congress learned, as other knowledgeable citizens and foreign policy elites did, that the Department of Defense had set up an intelligence team at the Pentagon, among other things, to search for terrorists and their links to Iraq and was at the same time channeling $340,000 per month to the Ahmed Chalabi-led Iraqi National Congress for intelligence collection. Yet Congress did not question the Pentagon about this unnecessary duplication of efforts, wasting of resources, and undermining of the CIA. Nor has any member of Congress so far required the Bush administration to respond to the independent reports mentioned above or proposed even a congressionally appointed independent investigation into how it led the nation to the Iraq War. It was not until November 2005 when Senate Democrats embarrassed the Republican Party-controlled Senate by a strategic parliamentary maneuver that the Republican leadership in that chamber agreed to reopen the Senate Intelligence Committee's investigation into the administration's use of prewar intelligence. The investigation had been put off until after the 2004 presidential election. The Republican leadership sought to bury it completely after the election. The leadership continued to December 2006, to drag its feet on the investigation.

There is fundamentally a lot that the American people, for the greater security of the nation and its political system, need to know from such investigation about the rush to the war in Iraq. At what point did the Bush administration decide to go to war in Iraq? Was the Iraq War of choice in accordance with the provisions of the Constitution of the United States? If not, what went wrong? What is the role and share of Congress in what went wrong? Was the justification for the war, as the nation was initially told, to disarm Iraq of its weapons of mass destruction or other reasons—to liberate Iraq, to fight terrorism, to democratize the entire Middle East—as the administration deftly shifted its rationale for the war? Did the nation go to war in Iraq to promote the ideology foisted on President Bush by his neoconservative advisers? Was dethroning Saddam Hussein and his regime worth the sacrifice (by 31 December 2006) of three thousand American soldiers, the maiming of more than twenty-two thousand others, the expenditure of more than $400 billion and counting, turning post-Saddam Iraq into a terrorist center, and the alienation and animosity of many members of the global community? How could any executive branch misbehavior or that of Congress be checked and prevented in the future and vital national resources preserved if the present administration and/or the Congress under whose watch the war was waged are not held accountable for their misdeeds? What are the implications of such a development and lack of accountability for the future of the American constitutional system? That these questions have not been raised or addressed by Congress is part of its culture of deference to the executive branch on foreign policy.

Chapter 6
Background to the George W. Bush Administration's War in Iraq

Why is it now so urgent that we should take military action to disarm a military capacity that has been there for more than 20 years, and which we helped to create?[175]

Since 1990, the United States has fought two major wars in the Persian Gulf against Iraq. The first war, from 1990 to 1991, was waged during the George H. W. Bush administration under the auspices of the United Nations Security Council. But, essentially, President Bush set the agenda of that war and was its driving force, as well as its most hawkish voice. Subsequently, several skirmishes, including bombings of no-fly zones and military installations, and covert actions were carried out in Iraq by the William Jefferson Clinton administration, assisted by the British government of Prime Minister Tony Blair, as offshoots of the first war. The second large-scale war that began in March 2003 and led to the conquest and occupation of Iraq was a war of choice waged by the George W. Bush administration. Unlike the first war, it was prosecuted without the authorization of the Security Council, and George W. Bush, unlike his father, was the agent and spokesman of its most hawkish voices—the neoconservatives in his administration led by Vice President Dick Cheney, Defense Secretary Donald Rumsfeld, and his deputy Paul Wolfowitz. As of the writing of this book, American troops are still occupying Iraq, although formal political authority was transferred to the Iraqis about eighteen months after the American invasion. To date (31 December 2006), the United States has spent more than $400 billion on its operations in the country. About three thousand US soldiers have been killed, and more than twenty-two thousand others have been severely wounded. No one knows for certain the number of Iraqi casualties, dead and wounded.

Among other reasons, the wars and skirmishes are rooted in the long history of US bungling in Iraq. The George W. Bush administration's war in that country is part of that history. It can be traced to the pattern of American policy for Iraq and for other countries in the Persian Gulf that emerged from the wreckage of Western European colonial empires in the twentieth century.

Some American leaders wanted nothing to do with them; others wanted to impose their will, while others yet thought that the locals would adopt [Western] democracy and become equal members of the world community. Few American leaders measured the ends they sought against the means they were willing to commit. All seemed more interested in getting discrete actions approved despite their domestic opponents.... Clashing priorities...produced results that none wanted.[176]

In the 1950s, US administrations, jointly with the British government, sponsored rulers in the Persian Gulf—Iran, Jordan, and Iraq—that they believed would lead their region to economic and political advancement while also contributing to the prevention of the spread of communism and Soviet influence to the region. During the Richard M. Nixon administration (1969–1974), Iraq became a pawn in the cold war with the Soviet Union. After its strongman, Saddam Hussein, had signed a letter of friendship with the Soviet Union, President Nixon ordered the CIA to provide covert assistance to the Kurds in order to check Soviet influence in the Middle East. America's friends—Britain, Israel, and Iran (under the rule of Shah Mohammad Reza Pahlavi) provided the Kurds additional covert assistance to further the goal. However, the covert operation against Iraq was not sustained. The shah of Iran reached an understanding with Saddam Hussein that enabled him to crush the Kurds, who were also abandoned by Nixon's successor, President Gerald Ford. This is, in part, how Saddam Hussein gradually, indirectly and directly, came to power in Iraq in 1979 with the help of subtle covert actions of America's CIA. But Saddam rejected the CIA's agenda. Under him, Iraq became a closer military and political ally of the Soviet Union. His secret services contributed logistics and money to the coalition that overthrew the American protégée, the Shah of Iran, Mohammad Reza Pahlavi in 1979. Following that event, the Jimmy Carter administration, which had earlier in its tenure sought in vain to renew diplomatic relations with Iraq,[177] approached Iraq again but was rebuffed. Baghdad remained uninterested in renewing diplomatic relations with the United States.

On 22 September 1980, Saddam Hussein invaded Iran because of a territorial dispute between the two countries over the Shatt al-Arab waterway.[178] The invasion followed months of increased tension between the Iranian Islamic Republic and secular nationalist Iraq. The Jimmy Carter administration stayed aloof and simply watched the war. At that time, the United States had no diplomatic relations with either of the belligerents. It had cut off diplomatic relations with Iran because of the Tehran embassy hostage crisis; Iraq had broken off ties with the United States during the 1967 Arab-Israeli War. Neither Saddam Hussein's dictatorial brand of Arab nationalism nor the Islamic fundamentalism espoused by Iran's Ayatollah Khomeini attracted any sympathy from the Carter administration officials. There was therefore no disposition for any US intervention in the war. Rather, Iraq was viewed by top officials of the administration as the enemy of a US enemy. The hope of the officials was that the two countries would exhaust themselves to a stalemate. This would ensure that neither country would emerge from the war with any additional power.

Ronald Reagan, who succeeded Jimmy Carter as president in January 1981, endorsed and followed this policy. His administration, just as its predecessor, was concerned with a likely interference with nonbelligerent shipping and critical oil productions and transshipment facilities in the Persian Gulf. However, a faction in his administration that was led by Secretary of State Alexander Haig and which saw Iran under Ayatollah Khomeini "as a bulwark" against Soviet and Arab expansion, allowed Israel to sell to Iran parts of its American weapons.

With the American munitions bought from Israel, Iran was able to beat back Saddam Hussein. Its troops advanced within a few miles of Iraq's second largest city, Basra. Given this outcome, the Reagan administration became apprehensive that an Iranian breakthrough on the Basra front, leading to a defeat of Iraq, might destabilize Kuwait, the Persian Gulf states, and even Saudi Arabia, thereby threatening the oil supplies to the United States and its allies. American friends in the region were even more deeply concerned that Iran's victory could upset and create instability in the entire area.

This apprehension, and Israel's use of American-supplied aircraft and intelligence to destroy Iraq's nuclear reactor at Osirak in 1981, prompted pro-Arab progressive elements in the Reagan administration to tilt US policy towards Saddam Hussein. Measures already underway to upgrade US-Iraq relations were accelerated; high-level officials exchanged visits. In February 1982, to facilitate channeling assistance to Baghdad, Iraq was removed from the US Department of State's list of states abetting international terrorism. Financial assistance was provided to Iraq through loan programs from the United States. The White House and the Department of State pressured the Export-Import Bank to provide Iraq with financing to enhance its credit standing and to enable it to obtain loans from other international financial institutions. Furthermore, the US Department of Agriculture "provided taxpayer-guaranteed loans for [Iraq's] purchases of American commodities, to the satisfaction of US grain exporters."[179] About two years later, on 5 April 1984, National Security Decision Directive 139, parts of which remain classified, stated that the United States "would do whatever was necessary and legal to prevent Iraq from losing the war with Iran."[180] The decision directive outlined measures the Reagan administration was to take to prevent an Iraqi collapse. Thus, the administration began to supply Iraq with battlefield intelligence on Iranian troop buildups, satellite photographs, logistical support, and cluster bombs through a Chilean front company.[181]

Furthermore, efforts had been initiated to restore full diplomatic relations with Iraq but were slowed down by Saddam himself. It was for that purpose that, in 1983 and 1984, President Reagan sent Donald Rumsfeld as his special envoy to Iraq. Rumsfeld was also to assure Saddam Hussein that his defeat by Iran would be against the interests of the United States and would be regarded "as a strategic defeat for the West."[182] Eventually, Rumsfeld met with Saddam Hussein on 21 December 1983. In their ninety-minute meeting, the two discussed regional issues of mutual interest, shared enmity towards Iran, and US efforts to find alternative routes to transport Iraq's oil to the West, as its facilities in the Persian Gulf had been shut down by Iran, and Iran's ally, Syria, had cut off a pipeline that transported Iraqi oil through its territory. Rumsfeld visited again in late March 1984. Full diplomatic relations were eventually restored by November 1984 after the US presidential elections. In the meantime, Vice President George H. W. Bush ensured that the flow of US arms, agricultural credits, and intelligence to Iraq was not interrupted.

Declassified documents show that, at the time Rumsfeld visited Baghdad in 1983 and 1984, Iraq was using chemical weapons on Iranians on an "almost daily" basis in defiance of international conventions.[183] "Actual rather than rhetorical opposition to such use was evidently not perceived to serve US interests; hence, the Reagan administration did not deviate from its determination that Iraq was to serve as the instrument to prevent an Iranian victory."[184] Also, it is known that between 1984 and 1988, when the Iran-Iraq War ended in a stalemate, the Reagan administration secretly supplied Iraq with supercomputers, machine tools, biological agents (including anthrax), and steel tubes that can have military and civilian applications.[185] The Departments of State and Commerce promoted trade in items such as these as a way to boost US exports and acquire political leverage over Saddam Hussein. This time, the tilt in US policy turned the tide of the war in favor of Iraq, perceived more generally by the Reagan-Bush administration as a bulwark against an Iranian conquest of the militarily weaker but oil-rich states of the Arabian Peninsula.

US policy was to tilt again in 1985 as a result of concerns within the Reagan administration's National Security Council (NSC) that the defeat of Iran by Soviet-supported Iraq would be disastrous to the goals of the US-Soviet ideological conflict. To allay this concern and to obtain funds to continue the administration's congressionally forbidden funding of the Contras of Nicaragua,

Admiral John Poindexter, Robert McFarlane, and Colonel Oliver North of the NSC traded arms with Iran in 1985 and 1986 in exchange for its influence over the release of Americans held hostage by pro-Iranian terrorists in Lebanon. The policy tilt towards Iran was also due to the belief by the Reagan administration officials that better relations with Iran were the key to stability in the Persian Gulf and that the sale of American arms was the key to better US relations with Iran.

Although the policy tilt infuriated Saddam, who vowed never to trust the United States again, it did not disrupt the flow of US arms to Iraq but was apparently a double-track policy. The exposure of the Iran-Contra scandal by a Beirut newspaper forced the departure of the pro-Iranian group from the Reagan administration and ended the two-track policy. Vice President Bush himself encouraged Saddam to intensify with vigor the bombing of Iran. The CIA continued to share intelligence with his regime. No vigorous protest was registered over Saddam's use of chemical weapons against Iranian troops. In 1987, in the guise of protecting freedom of navigation, the Reagan administration threw the weight of the US Navy behind Iraq's position in the Persian Gulf. Thus, a large American armada protected tanker traffic and crippled the Iranian navy. The war, however, ended in a draw in August 1988 after eight years, just as the US government had hoped. But it was estimated that nearly one million people had died in the course of the war, while tens of thousands more were displaced as refugees. After the war, a classified Department of State document stated,

> We can legitimately assert that our post-Irangate policy has worked. The outward thrust of the Iranian revolution has been stopped. Iraq's interests in development, modernity and regional influence should compel it in our direction. We should welcome and encourage the interest, and respond accordingly.[186]

With his country's war with Iran over, Saddam Hussein launched massive attacks, including the use of chemical weapons, against his fellow citizens—the Kurds. For this behavior, the US Senate sought to impose sanctions on Iraq. However, it was prevented from doing so by the Reagan-Bush administration. The administration had come to regard Iraq as a US friend, since it was the enemy of the US enemy, Iran.

When he became president in 1989, George H. W. Bush continued the Reagan administration policy towards Saddam Hussein. He "felt that America owed Saddam a debt for ever having bombed Iran."[187] Saddam's arms buildup continued. Regarding him as a valued ally and a bulwark against militant Shiite extremism, Bush ignored warnings by the Pentagon that Iraq was developing weapons of mass destruction. He hoped to bring Iraq into the family of nations and that Saddam's government would become less repressive and more responsible. For six months, his administration consistently opposed attempts by some members of Congress to impose sanctions on the Iraqi government for using chemical weapons against its own citizens at Halabja. This was the intent of National Security Decision Directive 25 signed by Bush in October 1989 to pursue a policy of carrots and sticks that assists Saddam in certain ways if his behavior conformed to US aspirations in the Middle East. Here is how Brent Scowcroft, the Bush administration's national security adviser explained the policy: "What we hoped was to continue the policy of the Reagan administration, which was first of all a balance between Iran and Iraq and then hoping perhaps to make Saddam Hussein a minimally useful member of the international community."[188] After the Iran-Iraq War, the administration knew, he continued, that Iraq had enormous reconstruction to undertake and it was the administration's hope that American business would be able to participate in that reconstruction, since Iraq was fundamentally a wealthy nation. The administration, Scowcroft added, had no illusion at all about the character of Saddam Hussein, but, at the same time, it did not see him necessarily as having serious unrequited aggressive aims. It thought it was useful to try a modest carrot and show him that the United States bore him no particular ill will but was prepared to have a normal kind of relations with him that would be at least commercially advantageous to both sides.

The administration continued this policy of cultivating Saddam as a "moderate" Arab leader until August 1990 when he invaded and annexed Kuwait. Richard Murphy, who was the Department of State's top Middle East diplomat for most of the 1980s, said in a PBS program,

> We all saw Iraq in the post-war [Iran-Iraq] era as a very valuable market for our business communities—potentially an enormous market once it got out from under the load of war debt that it had accumulated. And most experts predicted that that would happen in three to five years without invading Kuwait and raiding the Kuwaiti treasury. And I still think that was a reasonable time limit, that Iraq would have turned into, without this act of aggression, a state with whom one could have had very mutually profitable exchanges.[189]

The Reagan and Bush administrations were not alone in hobnobbing with Saddam Hussein as he was building and was using his massive arsenal of tanks, planes, missiles, and chemical weapons in the 1980s. The major European governments, as well as Western corporations, the Soviet Union, China, Czechoslovakia, and Brazil, were also complicit in creating the Iraqi military machine that the George W. Bush administration later saw as a grave danger to the United States and the world generally. Through the export of arms and technology, they all encouraged and contributed to the development and growth of Iraq's conventional and unconventional weapons.[190] Baghdad committed its worst human rights abuses during the period of its alliance with the United States and its allies. Apparently, the regime believed that committing those abuses against targets of no interest to the West, such as Iranian troops and the Kurds, would not result in serious consequences.

On 25 July 1990, eight days after a speech during which Saddam Hussein threatened Kuwait and the United Arab Emirates by saying, "Iraqis will not forget the maxim that cutting necks is better than cutting the means of living. Oh, God almighty, be witness that we have warned them," the US Ambassador April Glaspie met with him in Baghdad. In response to Saddam's furious anger at that meeting about Iraq's dispute with Kuwait over borders and low crude oil prices, the ambassador avoided any criticism of the Iraqi leader for threatening his neighbors. Rather, after expressing US concern about the massing of Iraqi troops on the Kuwaiti border, she informed him that President Bush "personally wants to deepen [the US] relationship with Iraq" and that the United States had not "much to say about Arab-Arab differences, like your border differences with Kuwait.... All we hope is you solve these matters quickly."[191] She added that President George H. W. Bush was not going to "to declare an economic war against Iraq."[192] Shortly after that meeting, the tide in US-Iraq relations turned for the worse. In August that year, Saddam invaded its smaller and weaker neighbor Kuwait, one of the world's largest producers of oil and a protégée of both Britain and the United States. The invasion reversed the apparent ongoing alliance between the United States and Iraq and triggered the demonization of Saddam Hussein and his regime by US administrators.

In the events leading up to that invasion, the US administration had committed a serious error: The George H. W. Bush administration failed to send Saddam Hussein a clear signal that the US government would consider using military force if Iraq invaded Kuwait. The failure to do so may have encouraged Saddam's behavior, although it is very likely that he might have disregarded such warning, as he may have persuaded himself to believe that the United States would be unwilling to risk a major war in the region. Also, Saddam himself committed a huge blunder in believing that the United States might not risk a war to protect its vital interests in such an oil-rich region and would allow Iraq to become the region's hegemon. He was additionally seriously mistaken in assuming that the other Persian Gulf states would accept his invasion, occupation, and annexation of Kuwait as a fait accompli. Those states and most of the Arab world did not.

Why Did Saddam Hussein Invade Kuwait?

Conflict between Iraq and Kuwait traces to the arbitrary and unsatisfactory manner (to Iraq) in which British colonial authorities drew the Iraqi-Kuwaiti boundaries. Iraq maintained a historical claim over Kuwait, arguing that British authorities had carved Kuwait out of Iraqi territory. Twice, in 1967 and 1973, Iraq had occupied small sections of northern Kuwait. However, the immediate cause of Saddam's invasion of Kuwait in 1990 was the aftermath of its war with Iran. After Iraq's eight-year war with Iran ended in 1988, Saddam Hussein, despite Iraq's $80 billion debt to Arab and Western countries, began to spend further amounts of money in rearming his depleted military arsenal. By 1990, Iraq had built the fourth-largest army in the world. The expenditure and low oil prices compounded Iraq's debt crisis. Suddenly, Saddam became angry with Iraq's Persian Gulf neighbors—Kuwait, Saudi Arabia, and the United Arab Emirates—mainly because of the low price of oil, its major source of revenue, and also because these neighbors had refused to renew an expiring ten-year pledge to provide financial assistance to Jordan and Iraq, the two Arab countries generally perceived in the Arab world to be the most directly threatened by Israel.[193]

Saddam harbored additional resentment against Kuwait because of disputes between Iraq and Kuwait over Babiyan and al-Warba, two strategically located islands that block Iraq's access to the Persian Gulf from its port at Umm Qasr and over the Rumaila oil field straddling their border. Saddam's anger against Kuwait was exacerbated by his accusation that Kuwait was exceeding its oil production quota and violating agreements on drilling rights in the Rumaila oil field. Specifically, Kuwait was accused of using so-called slant drilling to siphon off Iraqi oil.[194] It was asked to pay Iraq $10 billion in compensation. Furthermore, Saddam threatened to attack Kuwait and other Persian Gulf states that exceeded their oil production quota. Kuwait, encouraged by both Britain and the United States to stand firm, flatly rejected Saddam's demands.[195]

On 31 July and 1 August 1990, Iraqi and Kuwaiti officials met at Jedda, Saudi Arabia, to resolve their differences. The negotiations collapsed when Kuwaiti officials refused to cancel billions of dollars of Iraq's war debts and to concede disputed territories and agree to Iraq's demands that it reduce its oil production. The following day, 2 August 1990, Iraq, which already had massed thirty thousand troops on its border with Kuwait, invaded Kuwait with one hundred and twenty thousand troops and 850 tanks. On 3 August 1990, more Iraqi forces were massed between Kuwait and Saudi Arabia for defensive purposes, according to Saddam, but for possible invasion and occupation of

Saudi Arabia according to British and US governments. Not long after that, Saddam announced the annexation of Kuwait as the nineteenth province of Iraq.

Towards the Protection of Saudi Arabia
and the Liberation of Kuwait

Iraq's aggression, conquest, and occupation of Kuwait comprised a violation of its obligations under Article II of the UN Charter. Immediately, the UN Security Council met on 3 August 1990 and adopted Resolution 660 by a vote of fourteen to zero, with Yemen abstaining. The resolution condemned the invasion and demanded the immediate withdrawal of all Iraqi forces. Three days later, the Security Council passed its second resolution on the Iraqi invasion. Adopted by a vote of thirteen to zero, with Cuba and Yemen abstaining, Resolution 661 imposed a trade and financial boycott of both Iraq and Iraqi-occupied Kuwait.

For the United States and especially its European allies and Japan, which depend on oil imports from the Persian Gulf, the Iraqi invasion and occupation of Kuwait had ominous and unacceptable implications. The most foreboding implication was a possible control of oil supply in the Persian Gulf. Saddam's control of such supply in Iraq, Kuwait, and Saudi Arabia combined would place in his hands more than 40 percent of the world's oil supply and would enable him to manipulate the global economy. Similar concerns ten years earlier, after the Soviet Union invaded Afghanistan, had prompted President Jimmy Carter to warn that any attempt by any outside force to gain control of the Persian Gulf would be regarded as an assault on the vital interests of the United States and that such assault would be repelled by any means necessary, including military force.

Thus, although the United States had no defense treaty with Kuwait and had made no specific defense or security commitments to it, President Bush was resolved to protect vital US interests in the Persian Gulf. Thus, the issue of oil gave enormous urgency to his administration's policy on the Iraqi invasion of its neighbor. First, Bush declared that the "Iraqi invasion of Kuwait will not stand." Immediately, he signed an executive order freezing Kuwaiti assets to ensure that Iraqis could not draw and use those assets. His next task was the mobilization of members of the UN Security Council to adopt resolutions to force Iraq from Kuwait. Simultaneously, he began meticulously to build a worldwide coalition, including members of the Arab League, against Iraq. From the outset of the invasion, he received encouragement from the British Prime Minister Margaret Thatcher to take a bold stand against Saddam and to protect Saudi Arabia from any possible invasion. Similarly, less than forty-eight hours after the invasion, the Soviet leader Mikhail Gorbachev joined him to condemn Iraq for its aggression against Kuwait. On 7 August 1990, when Saddam proclaimed the annexation of Kuwait, President Bush, at the request of King Fahd, began the deployment of over two hundred thousand US troops to Saudi Arabia to protect the Kingdom and to deter further Iraqi aggression. The deployment was named Operation Desert Shield. Soon, armed forces from other members of the broad international coalition fashioned by President Bush joined the American troops in the operation.

In launching the operation, President Bush assured a joint session of Congress that US objectives in the Persian Gulf "are clear, our goals defined and familiar: Iraq must withdraw from Kuwait completely, immediately, and without condition.... No peaceful international order is possible if larger states can devour their smaller neighbors."[196] President Bush added,

> Vital issues of principle are at stake. Saddam Hussein is literally trying to wipe a country off the face of the Earth.... Vital economic interests are at risk as well. Iraq controls some 10 percent of the world's proven oil reserves. Iraq plus Kuwait [will control] twice that. An Iraq permitted to swallow Kuwait would have the economic and military power, as well as the arrogance, to intimidate and coerce its neighbors...who control the lion's share of the world's remaining oil reserves. We cannot permit a resource so vital to be dominated by one so ruthless a man. And we won't.

On 9 August 1990, two days after Saddam proclaimed the annexation of Kuwait, the UN Security Council, in a unanimous vote, fifteen to zero, adopted Resolution 662, which declared the annexation null and void. Because Saddam continued to defy the UN, the Security Council adopted two more resolutions to force Iraq from Kuwait and to restore Kuwait's legitimate government. Security Council Resolution 574 (26 October 1990) stipulated further measures, including military force, under the UN Charter, against Iraq if it continued to disregard previous resolutions; held Iraq responsible for all damages and personal injuries caused by its incursion into Kuwait; and called for Iraq to pay reparations for all the damages and injuries it had caused Kuwait. Resolution 678 adopted on 29 November 1990 authorized the United States and its allies to expel Iraq from Kuwait if Saddam Hussein failed to withdraw Iraqi forces by 15 January 1991.

Meanwhile, earlier in November 1990, a major debate had begun within the United States over the use of force to liberate Kuwait. Leaders of both US national political parties believed that any such use of force required the authorization of Congress. In the House of Representatives, forty-five members filed a legal suit on 20 November 1990 to require President Bush to seek congressional approval for any use of force. Debate on the issue intensified as

Congress held hearings on whether to use force or to wait for the sanctions and embargo already in place to force Iraq to withdraw its troops from Kuwait.

Conscious of the congressional concern, and desiring to make it clear to the American people that his administration had left no stone unturned to resolve the problem peacefully, President Bush, the day after the adoption of the Security Council Resolution 678, offered Saddam an open dialogue to resolve the Kuwait crisis peacefully. Saddam accepted the offer, but disagreement over the timing and place of the dialogue delayed its taking place until 9 January 1991, when US Secretary of State James Baker and his Iraqi counterpart, Tariq Aziz, met in Geneva. However, after six hours of deliberation, they remained deadlocked and were unable to agree on a peaceful resolution of the crisis. Iraq had insisted that it would only consider withdrawing if Israel withdrew from all the territories it was occupying since the Arab-Israeli War of 1967. It is apparent in all this that Saddam was being unrealistic in rejecting the Bush offer to resolve the crisis peacefully. Perhaps he believed that he could split the worldwide coalition the Bush administration had mobilized against his aggression and occupation of Kuwait and that the American people would not support any military action to expel Iraqi forces from Kuwait. If he held those beliefs, he was egregiously mistaken, as he eventually came to learn.

The day before the meeting, President Bush formally sought approval from Congress to use "all necessary means" to enforce Security Council Resolution 678 to expel Iraqi troops from Kuwait. Subsequently, on 12 January 1991, after three days of debate, the House voted to authorize the use of force by 250 to 183; the Senate followed suit by a vote of 52 to 47. The joint resolution reads, in part,

a. *The President is authorized*, subject to subsection (b), *to use United States Armed Forces pursuant to United Nations Security Council Resolution 678* (1990) in order to achieve implementation of Security Council Resolutions 660, 661, 662, 664, 665, 667, 669, 670, 674, and 677.
b. Before exercising the authority granted in subsection (a), the President shall make available to the Speaker of the House of Representatives and the President pro tempore of the Senate his determination that—(1) the United States has used all appropriate diplomatic and other peaceful means to obtain compliance by Iraq with the United Nations Security Council Resolutions cited in subsection (a); and (2), that those efforts have not been successful in obtaining such compliance.
c. *Consistent with* section 8 (a) (1) of *the War Powers Resolution, the Congress declares that this section is intended to constitute specific*

statutory authorization within the meaning of section 5(b) of the War
Powers Resolution.... Nothing in this resolution supersedes any
requirement of the War Powers Resolution.[197]

The measure by Congress set the stage for the war to liberate Kuwait, in
that, when Saddam continued to refuse to comply with Security Council
Resolution 678 requiring Iraqi forces to withdraw from Kuwait by 15 January
1991, the United States and the broad international coalition President Bush had
assembled launched Operation Desert Storm on 16 January 1991. It was in this
manner that the war for the liberation of Kuwait began. The war ended on 1
March 1991 after forty-three days, having involved the most intensive air and
armored operations since World War II.

The coalition forces launched the air war first. For six weeks, they bombed
Baghdad, military installations, and airfields in Iraq. Attacks on the ground
began on 24 February 1991 after Saddam had rejected an ultimatum to begin the
withdrawal of Iraqi forces from Kuwait by Saturday 23 February 1991. Iraqi
troops had set ablaze more than 150 oil wells inside Kuwait the previous day.
On 27 February 1991, three days after the ground assault began, Kuwait City
was liberated. A temporary cease-fire was agreed to the following day 28
February 1991. Iraqi troops had not shown much stomach for the fight, and
Colin Powell, chairman of the Joint Chiefs of Staff, had expressed concern that
their rout by the coalition would be seen by some as a massacre. President Bush
believed that this was needless, since the UN coalition had achieved the major
political objectives of the war—the liberation of Kuwait and the protection of
Saudi Arabia against a possible invasion by Iraq.

On 2 March 1991, the UN Security Council adopted Resolution 686, which
stipulated the coalition's conditions for a cease-fire. The resolution required
Baghdad to accept the Security Council's twelve previous resolutions against
Iraq and demanded that Iraq should renounce its annexation of Kuwait, agree
to pay reparations, release all prisoners, help remove land mines, and return
stolen property to Kuwait. The resolution further required that Iraq should cease
hostile acts against other countries and parties, including missile attacks and
flights of combat aircraft. Baghdad accepted these terms. Eventually, a
permanent cease-fire was signed on 3 March 1991.

What angered critics, especially some members of the George H. W. Bush
administration, who nine years later became members of the inner circle of his
son's administration, was why President Bush did not order the troops to march
to Baghdad to overthrow Saddam Hussein. The explanation offered by the
administration includes the following: The major political aims of the war—the

liberation of Kuwait and protecting Saudi Arabia against a possible invasion by Iraq—for which President Bush had mobilized the international coalition, including Arab states, under UN auspices had been achieved. The international coalition that had waged the war to achieve these objectives was fragile, and Bush was apprehensive that it would unravel if the aims were expanded to include the overthrow of Saddam. Here is, in part, how Bush's Secretary of State James Baker explained the administration's policy:

> We had promised the entire world in building what was an unprecedented international coalition, that we had no interest in occupying an Arab country. We weren't in this business to occupy Iraq. We were going to do what the UN Security Council said we should do, which was unconditionally eject Iraq from Kuwait. That was our war aim. That was our political aim.... [Going to Baghdad] to take out Saddam...would have involved...changing our war aims and political aims...[and] occupying Iraq. We might still be there fighting a guerrilla war.... Our military wanted no part of it.[198]

Baker added that the Arab members of the coalition may not have been willing to support an expanded war that would have killed more Iraqis and destroyed more equipment and economic and social infrastructure. Baker felt compelled to restate the reasons why the George H. W. Bush administration failed to remove Saddam Hussein from power in his 1995 publication *The Politics of Diplomacy*. The former secretary of state wrote:

> ...If Saddam were captured and his regime toppled, American forces would still have been confronted with the specter of a military occupation of indefinite duration to pacify a country and sustain a government in power. The ensuing urban warfare would surely have resulted in more casualties to American GIs than the war itself, thus creating a political firestorm at home. And as much as Saddam's neighbors wanted to see him gone, they feared Iraq would fragment in unpredictable ways that would play into the hands of the mullahs in Iran, who could export their brand of Islamic fundamentalism with the help of Iraq's Shiites and quickly transform themselves into a dominant regional power. Finally, the Security Council resolution under which we were operating authorized us to use force only to kick Iraq out of Kuwaitt, nothing more.[199]

Brent Scowcroft, Bush's national security adviser, pointed out that those Arab members with troops on the ground did not allow those troops to go into Iraq. Their troops stopped at the border of Kuwait. Scowcroft emphasized that it had not been the US objective to get rid of Saddam Hussein. He reinforced Baker's explanation that, had the United States tried to do so, it might still be occupying Baghdad. And "that would have turned a great success into a very messy, probable defeat."[200]

Dick Cheney who was secretary of defense during the war and later became vice president under George W. Bush, shared these views. He asserted in 1991

that a US invasion of Iraq would result in a quagmire. In 1992 he defended the
decision to leave Saddam Hussein in power. At that time he told an audience in
Seattle that capturing Saddam "Wouldn't be worth additional US casualties or
the risk of getting bogged down in the problems of trying to take over and
govern Iraq."[201] A decade later Cheney changed his views on Iraq and became
a leading architect of the Bush administration's war of regime change in Iraq.

However, what the George H.W. Bush administration did after the First
Gulf War was authorize the CIA to topple Saddam Hussein. It hoped that the
widespread anti-Saddam sentiment in Iraq, especially among the Kurds in the
North and the Shiites in the south of Iraq, would contribute to overthrow a
weakened Saddam Hussein. However, when these groups, responding to Bush's
call to revolt and topple the Saddam regime, did so in March 1991, the Bush
administration refused to go to their aid, thus allowing Saddam to crush the
rebellion.[202] It was concerned with political instability within Iraq and the
region. A civil war among Iraq's antagonistic ethnic and religious groups—a
Kurdish north, a Shiite south, and a Sunni center—could easily spread
instability throughout the Persian Gulf and consequently affect the global
economy. There was also the question of what the United States would do if the
Kurds and the Shiites declared independence: Would the United States "go to
war against them to keep a unified Iraq?" Scowcroft asked.[203] What the
administration did, in collaboration with Great Britain and France, was to
establish and patrol no-fly zones in northern and southern Iraq to protect the
Kurds and the Shiites against further repression by the Saddam Hussein regime
in Baghdad. Iraq was banned from using all civilian and military aircraft,
including helicopters, in the air exclusion zones. Finally, President Bush feared
that the domestic political support he had built for prosecuting the war would
not continue if, after expelling Iraq from Kuwait and depriving it of much of its
military power, he continued the war in order to remove Saddam from power.

Towards the Containment of Iraq

For the reasons summarized above, Saddam Hussein, although severely
weakened, remained in political control of Iraq. To further weaken and contain
him, a number of measures were adopted. The most prominent measures were
the following:

1. The patrolling of the above-mentioned no-fly zones established for the
    protection of the Kurds and the Shiites. Although criticized as illegal and
    unauthorized by the Security Council, and although France later withdrew
    from its enforcement because, in its view, changes in the mission had

eliminated its humanitarian aspects, the zones became crucial to the US and British policy of containing Saddam. Their governments continued to order daily patrols in the zones until 15 January 2003. For his part, Saddam Hussein refused to recognize the legitimacy of the no-fly zones and occasionally breached the ban with adverse consequences. For example, the United Nations reported that US bombings in the no-fly zones killed 144 Iraqi civilians in 1999, the only year for which it had reliable figures.

2. A continuation of the comprehensive economic sanctions imposed on Iraq before the start of the war. The Security Council did not lift its comprehensive economic sanctions; rather, it left them in place as leverage to foster Iraqi disarmament. The sanctions remained in place for a long time. Tightly enforced, they severely hurt innocent Iraqi civilians, because they prohibited the export of all Iraqi oil, which provided all but a small fraction of Iraq's access to hard currency. Meanwhile, Saddam remained deceptively intransigent on compliance with the resolution requiring Iraq to disarm of its weapons of mass destruction. To alleviate the harsh impact of the sanctions on innocent civilians, the UN initiated an Oil-for-Food Program in 1995 after widespread criticism of the humanitarian crisis. The program allowed Iraq to sell oil for food, medicine, and other essentials. Its purpose, to reemphasize, was to force Saddam Hussein to his knees without causing Iraqi people continued suffering. Thirty percent of the income from the oil (later reduced to 25 percent) was earmarked to pay for reparations incurred by Iraq's invasion of Kuwait. The program went into effect in late 1997. Between that date and 2003, Iraq earned $64 billion in oil revenue that qualified for the UN program. This provided some relief to the Iraqis but failed to eliminate the humanitarian crisis that followed the 1991 Gulf War. Ironically, the program's biggest beneficiary was Saddam Hussein himself. This was because the program was abused through bribes and a secret kickback scheme of Oil-for-Food contracts and illegal smuggling orchestrated by the Saddam Hussein regime in collaboration with a cabal of oil dealers and states. Saddam Hussein managed to funnel most of the illegal shipments through American friends—Turkey and Jordan. Rather than strictly monitor the program and stop the abuse, UN member states, especially the United States, focused more attention on their own Iraq policies. Calls to lift the sanctions were effectively resisted by the US and British governments of Bill Clinton and Tony Blair. The two governments kept their vow to block any lifting or serious reform of the sanctions so long as Saddam remained in power.

The Oil-for-Food Program was suspended during the US-led invasion of Iraq and was adjusted soon after the conquest and occupation of Iraq to provide the Iraqis temporary humanitarian relief. Eventually, the sanctions were lifted in May 2003 after the overthrow of Saddam in March 2003 by the Bush administration's "Coalition of the Willing." This was accomplished by Security Council Resolution 1483 (28 May 2003), despite the concern of some members of the council that a resolution lifting the sanctions would indirectly justify the war and acknowledge US occupation of Iraq. The resolution gave the Bush administration and its coalition partners occupying Iraq control over the country and its oil.

3. Tough inspections and elimination of all of Iraq's weapons facilities. On 3 April 1991, the Security Council adopted Resolution 687. Section C of the resolution required that Iraq should unconditionally accept, under international supervision, the destruction, removal, or rendering harmless of its weapons of mass destruction, ballistic missiles with a range over 150 kilometers (about ninety-four miles), and related production facilities and equipment. The section also provided for the establishment of a system of ongoing monitoring and verification of Iraq's compliance with the ban on these weapons and missiles. For this purpose, the UN Special Commission (UNSCOM) was established. Finally, the section required Iraq to declare, within fifteen days, the locations, amounts, and types of all its weapons and missiles.

Although the Iraqi leader Saddam had no intention of complying fully with the inspections, he formally accepted the resolution on 6 April 1991, having, however, two days earlier ordered Iraqi nuclear scientists to hide nuclear weapons materials from inspectors, collect and move computer data, and formulate a justification for the existence of Iraqi nuclear labs. Twelve days later (18 April 1991), Iraq declared some chemical weapons and materials as required by the resolution but stated that it had no biological weapons program. Thus began what the George W. Bush administration described in several speeches after the terrorist bombings of 11 September 2001 as "a decade of deception and defiance" of the international community by Iraq.

In spite of Saddam's denials and maneuvers, UNSCOM began inspections in Iraq on 9 June 1991. For seven years, the process was a tortuous game of hide and seek, intimidation and withholding of information, threats and counterthreats, and spying beyond the agenda and purpose of the UN mission. During that period, Iraq cooperated with UNSCOM and the International Atomic Energy Agency in some areas but flatly refused cooperation at times in other areas. Iraq maintained that it had destroyed all its weapons but could not produce a paper trail to fully document their destruction.

In the meantime, under the Clinton administration, the CIA continued to support various efforts to overthrow Saddam Hussein. In 1996, one such anti-Saddam effort by former Iraqi military officers was penetrated by Saddam's security service. About 120 of those plotters were executed by the Saddam regime.[204]

Later, the revelation that UNSCOM was illegally spying for the United States and Israeli intelligence agencies severely compromised the inspection process and the UN agency itself. That UNSCOM inspectors were acquiring and turning over to the US and Israeli governments information that had nothing to do with the UN agenda—the prohibited weapons program—but with the movements of Saddam, the patterns of his high-ranking officials, and the locations of his Republican Guard, enraged Saddam. Attempts by US officials to micromanage the inspection process and control its pace, intrusiveness, and site selection had a similar effect and further complicated the process.

Despite these complications and the lack of full Iraqi cooperation, by December 1998, when UNSCOM's inspection team was withdrawn from Iraq on the eve of the Clinton administration's Desert Fox bombing of Iraq, the bulk of Iraq's weapons programs had been found and destroyed or rendered harmless. And the Saddam regime had been effectively contained and isolated. But for the US and British governments, suspicious accounting of the destroyed munitions and Saddam Hussein's elaborate concealment mechanism left several unanswered questions. The two governments had already become very frustrated with the inspection process, so that, on 17 December 1998, their military forces launched a four-day air and cruise missile campaign against approximately one hundred key Iraqi military targets in order to punish Saddam for defying UNSCOM inspectors. Saddam became so enraged by the four-day Desert Fox bombing of Iraq that he flatly refused to allow UNSCOM inspectors back into Iraq. Thereafter, disarming Iraq was left in limbo. UN inspections in Iraq did not resume until after the passage of UN Security Council Resolution 1441 in November 2002. This followed the assumption of the US presidency by George W. Bush in January 2001 and the subsequent terrorist attacks on US territory that transformed his administration.

Prior to those events, though, some neoconservatives who became members of the Bush administration had already developed a deep and abiding interest in regime change in Iraq, as well as in new directions in the US role in the post–cold war world. In 1992, after the 1990-to-1991 Gulf War, Dick Cheney, Paul Wolfowitz, and Lewis "Scooter" Libby articulated views in a document entitled the Defense Planning Guidance (DPG) that, although rejected by President George H. W. Bush at the time, was to become the bedrock of President George W. Bush's administration's National Security Strategy of the United States of America (2002). Among other things, the DPG introduced explicitly the possible necessity of US unilateral action in some aspects of world affairs. It stressed the preventive use of force to promote US goals and highlighted the usefulness of a nuclear arsenal powerful enough to deter the development of nuclear programs in other countries. The belief by the neoconservatives in the Bush administration that Iraq, under the regime of Saddam Hussein, had a nuclear weapons program and had refused to comply with UN Security Council resolutions that required it to disarm made the country a target of implementing key aspects of the views articulated in the original DPG (1992). These same Bush administration officials were members of a group that had sent President Clinton an open letter in January 1998 recommending the removal of Saddam and his regime by military force. Now, as part of the Bush administration, they only waited for an opportune moment to realize their dream. The 11 September 2001 terrorist attacks on US territory gave special urgency to doing so.

True or false, the neoconservatives in the Bush administration perceived a link between those terrorist attacks and Iraq. But without doubt, the attacks triggered an immediate shock on the American people, who had not experienced a true conflict on American soil in a hundred years, especially not one that involved the death of three thousand people. They provided President Bush, who believed they had given him a mission, an excellent opportunity for political mobilization of the American people. Indeed, his political strategist, Karl Rove, assured him that those attacks had provided him the leverage he needed in the political system. Bush began to use that leverage to mobilize the American electorate in a series of speeches to the nation. One conspicuous example is his first State of the Union address (29 January 2002), when he vowed to extend the war he had declared on terrorism to states sponsoring or providing safe havens to terrorists. Iraq, to which he devoted five sentences in that address, was ostensibly a prominent target of that extension.

Earlier, in 1998, the US Congress had demonstrated interest in regime change in Iraq. At that time, it passed, and President Clinton signed, the Iraqi Liberation Act. The act authorized the expenditure of $97 million to support opposition groups against Saddam Hussein and to promote the emergence of a democratic government after his removal. The Bush administration later invoked this act. On 16 February 2002, President Bush signed a top-secret intelligence order directing the CIA to support military action to overthrow

Saddam Hussein. Congress approved $189 million to finance the operation for the first year. The administration made great efforts during its first two years at unifying fractious Iraqi opposition groups. It relied heavily upon them as it sought to develop a strategy for toppling Saddam Hussein. A high-profile meeting with the groups in London in mid December 2002 to explore how to establish an Iraqi government in exile, expecting a war for regime change, demanded that the United States should refrain from imposing a military occupation on a post-war Iraq. These were the events that provided the immediate background to the George W. Bush administration's war in Iraq.

Chapter 7
The George W. Bush Administration's Case for War in Iraq

We know that the Iraqi regime is led by a dangerous and brutal man. We know he's actively seeking the destructive technologies to match his hatred. We know he must be stopped. The dangers we face will only worsen from month to month and from year to year. To ignore these threats is to encourage them. And when they have fully materialized it may be too late to protect ourselves and our friends and our allies. By then the Iraqi dictator would have the means to terrorize and dominate the region. Each passing day could be the one on which the Iraqi regime gives anthrax or VX—nerve gas—or some day a nuclear weapon to a terrorist ally.[205]

[After 11 September 2001] President Bush, with obvious relish, declared himself a "war president." And he kept the nation focused on martial matters by morphing the pursuit of Al Qaeda into a war against Saddam Hussein.[206]

I have never covered a president who actually wanted to go to war. Mr. George W. Bush is the exception.[207]

My country seems to be on the verge of making a historical mistake, one that will forever change the political dynamic which has governed the world since the end of the Second World War, namely the foundation of international law as set forth in the United Nations charter, which calls for the peaceful resolution of problems between nations.[208]

About nine months after he had taken office, President George W. Bush, untrained and untested in national security, found himself about to embark on a complicated and prolonged road to war, first in Afghanistan and then in Iraq. This meant that he had to rely heavily on the advice of others. Whereas the war in Afghanistan was provoked by terrorist attacks on US territory and required little or no justification, the one in Iraq was a war of choice. The case the Bush administration made for it was heavily influenced by the views of twenty neoconservatives within and outside the administration, including some in the pages of *Commentary* and the *Weekly Standard* and in the studios of Fox News. The war that began in March 2003 against Iraq was a triumph of their clearly and forcefully articulated views. It had been planned for a decade by neoconservatives and was argued for by such leading foreign policy ideologues as Paul Wolfowitz, Donald Rumsfeld, Lewis "Scooter" Libby, Douglas Feith, and Richard Perle. It is therefore appropriate to start this chapter by shedding some light on those views in order to appreciate their role and impact on the case the Bush administration collectively and relentlessly made before the American people and the world generally for war against Iraq.

Doing so is critical, among other reasons, because George W. Bush, as he himself publicly acknowledged, was very weak on foreign policy issues and had a lot to learn about world affairs when he assumed the US presidency on 21 January 2001. During the campaign for that office, he promised a humble approach to foreign policy and repeatedly endeavored to reassure the electorate that he would compensate for his weakness in foreign affairs issues by surrounding himself as president with seasoned advisers. In an opinion editorial in the *New York Times* (26 July 2000) Maureen Dowd, anticipating that neoconservatives might take advantage of Bush's inexperience in foreign policy matters to promote their own agenda, wrote that Dick Cheney, whom Bush had selected as his running mate, would be his "baby sitter." Although he told Cheney, upon selecting him as such, that, if times were good, he was going to need his advice but not merely as much as he would need him if times were bad,[209] Bush minimized such a view in the course of the campaign by consulting foreign policy experts. He not only consulted such experts as former secretaries of state Henry Kissinger and George Shultz, but he also assembled a group of eight foreign policy advisers named the *Vulcans* by its chair, Condoleezza Rice. Six members of the group with neoconservative credentials became part of the Bush administration's foreign policy team.[210]

It is important to observe that two of those members—Paul Wolfowitz and Richard Perle—in addition to Vice President Dick Cheney and Defense Secretary Donald Rumsfeld, already had an ax to grind against Bush's predecessors—his father George H. W. Bush, Colin Powell, and Bill Clinton—for not forcefully removing the Iraqi leader Saddam Hussein from power. Of this group, Paul Wolfowitz, who may have spent more time with Bush during the 2000 presidential campaign than any other foreign policy adviser except Condoleezza Rice, was the most prominent intellectual proponent of ousting Saddam Hussein from power by military force. Also, George Schultz, one of the foreign policy consultants, was on the board of directors of the Bechtel Group, the largest contractor in the United States. In 2002, he became the chairman of the advisory board of the Committee for the Liberation of Iraq. The fiercely pro-war Committee had very close ties to the Bush White House and clearly was not just seeking the ouster of Saddam Hussein but was also committed "to work beyond the liberation of Iraq to the reconstruction of the economy."[211] Vice President Dick Cheney himself had been chief executive officer of Halliburton, a prominent Texas oil company with corporate offices in the Washington, D.C., Beltway. But conspicuously absent from Bush's core foreign policy advisers and consultants were such political realists as James Baker, Brent Scowcroft, and Lawrence Eagleburger, who had served as key members of his father's foreign policy team.

Neoconservatives and the Bush Administration's Case for War in Iraq

In the United States, neoconservatives are intellectuals or leaders of thought who broke ranks with liberals and moderates on major domestic and, especially, foreign policy issues to become ultraconservative in the 1960s and 1970s.[212] They were initially anti-Soviet liberals with a pro-Israel wing and a focus on confrontation with the Soviet bloc. From the 1980s, they began to manifest a growing contempt for international law and hostility towards the United Nations. Inspired by the example of Israel, they embraced and espoused the tactics of preventive war after the end of the cold war. Their ranks, voice, and influence in US government increased slowly but significantly thereafter.[213] The increase in their influence is a function of two forces: their unexpected alliance with the religious right, which emerged as a substantial base of the Republican Party, and the 11 September 2001 attacks on the World Trade Center and the Pentagon, which they believed gave them and President Bush a mission to repel Islamic terrorists and transform the Middle East. Even so, they are unrepresentative of either the US population or the mainstream of the American foreign policy establishment.

Characteristically, neoconservatives are supremely confident and inclined towards an interventionist foreign policy and a unilateralism that is frequently at odds with traditional conceptions of diplomacy and international law. They describe themselves as realists and often articulate their views through such neocon think tanks as the Project for a New American Century and the American Enterprise Institute. Such views invariably tend to deviate from the political mainstream and further distinguish the group sharply from liberals and conservatives, for example, on the use of military force to pursue foreign policy goals, as hawks. As unilateralists, who also want to impose moral clarity on world politics, they dismiss multilateralists as sentimental and naive. But they take seriously old-fashioned foreign policy realists, who, however, disagree with their extreme and triumphalist views, and consider themselves as pragmatist enough to discuss American foreign policy on the grounds of practical matters, such as national security interest and balance of power. Professor Stanley Hoffmann of Harvard University described them as truly "no more than realists drunk with America's new might as the only superpower....

But that headiness," the professor wrote, "makes all the difference. For, whereas the hallmark of past realists...was the kind of discerning prudence and moderation that Thucydides once praised, the new voices are nothing if not excessive and triumphalist."[214]

Long-term ties of neoconservatives to Republican Party circles helped many of their group, who had known, worked together, and reinforced each other for a long time, to be appointed to key posts in the George W. Bush administration. More responsible for their appointment to those posts in the administration was the role of Dick Cheney. Cheney was in charge of Bush's presidential transition, the period between the election in November 2000 and Bush's accession to the presidency on 21 January 2001, and Bush had tasked him with a robust national security portfolio. Cheney used that opportunity and assignment to pack the administration with his neoconservative allies, including such individuals as Donald Rumsfeld, Paul Wolfowitz, Richard Perle, Douglas Feith, John R. Bolton, and a protégé of Wolfowitz, Lewis "Scooter" Libby, who became Cheney's chief of staff and national security adviser. Note that these individual neoconservatives were all linked together by the Project for the New American Century formed in the 1990s. They brought into the administration others—like Under Secretary of Defense William Luti and Abram Shulsky, director of the Office of Special Plans created to rival the traditional intelligence agencies—that shared their views and attitudes.

The neoconservatives share a number of beliefs and key attitudes in foreign policy that shape their foreign policy prescriptions.[215] Prominent among these include the following:

1. A contempt for multilateralism and a passion for unilateralism in addressing global issues that have a bearing on US security and global dominance, using America's unparalleled military power.
2. A lack of faith in the legitimacy and effectiveness of international law and institutions to achieve either security or justice.
3. A belief that the United States should not limit itself to a purely defensive strategy, such as was the case against the Soviet Union during the cold war.
4. A disdain and distrust for Europeans, especially the French.
5. A conviction that fundamentalist Islam poses a major threat to the United States and its Western European allies.
6. An obsession with specific flaws of the Arab world that needed to be rectified in their desire to change the political status quo in the Middle East through democratization of the entire region.
7. Support for the Jewish state of Israel.

8. A belief that the People's Republic of China is a long-term strategic threat to the United States that should be confronted sooner rather than later.

With effective bureaucratic skill, relentlessness, and intellectualism, members of the group were able to articulate these beliefs and outflank the moderates in the administration with a less hawkish and imperial world view. Evidently, from its start, the administration was riven by ideological disputes between the hawks—the Rumsfeld-Cheney group—and the moderates—the Powell group—on foreign policy. President Bush, however, chose to stay quite at home in the political environment of the neoconservative hawks, who persuaded him of the need to adopt a new national security policy. Thus, their beliefs and attitudes began to shape his foreign policy decisions. Indeed, his foreign policy speeches and approach, especially during his first term, reflected their language, thought, arrogance, strong support for the Israeli Prime Minister Ariel Sharon, rejection of various multilateral treaties and institutions, and push for regime change in Iraq and other Middle Eastern countries. The following statements are typical neoconservative phraseology replicated in his speeches on Iraq and its Saddam Hussein regime: "Iraq is a gathering threat to the United States." "I don't care what the international lawyers say. We don't want the smoking gun to become a mushroom cloud." "Iraq is a danger that is gathering momentum." "This is a regime that has lied and cheated." "This is not a regime that can be trusted."

Here is a succinct summary of the views of neoconservatives on the US role in post–cold war world affairs, although they are not monolithic on all issues. Neoconservatives have complete faith in the ability of American power to bend the world to America's will. They advocate a robust US military defense budget in order to perpetuate the nation's unprecedented and unrivaled military and political power and aggressively challenge regimes deemed hostile to its values and interests. They believe and espouse the view that, in the current new world order, the United States should assertively and unabashedly act as a benevolent global hegemon, charting a bold course for itself in world affairs.[216] It should regard with deepest suspicion international institutions that point to an ultimate world government. At the same time, it should inhibit the rise of another superpower that could rival it and should not even allow any other power to attempt to match US military capacity. Therefore, it should neither hesitate nor be ashamed to use its unrivaled military power to defend its global interests and to promote its values around the world. It should do so not necessarily with or through allies, treaties, and multilateral organizations that would define and legitimize common goals, but, instead, it should necessarily act alone as the world's sole superpower, thereby avoiding the constraints allies, international law, and multilateral organizations could impose.

Essentially, this foreign policy approach undermines one of the critical sources of the legitimacy of US behavior in the post–World War II world: the pledge of the use of US power to uphold international law. Instead, by rule of thumb, the United States may organize coalitions—"coalitions of the willing"—when necessary but should not hesitate to act alone in defense of its self-interest. This approach, the neoconservatives claim, is not only best for the United States, it is best for the world, which can only achieve peace through US leadership backed with credible force, not weak treaties to be disrespected by tyrants.

Additionally, such neoconservatives as Charles Krauthammer and William Kristol believe that not just the power of the United States alone, but also its exceptionalism and the good it does for the world, justifies its international behavior. Another neoconservative, Robert Kagan, added, "It was not international law and institutions but the circumstances of the Cold War and Washington's special role in it, that conferred legitimacy on the United States, at least within the West."[217] In that same vein, W. Michael Reisman also argued that "because the United States, as a result of its strength, is responsible for world order, it is justified in rejecting whatever parts of international law it decides would make that order more difficult."[218] Defense Secretary Donald Rumsfeld and John R. Bolton, as the Bush administration's undersecretary of state for arms control and international security, similarly asserted that the United States, as powerful as it is, should ignore international law and organizations that stand in its path.[219] Before becoming an official of the Bush administration, Bolton had noted in the late 1990s "that it is a big mistake for us to grant any validity to international law even when it may seem in our short-term interest to do so—because over the long-term, the goal of those who think that international law really means anything are those who want to constrict the United States."[220]

In these views, one detects a similar fundamentally contemptuous attitude towards the principles of international law manifested by the German regime that brought on World War II. To start that war, the German regime had acted on the principle that might, not international law, makes right. Influenced by similar neoconservative views, President George W. Bush declared that the United States did not need anybody's permission slip to defend its national security interests. Surely, he cast profound doubt over whether his administration would consult America's traditional allies or simply summon them to follow their leader when, in his statement on the war on terrorism, he declared: "Either you are with us, or you are with the terrorists." Bush manifested the same bluntness when he repeatedly warned the United Nations that it risked irrelevance unless it disarmed Iraq by military force as his administration demanded.

Neoconservatives also stress that contemporary threats to the United States can no longer be successfully confronted by the cold war strategy of containment but must be prevented essentially through preemptive military action. They believe that the new security challenges confronting the United States and the strategy for addressing them require a reorganization and restructuring of US armed forces that they insisted remained still oriented entirely to the cold war strategy of deterrence and so are inadequate for meeting the newer challenges and other contingencies. In addition, defending America, as championed by such neoconservatives as Defense Secretary Rumsfeld and his deputy Paul Wolfowitz, requires a national missile defense system, space weaponry, and preventive warfare.

These views had been forcefully articulated in 1992 by Paul Wolfowitz and Lewis "Scooter" Libby in the Defense Planning Guidance at the direction of Dick Cheney, who was then President George H. W. Bush's defense secretary. The radical philosophy espoused in the document was rejected by Cheney's boss. The views, however, were resurrected when President George H. W. Bush's son, George W. Bush, became president. They became the dominant feature of his National Security Strategy of the United States of America released in September 2002 and essentially laid the foundation for every major theme of his administration's post–11 September 2001 foreign policy. Neoconservative ideology imbedded in the National Security document reserved for the United States the right of preemptive military action, while it warned others nations not to use preemption as a pretext for aggression. Furthermore, the neoconservative authors of the document presumed that "the United States is the sole judge of the legitimacy of its own or anyone else's preemptive strikes."[221] In sum, the Bush doctrine of preemption championed by the conservatives and enunciated in the National Security strategy document "proclaims the emancipation of a colossus from international constraints (including from the restraints that the United States itself enshrined in networks of international and regional organizations after World War II). In context, it amounts to a doctrine of global domination."[222]

The neoconservatives recognized the strategic importance of the Middle East in world affairs in general and to US national security interests, including its identity of interests with the Jewish state of Israel, in particular. But, for a long time, the region had problems of political instability, repression, conflicts, and terrorism and remained very hard to transform in spite of its potential. Neoconservatives saw the absence of democracy, as practiced in the Western world, in the region as a major cause of these problems and a factor contributing to the region's instability.

Most neoconservatives shared the belief that authoritarianism and theocracy in the Middle East prompted hostile feelings towards the United States and Israel, a key outpost of democracy in the region. A loose collection of the friends of Israel, including such Bush administration officials as Paul Wolfowitz, Richard Perle, Douglas Feith, and Elliott Abrams, concluded that the 1991 Gulf War, provoked by Saddam Hussein's invasion and occupation of Kuwait, provided an auspicious opportunity to initiate a transformation of the greater Middle East into a land of free-market, pro-Western democracies living at peace with Israel. In their view, the identity of interest between Israel and the United States, both of which are forced to cooperate and rely on military power for their survival, called for such a transformation. That transformation, they claimed, would secure reliable petroleum supply and military bases for the United States and could begin through a regime change in Iraq and the establishment of a democratic government in the country. Indeed, Richard Perle stressed that there was "tremendous potential to transform" the Middle East if the Saddam Hussein regime were removed and replaced with a group of Iraqis who would move the country in the direction of a humane and open politics. Such a process, he held, would inspire the opponents of the regimes in Iran and elsewhere in the greater Middle East to bring down the tyrants who were afflicting them in pretty much the way Saddam Hussein was oppressing the Iraqis.[223] It would also force the autocratic regimes in the region to accelerate efforts to reform themselves. He stressed that a democratic Iraq that moved from the column of opponents of the peace process between the Israelis and the Palestinians into the column of proponents for negotiating a settlement would have a major effect on prospects for negotiating a settlement to the very difficult conflict. Israeli leaders shared these views and unreservedly supported a war against Iraq. They and pro-Israel groups in the United States worked together to shape the Bush administration's policy towards Iraq.[224]

Douglas Feith, Bush's undersecretary for defense policy, was very prominent in that role, especially in promoting an alternative analysis on the Saddam Hussein-Al Qaeda relationship. His alternative analysis totally ignored the consensus of the intelligence community that the two had not been working together. For long, Feith had shared the notion that regime change in the Arab world would ensure Israel's security. A 1996 report—A Clean Break: A New Strategy for Securing the Realm—that he co-authored with Richard Perle "spelled out a rosy scenario under which a post-Saddam Iraq with a Shiite majority government would support a pro-Israel position."[225] The close ties that emerged after regime change in Iraq between the Iraqi Shiite leadership and Iran which publicly called for the elimination of Israel demonstrated the absurdity of the Feith expectation.

It was in this manner, according to some observers, that the neoconservatives in the administration manipulated the nation and the inexperience of President Bush in foreign affairs into a war in Iraq to transform the Middle East, secure oil and strategic bases for the United States, and make the region safe for Israel. To them, the Bush administration critics argued, Bush was malleable to the extent of trying to distinguish himself from his father and his "mistakes" in the 1991 Gulf War of not removing Saddam Hussein from power in Baghdad. Furthermore, the critics surmised, "It is not clear that George W. Bush fully [understood] the grand strategy Paul Wolfowitz and his aides [were] unfolding. He seems genuinely [to have believed] that there was an imminent threat to the United States from Saddam Hussein's 'weapons of mass destruction' something the neoconservatives [said] in public but [were] far too intellectual to believe themselves.[226] But it was uncertain that he fully grasped the potential consequences of the decision to bring about regime change in Iraq by military force, which the neoconservatives were urging on him.

President George W. Bush accepted the recommendation that removing Saddam Hussein from power by force would transform the Middle East into a land of pro-Western democracies living at peace with Israel. He reiterated this view in December 2005, more than two years after launching the war against Iraq.[227] The justification for Saddam Hussein's forced removal, Bush persistently told the nation and the world, was that the Iraqi ruler had and was building and hiding weapons of mass destruction "that could enable him to dominate the Middle East and intimidate the civilized world"; he had "close ties to terrorist organizations, and could supply them with terrible weapons to strike" at the United States; and he had deceived and defied the United Nations for over a period of eleven years. Therefore, he had to be forcibly disarmed and removed from power. In an address on 26 February 2003 to members of the American Enterprise Institute, regarded as the de facto headquarters for neoconservative foreign policy, Bush said, "a liberated Iraq can show the power of freedom to transform [the vital Middle East] by bringing hope and progress into the lives of millions.... A new regime in Iraq would serve as a dramatic and inspiring example of freedom for other nations in the region.... Success in Iraq could also begin a new stage for Middle Eastern peace, and set in motion progress toward a truly democratic Palestinian state."[228] Evidently, the president joined the neoconservatives to substitute the neoconservative moral purpose—promoting change and "the extension of democracy, through force, if necessary—for that favored by the architects of post–World War II order, which emphasized the protection of democratic community through rules constraining the use of force."[229]

The Bush administration's policy to implement the views and recommendations of the neoconservatives—to replace by military force a tyrannical regime with a democracy—was personally for him an afterthought. Until the invasion, conquest, and occupation of Iraq, he had showed no interest in nation building. He was critical of Clinton for attempting to build nations in Somalia, Bosnia, and Kosovo. The afterthought was tantamount to claiming that "a well-placed stick of dynamite can turn a redwood forest into charming Victorians."[230] It was equally unrealistic to suggest that forcefully getting rid of an Arab leader, no matter how tyrannical he was, would resolve the intractable problems of the Middle East. Furthermore, the policy unrealistically assumed that the United States could very successfully project on the Middle East countries—the Arab world—a model of democracy that has worked for it. Very seldom has democracy been bestowed upon a people by a paternal outside hand. Rather, democracy is essentially homegrown; it is not an easy transplant, at least not in the short run. Even in the long term, it is doubtful that the United States could compel other societies to become democratic. Few rational Americans, if any, would view their "nation as a mere staging platform for a 'global democratic revolution,' to be promoted by invading foreign countries and arming foreign insurrections where no 'calculations of national interest are necessary.'"[231] It is no wonder that "most of the career professionals in the national security agencies—the military, the intelligence community and the Foreign Service—opposed the grand strategy of Bush and his neocon appointees."[232]

Even though the neoconservatives persisted in their drive for regime change in Iraq, no definite policy recommendation was immediately submitted to President Bush. This was because of deep division and tensions between the hawks, as represented by Vice President Dick Cheney and Defense Secretary Donald Rumsfeld, on the one hand, and the moderates, whose major voice was Secretary of State Colin Powell. The terrorist attacks of 11 September 2001 changed all that. They provided the neoconservatives a golden opportunity, forced Bush's hand, and handed his administration what it passionately came to believe was a mission. That said, it should be made clear that the subsequent George W. Bush administration war in Iraq was a war of choice. The United States did not have an immediate need to wage war against Iraq in March 2003.

Nor did it have an immediate need to wage war in the manner that it did so. Besides domestic political calculations—the vagaries of domestic politics—top policy makers within the administration had differing motivations about the perceived threat Iraq posed to the United States and how to respond to it. While some advocated a unilateral US response using military force, others preferred a multilateral approach under the auspices of the UN Security Council. Nevertheless, the Bush administration decided on a war. It produced a rationale and justification for the war it eventually waged against the Persian Gulf state.

The Bush Case for War: Avenues and Forums Used

Given the ongoing hostile relations between the regime of Saddam Hussein and the United States and the beliefs and views of neoconservatives regarding the US role and national security strategy in the post–cold war world that was shaping the Bush administration's foreign policy, it is plausible that President George W. Bush had already made up his mind to bring about regime change in Iraq before the terrorist attacks of 11 September 2001. Before he became president, Bush told a writer and long-time family friend, Mickey Herskowitz,

> One of the keys to being seen as a great leader is to be seen as a commander-in-chief.... My father had all the political capital built up when he drove the Iraqis out of Kuwait and he wasted it.... If I have a chance to invade...and if I had that much capital, I'm not going to waste it.[233]

From this, it is apparent that Bush was eagerly looking for a convenient pretext to exploit a political capital—a perceived threat to national security. The terrorist attacks of 11 September 2001 provided that pretext. This perspective is documented by a number of evidences: First, before the attacks, Iraq had already become an important concern of the Bush administration. Bush and three senior officials of his administration—Vice President Cheney, Defense Secretary Rumsfeld, and his deputy Paul Wolfowitz—were so focused on that concern that they ignored the series of briefings and warnings provided them about al-Qaeda by the outgoing Clinton administration and the Intelligence Community. Therefore, one of the administration's earliest foreign policy decisions was a review of Iraq policy. Before and after that review on the seventeenth day of the Bush presidency (5 February 2001), leading officials of the administration remained angry that a "totally risk-averse" Clinton administration had allowed Saddam Hussein more than eight years to grow in strength and openly defy the United States and the UN Security Council resolutions requiring Iraq to disarm. Various options for dealing with him were contemplated. In fact, within two weeks of the administration's inauguration,

Vice President Dick Cheney helped to free funding for opponents of
Saddam—the Iraqi National Congress (INC)—held up by the Department of
State. His office enthusiastically supported further efforts to empower the INC
to overthrow Saddam. He had become so exasperated with the failure of
measures—economic sanctions, imposition of no-fly zones, and bombings—to
eliminate Saddam that he decided that the Iraqi leader had to be taken out by
military force.[234]

Secondly, at the Principals Meeting on 4 September 2001, when Richard A.
Clarke and George Tenet spoke passionately about the urgency and seriousness
of the al-Qaeda terrorist threat to the United States, Rumsfeld and Wolfowitz
argued that there were other terrorist concerns, like Iraq, that required the
administration's action.[235] Clarke testified before the 9/11 Commission and later
wrote that, from discussions held immediately after the terrorist attacks of 11
September, he "realized with almost a sharp physical pain that Rumsfeld and
Wolfowitz were going to try to take advantage of this national tragedy to
promote their agenda about Iraq."[236]

Immediately after 11 September, Rumsfeld and Wolfowitz brought up the
possibility of military action against Iraq, using the occasion of the attacks as
an opportunity to do so. They and eight other members of the Bush
administration had been among the signatories to a 26 June 1998 letter to
President Clinton calling for the ouster of Saddam Hussein by military force.[237]
Rumsfeld had been the only member of Bush's war council to abstain from
voting on the Colin Powell position that the US focus at the time should be on
dealing with Osama bin Laden and his al-Qaeda terrorist network that had
attacked the United States. Two days after the attacks, and before a decision was
made to respond militarily to the perpetrators of the 11 September attacks,
Rumsfeld continued to talk about broadening the objectives of US response to
them and "getting Iraq." Furthermore, he complained that "there were no decent
targets for bombing in Afghanistan," which had provided a haven for al-Qaeda.
The United States, therefore, he proposed, should consider bombing Iraq, which
had better targets. President Bush did not reject out of hand Rumsfeld's idea of
attacking Iraq. Rather, he observed that what was needed to be done with Iraq
"was to change the government" there and not to bomb it with cruise missiles,
as Rumsfeld had implied. President Bush did not stop at that. On the evening
of 12 September, he ordered Richard A. Clarke and his colleagues to go back
and review everything about the attacks to see if they had been carried out by
Saddam. A reassurance that the attacks were the work of al-Qaeda failed to
convince him. He insisted "testily" on further review.[238]

Thirdly, with speed and tenacity but without credible evidence, high-ranking officials of the administration linked the 11 September attacks on US territory to Saddam Hussein. They rejected evidence to the contrary. Systematically and selectively, they used and distorted some intelligence on Iraq's biological and chemical weapons program to make it seem more alarmist and more dangerous.[239] Indeed, Joseph C. Wilson, a retired ambassador and former director of Africa policy in the National Security Council, asserted, as later was confirmed by the Downing Street Memo, that the administration had manipulated and twisted aspects of the intelligence to support a political goal that had already been established.[240]

Fourthly, Richard Perle, chair of Rumsfeld's Defense Policy Board and an outspoken public advocate for war against Iraq, contributed to the language on punishing sponsors of terrorism that was included in the president's 20 September 2001 speech by one of his speech writers David Frum. Specifically, Perle had suggested that the failure to impose a penalty on states harboring terrorists meant that those states operated far more effectively and that punitive action against them would eliminate such behavior.[241]

Finally, barely two months after the terrorist attacks, President Bush set his Defense Secretary Donald Rumsfeld in motion on Iraq War plans. At that time, Bush asked Rumsfeld to "get Tommy Franks [of the Central Command based in Tampa, Florida] looking at what it would take to protect America by removing Saddam Hussein if we have to." He further inquired of Rumsfeld whether that "could be done on a basis that would not be terribly noticeable,"[242] and requested that he should not talk to others about what he was doing. A leak of the secret, Bush told Rumsfeld, "would trigger enormous international angst and domestic speculation," especially "if people thought we were developing a...war plan for Iraq."[243]

Bush's first step, with the intimate involvement of his secretary of defense, in embarking on a war for regime change in Iraq was buttressed by the position of Vice President Dick Cheney for whom removing Saddam Hussein from power had become a high necessity. Dick Cheney was described as "a powerful, steam rolling force" on Bush's long walk-up to war in Iraq.[244] He and the hawks in the Pentagon—Deputy Defense Secretary Paul Wolfowitz and Under Secretary of Defense for Intelligence and Chairman of the Defense Policy Board Richard Perle—had harbored a sense of unfinished business in the 1991 Gulf War. He had served the president's father as defense secretary during that war. After the terrorist attacks on the United States, Cheney developed an intense focus on the threats he perceived to be posed to the United States by Saddam Hussein and Osama bin Laden's terrorist network that was responsible for the attacks, even as he remained very close to President Bush. The task after the attacks was therefore how to convince the American people of the need to remove this threat.

To carry out this task, the George W. Bush administration literally plunged into a crusade. It used its leading members and every available venue and forum to make its case for war in Iraq. At times, it abandoned the language of diplomacy and attacked opponents of preemptive war, including UN weapons inspectors and nations, such as France and Germany, that refused to support such a war in the Security Council, in phraseology usually reserved for political campaigns. In its attempts to convince the American public of the need to go to war in Iraq, the administration used the politics of fear and division to manipulate public opinion. It exploited the terrorist attacks of 11 September 2001 to effectively make its case. "Without September 11," a senior official of the administration said, "we never would have been able to put Iraq at the top of our agenda. It was only then that this president was willing to think about the unthinkable—that the next attack could be with weapons of mass destruction supplied to terrorists by Saddam Hussein."[245]

Critically, the administration took measures to neutralize the CIA and other members of the Intelligence Community as an objective voice on foreign affairs. It tried to intimidate the agencies to produce intelligence that would suit its policy on Iraq rather than intelligence that should inform and guide the policy. As an eyewitness, Paul R. Pillar, who served from 2000 to 2005 as the national intelligence officer responsible for the Middle East, wrote,

> In the wake of the Iraq war, it has become clear that official intelligence analysis was not relied on in making even the most significant national security decisions, that intelligence was misused publicly to justify decisions already made, that damaging ill will developed between policymakers and intelligence officers, and that the intelligence community's own work was politicized....
>
> The Bush administration deviated from the professional standard not only in using policy to drive intelligence, but also in aggressively using intelligence to win public support for its decision to go to war. This meant selectively adducing data—"cherry-picking"—rather than using the intelligence community's analytic judgments. In fact, key portions of the administration's case explicitly rejected those judgments.[246]

Apparently, the Director of Central Intelligence George Tenet, eager to ingratiate himself with the administration and to please it on Iraq, fell prey to this strategy of intimidation and politicizing of intelligence. After the failure of his agency to provide any effective warning of the attacks of 11 September, Tenet, whose tenure had become less secure, became so subdued that he succumbed to the pressures of the Bush administration to provide it suitable intelligence. The administration's Secretary of Defense Donald Rumsfeld "had sized him up and decided he could run right over him."[247] Many CIA analysts viewed him as being so "eager to endear himself" to the hawks in the administration and to improve his standing with President Bush and Vice President Cheney that he obliged them and abandoned his analysts.[248]

Besides intimidating the Intelligence Community, the administration created an alternate agency—including the leaders of the Iraqi National Congress and defectors from Iraq with a stake in overthrowing Saddam—to provide the kind of intelligence that would justify its policy.[249] The major alternate agency, the Pentagon's Office of Special Plans, engineered a crucial change of direction in the US Intelligence Community. Its chief advisers and analysts produced a labyrinth of intelligence reviews that the administration used to engage in an elaborate campaign of orchestrated public intelligence sharing as part of its efforts to shape public opinion and build support on its policy towards Iraq.[250] Vice President Dick Cheney's chief of staff, Lewis Libby, was authorized to leak sanitized classified intelligence to a few trusted journalists in an effort to bolster the administration's case for war in Iraq.[251] In August 2002, the administration established a White House Iraqi Group to market and bolster public support for war in Iraq. In addition, the Policy Counterterrorism Evaluation Group within the Pentagon was charged with finding links between al-Qaeda and Iraq that the Intelligence Community had possibly missed.

Furthermore, the administration allowed civilians in the Pentagon to dominate the administration's foreign and national security policy, while the Defense Secretary Rumsfeld undertook to shape presidential briefings on Iraq and their ultimate results. The White House itself twisted facts and ignored contradicting evidence as it strove to convince the American public of the impending nuclear weapon's threat from Iraq. A glaring example is the selective and distorting use it made of the record of the debriefing of General Hussein Kamel by the UN weapons inspectors. It totally ignored the credit the defector, Saddam Hussein's son-in-law, had given to the inspectors for the important and effective role they had played in destroying Iraq's weapons of mass destruction.

Deliberately and repeatedly, the administration presented its case for the war in simple terms and in the name of American vital national security interests and American values and ideals, that is, in the name of survival and messianic idealism. It exploited the "shock and awe" inflicted on the nation by the 11 September terrorist attacks in explaining that Saddam Hussein's weapons of mass destruction posed a very serious threat to the nation, especially when placed in the hands of terrorists. It insisted that there existed a link between Saddam Hussein and al-Qaeda terrorists that viciously attacked the United States. The administration's effectiveness in making this link is indicated by the fact that, whereas, in reality, it was Saudi Arabian and Egyptian nationals who had hijacked and used American airplanes as their weapons of destruction on 11 September 2001, more than half of the American people believed that the Iraqis had been deeply implicated in those horrendous acts. Those attacks also essentially wiped away the tolerance of many more Americans for Iraq's alleged possession of weapons of mass destruction.

The administration's strategy was effective because, after 11 September,

> there was the rebirth of a wounded and indignant patriotism, a rallying behind the president who promised decisive victory, had taken a hard line and [was offering] firm leadership. Thus opinion came to accept the arguments linking Iraq to terrorism, and the media put themselves at the service of the administration and of the public…. For a country half of whose [eligible] voters do not vote, and for whom politics is not the condition of their lives, it takes a major crisis and a president who presents himself as a savior [as George W. Bush did] to [achieve] public mobilization."[252]

Furthermore, the administration exploited the humanitarianism of the American people when it presented in lucid terms the crimes of the Saddam Hussein regime against its citizens and neighbors. The horrendous violations of the citizens' fundamental rights required that the victims should be liberated and democracy promoted in the nation and the entire Persian Gulf region, as the administration was advocating. To the average American, the cause of maintaining national security and promoting democracy was just and worthy of support. The media emphasized the worthiness of the cause, and the success in Afghanistan gave it a further boost.

While more conventional foreign policy experts argued that Iraq could be restrained by multilateral action, including enforcing the US- and British-imposed no-fly zones and a policy of smart sanctions and aggressive inspection by the UN inspectors to restrain its ability to possess weapons of mass destruction, the administration rejected such an approach as ineffectual. It saw the approach as an appeasement that had sustained Saddam Hussein's eleven years of deceit and defiance of the international community.

Administration insiders like Paul Wolfowitz, Vice President Dick Cheney, Donald Rumsfeld, and Chairman of the Defense Advisory Board Richard Perle, for example, used the Project for the New American Century and Fox Television News network to disseminate their views and make their case for the war. The American Enterprise Institute and the Veterans of Foreign Wars were similarly used by President Bush and Vice President Dick Cheney themselves and several of the administration's top officials. Richard Perle was a fellow of the American Enterprise Institute. Furthermore, the administration used the electronic media very effectively. The president and his high-ranking officials granted several media interviews. Rumsfeld and Douglas Feith created the Office of Strategic Influence in the Pentagon to manipulate the media and the American public. The president made several radio addresses to the nation, as well as other orchestrated public speeches and joint addresses to both chambers of the US Congress, press conferences, and addresses to the United Nations. He authorized Ari Fleischer and Scott McCllelan, his successive White House spokesmen, to give frequent press briefings on Iraq. Also, the administration provided members of relevant committees of Congress briefing sessions to receive so-called confidential information about so-called threats to the United States from Iraq that were actually unsubstantiated. After the sessions, the legislators said they had heard little that was new or little threat from Iraq that was imminent. The administration was undeterred. It continued relentlessly to release various accounts to demonstrate how and why Iraq was an imminent threat to its neighbors, the world, and the United States.[253]

In his address to the nation from the Oval Office on the evening of 11 September 2001 after the terrorist attacks, Bush included a tough passage about punishing those who harbor terrorists. He asserted that the United States would make no distinction between those who commit such acts and those nations, organizations, or persons who harbor or assist them. Two days after his address, Deputy Defense Secretary Paul Wolfowitz elaborated on the proclamation at a Pentagon briefing. Wolfowitz signaled that the United States would enlarge its campaign against terrorism to include Iraq; getting rid of Saddam Hussein was necessary and would be relatively easy. He added, "one has to say it's not just simply a matter of capturing people and holding them accountable, but removing the sanctuaries, removing the support system, ending states [which] sponsor terrorism. And that's why the campaign has to be broad and sustained."[254]

President Bush reinforced the Wolfowitz elaboration in his speech to a joint session of US Congress (20 September 2001) and in his State of the Union address in January 2002. In the former, Bush vowed that the United States "will pursue nations that provide aid or safe haven to terrorists. Every nation in every region, now has a decision to make. Either you are with us, or you are with the terrorists. From this day forward, any nation that continues to harbor or support terrorism will be regarded by the United States as a hostile regime."[255] Bush went on in his State of the Union speech in January 2002 to identify Iraq, Iran, and North Korea as constituting an "axis of evil," arming to threaten the peace of the world. He accused Iraq specifically of continuing to "flaunt its hostility toward America and to support terror."[256] Later in the year, he proclaimed, "There are many dangers in the world, the threat from Iraq stands alone because it gathers the most serious dangers of our age in one place. Iraq could decide on any given day to provide a biological or chemical weapon to a terrorist group or individual terrorists."[257] In his remarks at the UN General Assembly on 12 September 2002, Bush warned that the first time the world may be completely certain that Saddam Hussein has a nuclear weapon "is when, God forbid, he uses one."[258] In his State of the Union Address on 28 January 2003, Bush told the nation and the world that the British government had learned that Saddam Hussein had recently sought significant quantities of uranium from Africa for his nuclear weapons program.[259] Saddam, he added, had not credibly explained those activities and clearly had much to hide.

Finally, the Bush administration worked closely with British Prime Minister Tony Blair to make its case that Saddam Hussein threatened his neighbors with Iraq's arsenal of weapons of mass destruction and so had to be disarmed by military force. Before Bush became president in 2001, Blair's government, among other actions it took against Iraq in collaboration with the Clinton administration, had resorted to spreading false information about Iraq. It began to do so in 1996 after an impasse over UN inspections in Iraq put the British and US governments on the losing side of the battle for international public opinion.[260] Blair had several strategic meetings with Bush on Iraq after Bush became president. He walked a tightrope between the Bush administration's determination to remove Saddam from power by military force and the conviction of other European allies of the United States that Iraq should be disarmed through peaceful means. Yet he remained the staunchest supporter of the Bush administration's Iraq policy. On 24 September, his government issued a dossier that dramatized the threat of weapons of mass destruction posed by Iraq. The dossier claimed that assessed intelligence had established beyond doubt that Saddam had continued his efforts to develop nuclear weapons and had sought to purchase uranium from an African country for his nuclear weapons program. However, in order to mute division within his government and strong opposition by his compatriots against war in Iraq, Blair persuaded President Bush to seek Security Council authorization for such war. When the effort to do so failed, Blair's government joined the Bush administration as the strongest member of its coalition of the willing to invade Iraq.[261]

The Bush Administration's Specific Charges against
Saddam and Rationale for War

In the manner described above, the Bush administration, using its resources, several venues, and occasions, made its case for war in Iraq: to eliminate threats to the United States and the world associated with Saddam Hussein. The threats, the nation and the world were told, included Saddam Hussein's possession of stockpiles of weapons of mass destruction—UN weapons inspectors had determined that Iraq had those weapons—Iraq's ties to terrorists, repeated suggestions that Saddam Hussein might offer some of his arsenal of weapons of mass destruction to terrorists like those who had attacked US territory in September 2001 with devastating effect, and the danger that Iraq, under Saddam's repressive regime, was perceived to pose to its neighbors, including Israel. Thus, the original justification for war was to disarm Iraq of its weapons of mass destruction, which posed a dire and gathering danger to the interests and security of the United States and the world, and to uphold the sanctity of UN Security Council resolutions.

However, the gathering danger posed by Saddam Hussein's regime, whether it was in fact what the Bush administration affirmed or not, was not enough to convince the overwhelming majority of the international community and the American people to support unreservedly an unprovoked war against Iraq. Therefore, the administration and its supporters were compelled to exaggerate the threat and to marshal other justifications in order to win national and international support. After obtaining the congressional resolution on Iraq in October 2002, the administration began to emphasize moral[262] and other rationales for regime change in Iraq. For example, it stressed the plight of the Kurds and Iraqi Shiites under a murderous Saddam Hussein regime that brutalized its own citizens, the removal of Saddam Hussein as a key ally of al-Qaeda and Osama bin Laden, and the democratization of the greater Middle East. Here, in an outline format, is a summary of the case—the charges against Saddam Hussein—the administration made to justify war for regime change in Iraq:

1. Saddam Hussein is a grave and gathering danger with an extreme animus for the United States. He is clearly a gathering threat against the United States, against US allies, and against his neighbors. Assessed intelligence leaves no doubt that his regime continues to possess and conceal some of the most lethal weapons ever developed. His regime has already used chemical weapons against the Iranians and against his own citizens.
2. For eleven years, under the regime of Saddam, Iraq deceived and defied the United Nations and failed to comply with resolutions of the Security Council requiring it to disarm. It continues "to thumb its nose at the world." Iraq remains a serious threat to peace, stability, and security in the Persian Gulf.

3. Saddam is actively pursuing a nuclear weapon and actively seeking to blackmail the United States and to strike it with weapons of mass destruction. He is developing weapons of mass destruction with one intention: to hold America hostage and to harm its citizens, friends, and allies.

4. Saddam has the infrastructure and nuclear scientists to make a nuclear weapon.

5. Saddam has stored biological and chemical weapons and has looked for ways to weaponize those and deliver them.

6. Saddam's regime has large, unaccounted-for stockpiles of chemical and biological weapons —including VX, sarin, cyclosarin and mustard gas, anthrax, botulism, and, possibly, small pox—and he has an active program to acquire and develop nuclear weapons.

7. Saddam has a history of reckless aggression in the Middle East. He cavorts with terrorists and aids, trains, and provides safe haven to terrorists, such as Abu Nidal. He had links with al-Qaeda. Mohamed Atta, the leader of the 11 September 2001 attacks on US territory, met with Iraqi intelligence officers at Prague prior to the attacks of that date. Later, some officials of the administration, except Vice President Cheney, conceded that Saddam may not have had "operational control" of what happened on 11 September 2001.

8. Saddam was paying $25,000 apiece to Hamas suicide bombers.

9. Saddam is a man who would use weapons of mass destruction at the drop of the hat and would team up with terrorist organizations with weapons of mass destruction to threaten America and its allies. The cause of peace will be advanced only when the terrorists lose a wealthy patron and protector and when the dictator is fully and finally disarmed.

10. Saddam Hussein was involved in attempts to assassinate US leaders, including former President George H. W. Bush.

11. Saddam's regime has something to hide from the civilized world. His is a regime that cannot be trusted.

12. The Saddam regime has a tragic record of violence against Iraqi women.

13. Iraq is part of the axis of evil that represses its own people and threatens its neighbors. Under the ruthless regime of Saddam, as demonstrated by recent history, it twice invaded its neighbors without provocation and caused death and suffering on a massive scale.

14. On many thousands of occasions, Iraq fired on US and coalition armed forces engaged in enforcing the resolutions of the UN Security Council.

15. Iraq has at least seven mobile factories for the production of biological agents—equipment mounted on trucks and rails to evade discovery.

16. According to the British government, the Iraqi regime could launch a biological or chemical attack in as little as forty-five minutes.

17. Iraq refuses to return to Kuwait state archives and museum pieces it had carted away during its invasion, conquest, and occupation of the country in 1990.

18. Iraq refused to allow visits by human rights' monitors.

19. Iraq expelled UN humanitarian relief workers after the first Gulf War.

20. Iraq is practicing child labor and forced labor.

21. There is lack of freedom of speech or press in Iraq.

22. Two days before the House of Representatives voted on the Iraq Resolution, President Bush declared at Cincinnati, Ohio, on 8 October 2002, "In light of the devastating attacks [of 11 September 2001] and facing *clear evidence of peril* America is unwilling to wait for the final proof, the smoking gun, that could come in the form of a mushroom cloud. Having every reason to assume the worst and…an urgent duty to prevent the worst from occurring, it simply cannot and will not resume the old approach to inspections, and applying diplomatic and economic pressure" (emphasis added).[263]

23. "The purposes of the United States in Iraq should not be doubted: The Security Council resolutions [on Iraq] will be enforced…the just demands of peace and security will be met—or action will be unavoidable. And a regime that has lost its legitimacy will also lose its power."[264]

24. America's security, the safety of its friends, and its values lead it to confront the Iraqi gathering threat. The high risk that Saddam Hussein's regime will either employ Iraq's weapons of mass destruction to launch a surprise attack against the United States or its armed forces or provide them to international terrorists who would use them to do so and the extreme magnitude of harm that would result to the United States and its citizens from such an attack combine to justify the use of force by the United States against Iraq to defend itself. The terrorist threat to America and the world will be diminished the moment that Saddam Hussein is disarmed.

25. "In all these efforts, however, America's purpose is more than to follow a process—it is to achieve results: the end of terrible threats to the civilized world. All free nations have a stake in preventing sudden and catastrophic attacks…. Yet the course of this nation does not depend on the decisions of others. Whatever action is required, whenever action is necessary, I will defend the freedom and security of the American people."[265]

26. "The danger posed by Saddam Hussein and his weapons cannot be ignored or wished away. The danger must be confronted. We hope that the Iraqi regime will meet the demands of the United Nations and disarm, fully and peacefully. If it does not, we are fully prepared to disarm Iraq by force. Either way, this danger will be removed."[266]

27. "The safety of the American people depends on ending this direct and growing threat. Acting against the danger will also contribute greatly to the long-term safety and stability of our world. The current Iraqi regime has shown the power of tyranny to spread discord and violence in the Middle East. A liberated Iraq can show the power of freedom to transform that vital region, by bringing hope and progress into the lives of millions. America's interest in security, and America's belief in liberty, both lead in the same direction: to a free and peaceful Iraq."[267]

28. On 19 March 2003, when the US invasion of Iraq began, President Bush told the nation, "The people of the United States...will not live at the mercy of an outlaw regime that threatens the peace with weapons of murder. We will meet that threat now, with our [military forces] so that we do not have to meet it later with armies of fire fighters and police and doctors on the streets of our cities."[268] In his letter to Congress on the same day, Bush sought to tie Iraq specifically to the terrorist attacks of 11 September 2001. He asserted that the war he had just initiated against Iraq was permitted by legislation authorizing force against nations, organizations, or persons who planned, authorized, committed, or aided the terrorist attacks that occurred on 11 September 2001.

29. Two days earlier (17 March 2003), in an address to the nation from the Cross Hall, when he demanded that Saddam Hussein and his sons should leave Iraq within 48 hours, President Bush extended the following message to the Iraqis: "If we must begin a military campaign, it will be directed against the lawless men who rule your country and not against you. As our coalition takes away their power, we will deliver the food and medicine you need. We will tear down the apparatus of terror and we will help you to build a new Iraq that is prosperous and free. In a free Iraq, there will be no more wars of aggression against your neighbors, no more poison factories, no more executions of dissidents, no more torture chambers and rape rooms. The tyrant will soon be gone. The day of your liberation is near."[269]

In Their Own Words

The Bush administration's collective and general rationale for war in Iraq is summarily outlined above. Here, excerpts are provided from speeches and statements of selected top officials of the administration—*in their own words*—indicting the regime of Saddam Hussein and/or justifying a war against Iraq. The selected officials include Vice President Dick Cheney, Defense Secretary Donald Rumsfeld, Deputy Defense Secretary Paul Wolfowitz, Chairman of the Pentagon's Defense Policy Board Richard Perle, President Bush's adviser on national security Condoleezza Rice, Director of Central Intelligence George Tenet, and Secretary of State Colin Powell.

Vice President Dick Cheney

A distinctive player in the Bush administration, Dick Cheney exerted an unusually strong influence on every major foreign policy question the administration confronted. His willingness and ability to circumvent typical bureaucratic channels to gain advantage over his rivals facilitated that influence. Political observers agreed that there had "never been a time when a vice-president had played such a dominant, powerful role inside the national security policy making process."[270] A 23 January 2006 special report by *US News and World Report* described him as the "leading architect of the war in Iraq."[271] In *Worse Than Watergate*, John W. Dean describes the relationship between Bush and Cheney in national security as one in which Cheney is not only "the senior partner [but also] is prime minister *sub silentio*."[272] According to President Bush himself, Dick Cheney "was a rock...he was steadfast and steady in his view that Saddam Hussein was a threat to America and we had to deal with him."[273] Bush would not testify before the 9/11 Commission unless Vice President Cheney accompanied him. The 9/11 Commission accommodated him.

From the perspectives of Bush's first Secretary of State, Colin Powell, Dick Cheney, "the cool operator" during the first Gulf War, had undergone "a sad transformation" on the issue of regime change in Iraq. On that issue, "he just would not let go." Rather, he had "the fever" and "an unhealthy fixation" not only on overthrowing Saddam Hussein but also on the existence of a connection between al-Qaeda and Iraq. He "took intelligence and converted uncertainty and ambiguity into fact."[274] Thus, he became "the evil genius behind the [Iraq] war."[275] In this role, Cheney was particularly assisted by his chief of staff and national security adviser I. Lewis Libby. An influential national security thinker, Libby also served as an adviser to President Bush and was a powerful advocate of some of the administration's most far-reaching foreign policy decisions after the terrorist attacks of 11 September 2001.

Hans Blix, the former chief UN weapons inspector, described the vice president as his "chief tormentor in the White House" who was "disdainful" of the inspection process. Cheney's position, from what he told Blix in a meeting in October 2002, was that inspections could not go on forever; if they did not produce results, the United States was ready to discredit them in favor of disarmament. Hans Blix interpreted this as a pretty straight way of insisting that, if the UN weapons inspectors did not find the weapons of mass destruction that the Bush administration believed Iraq possessed, the United States was ready to say that the inspectors were useless and would embark on disarmament by other means.[276]

After the terrorist attacks of 11 September 2001 on US territory, Dick Cheney decided that the United States would confront the threat of terrorism by resorting to two fundamental approaches. First, the government would have to lower the standard of proof. "Smoking gun, irrefutable evidence would not have to be required for the United States to act to defend itself." Secondly, defense alone would not be enough. Rather, offense would be the nation's major response to every threat, especially the threat of a nuclear weapon or biological or chemical agent in the hands of a terrorist inside America's borders.[277]

Vice President Dick Cheney became the Bush administration's most vocal advocate of military action against Iraq, although, initially, on 16 September 2001, he had told NBC's Tim Russert on *Meet the Press* that Saddam Hussein was bottled up. In early 2002, as a new interim government replaced the Taliban and al-Qaeda in Kabul, Afghanistan, Cheney told President Bush that toppling Saddam Hussein would be the next phase in the war on terrorism. "He said simply that he had been part of the team that created what he now saw as a flawed policy—leaving Saddam in power at the end of the Gulf War—and now Bush had a chance to correct it."[278] To facilitate the correction, the vice president adamantly opposed the ongoing multilateral approach to Iraq through the United Nations. He preferred a US unilateral military action against Iraq over a UN authorized approach. Following allegations that most Arab or Muslim countries that would publicly oppose US invasion of Iraq privately wanted Saddam Hussein removed from power, Cheney undertook a diplomatic tour of the Middle East in March 2002. During the tour, he offered the governments of the region assurances of the Bush administration's determination to bring about regime change in Iraq and solicited assistance from them in a war against Iraq.

At home in the United States, Cheney used several forums to urge for war to bring about regime change in Iraq. On the speech circuit and Sunday television interviews, he delivered such chosen lines as the following: "There is no doubt that Saddam Hussein now has weapons of mass destruction." "We believe he has, in fact, reconstituted nuclear weapons." "We know he has a long-standing relationship with various terrorist groups, including the al-Qaeda organization." Speaking in California on 7 August 2002, he told his audience, "What we know now, from various sources, is that [Saddam Hussein] continues to pursue a nuclear weapon."[279] About two weeks later, on 26 August 2002, he asserted that Saddam had nuclear capability that "could directly threaten 'anyone he chooses, in his own region and beyond.'"[280] In a television interview on 8 September 2002, the Vice President insisted, "We do know, with absolute certainty, that [Saddam Hussein] is using his procurement system to acquire the equipment he needs in order to enrich uranium to build a nuclear weapon."[281]

In a speech at Nashville, Tennessee, to Veterans of Foreign Wars on 26 August 2002, Cheney warned that a return of UN inspectors to Iraq would not provide any assurance whatsoever that Saddam Hussein would comply with UN resolutions. He insisted that the old doctrines of security strategy do not apply to the case of Saddam Hussein, "a sworn enemy" of the United States, who was threatening his region, the world, and the United States with weapons of mass destruction. Rather, a different strategy was needed: elimination of the threat through preemptive action and regime change. Cheney went further to stress to his audience the benefits to the Middle East of regime change in Iraq:

> Regime change in Iraq would bring about a number of benefits to the region. When the gravest of threats are removed, the freedom loving peoples of the region will have a chance to promote the values that bring lasting peace. As for the reaction of the Arab "street," the Middle East expert Professor Fouad Ajami predicts that after liberation, the streets in Basra and Baghdad are "sure to erupt with joy in the same way the throngs in Kabul greeted the Americans." Extremists in the region would have to rethink their strategy of Jihad. Moderates throughout the region would take heart. And our ability to advance the Israeli-Palestinian peace process would be enhanced, just as it was following the liberation of Kuwait.[282]

On the same occasion, Vice President Cheney elaborated on the capabilities of Iraq and the nature of the threat it posed to the United States and rebuffed arguments by those who opposed preemptive action against Iraq. He asserted the following:

> The Iraqi regime has in fact been busy enhancing its capabilities in the field of chemical and biological agents, and they continue to pursue an aggressive nuclear weapons program they began years ago. These are offensive weapons for the purpose of inflicting death on a massive scale, developed so that Saddam Hussein can hold the threat over the head of any one he chooses. What we must not do in the face of this mortal threat is to give in to wishful thinking or willful blindness....
>
> What [Saddam Hussein] wants is more time, and more time to husband his resources to invest in his ongoing chemical and biological weapons program, and to gain possession of nuclear weapons.
>
> Should all his ambitions be realized, the implications would be enormous for the Middle East and the United States and for the peace of the world. The whole range of weapons of mass destruction then would rest in the hands of a dictator who has already

shown his willingness to use such weapons and has done so, both in his war with Iran and against his own people. Armed with an arsenal of the weapons of terror and a seat atop ten percent of the world's oil reserves, Saddam Hussein could then be expected to seek domination of the entire Middle East, take control of a portion of the world's energy supplies, directly threaten America's friends throughout the region, and subject the United States or any other nation to nuclear blackmail.

Simply stated, there is no doubt that Saddam Hussein now has weapons of mass destruction; there is no doubt that he is amassing them to use against our friends, against our allies, and against us. And there is no doubt that his aggressive regional ambitions will lead him into future confrontations with his neighbors, confrontations that will involve both the weapons he has today and the ones he will continue to develop with his oil wealth....

Some concede that Saddam is evil, power hungry, and a menace, but that until he crosses the threshold of actually possessing nuclear weapons, we should rule out any preemptive action. That logic seems to me to be deeply flawed. The argument comes down to this: Yes, Saddam is as dangerous as we say he is. We just need to let him get stronger before we do anything about it. Yet if we did wait until that moment, Saddam would simply be emboldened and it would become even harder for us to gather friends and allies to oppose him. As one of those who worked to assemble the Gulf War Coalition, I can tell you that our job then would have been infinitely more difficult in the face of a nuclear armed Saddam Hussein. And many of those who now argue that we should act only if he gets a nuclear weapon would then turn around and say that we cannot act because he has a nuclear weapon. At bottom that argument counsels a course of inaction that itself could have devastating consequences for many countries, including our own.[283]

On three separate occasions—29 August 2002, 30 January 2003, and 31 January 2003—Dick Cheney asserted, "Iraq poses terrible threats to the civilized world" and is a "serious threat to our country," and "there is no doubt that Saddam Hussein now has weapons of mass destruction...to use against our friends, against our allies, and against us." Finally, on *Meet the Press* with NBC's Tim Russert on 14 March 2003, five days before the administration launched its war against Iraq, he claimed, "We know that [Saddam Hussein] is out trying once again to produce nuclear weapons, and we know that he has a long-standing relationship with various terrorist groups, including the al-Qaeda organization."[284] His argument here was that the Bush administration necessarily had an obligation to act to prevent Saddam Hussein from sharing his alleged arsenal of the world's most dangerous weapons with terrorists.

Defense Secretary Donald Rumsfeld

Donald Rumsfeld and Dick Cheney had worked together in Washington during the Richard M. Nixon administration when Rumsfeld was President Nixon's director of the Office of Economic Opportunity and Cheney served as his aide. Later, Cheney served as deputy chief of staff under Rumsfeld in the Gerald Ford administration. They both continued to work for the administration until

January 1977 as chief of staff and secretary of defense, respectively. Both shared neoconservative beliefs and views about America's post–cold war role in the world and were like-minded about threats posed by terrorists and alleged weapons of mass destruction in the hands of Saddam Hussein of Iraq. It was largely the previous association and the sharing of those beliefs and views that brought them together to work in the Bush administration. While Cheney had what has been described as "an enveloping influence on [President] Bush and national security," Rumsfeld was identified as "a defense chief who has definite Napoleonic tendencies" and is prone to undercutting or reinterpreting already-made decisions, especially on Iraq.[285] Both officials "managed to keep a heavy 'thumb on the scales' of high-level deliberations, particularly on critical issues such as Iraq."[286]

After the 11 September terrorist attacks, Rumsfeld repeated categorically that defense was not enough, that the United States needed an offense. He was one of the early proponents of war in Iraq. A day after the attacks of 11 September 2001, he had asked, characteristically, whether there was a need to address Iraq as well as Osama bin Laden. He compared Saddam Hussein with Adolf Hitler and likened the "tolerance" of the Iraqi leader to the 1930s appeasement of the German leader. He and his neoconservative supporters argued that developments in the Middle East pointed undoubtedly to Saddam Hussein's aggressive behavior and the threat his regime posed to Iraq's neighbors and to world stability. The alleged "reconstitution" of Iraq's weapons of mass destruction program and its "sponsorship" of terrorists, he believed, signaled that it was only a question of time before the Iraqi regime initiated some sort of aggressive action in the Middle East. It was therefore prudent for the United States to invade Iraq preemptively to oust Saddam Hussein from power.

Here are some typical excerpts from Rumsfeld's statements justifying war in Iraq:

> The policy of our country, and of many [other] countries, is that there should be a change of regime, that in fact, [Saddam Hussein] is so repressive to his people, he's killed so many of his own people, he's used gas on his own people, chemicals, he's invaded his neighbors, he's developing weapons of mass destruction, he's a person who threatens his neighbors, he describes them as illegitimate repeatedly. You know, you could live with that in an earlier era where a person was a dictator and a vicious, repressive person, as long as he was basically harming his own people, and didn't have weapons of mass destruction, the world kind of set it off to the side and said, that's not right, and we recommend against it, but we're not going to do anything about that. And they would not use diplomacy or economic sanctions or military power to change it [12 April 2002].[287]

They [Iraqis] have weaponized their chemical and biological weapons, we know that. They've had an active program to develop nuclear weapons.[288]

Some have argued that the nuclear threat from Iraq is not imminent—that Saddam is at least five to seven years away from having nuclear weapons. I would not be so certain. And we should be just as concerned about the immediate threat from biological weapons. Iraq has these weapons [18 September 2002].

No terrorist state poses a greater or more immediate threat to the security of our people and the stability of the world than the regime of Saddam Hussein in Iraq [19 September 2002].[289]

We know that Saddam Hussein has chemical and biological weapons. And we know he has an active program for the development of nuclear weapons. I suppose what it would prove [if UN weapons inspectors find no weapons of mass destruction in Iraq] would be that the inspection process had been successfully defeated by the Iraqis if they find nothing. That's what one would know if that turned out to be the case. There's no question but that the Iraqi regime is clever. They have spent a lot of time hiding things, dispersing things, tunneling underground, taking documentation and moving it to different locations in the past, preventing inspectors from getting access, listening in on what inspectors intend to do. And before the inspectors arrive to do it, seeing that what was there is moved or that effort is frustrated in some way [14 November 2002].

I would look you in the eye and I would say, go back before September 11 and ask yourself this question: Was the attack that took place on September 11 an imminent threat the month before or two months before or three months before or six months before? When did the attack on September 11 become an imminent threat? When was it sufficiently dangerous to our country that had we known about it that we could have stepped up and stopped and saved 3,000 lives? Now, transport yourself forward a year, two years, or a week or a month, and if Saddam Hussein were to take his weapons of mass destruction…either use them himself, or transfer them to the al Qaeda, and somehow the al Qaeda were to engage in an attack on the United States…. So the question is when is it such an immediate threat that you must do something? [14 November 2002].[290]

Saddam Hussein possesses chemical weapons. Iraq poses a threat to the security of our people and to the stability of the world that is distinct from any other. It's a danger to its neighbors, to the United States, to the Middle East and to international peace and stability. It's a danger we cannot ignore. Iraq and North Korea are both repressive dictatorships to be sure and both pose threats. But Iraq is unique. In both word and deed, Iraq has demonstrated that it is seeking the means to strike the United States and our friends and allies with weapons of mass destruction [3 January 2003].[291]

Saddam Hussein possesses chemical and biological weapons. Iraq poses a threat to the security of our people and to the stability of the world that is distinct from any other. Iraq has demonstrated that it is seeking the means to strike the United States and our allies with weapons of mass destruction [20 January 2003].[292]

Deputy Defense Secretary Paul Wolfowitz

Paul Wolfowitz was "the intellectual godfather and fiercest advocate for toppling Saddam Hussein" from power.[293] He was "like a drum that would not stop,"[294] and, for many years, he was one, if not the most outspoken and persistent, advocate of ousting Saddam Hussein from power. Indeed, before joining the George W. Bush administration, he had coauthored a policy paper with I. Lewis Libby asserting that the United States should act alone, if necessary, to deter nations from acquiring weapons of mass destruction. Once in the administration, he had easy access to his superiors in office to make his case against Saddam. To him, and he so pleaded, Saddam and his Baath Party were like Adolf Hitler and his Nazi organization of gangsters and sadists. Removing his regime from power, Wolfowitz argued, would not only remove a threat to US security but would also usher an opening to a better world. Eliminating him from power, he urged, was absolutely necessary and would be relatively easy.[295] It would also pave the way for a grand reordering of the Middle East, pushing the region away from tyranny and anti-Americanism towards modernity and democracy. He framed the future invasion of Iraq while he was at John Hopkins University after twelve years of serving in the Republican Party-controlled White House.

Wolfowitz was perhaps the foremost believer that President Bush's father George H. W. Bush had blundered when he decided to end the Gulf War (1991) without overthrowing Saddam Hussein. He was particularly angry with General Colin Powell for his role in that decision. He nursed that anger for more than ten years and hoped for an opportunity to undo the decision. As indicated in preceding chapters, he was one of the signatories to a letter calling upon President Clinton in 1998 to remove Saddam from power by military force. He demanded that Clinton should adopt a strategy to control Iraq's southern oil fields, install Ahmed Chalabi's Iraqi National Congress in Baghdad, and fund it with proceeds from the oil exports.[296] Also, he had signed on, in February 1998, to a Steve Forbes-led memo warning Congress that Saddam Hussein was continuing to develop biological and chemical weapons, might be experimenting on human prisoners with deadly biological toxins, and was threatening a million-man holy war against the United States, while, at the same time, he was making a deal with UN bureaucrats to buy time to accelerate his production of weapons of mass destruction.

Wolfowitz's appointment as deputy secretary of defense in the George W. Bush administration became a stepping stone to undoing the elder Bush-Powell blunder. "Powell," he told enquirers, was his reason for accepting to serve in that office.[297] Having accepted to serve in the Bush administration, a coup led by Ahmed Chalabi was seen by him and other hawks in the administration as the best means of getting rid of Saddam Hussein and his regime. But, after the terrorist attacks on US territory on 11 September 2001, the notion of a coup gave way to the idea of an American invasion of Iraq. On 15 September 2001, four days after the terrorist attacks, Wolfowitz advocated attacking Iraq before Afghanistan, even though there was no evidence that Saddam was involved in the attacks on US territory. Bush rejected the proposal but later embraced it after a quick victory in Afghanistan. Henceforth, Wolfowitz argued that the attacks had convinced him that terrorism was no longer a manageable evil, that its intersecting worldwide networks and its state sponsors (of which Saddam Hussein's Iraq, he insisted, was one) had to be attacked. He believed that Saddam Hussein's regime had long deserved to be overthrown and that, after the quick military victory in Afghanistan, his removal was important enough to risk American lives directly.[298] His plea for the removal of Saddam Hussein and his regime was implemented in March 2003 when the Bush administration invaded Iraq. He hailed the subsequent seizure of Iraq's southern oil fields and asserted that the oil would generate about $100 billion over two years for the reconstruction of the country.

In the midst of the continuing insurgency after the overthrow of Saddam and his own narrow escape when his hotel in Baghdad was bombed in late 2003, Wolfowitz "found himself," he said, "asking with some frequency whether the war [in Iraq] had been worth it."[299] However, in spite of his personal anguish and the US failure to find any weapons of mass destruction in Iraq, Wolfowitz firmly insisted that the war was justified. By then, he had switched his major rationale for the war from disarming Saddam to promoting the freedom of the Iraqis and the building of free institutions in Iraq and the entire Middle East.

Richard Perle, Chair, Pentagon's Defense Policy Board

Richard Perle, chair of the Pentagon's Defense Policy Board, was a relentless critic of the Clinton administration's policy towards Iraq and a staunch supporter of Iraqi exile groups that sought US assistance for the overthrow of Saddam Hussein. He was one of the drafters of the 1998 letter to President Clinton urging the overthrow of Saddam Hussein by military force. He later accused the Clinton administration of leaving his successor George W. Bush in a very difficult position by allowing Saddam Hussein eight years to outlast all efforts to discipline him.

Shortly after the inauguration of George W. Bush as president in January 2001, Richard Perle became chair of the Pentagon's Defense Policy Board. He is known to have the ability to "radically change government policy even though he is a private citizen."[300] His influence on the Bush administration "was buttressed by close association, politically and personally, with many important [neoconservative] figures in that administration, including Paul Wolfowitz and Douglas Feith."[301] As chair, Perle turned the Defense Policy Board, which advised the Pentagon on strategic issues, into a bully pulpit from which he advocated the overthrow of Saddam Hussein and a policy of preemptive war for the security of the United States and that of Israel.

Before the terrorist attacks on 11 September 2001, Richard Perle, as chairman of the Pentagon's Defense Policy Board, provided a subcommittee of the Senate Foreign Relations Committee robust information regarding his claim that Iraq possessed weapons of mass destruction. In an earlier hearing before the subcommittee in March 2001, he asked rhetorically, "Does Saddam have weapons of mass destruction? Sure, he does," he affirmed. "We know he has chemical weapons. We know he has biological weapons.... How far he has gone on the nuclear weapons side I don't think we really know. My guess is that it's further than we think. It's always further than we think, because we limit ourselves, as we think about this, to what we're able to prove and demonstrate.... And, unless you believe that we uncovered everything, you have to assume there is more than we're able to report."[302]

Richard Perle was one of those who, together with neoconservatives in the Bush administration, spread the view that Saddam had weapons of mass destruction and harbored terrorists as well. He insisted, as Vice President Dick Cheney did, that the Bush administration had evidence that there were "clearly established links between al-Qaeda and Iraqi intelligence."[303] In a speech on 14 November 2001 (before a meeting of a conservative think tank: the Foreign Policy Research Institute at Philadelphia), as the Taliban was being routed in Afghanistan, Perle articulated what became the Bush administration's most compelling argument for going to war in Iraq. He asserted that there was the possibility that, with enough time, Saddam Hussein would be capable of attacking the United States with a nuclear weapon. He cited testimony from an Iraqi defector, Khidhir Hamza, that, in response to the 1981 Israeli bombing of the Osiraq nuclear reactor near Baghdad, Saddam Hussein had ordered future nuclear facilities to be dispersed at four hundred sites across Iraq. He went on,

> Every day, these sites turn out a little bit of nuclear materials. The question in my mind is: Do we wait for Saddam and hope for the best? Do we wait and hope he doesn't do what we know he is capable of, which is distributing weapons of mass destruction to anonymous terrorists, or do we take preemptive action?.... What is essential here is not to look at the opposition to Saddam Hussein as it is today, without any external

support, without any realistic hope of removing that awful regime, but to look at what
could be created with the power and authority of the United States.[304]

In December 2001, Perle and former Director of Central Intelligence James
Woolsey inspired a surge of articles and newspaper columns advocating the
extension of the war in Afghanistan into Iraq. Perle specifically argued that, if
the United States recoiled from dealing effectively with Saddam, it would be
setting a dangerous threshold, empowering terrorists to carry on their mischief
freely any place they choose to do so. Failing in that manner to come to grips
with Iraq would gravely diminish the US ability to win the war on terrorism.

Early in 2002, at a panel discussion at the neoconservative American
Enterprise Institute where Ahmed Chalabi was one of the panelists, Richard
Perle asserted that the evidence was mounting that the Bush administration was
looking very carefully at strategies for dealing with Saddam Hussein. He went
on to declare that the "war on terrorism will not be complete until Saddam is
successfully dealt with. And that means replacing his regime...that action will
be taken, I have no doubt."[305] In November 2002, he told an audience of British
parliamentarians that "even a clean bill of health" from the UN weapons
inspectors would not stave off a US war against Iraq.[306]

Condoleezza Rice, Adviser on National Security

Condoleezza Rice was so close and deferential to President George W. Bush on
Iraq that she became his cheerleader on the issue of regime change in the
country. In a memorandum, David Manning, foreign policy advisor to British
Prime Minister Tony Blair, describes her "enthusiasm for regime change" in
Iraq as "undiminished."[307] She would become "excited over any news that did
not conform with [Bush's] position."[308] In her neutral post as Bush's adviser on
national security, she was the one person that could and should have warned
him on two issues: first, to be wary of the pressures that were being exerted on
him by the neoconservatives in his administration to pursue a policy of regime
change in Iraq, and, second, given the nature of available intelligence, to
moderate his categorical statements of the certainty of Saddam Hussein's
possession of weapons of mass destruction and links to al-Qaeda. Instead, she
became a blunt advocate of tough action and concurred with the president's
pronouncements and reinforced them in her own speeches. In 2002, the
National Security Council (NSC), of which she was the head, directed that
funding for the Iraqi National Congress should continue "despite the warnings
from both the CIA, which terminated its relationship with the INC in December

1996, and the DIA (Defense Intelligence Agency), that the INC was penetrated by hostile intelligence services, including the Iranians."[309]

Besides her office as national security adviser, Rice served as a member of the White House Iraqi Group. The group included Karl Rove; I. Lewis Libby; White House Chief of Staff Andrew Card; Rice's deputy, Stephen Hadley; and Mary Matalin, Cheney's media adviser, and had been established to coordinate and promote the Bush administration's Iraq policy. Before the war, Rice and other members of the group promoted the view that Saddam Hussein had weapons of mass destruction and was seeking more such weapons. Also, she shared the view of neoconservatives that the United States should move aggressively to reshape other countries and accommodated their pressures on the president for regime change in Iraq. She frequently used the phraseology of the neoconservatives in her own speeches and lecture circuits making the administration's case for war in Iraq. Saddam Hussein had to be overthrown, she recommended to President Bush, not just because the credibility of the United States was on the line, but also because the credibility of everybody else would be on the line if Saddam were yet again allowed to beat the international system. To allow Saddam's threat "to play volley ball with the international community," she suggested, would come back to haunt the administration."[310] Therefore, Bush had to implement his threat to overthrow Saddam Hussein by force and live with that decision.

After the terrorist attacks on 11 September 2001, which she regarded as "one of those great earthquakes that clarify and sharpen," Condoleezza Rice asserted that opposing terrorism and preventing the accumulation of weapons of mass destruction in the hands of irresponsible states define the US national interest.[311] Also, after those attacks, she assembled the staff of the National Security Council and asked them to think seriously about how the Bush administration could capitalize on those events to change fundamentally American foreign policy doctrine and "the shape of the world." She advocated the view that the United States should assemble "coalitions of the willing" to support its international behavior rather than believe it had to work within the existing infrastructure of international treaties and organizations.[312]

As Bush's national security adviser, Rice endorsed and reinforced the policy advocated by Vice President Dick Cheney that the Bush administration had to lower the standard of proof and jettison reliance on irrefutable evidence—the smoking gun—in order to defend and protect American interests. She argued that it would be irresponsible and catastrophic for the administration to wait until a "mushroom cloud" awakened it to Saddam Hussein's menace. Furthermore, the administration, she asserted, could not wait for help from the

UN Security Council. UN members, she claimed, often expressed disdain for the United States and were apparently willing to appease the Iraqi regime. Thus, she unequivocally supported the proposal by Cheney that the administration should first seek from the US Congress, rather than the UN Security Council, a resolution authorizing the use of military force in Iraq. Part of the rationale for this was political: In an election year, it would be to the administration's advantage if the voters knew before casting their ballots where members of Congress stood on the threat posed to the United States by Saddam Hussein and his dangerous regime. She further rationalized the administration's draft resolution on Iraq on the need for the United States "to speak so that the UN knows that America is capable of acting with or without UN authorization."[313] It would be a mistake, she argued, for the US Congress to somehow tie its action to UN action.

Along the same lines, Rice was opposed to sending Hans Blix and other UN weapons inspectors back to Iraq. The danger in doing so, she believed, was that, if the inspectors went back and found no weapons of mass destruction, some countries would demand the lifting of the sanctions imposed on Iraq. That would play into the hands of the Iraqis, who love the game and are comfortable with it. The Security Council would split if the process continued in that fashion.

Condoleezza Rice's role in making the Bush administration's case for war in Iraq can be gleaned from her speeches to various groups in the United States, presentations to key members of Congress, and news media interviews. Before the Conservative Political Action Conference at Arlington, Virginia, shortly after President Bush's 2002 State of the Union address, Rice proclaimed that the United States "will do everything in its power to deny the world's most dangerous powers the world's most dangerous weapons."[314] In a presentation to twenty key members of Congress in the Cabinet Room on 5 February 2003, she explained why, besides the threat posed to the United States, the Bush administration had to go to war in Iraq: The UN would become impotent if it could not resolve the Iraq problem after a dozen resolutions. At that point, the United States would have to resolve the problem on its own because "Iraq is critical to reestablishing the bona fides of the Security Council."[315] War was the active option. Sanctions, limited military operations, and resolutions, all had been tried. At some point, war becomes the only option.

On Sunday, 8 September 2002, Rice went on the TV talk circuit proclaiming that Iraq was attempting to obtain aluminum tubes from Africa suitable for uranium centrifuges for nuclear weapons. Four days later, President Bush repeated the charges before the UN General Assembly. In an exclusive interview (15 August 2002) for the BBC's 11 September 2001 anniversary series, Rice made her moral case for regime change in Iraq:

> The Iraqi leader [Saddam Hussein] had developed biological weapons, lied to the UN repeatedly about the stockpiles…and had used chemical weapons against his own people and against his neighbors.
>
> He had invaded his neighbors twice. He had killed thousands of his own people.
>
> He shoots at our [British/US] planes…in the no-fly zone where we're trying to enforce UN Security Council resolutions. And he, despite the fact that he lost the [1991] war—a war which he started—negotiates with the UN as if he won the war.
>
> This is an evil man [Saddam Hussein] who, left to his own devices, will wreak havoc again on his population, his neighbors and, if he obtains weapons of mass destruction and the means to deliver them, on all of us.
>
> This is a very powerful moral case for regime change in Iraq. Saddam…is too great a security risk to leave in power. We certainly do not have the luxury of doing nothing…if Saddam Hussein is left in power, doing the things he's doing now, this is a threat that will emerge, and emerge in a very big way. [316]

In an interview conducted by Wolf Blitzer, *CNN Late Edition*, on 8 September 2002, Rice continued the Bush administration's "we know" indictment of Saddam Hussein and his regime:

> There is no doubt that Saddam Hussein's regime is a danger to the United States and to its allies, to our interests. It is a danger that is gathering momentum, and it simply makes no sense to wait any longer to do something about the threat that is posed here…. The one option that we do not have is to do nothing.
>
> There is certainly evidence that al-Qaeda people have been in Iraq. There is certainly evidence that Saddam Hussein cavorts with terrorists.
>
> We know that in the last four years there have been no weapons inspections in Iraq to monitor what [Saddam Hussein] is doing, and we have evidence, increasing evidence, that he continues his march toward weapons of mass destruction.
>
> We know that he stored the biological weapons. We know that he has used chemical weapons. And we know that he has looked for ways to weaponize those and deliver them.
>
> This is a regime that cannot be trusted; that very much wants to blackmail us, the United States, because our interests clash. It wants to blackmail its neighbors, and it will eventually want to blackmail the entire international community. If we wait until that blackmail includes the ability to blackmail with a nuclear weapon, we will have made a grave mistake. [317]

Director of Central Intelligence George Tenet

George Tenet, director of Central Intelligence and the Central Intelligence Agency, was the only high-level Clinton administration holdover on the George W. Bush administration's national security team. He bonded quickly with President Bush, who liked him and had full confidence in him. A friend and former colleague of his said that Tenet was "a politician."[318] Conscious of the importance of forging personal relationships, "he devoted time to the people important in his professional and personal life."[319] Contextually, in the Bush administration, he observed a new factor: "the absence of doubt at the top. [President] Bush displayed no hesitation or uncertainty.... Suddenly there seemed to be no penalty for taking risks and making mistakes."[320] Tenet therefore decided to capitalize on the new factor and on the mutual admiration and trust between him and the president. Accordingly, throughout his tenure in the Bush administration, Tenet remained publicly loyal to President Bush. He acted as if he were a member of the Bush administration rather than an independent, detached, and objective conveyor of factual information to it.

Before the terrorist attacks on 11 September 2001, Tenet had observed that Iraq was a particularly important concern for the Bush administration. Iraq, therefore, became a major part of his briefings to Bush. Also before 11 September, a special group—the Iraqi Operations Group—Tenet had set up reached the following conclusion: Covert action would not remove Saddam from power, because he had erected a nearly perfect security apparatus to protect himself and to foil a coup attempt. Therefore, it would require the "concentration of the entire US government to remove him." The CIA would have to support a full military invasion of Iraq to bring that about.[321] The president and Vice President Cheney, who were to be briefed on this conclusion on 11 September 2001, received the briefing in detail after that fateful date. Given the terrorist attacks and the administration's animus for Saddam Hussein, the briefing added substantial pressure on President Bush for war in Iraq.

There was widespread belief, within and outside the Intelligence Community, that George Tenet had been far too deferential rather than straightforward about Iraq in his dealings with the Bush administration. Critics of this relationship claimed that Tenet was flatly refusing to speak truth to power—the administration—to warn President Bush that his agency's evidence on the presence of weapons of mass destruction in Iraq was not ironclad and did not include a so-called smoking gun. Could it be that Tenet wanted to make it possible for President Bush to do what he knew the president wanted, and had already decided, to do? Although Tenet denied it all, anonymous CIA insiders charged that intelligence on Iraq had been slanted to buttress President Bush's policy on Iraq, that, under the administration's pressure, Tenet had failed to protect analysts whom the administration had beaten down defending their analysis and had thus allowed the CIA to be subverted (through intimidation and undermining by the offices of Vice President Cheney and Defense Secretary Rumsfeld) from serving its role as an independent agency for ensuring US national security.[322] Later, in July 2005, Tenet himself told the Senate Intelligence Committee that, even though it was wrong to do so, he had complied with the Bush administration's request to say something about there not being any inconsistency between what the president had said about the Saddam-terrorist link and the CIA viewpoint.

Tenet had continued his support of Bush's intentions on Iraq. Earlier, when President Bush appeared to be not overly impressed with the CIA's intelligence on Saddam's weapons of mass destruction and told the director to make sure that no one stretched to make the administration's case, George Tenet assured him that he should not worry. It was a slam dunk case. Yet, the CIA had no concrete evidence or a smoking gun of the slam dunk. If it had such evidence, it never told the UN weapons inspectors where to find the weapons. This said, well-placed officials in the Bush administration were skeptical about Iraq's possession of weapons of mass destruction after the 1991 Gulf War. Among such officials were some senior military officers, the Deputy Secretary of State Richard Armitage and the CIA spokesperson Bill Harlow. Harlow repeatedly warned the news media that, although the Intelligence Community in general asserted that Saddam Hussein had weapons of mass destruction, it lacked a credible evidence, a smoking gun. The skepticism failed to convince President Bush. Rather "the ambiguous [and unsubstantiated] pronouncements of the heavyweights—George Tenet, Vice President Dick Cheney, and Defense Secretary Donald Rumsfeld—prevailed."[323] Given these circumstances and the failure to find stockpiles of weapons of mass destruction in Iraq, it is not unrealistic to conclude that George Tenet tailored the intelligence he produced on Iraq either to fend off political pressures or to suit the political needs of a president with whom he had bonded so well. Not long after he resigned as the Director of Central Intelligence, he was honored by President George W. Bush with the award of the highest national honor—the civilian Medal of Freedom.

Secretary of State Colin Powell

Colin Powell had been intimately involved in the first Gulf War during the George H. W. Bush administration as the chairman of the Joint Chiefs of Staff. As head of the US armed forces at the time, he had participated in the decision to end that war without removing Saddam Hussein from power. To him, continuing the war to Baghdad in order to end Saddam Hussein's regime was imprudent. The political purpose of the war—to liberate Kuwait—and the military objective that flowed from it—to eject the Iraqi army from Kuwait—had been achieved. To continue the war would cause the expenditure of more American resources and more Iraqi casualties, making it look like a massacre, as many Iraqi soldiers had already died and others had fled. Besides, going beyond the liberation of Kuwait would destroy the international coalition against Saddam Hussein and thus would be counterproductive to US goals. This decision had infuriated the neoconservatives and hawks Vice President Cheney had brought into the George W. Bush administration who sought to reverse it.

On the subsequent George W. Bush administration's conflict with Iraq, Powell maintained a low profile compared to the more outward and more hawkish and unilateralist Vice President Cheney; Defense Secretary Rumsfeld; and his deputy, Paul Wolfowitz. He preferred resolving the conflict through multilateral diplomacy and patience over a military option. In his view, Iraq, after the Gulf War, had become exhausted by a decade of UN sanctions; UN arms inspectors had effectively controlled Saddam Hussein, and Saddam had demonstrated neither a capability nor an overt intention to threaten the United States. In February 2001, he said that the Bush administration ought to declare that the policy of containment had worked; it had contained Saddam Hussein and kept him in his box and unable to project conventional power against his neighbors.

Because he believed that cooperation with allies and international institutions was important, Powell, in contrast to his more hawkish colleagues in the Bush administration, sought to broaden international support for more stringent measures against Iraq. He believed that an agreement in the UN Security Council was indispensable to any military operation to depose the Iraqi regime of Saddam Hussein. He argued that US diplomatic efforts at the United Nations would be helped enormously by a strong congressional resolution authorizing President Bush to take necessary and appropriate action. Such a resolution, he maintained, would show the world that the United States was united on the effort to disarm Iraq.[324] When he perceived the intense pressure the administration's neoconservatives were exerting on Bush to undertake military incursions into Iraq to oust Saddam, Powell advised the president not to allow himself to be "pushed into anything" until he was "ready for it" or thought there was a real reason for it.[325] Alarmed that neoconservative pressure on President Bush for military action in Iraq had intensified, Powell again urged Bush not to allow himself to be bullied into a quick strike or incursion into Iraq.

But Powell's views were overshadowed by those of Cheney, Rumsfeld, and Wolfowitz. As a result, Powell was not privy to the initial decision to go to war in Iraq, even at the time that his diplomatic efforts led to UN Security Council Resolution 1441 in the fall of 2002. Knowing his inclinations, Bush never asked Powell for any recommendation on war in Iraq. Rather, he treated him as a secondary actor but allowed him, contrary to the position of Vice President Cheney, to negotiate a diplomatic option in the UN Security Council. The result was Resolution 1441, adopted unanimously by the Security Council on 8 November 2002 to verify Iraqi disarmament by UN arms inspectors. As it turned out, this move appeared to have been designed or used by Bush to serve as a kind of decoy to enable his administration to complete its military preparation for a war in Iraq.

In time, despite his reluctance for the military option the hawks advocated, Powell, as a loyal soldier, became influenced by the case Bush and the hawks and neoconservatives in his administration were making for that option. In a speech at the World Economic Forum in Davos, Switzerland, on 23 January 2003, he stressed the adoption, purpose, and provisions of the Security Council Resolution 1441. He explained how Saddam had systematically and utterly failed to comply with the requirements of the resolution but instead had defiantly and deceptively "attempted to conceal with volume what it lacked in veracity" to the extent that not a single member of the Security Council defended its response to the resolution. Powell went on to argue that the Bush administration's policy of regime change in Iraq was dictated by the repeated violations of the trust of the UN by Saddam and his regime. The violations, including the absence of any indication whatsoever that Iraq had made the strategic decision to come clean and to comply with its international obligation to disarm, he stressed, had reached such a height that they posed a grave danger to international peace and security.[326]

Powell repeated before his Davos audience other allegations he had made earlier before the Security Council and asserted that the Bush administration believed that time was running out for Saddam Hussein. The integrity of the UN and its resolutions must be sustained to prevent its irrelevance. The administration would not shrink from war if that was the only way to disarm Iraq of its weapons of mass destruction. It reserved its sovereign right to use military force alone against Iraq or in a coalition of the willing. "History," he concluded, "will judge harshly those who saw the coming danger but failed to act."[327]

Flanked by Director of Central Intelligence George Tenet to bolster the certainty of his presentation, Powell made the administration's most eloquent and persuasive case for disarming Iraq by military force before the Security Council on 5 February 2003 for about one and a half hours. He affirmed before the Council, "Every statement I make today is backed by sources, solid sources.... These are not assertions. What we are giving you are facts and conclusions based on solid evidence."[328] He assured the Council that Iraq had large stockpiles of chemical and biological weapons and was reconstituting its nuclear weapons program and building a fleet of advanced missiles. He presented photographs, intercepts, and assertions from informants about Iraq's weapons of mass destruction programs. Here are selected highlights from his presentation:

> We have first-hand descriptions of *biological weapons factories on wheels and on rails.*
>
> We know from sources that a missile brigade outside Baghdad was dispersing rocket launchers and war heads containing biological agents to various locations.
>
> Our conservative estimate is that Iraq today has a stockpile of *between 100 and 500 tons of chemical weapons agents.*
>
> He [Saddam Hussein] *remains determined to acquire nuclear weapons....* He is so determined that he has made repeated covert attempts to acquire high-specification *aluminum tubes* from 11 different countries.
>
> What I...bring to your attention today is the potentially much more *sinister nexus between Iraq and the al-Qaeda terrorist network....* Iraqi officials deny accusations of ties with al-Qaeda. These denials are simply not credible.[329]

Powell included the aluminum tubes argument even though he had been expressly told by the Department of State's Bureau of Intelligence and Research that the allegation was not credible. He also referred to terrorist activity described as taking place in Iraq when he knew that activity was taking place in an area controlled by the Kurds and not under the control of Saddam Hussein. He also had been told by his own terrorist experts that there was no credible evidence of links between Saddam and the al-Qaeda terrorist network. On 7 March 2003, about three weeks after his remarks before the Security Council on 5 February 2003, after UN weapons inspectors had submitted their report, including a statement contradicting the aluminum charges against Iraq, and requested additional time to complete their work, Powell made another eloquent case before the Security Council.[330] He characterized the report of progress by the UN weapons inspectors as "a catalog still of non-cooperation" by the Iraqi regime. He insisted that Iraq had made no strategic decision to disarm but was still intent on maintaining its stockpiles of weapons of mass destruction. He therefore called for disarming it by military force, since it was refusing to disarm peacefully. Given his earlier stance on the Iraqi conflict, some observers wondered whether Powell might not have been true to his own conscience but simply made the administration's case as a loyal secretary of state and good soldier.

On 19 March 2003, after Powell's persuasion and vigorous diplomacy had failed to produce a second Security Council resolution to authorize war in Iraq, the Bush administration, with a coalition of about thirty-four countries, of which Britain was the most significant, invaded Iraq.

In view of his early reluctance to support a military option and the subsequent case he made for the administration's justification of that option, some political observers opined that Powell, the most politically credible official of the George W. Bush administration, had really failed the nation and the international community. Instead, he had become an enabler, "providing cover for an appearance of reasonableness so Cheney and Rumsfeld worked their will."[331] The appropriateness of this observation became abundantly clear after 28 January 2004 when David Kay, who had recently resigned as head of the Bush administration's Iraq Survey Group, informed the Senate Armed Services Committee that 85 percent of the work of the group had been completed and that he did not expect to find any weapons of mass destruction stockpile in Iraq. Powell was disappointed at the news regarding the one key reason the Bush administration launched a war against Iraq. Yet, he said, the decision to go to war was the right thing to do. However, he added that the absence of a stockpile of weapons of mass destruction in Iraq "changes the political calculus...because it was the stockpile that presented the final little piece that made [Iraq] more of a real and present danger and threat to the [Persian Gulf] region and the world."[332] In a television interview with ABC's Barbara Walters in September 2005, Powell lamented his 5 February 2003 speech to the United Nations giving a detailed description of an Iraqi weapons program that turned out not to exist. The speech, he said, was painful for him personally and would be a lasting blot on his record.[333]

In spite of the failure by the Bush administration itself to find any stockpiles of weapons of mass destruction in Iraq, more than three years after it launched a war to disarm Iraq's Saddam Hussein of his alleged weapons of mass destruction, President Bush was still making a case to stay the course in Iraq. He resurrected the discredited domino theory, which was the basis of US intervention in Southeast Asia, as he continued to harp on the terrorist attacks of 11 September 2001. If the United States did not defeat communism in Vietnam (or in similarly perceived threatened countries, like Grenada), the domino theory postulated, the whole of Southeast Asia (or the Caribbean, in the case of Grenada) might fall under Communist control. Therefore, the United States must defeat the Communists, or terrorists, hitherto weapons of mass destruction in Iraq, in the Bush administration's case, before they attack the United States on its own territory. Thus, neither President Bush nor Secretary of State Rice has ceased to evoke the cause of democracy and freedom, as well as the memory of the terrorist attacks of 11 September 2001, in his administration's policy of staying the course in Iraq. "We fight [in Iraq today]," he said in two addresses at Fort Bragg, North Carolina (28 June 2005), and West Virginia (4 July 2005), "because terrorists [no longer Saddam Hussein's weapons of mass destruction] want to attack our country and kill our citizens, and Iraq is where they are making their stand."[334]

Chapter 8
An Evaluation of the George W. Bush Administration's Case for War in Iraq

It is worth recalling the events of 1962, when John F. Kennedy sent former Secretary of State Dean Acheson to brief Charles de Gaulle about the Soviet deployment of nuclear missiles in Cuba. Acheson offered de Gaulle a full intelligence briefing, but the French president told him it wasn't necessary, saying he trusted Kennedy never to risk war unless he was sure of his facts. After the diplomatic debacle over Iraq, it is hard to imagine a similar level of trust today.[335]

The previous chapter chronicled how the George W. Bush administration made a comprehensive and persistent case to justify a war against Iraq in US national security interest. This chapter attempts an evaluation of that justification from the following angles: its accuracy and consistency, its reception at home in the United States and abroad in the international community, and its impact on US credibility at home and abroad as a global leader.

The Bush administration's major justification for war in Iraq, namely that Iraq had stockpiles of weapons of mass destruction and ties to terrorist groups that might use those weapons against the United States, for the most part, lacked credible evidence. The informed and attentive public did not have much faith in the intelligence the administration used to make its case, in spite of the aggressive manner by which the justification was presented. Credible members of the US Intelligence Community had doubts about Iraq's weapons of mass destruction and believed that the administration had cherry-picked and politicized the prewar intelligence to make its case for war. Even CIA Director George Tenet, who had assured Bush that Iraq had weapons of mass destruction, said later that the CIA never affirmed that Iraq was an imminent threat to the United States.

The evidence gathered by the UN inspection teams and the International Atomic Energy Agency, which monitored Iraq's weapons of mass destruction programs, was far more accurate than US intelligence and CIA estimates. The Bush administration's evidence was a mixed bag of inaccuracies and dated accuracies. Iraq had used chemical weapons on its people and on Iranian soldiers, but its stockpiles of chemical weapons had been destroyed, and it had no nuclear weapons at the time the Bush administration was calling for war to disarm it. The administration's campaign for war against the country "was dominated more by fear than facts, more by assertions of what might be, or could be, or used to be, than by what actually existed."[336]

The fact that the administration's evidence was a mixed bag was a function of the combination of several factors: the nation's contemporary security concerns after the shock of the September 2001 terrorist attacks on US territory, the inherent uncertainties of intelligence, and the motivations and political ideologies of the personalities who used the available intelligence and chose the military option for dealing with Iraq. The individuals who decided for war exploited every propitious circumstance and the fears, hopes, humanitarianism, values, and ideals of the American people in making a calculated, elaborate, persistent, and effective case for war. But, in doing so, they totally ignored the inherent uncertainties and timing of intelligence and seldom factored those uncertainties into their justification for war. More often than not, they selected intelligence to suit their case.

Certainly, some of the charges the Bush administration officials enumerated as justification for regime change in Iraq through military force were accurate. There was no dispute that Saddam Hussein was a menace to large sections of his own people. He terrorized and brutalized opponents of his regime and spent large sums of money waging war and rebuilding his military forces at the expense of civil society. His opponents and impartial political observers felt a need for a change of government in Iraq but not necessarily by war. But some charges against him, while accurate, were also dated and history. They did not constitute an immediate casus belli by any other sovereign state against sovereign Iraq. Furthermore, Saddam Hussein's wars with Iraq's neighbors—Iran and Kuwait—were a historical fact but were not ongoing. Saddam had used chemical and biological weapons against Iranians and his own people. His nuclear and biological weapons programs and his contacts with international terrorists date back to a period when Saddam Hussein was seen in Washington as a valued ally. His brutality to large sections of his own people was ignored. Trade with Iraq in chemical arms agents was allowed by the US administrations of Ronald Reagan and George H. W. Bush despite their use on Iranians and Kurds (see chapter 6).[337] So, what triggered the change of US policy towards him?

Some alleged offenses of Saddam Hussein and Iraq were inaccurate. Several official reports, including those by the CIA, declassified information, the 9/11 Commission, the UN Security Council Monitoring Group tracking al-Qaeda, and US allies fighting al-Qaeda in Europe, did not find any evidence of collaboration between Iraq and al-Qaeda terrorist network. The allegation (based on what President Bush described in his 2003 State of the Union address as "our intelligence" and British government sources) that Saddam Hussein sought sufficient quantities of uranium from Africa for his nuclear weapons program was inaccurate. The Department of State's Bureau of Intelligence and Research had said so before President Bush made the statement in his State of the Union address. Also, Mohamed El Baradei, director of the International Atomic Energy Agency, said the uranium claim was based on false documents. And former US Ambassador Joseph Wilson, after a CIA-authorized investigation, concluded that the allegation was untrue. After the administration continued to repeat it, Wilson wrote an opinion editorial in the *New York Times* (6 July 2003) asserting that the administration had twisted some of the intelligence related to Iraq's nuclear weapons program to exaggerate the Iraqi threat. Similarly, British foreign intelligence reported to Prime Minister Blair that the Bush administration was so obsessed with overthrowing Saddam Hussein that it fixed intelligence around the policy.

The administration became very infuriated by the Wilson opinion editorial in the *New York Times*. The Office of Vice President Cheney viewed the editorial as a direct attack on the credibility of the Bush administration "on a matter of signal importance: the [administration's] rationale for war in Iraq."[338] Lewis Libby, Vice President Cheney's chief of staff, was tasked to rebut the attack by leaking parts of a classified prewar intelligence estimate on Iraq, sanitizing others that argued against war. Libby complied and shared the sanitized classified prewar intelligence with a few trusted journalists.

Finally, the initial and major justification for war—stockpiles of weapons of mass destruction in Iraq—did not exist. Saddam Hussein had no weapons of mass destruction when the Bush administration and its symbolic "coalition of the willing" invaded his country. The UN weapons inspectors had successfully accomplished the task of disarming him. The head of the Bush administration's Iraq Survey Group, David Kay, who later resigned from the team responsible for finding Iraq's weapons of mass destruction, testified before the Senate Intelligence Committee that, in his judgment, "we were all wrong " about Saddam Hussein's weapons capability. He reported that his group had not "uncovered evidence that Iraq undertook significant post-1998 steps to actually build nuclear weapons or produce fissile material" and that it was highly unlikely that there were large stock piles of deployed, militarized chemical and biological weapons in the country. His group was unable to corroborate the existence of a mobile biological weapons production effort. Technical limitations, he said, would prevent any of those processes from being ideally suited to mobile trailers. Finally, he stated,

> Iraq did not have a large, ongoing, centrally controlled chemical weapons program after 1991…. Iraq's large-scale capability to develop, produce, and fill new chemical munitions was reduced—if not entirely destroyed—during Operations Desert Storm and Desert Fox, 13 years of UN sanctions and UN inspections.[339]

Furthermore, there was no iron-clad or credible evidence that Saddam had any ties with al-Qaeda terrorists. The Senate Intelligence Committee report on prewar intelligence (released September 2006) affirmed that he had no ties with al-Qaeda but was distrustful of it and, at the same time, "viewed Islamic extremists as a threat to his regime." The report added that postwar findings did not support a 2002 intelligence report that Iraq was reconstituting its nuclear program, possessed biological weapons, or had ever developed mobile facilities for producing biological warfare agents.[340] Thus, at the time the Bush administration invaded Iraq, Saddam Hussein posed an imminent nuclear or biological weapons threat neither to the United States nor to Iraq's neighbors. In view of this, David Kay suggested that it was "time to begin the fundamental analysis of how we got here, what led us here and what we need to do in order to ensure that we are equipped with the best possible intelligence as we face these issues in the future."[341] This sentiment was echoed by the Coalition for a Realistic Foreign Policy comprising foreign policy experts in Washington drawn together from the Cato Institute, the New American Foundation, and the Carnegie Endowment for International Peace. In its founding statement after the disastrous invasion and occupation of Iraq, the Coalition called for a restraint and focused foreign policy that would best protect the liberty and safety of the American people in the twenty first century.[342]

Reception of the Case for War at Home

How did the American people and the international community receive the Bush administration's case and justification for war in Iraq? Because of the administration's high secrecy and foreign policy management style, we do not know exactly the critical details of the process by which it reached its decision for war in Iraq (see the section on the Bush administration's policy approach to the war in Iraq, in chapter 10). However, we know that the decision was controversial within the administration itself and within the nation,while it was widely rejected by the international community.

There were policy differences within the administration. John Brady Kiesling, for nineteen years a career foreign service officer with wide experience in the Middle East and Greece, resigned from his office publicly when he became convinced that the administration was determined to invade Iraq.[343]

Vice President Cheney and his neoconservative advisers, as well as the neoconservatives in the Department of Defense, who, before the events of 11 September 2001, had believed that Iraq posed an imminent danger to US security, were unwilling to tolerate any longer the Saddam Hussein regime in Iraq. Therefore, determined, among other reasons, that they could not continue to live with uncertainty about Iraq's chemical, biological, and nuclear weapons capabilities, they unilaterally decided on regime change in the country by military force. They and President Bush cherry-picked the intelligence data to make the case for invading Iraq. They deliberately kept the public in the dark as to countervailing analysis at the highest level of the Intelligence Community.

Other members of the administration—Secretary of State Colin Powell and top experts in the Department of State and its Bureau of Intelligence and Research (INR)—never believed that Iraq posed an imminent danger to the United States. Differing with the ardent advocates for war, they believed that Saddam Hussein was under control. They did not see him as an imminent threat and were concerned about the political and other costs of unilaterally going to war to depose him. Therefore, they preferred to deal with him through more stringent diplomatic/coercive measures short of war under UN auspices. In the October 2002 Intelligence Estimate on Iraq, INR experts wrote that the activities they had detected did not add up to a compelling case that Iraq was pursuing, at the time, what they could consider to be an integrated and comprehensive approach to acquire nuclear weapons. The Department of Energy, which is in charge of the US nuclear weapons program, agreed with this conclusion. It considered as absurd the claim of a near-term Iraqi nuclear threat and the images of a mushroom cloud over American cities being spread by the president and his adviser on national security Condoleezza Rice. The department also concluded that the aluminum tubes the Bush administration claimed Iraq had sought from Africa for uranium enrichment were poorly suited for that purpose. The Department of State's INR concurred with that conclusion and further asserted that the claims of Iraqi pursuit of natural uranium from Niger were, in its assessment, highly dubious.

In addition, there were differences between the Departments of Defense and State in other areas as well. The Department of State stressed Iraq's violations of UN sanctions, while the Pentagon focused on the al-Qaeda link, which did not resonate anywhere outside the United States, as a justification for war in Iraq. Their other differences included: the number of American troops to be deployed, the role of the Iraqis after the initial phase of the war, differences in expectations regarding the reaction of the Iraqis, the nature of likely resistance and insurgency by the Iraqis, postwar reconstruction, and the role of the United Nations. The Department of State favored using a more robust number of troops for the invasion; using Iraqis as part of the administration after the ouster of Saddam Hussein. It also expected the United Nations to play some role in the post–war reconstruction of Iraq. The Department of Defense, on the other hand, rejected these approaches as well as the notion of an insurgency in Iraq after regime change in the country.

The US Army War College and officials at the Department of State differed with the civilian hawks in the Pentagon in the need for postwar reconstruction and the expectation that the US soldiers would be regarded by Iraqis as liberators. They warned about likely resistance and insurgency against occupation. But their views in these matters were ignored. The Department of State, which was regarded as the enemy, was sidelined, while the Department of Defense and the Office of Vice President Cheney, which insisted on controlling the planning, prevailed in most of the controversies.

There was a steady feud between the White House, the office of Vice President Cheney, and the civilian leaders of the Pentagon, on the one hand, and the CIA on the other. The feud was stoked by friction over the merits of a war in Iraq, over whether links existed between Saddam Hussein's government and al-Qaeda, and over the CIA-instigated criminal inquiry of White House officials suspected of leaking the name of covert CIA officer Valerie Plame. The bickering escalated. On the one hand, some CIA officials believed that the administration's preoccupation with Iraq had dangerously diverted US counterterrorism policy. On the other hand, the Bush administration deviated radically from professional standards not only in using policy to drive intelligence, but also in aggressively using intelligence to win public support for its decision to go to war in Iraq. As the Intelligence Community struggled to maintain its objectivity, the Bush administration policy makers pressed for more and more material at multiple levels on Saddam's link to al-Qaeda. Vice President Cheney and civilian leaders of the Pentagon distrusted the CIA and apparently co-opted its director into providing intelligence that supported their policy. They created an alternate agency—the Pentagon's Office of Special Plans—to find every possible link between Saddam and al-Qaeda.

In its briefings, the special Pentagon unit accused the CIA of faulty analysis for failing to see the purported alliance. Thus, dissenting opinion from CIA analysts was never publicized in the drive to remove Saddam Hussein from power. Much of the accusations leaked out to create a public perception of rancor between the administration and the Intelligence Community. This, in turn, encouraged some supporters of the administration to accuse intelligence officers of attempting to sabotage President Bush's policies.[344] Lastly, CIA-instigated criminal inquiry of White House officials suspected of leaking the name of CIA covert officer Valerie Plame exacerbated the friction between the agency and the administration.

From these internal differences, perceptive and seasoned analysts of the administration's case for war, like those in the Carnegie Endowment for International Peace, a nonpartisan think tank, concluded that the administration had made a reckless use of prewar intelligence in pursuit of a predetermined conclusion. They asserted that, in doing so, the administration failed to share with Congress intelligence agency doubts, caveats, and probabilities on its key claims about Iraq's weapons of mass destruction, as well as its leaders' ties to terrorist groups. Thus, before the war, there was clear concern that its main advocates had been intent upon such a conflict from the moment they entered office. Evidence for such concern became overwhelming after the war.

In spite of the George W. Bush administration's exploitation of the events of 11 September 2001 as a political opportunity to whip up national emotion for war, the American people responded to its case for war with no enthusiasm. Rather, they were deeply divided in their response to its justification for war in Iraq despite its breadth and tenacity (see chapter 9). About 20 percent of the American population rejected war out of hand, while 40 percent favored war, and 40 percent favored war if it was authorized by the UN Security Council. More than 160 cities and counties approved resolutions opposing the administration's preventive war against Iraq. Some of the cities resolved that a military invasion of Iraq would "divert attention from economic issues and challenges confronting the American people and American cities."[345] Two and a half years after the war was launched, a wide spectrum of public opinion surveys showed that more than half of the American people believed that the war was a mistake. Some 57 percent believed the president, his vice president, and their allies had "deliberately misled" them to justify the invasion of Iraq.[346] About the same percentage of the American public no longer believed in the president's honesty. While fewer than 40 percent of the American people continued to approve of the Bush administration's handling of the war, 55 percent thought the United States should not have gone to war against Iraq in the first place.[347]

A survey conducted in June 2005 by Public Agenda, a nonprofit survey organization, with the support of the Ford Foundation, reported that 50 percent of the respondents to its survey said they were misled about the Bush administration's reasons for invading Iraq. Only 22 percent of Americans surveyed, the organization said, felt that the Bush administration had the ability to create a democracy in Iraq. A majority of those surveyed (58 percent) felt that "democracy is something that countries come to on their own."[348]

Much of the nation's foreign policy elite had serious reservations about a unilateral war to foster regime change and democracy in Iraq. Brent Scowcroft, the former national security adviser to Bush's father, spoke against such a war in Iraq. Also two prominent individuals—James A. Baker III and Lawrence Eagleburger—who had successively served the elder Bush as secretaries of state questioned President Bush's Iraqi moves. Baker cautioned the Bush administration against launching a unilateral war for regime change in Iraq. Although he believed that the United States could certainly succeed in such a move, he urged President Bush to reject the advice of those who counseled doing so. The cost in all areas, he warned, would be much greater as would the political risks for both the United States and the international community. Therefore, he suggested that the administration should pursue a UN Security Council resolution requiring Iraq to submit to an "intrusive inspections regime" and authorizing "all necessary means" to enforce those inspections. For his part, Eagleburger asserted that the Bush administration had not yet made a convincing case for a military action against Saddam Hussein. The American people, he urged, had to be presented with a credible evidence that Saddam had weapons of mass destruction before any attempt to remove him from power with massive force. These views support an unmistakable inference that the president's father, George H.W. Bush, who remained intimately associated with their authors who had served him well during his presidency, did not support a war for regime change in Iraq.[349] Former President Jimmy Carter did not support a war for regime change in Iraq but rather spoke publicly against such a war. Former President Gerald R. Ford (now late) did not reveal his position on the war advocated by the George W. Bush administration until a year after the war had been launched. In an embargoed interview in July 2004 Ford told Bob Woodward that the war was not justified; he strongly disagreed with the Bush administration's justification for it. He believed very strongly that the administration's emphasis on stockpiles of weapons of mass destruction in Iraq and how it justified "what it was going to do" was an error. As president, he would not have invaded Iraq on the basis of the information publicly provided by the Bush administration but would have pushed for alternatives such as sanctions more vigorously.[350]

It was on rationale similar to Ford's that secretly, elements of the Intelligence Community challenged virtually all the intelligence the administration publicized in justification for war as either exaggerated or taken out of context. Some, who called for a thorough analysis of the relationship between Iraq and the nation's pressing realities, surmised that any campaign against Iraq might divert critical attention from the ongoing war on terrorism and might also produce complicating consequences in the Middle East.[351]

Opponents of a preemptive war, including academics and American leaders of thought, flooded Congress with messages and newspaper advertisements as that body deliberated on the Bush administration's draft resolution to authorize war in Iraq. MoveOn.Org and similar protest organizations rejected a military option for the conflict over Iraq's weapons of mass destruction. Some opponents rejected a war they thought was to promote the interests of oil companies and contractors, such as Halliburton. On the other hand, neoconservatives and supporters outside the administration endorsed and contributed to the justification.

For their part, the news media generally devoted little analysis to the Bush administration's justification for war in Iraq. They accommodated the administration and became channels through which it made its case for war. It was only after the invasion and the administration's failure to find the alleged stockpiles of weapons of mass destruction in Iraq that such leading national dailies as the *New York Times* and the *Washington Post* expressed regret for not probing deeper into the Bush administration's case for war for regime change in Iraq.

As discussed in chapters 1 and 9, Congress accepted the administration's justification for war in Iraq. It did so when it passed overwhelmingly its Iraq Resolution authorizing President Bush to use the armed forces of the United States as he determined to be necessary to defend the national security of the United States against the continuing threat posed by Iraq. Given the recent terrorist attacks at the New York World Trade Center and the Pentagon and the timing of the resolution, a few weeks before a midterm congressional election, several members of Congress voted for the resolution to avoid the political damage of being stigmatized as unpatriotic and weak on national security. But after all this, the US Army War College offered a perceptive and prescient analysis of the impending war in Iraq and its justification by the administration as a war of liberation for which the Iraqi people would be grateful to the United States. According to the analysis,

Long-term gratitude is unlikely and suspicion of the US motives will increase as the occupation continues. A force initially viewed as liberators can rapidly be relegated to the status of invaders should an unwelcome occupation continue for prolonged time. Occupation problems may be especially acute if the United States must implement the bulk of the occupation itself rather than turn those duties over to a postwar international force.... After the first year, the possibility of a serious uprising may increase should severe disillusionment set in and Iraqis begin to draw parallels between US actions and historical examples of western imperialism.[352]

Three years into the war (March 2006), WorldPublicOpinion.Org and Knowledge Networks conducted and in-depth poll of the American people on the Iraq war. On the decision to go to war, the study found that by a two-to-one margin Americans had come to believe that "the Iraq war was of choice, not a war of necessity—i.e., it was not necessary for the defense of the US—and that [it] was not the best use of US resources."[353] A majority of the 851 Americans polled believed that Iraq had no weapons of mass destruction program. A large number of the majority believed that President Bush "was determined to go to war with Iraq independent of whether Iraq had WMD or was providing substantial support to Al-Qaeda." Bush was perceived by a modest majority to be "so intent on doing so that he did not give the country the most accurate information that he had and thus misled the people."[354] He would still have gone to war, 66 percent of the poll participants affirmed, even if before the war US intelligence services had told him that there was no reliable evidence that Iraq possessed or was building weapons of mass destruction or was providing substantial support to al-Qaeda terrorist networks. The findings of the poll were reinforced by the verdict of the mid-term elections of November 2006 which was the electorate's repudiation of the Bush administration's war in Iraq.

Reception of the Case for War outside the United States

While the Bush administration's justification for war in Iraq was ultimately accepted by the American people as represented by the US Congress, it failed to convince the international community, at least as represented by the UN Security Council. Several members of the Council were alienated by the Bush administration's provocative policies. They were dubious about Bush's war aims: whether they were to disarm Iraq or to defeat its leaders or to implement his administration's dream of remaking the greater Middle East, starting with Iraq, in America's image of democracy. Even the administration's greatest European supporter, the British government of Tony Blair, did not agree with the belief on which the administration relied to justify a preemptive war against Iraq: specifically, that any state could enforce UN resolutions, in this case, on Iraq.[355]

Bush did not help matters when his administration undercut the entire process of trying to avoid a war through inspections and negotiations by undertaking a military buildup it said was necessary to force Iraq to comply.

The buildup could not be reversed without the United States losing face. It simply accented its eagerness for war. Thus, outside the United States, many critics of the US impending invasion of Iraq concluded that the series of sanctions and diplomatic maneuvers sought against Iraq by the Bush administration were not made in good faith. Rather, in their view, the Bush administration had evidently decided to invade Iraq shortly after the 11 September 2001 terrorist attacks, and its alleged weapons of mass destruction evidence was produced in order to provide a pretext for an invasion that was already a certainty. It is no wonder that the Bush administration's invasion of Iraq unleashed waves of anti-Americanism, particularly in Europe and the Middle East. The fallout from the invasion greatly complicated for the administration the already difficult task of managing US power in a world that had grown suspicious of US ambitions.

The administration had assembled a worldwide coalition after the tragedy of 11 September 2001 to overthrow the Taliban in Afghanistan and to put al-Qaeda in flight if not to destroy it. But most of the world, including most of the European nations, China, India, and Russia, who had supported that effort refused to support the Bush administration's subsequent call for war in Iraq. They bluntly opposed such war. Thus, widespread international opposition to the war made it difficult for the administration to attract foreign troop contributions to help stabilize post-Saddam Hussein Iraq.

The administration's case for war in Iraq was overwhelmingly rejected by most of the international community for a variety of reasons. President Jacques Chirac of France succinctly explained his country's opposition to the war:

> France is not pacifist. We are not anti-American either. We are not just going to use our veto to nag and annoy the US. But we just feel that there is another option, another way, another more normal way, a less dramatic way than war, and that we have to go through that path. And we should pursue it until we've come [to] a dead end, but that isn't the case.[356]

The administration's claim that it sought to uphold the sanctity of UN Security Council resolutions and thus enhance UN authority sounded hollow. Security Council resolutions had been defied time after time by some states without incurring any punitive military action. The administration's claim was contradicted by the disdain of its neoconservative officials for the UN arms inspectors, international law, and institutions and by its record, for example, on the Kyoto Protocol on Climate Change and the International Criminal Court. The administration's record seemed to be more in accord with its preemptive strike doctrine.

It was clearly apparent that the administration's justification for regime change in Iraq generally "seemed to shift as occasion demanded and led many outside observers to question [its] motives and to doubt it would ever accept Iraq's peaceful disarmament."[357]

Administration officials themselves acknowledged that, as the White House switched its signals—was the aim to disarm Iraq or to overthrow the Saddam Hussein regime or to democratize the Middle East?—the mixed message undercut the claim that the United States wanted to avoid war. Moreover, the administration was unable and impatient to produce credible evidence of the presence of weapons of mass destruction in Iraq. Its allegations of close ties and cooperation between Saddam Hussein and al-Qaeda were never proved. No other country accepted that such a link existed. Its own CIA doubted the allegations. Its belated effort to obtain a second resolution, subsequent to Resolution 1441, which could have helped to produce or negate evidence of stockpiles of weapons of mass destruction failed, because the administration was in a rush for war and unwilling to compromise. The unwillingness to compromise and the administration's shifting justifications for war contributed to the belief by most of the world that Washington was determined to go to war in Iraq regardless of what Saddam Hussein did. In light of the administration's two-year history of scorn for international institutions and agreements, its rhetoric and style about Iraq alienated rather than persuaded other members of the international community. It is no wonder, therefore, that the levels of anti-Americanism around the world rose to unprecedented levels.

Impact of the Case for War at Home and Abroad

The Bush administration's justification for war in Iraq and its approach had definite results at home and abroad. At the 1945 Nuremberg trials of the major Nazi criminals, one of the prosecutors, the US Supreme Court Justice Robert Jackson, asserted that "no grievances or policies...justified resort to aggressive war. It is utterly renounced and condemned as an instrument of policy."[358] The US-inspired Charter of the United Nations maintains the same position. The charter obligates individual member states to "refrain from the threat or use of force against the territorial integrity or political independence of any state."[359] It permits only one clear exception: Force could be used in self- or collective defense against an armed attack. The Bush administration abandoned this well-established principle in its case for war in Iraq. Possessing weapons of mass destruction did not constitute proof of an impending attack by Iraq or credible evidence of its intention to share the weapons with terrorists. In making its case for war, the Bush administration ignored this side of the argument. In doing so, it undermined four major pillars that supported the credibility and legitimacy of US behavior in post–World War II world affairs: "its commitment to international law, its acceptance of consensual decision-making, its reputation for moderation, and its identification with the preservation of peace."[360]

Several surveys conducted in 2003 and 2004 found that the United States was widely considered to be a global threat rather than the agent of peace the Bush administration had proclaimed it to be. Perhaps, this consideration was a consequence of two events: the Bush administration's war in Iraq and its doctrine of US preemptive strikes and primacy, rejecting the emergence of other powers to compete with or rival the United States. The doctrine of US primacy rejected the notion that, in order to maintain global peace and stability, it is essential that power should counteract power.

Within the United States itself, a *Washington Post*-ABC News survey conducted in June 2004 revealed that 52 percent of the American people believed that the Bush administration deliberately misled them about the possession of weapons of mass destruction by Saddam Hussein.[361] There was also the view that the possession of weapons of mass destruction by Saddam Hussein "never was the prime mover" for the war. At best, it only offered the administration "a rationalizing capacity.... And when the intelligence did not go [its] way, it fixed it" with the cooperation of the nation's "professional institutions which allowed themselves to be bullied or worse."[362]

Many other US nationals believed that the consequent invasion, conquest, and occupation of Iraq, contrary to the justification for the war, provided terrorism a big boost and caused Iraq to become the world's leading terrorist recruiting and training center. It had not made America safer but had damaged America's domestic and international credibility. In "A Tragedy of Errors" (*Nation* [23 February 2004]), a writer laments,

> They said Saddam had WMDs. He didn't. They said he was in league with Osama bin Laden. He wasn't. They predicted that no major post-war insurgency in Iraq would occur. It did. They said there would be a wave of pro-Americanism in the Middle East and the world if the United States acted boldly and unilaterally. Instead, there was a regional and global wave of anti-Americanism.[363]

Rashid Khalidi, a leading historian of the Middle East, argues that major aspects of the Bush administration's justification for war in Iraq—disarming Saddam Hussein of never-found weapons of mass destruction, the nonexistent "links between Saddam Hussein and Al-Qaeda terrorists," ending terrorism by depriving terrorists of their sponsor—masked the administration's "unacknowledged war aims." In his view, the war was a war fought firstly to demonstrate that it was possible to free the United States from subordination to international law or the UN Charter, from the need to obtain the approval of the United Nations for American actions, and from the constraints of operating within alliances. In other words, it was a war fought because its planners wanted to free the greatest power in world history from these Lilliputian bonds, and saw the tragedy of 9/11 as a golden opportunity to achieve this long-cherished goal. For them this was a war of choice, and Iraq was a suitable guinea pig for a new hyperunilateral American approach that would "shock and awe" the rest of the world.[364]

Khalidi adds that a secondary unacknowledged war aim of the Bush administration in Iraq was to establish long-term American military bases in a key Arab country in the heart of the Middle East. In a comment entitled "Plan for Quagmire," the *Progressive* (January 2006) expressed similar views. The comment concluded that the Bush administration's "motives for the war include[d] the control of oil, the privatization of Iraqi's economy, the establishment of permanent US military bases, the projection of US power, and the reputation of America's military."[365]

In making its case for war and regime change in Iraq, the Bush administration showed no deep appreciation for the virtues of the existing international order that it desired to replace. Its vision of the world order was one in which sovereignty became "more absolute for America even as it [became] more conditional for countries that challenged Washington's standard of internal and external behavior."[366] Hence, only America needs no permission slip in order to protect its interests. Other states are either with the United States, or they are against it. The United States should operate in the world on its own terms. It "is to be less bound to its partners and to global rules and institutions while it steps forward to play a more unilateral and anticipatory role in attacking terrorist threats and confronting rogue states seeking WMD. The United States will use its unrivaled military power to manage the global order."[367]

The administration argued that to wait until all the evidence was in or until authoritative international bodies supported military action in Iraq was to wait too long. Yet that approach was the only basis that the United States could use if it needed to appeal for restraint in the actions of other nations. It was therefore opening a Pandora's box in which other nations might foreswear restraint. Finally, in its approach to Iraq, the administration failed to appreciate the likelihood that the overwhelming conventional might of the United States, combined with a policy of preemptive strikes, could lead the states it stigmatized as evil and hostile to accelerate programs to acquire their own possible deterrent—weapons of mass destruction—to the United States.

Chapter 9
Congress Defers to the George W. Bush Administration on War in Iraq

If the president goes to the American people and wraps himself in the American flag and lets Congress wrap itself in the white flag of surrender, the president will win.... The American people had never heard of Grenada. There was no reason why they should have. The reason we gave for the intervention—the risk to American medical students there—was phony but the reaction of the American people was absolutely and overwhelmingly favorable. They had no idea what was going on, but they backed the president. They always will.[368]

Two surveys by the Chicago Council on Foreign Relations (CCFR) in the fall of 2002 and in July 2004 exploring attitudes about foreign policy issues among a wide range of the general public and American leaders uncovered a dissonance between public will or interest and official goals and behavior. Specifically, the surveys found that large majorities of the public and leaders agreed that the United States, contrary to President George W. Bush's stance, should participate with the rest of the world in dealing with global security and other issues, such as environmental degradation and climate change, international criminal justice, and prevention of the proliferation of weapons of mass destruction. The majorities even showed "a readiness to accept multilateral decisions that are unfavorable to the US."[369] Also, the surveys found that a percentage of the public, ranging from 49 percent to 65 percent, incorrectly thought that the majority of Congress would vote on the issues in keeping with the preferences of the people. An earlier February 2003 University of Oregon Survey Research Laboratory survey also showed that the vast majority of respondents supported the Kyoto Protocol on Climate Change and thought that the United States should take measures to reduce emissions of carbon dioxide regardless of what other nations did.[370]

Strikingly, the two Chicago Council on Foreign Relations surveys and others found that "many of these consensus positions were quite at odds with the way the US Congress had voted on the foreign policy issues." A similar behavior occurred in the fall of 2002 as Congress was debating a draft resolution which the Bush administration had submitted to it asking for authorization, literally, to go to war in Iraq. At the time Bush submitted the draft resolution, public opinion polls revealed that, in spite of their anger at the criminal acts of 11 September 2001, the American people were more worried than really enthusiastic about a war with Iraq. The polls showed deep divisions within the American public—40 percent favored war, 40 percent favored war only on the condition of a legitimation by the UN, and 20 percent were against war. In spite of this the 107th Congress authorized the war and President Bush waged it. Three months after a November 2006 congressional elections in which voters registered their anger over the war by sweeping Democrats into power in both chambers of Congress, some rank-and-file Republicans in the Congress ignored the message. They continued to support the Bush administration's decision to deploy more U.S. troops to Iraq in the grip of a sectarian war. In the Senate, they successfully maneuvered to prevent a debate on a non-bonding resolution co-written by Republican Senator John Warner and Senate Democrat Ben Nelson on the president's decision to escalate the war.

Beyond America's domestic environment, the Bush administration's draft resolution to enable it to enforce the doctrine of unilateral and preemptive war that President Bush had advocated in his National Security Strategy of the United States of America was perceived as self-serving. More importantly, it was believed to be in disregard of both the UN Charter and the sovereignty of states alleged to be building weapons of mass destruction and harboring terrorists. These facts, together with the deep divisions within the American public regarding war, required the Congress and the American people as a whole to reflect deliberately and carefully about where the doctrine and the resolution to enforce it might lead. Above all, they required Congress to factor into its deliberations and decisions on the draft resolution its solemn constitutional responsibility regarding war, as well as the potential consequences of the unilateralist and imperial tendencies of the Bush administration on the major problems, such as global security, terrorism, crimes against humanity, and climate change, confronting the world.

As Congress debated the draft resolution, opponents of a unilateral preemptive war bombarded its members with messages opposing any passage of the draft resolution. Also, a number of prominent American academics and leaders of thought appealed to it by various means—telephone calls, electronic mails, public lectures, newspaper editorials, and advertisements in the nation's leading newspapers—to deny the requested authority. Even within the professional military, which, in the US political system, is under civilian control, there were indications of voices of dissent on an American unilateral preemptive war in the Persian Gulf. Congress defied all of these voices and voted to give the president the authority to decide at his own discretion to wage a preventive war against Iraq.

Arthur Schlesinger Jr. writes that the issue of preventive war as a presidential prerogative is hardly new. However, he relates how, contrary to the speedy action of Congress in granting President Bush his request for a preventive war against Iraq, Representative Abraham Lincoln had responded to a similar request by President James Polk in the nineteenth century. Schlesinger writes,

> In February 1848 Representative Abraham Lincoln explained his opposition to the Mexican War: Allow the President to invade a neighboring nation, whenever he shall deem it necessary to repel an invasion and you allow him to do so *whenever he may choose to say* he deems it necessary for such purpose—and you allow him to make war at pleasure.... If, today, he should choose to say he thinks it necessary to invade Canada to prevent the British from invading us, how could you stop him? You may say to him, "I see no probability of the British invading us"; but he will say to you, "Be silent; I see it, you don't" (emphasis added).[371]

Schlesinger also contrasts the Bush approach to those of three post–World War II presidents—Harry S. Truman, Dwight D. Eisenhower, and John F. Kennedy. Both Presidents Truman and Eisenhower, veterans of World War I, he recalls, explicitly ruled out preventive war against Joseph Stalin's attempt to dominate Europe. Similarly, in the Cuban Missile Crisis of October 1962, Schlesinger adds, President Kennedy, himself a hero of World War II, rejected the recommendations of the Joint Chiefs of Staff for a preventive strike against the Soviet Union in Cuba. The approach of the cold war presidents, Schlesinger concludes, was compatible with the George F. Kennan formula of containment plus deterrence. It worked effectively to avoid a nuclear clash. It is obvious that, in October 2002, the US Congress, a deliberative body such as it is, forgot to consider the wisdom of the approach of these three presidents when it rushed to authorize a preventive war at the discretion of a president who, earlier, while campaigning for the office of the presidency in 2000, had publicly acknowledged his inexperience in foreign policy.

The Iraq Resolution

At the administration's first war cabinet meeting at Camp David on 14 September 2001, after the terrorist acts of 11 September, Secretary of State Colin Powell argued against the view put forward by Deputy Defense Secretary Paul Wolfowitz. Specifically, Wolfowitz had advocated that the events of 11 September provided a perfect opportunity to move against state sponsors of terrorism, including Iraq. Powell insisted that an international coalition could be mobilized only for an attack on al-Qaeda and the Taliban government in Afghanistan, not for an invasion of Iraq. President Bush accepted this position after the war cabinet, except Defense Secretary Donald Rumsfeld, who abstained, had voted with Powell. However, the hawks in the administration—Vice President Cheney, Defense Secretary Rumsfeld, his deputy Wolfowitz, and Chairman of the Defense Policy Board Richard Perle—continued to build a case for war against Iraq in various forums. President Bush hinted at this goal on several occasions: his speech to Congress on 20 September 2001, news conferences, and his State of the Union address on 20 January 2002, on which occasion he referred to Iraq, Iran, and North Korea as comprising an "axis of evil" with which the United States would have to deal preemptively.

Referring specifically to Iraq, President Bush said,

> Iraq continues to flaunt its hostility toward America and to support terror. The Iraqi regime has plotted to develop anthrax, and nerve gas, and nuclear weapons for over a decade. This is a regime that has already used poison gas to murder thousands of its own citizens—leaving the bodies of mothers, huddled over their dead children. This is a regime that agreed to international inspections—then kicked out the inspectors. This is a regime that has something to hide from the civilized world.[372]

He warned that his administration would be deliberate but would not wait on events while dangers gathered. He would not stand by as peril drew closer and closer. The United States, he said, "will not permit the world's most dangerous regimes to threaten [it] with the world's most destructive weapons."[373] Surely enough, his administration's military planning for war against Iraq began as early as 21 November 2001, after he directed Defense Secretary Rumsfeld to begin a review of what would be required to oust the Iraqi leader Saddam Hussein from power. Four months later, an article in the *Los Angeles Times* (10 February 2002) reported that the Bush administration was considering action against Saddam that might require a massive number of US troops. This was corroborated by published accounts by Bob Woodward and former US Counterterrorism Chief Richard A. Clarke. The war planning was sufficiently advanced that the nearly unanimous conventional wisdom in Washington held that the Bush administration was determined to remove Saddam from power by any means it deemed necessary. By July 2002, newspaper accounts were reporting some details of the war measures that were being considered by the administration.[374]

Vice President Cheney became the most vocal and persistent advocate of a unilateral preemptive action to bring about regime change in Iraq and to transform the Middle East. He and other hawks in the administration continued to build the case for war against Iraq. The result was that the administration decided on war against Iraq months before it submitted its draft resolution for that purpose to Congress in September 2002. In the *New Yorker* (31 March 2003), the Department of State's director of policy planning at the time, Richard N. Haas, wrote that, in early July 2002, he had asked Condoleezza Rice, then national security adviser, whether it made sense to place Iraq at the center of US foreign policy agenda while a global campaign against terrorism was already underway. Rice's response, Haas said, was essentially that that decision had been made; he therefore shouldn't waste his breath. The question then was, "How do we do it intelligently, how do we do it wisely? How do we prepare for the run-up to war so that diplomatically we will have maximum support if indeed we go to war? How do we prepare for the aftermath?"[375] Also, in a 14 March 2002 memorandum labeled "secret—strictly personal," David Manning, British Prime Minister Tony Blair's chief foreign policy advisor, described to Blair a dinner conversation he had had with Rice:

> We spent a long time at dinner on Iraq. It is clear that Bush is grateful for your support and has registered that you are getting flack. I said that you would not budge in your support for regime change but you had to manage a press, a Parliament and a public opinion that was different from anything in the States. And you would not budge either in your insistence that, if we pursued regime change, it must be very carefully done and produce the right result. Failure was not an option....
>
> Condi's enthusiasm for regime change is undimmed. But there were some signs...of greater awareness of the practical difficulties and political risks.... From what she said, Bush has yet to find answers to the big questions:
>
> - How to persuade international opinion that military action against Iraq is necessary and justified;
> - What value to put on the exiled Iraqi opposition;
> - How to coordinate a US/allied military campaign with internal opposition (assuming there is any);
> - What happens the morning after?[376]

Further evidence of the Bush administration's early decision to invade Iraq is provided by leaked British documents that show that British Prime Minister Tony Blair, the Bush administration's strongest ally in the quest for regime change in Iraq, told Bush at his Texas ranch in April 2002 that London would support military action to oust Saddam Hussein. But Blair set conditions: Bush had to seek reentry of UN weapons inspectors—which Saddam was expected to refuse—and then necessitating Security Council authorization for military action.[377] Supporting this evidence of an early decision for regime change in Iraq were the minutes of a meeting Prime Minister Tony Blair had with his cabinet colleagues on 23 July 2002. According to the minutes of that meeting, the Bush administration had already decided before that date to remove the Saddam regime through military action.[378] A copy of a memorandum detailing the minutes of that meeting was leaked to the *Sunday Times of London*, which published it in May 2005 on the run-up to the British parliamentary elections in that month. The minutes recorded that one of the officials at that meeting, Sir Richard Dearlove, head of the British equivalent of the CIA, reported on his recent talks in Washington, affirming that

> there was a perceptible shift in attitude. Military action was now seen as inevitable. Bush wanted to remove Saddam, through military action, justified by the conjunction of terrorism and WMD. But the intelligence and facts were being fixed around the policy. The NSC had no patience with the UN route, and no enthusiasm for publishing material on the Iraq regime's record. There was little discussion in Washington of the aftermath after military action.[379]

The passage quoted above from the leaked secret Downing Street Memo establishes six points:

1. "By mid-July 2002, eight months before the [Iraq] war began, President Bush had decided to invade and occupy Iraq."
2. Bush had decided to "justify" the war "by the conjunction of terrorism and WMD."
3. Already "the intelligence and facts were being fixed around the policy."
4. Many at the top of the administration did not want to seek approval from the United Nations ("going the UN route").
5. "Few in Washington seemed much interested in the aftermath of the war."[380]
6. The Bush administration deliberately refused to heed the concerns and warnings of its Secretary of State Colin Powell against a unilateral preemptive war to topple the Saddam regime in Iraq.

The report of Sir Richard Dearlove, as quoted above, corroborates the written accounts of two former Bush administration officials—Richard A. Clarke, the former terrorism adviser, and Paul H. O'Neill, the former treasury secretary. Both former officials wrote in their books that Bush had decided, at least by July 2002, to invade Iraq.[381] But his administration continued to tell members of Congress, the American people, and the world generally that war with Iraq was not inevitable as long as Iraq declared and destroyed all its weapons of mass destruction, none of which, to date, has been found. However, the truth was that President Bush's public speeches, including weekly radio addresses, indicated otherwise: that he wanted war and was determined to wage war against Iraq.

A lone voice in the administration in all this was that of Secretary of State Powell, who continued to counsel the need to consult the UN Security Council. Powell warned that the United States should not act unilaterally and should fully consider the economic and political consequences of war in the Middle East in particular. Brent Scowcroft, former advisor on national security to former President George H. W. Bush, publicly endorsed this position and the need for the return of UN weapons inspectors to Iraq.

When he addressed the United Nations on 12 September 2002, President Bush displayed an arrogant and bellicose attitude. He warned the United Nations against becoming irrelevant by not enforcing its resolutions on Iraq. He called for a new Security Council resolution on Iraq and also warned that the purposes of the United States should not be doubted. The Security Council resolutions on Iraq, he said, "will be enforced—the just demands of peace and security will be met—or action will be unavoidable. And a regime that has lost its legitimacy will also lose its power."[382]

It was after his speech at the United Nations that President Bush submitted his draft resolution to Congress on 19 September 2002 asking for authority to go to war in Iraq.[383] Some thought that he had taken this step as a ploy to ensure the passage of a new resolution on Iraq by the Security Council, some of whose members disagreed with the Bush approach to Iraq. But, initially, the administration had concluded that President Bush, as commander in chief of US armed forces, did not require authority from Congress for a military action against Iraq. The administration's legal counsel argued, too robustly in the opinion of some constitutional authorities, that the 1991 Iraq Resolution provided the president continuing authority for war against Iraq.[384]

Congress redrafted the resolution. In its final version, the Iraq Resolution authorized President Bush

1. ...to use the Armed Forces of the United States *as he determines to be necessary and appropriate* [emphasis added] in order to: (1) Defend the national security of the United States against *the continuing threat posed by Iraq* [emphasis added] ; and (2) Enforce all relevant United Nations Security Council resolutions regarding Iraq.

2. ...In connection with the exercise of the authority granted in subsection (a) to use force the President shall, prior to such exercise or as soon thereafter as may be feasible, but not later than 48 hours after exercising such authority, make available to the Speaker of the House and the President *pro*

tempore of the Senate his determination that: (1) Reliance by the United States on further diplomatic or other peaceful means alone either (A) will not adequately protect the national security against the continuing threat posed by Iraq or (B) is not likely to lead to enforcement of all relevant United Nations Security Council resolutions regarding Iraq; and (2) Acting pursuant to this joint resolution is consistent with the United States and other countries continuing to take the necessary actions against international terrorism and terrorist organizations, including those nations, organizations, or persons, who planned, authorized, committed or aided the terrorist act that occurred on 11 September 2001.[385]

The House of Representatives voted 296 to 133 for the resolution on 10 October 2002. The Senate, where the resolution was introduced on 2 October 2002, voted seventy-seven to twenty-three on 11 October 2002. The measure passed both chambers of Congress by wider margins than the 1991 Resolution that authorized the first Gulf War (see chapter 6 for the wording of the earlier 1991 Iraq Resolution). The Senate vote sharply divided the Democrats, with twenty-nine voting for the resolution and twenty-one against. All Republican senators, except Lincoln Chafee of Rhode Island, voted for passage. In the House, six Republicans joined 127 Democrats to vote against the resolution.[386] After passing the resolution in this manner, leading members of Congress explained that they had voted in a nonpartisan way in order to support President Bush and to speak with one voice at a critical moment in history. In addition, echoing the voice of an earlier Congress after passing the 1964 Gulf of Tonkin Resolution, a key section of the House of Representatives International Relations Committee report on the Iraq Resolution asserted,

> The Committee hopes that the use of military force can be avoided. It believes, however, that providing the President with the authority he needs to use force is the best way to avoid its use. A signal of our Nation's seriousness of purpose and its willingness to use force may yet persuade Iraq to meet its international obligations, and is the best way to persuade members of the Security Council and others in the international community to join us in bringing pressure on Iraq or, if required, in using armed force against it.[387]

After Congress had authorized him in this manner to decide at his own discretion to go to war in Iraq, President Bush declared that America had spoken with one voice. Congress, he said, "has spoken clearly to the international community and the United Nations Security Council.... Saddam Hussein and his outlaw regime pose a great threat to the [Persian Gulf], the world and the United States. Inaction is not an option, disarmament is a must."[388]

In the presence of members of his cabinet and those of Congress in the East Room of the White House, President Bush addressed the American people:

> The 107th Congress has just become one of the few called by history to authorize military action to defend our country and the cause of peace. But no one should assume that war is inevitable. Though Congress has now authorized the use of force, I have not ordered the use of force. I hope the use of force will not become necessary. Our goal is to fully and finally remove a real threat to world peace and to America. Hopefully this can be done peacefully. Hopefully we can do this without military action. Yet, if Iraq is to avoid military action by the international community, it has the obligation to prove compliance with all the world's demands. It's the obligation of Iraq. Iraq still has the power to prevent war by declaring and destroying all its weapons of mass destruction. But if it does not declare and destroy those weapons, the United States will go into battle, as a last resort.[389]

As it turned out, President Bush did not go to war against Iraq as a last resort. He chose to go to war at the time he did and in the manner he wanted. After Congress had authorized him to decide at his own discretion to go to war in Iraq, Louis Fisher, a constitutional authority, concluded that the process looked like a monarchy and not a republic. "A nation dedicated to 'We the People,'" he wrote, "places ultimate authority in elected lawmakers. Members of Congress take an oath to defend the Constitution, not the president. Nevertheless, in this area of the war power, the United States has been drifting toward monarchy and away from a republic."[390] Surely, in delegating the awesome responsibility to the discretion of President Bush, Congress abdicated its constitutional war powers by transferring the choice or decision it should have made in whether or not to go to war in Iraq to the president. Former Indiana Representative Lee Hamilton, who had served as chairman of the House International Relations Committee and had compiled a distinguished record in the House during a period of thirty-four years, reached a similar conclusion when he observed that, in passing the resolution, Congress had "really handed over to the president not just the question of how...to conduct the war, but the authority to decide whether or not to go to war."[391]

All of this was done in spite of serious reservations of much of the foreign policy establishment and the professional military, and widespread international opposition, including many North Atlantic Treaty Organization (NATO) allies. Even more importantly, the authority was granted even though, in the run-up to the vote on the resolution, the Bush administration had refused to declassify essential intelligence assessing the threat from Iraq that the chairman of the Senate Select Intelligence Committee, Senator Bob Graham, had believed contradicted the administration's justification for the resolution. This denial to Congress of the flow of information it needed to fulfill its constitutional role in debating Bush's draft resolution reflected the secrecy with which the Bush administration was pursuing its Iraqi policy. It indicated that the administration had something to hide and set off an alarm for caution that Congress obviously either failed to recognize or, more probably, chose to ignore.

Congressional behavior in passing the resolution, while not laudable, was a function of the general situation and prevailing circumstances at the time. The climate of fear induced by the 11 September 2001 terrorist attacks was still very pervasive and was capitalized upon by the Bush administration. Concern for victory at the impending congressional and later presidential elections was a political factor. The maneuvers of the Bush administration, for political purposes, in grossly exaggerating Iraq's weapons of mass destruction in order to frighten and induce Congress into endorsing an invasion of Iraq were adroitly presented to the nation as in the vital national security interests of the United States. This had the patriotic effect of rallying around the administration, whether it was right or wrong. The failure of Congress to deliberate and ask hard questions of both the administration and the intelligence agencies, especially the CIA, about the nature and use of intelligence about Iraq's weapons of mass destruction shared with it was a major factor. Finally, a culture of deference and abdication of constitutional responsibility by timid politicians of both major political parties in Congress was the most profound factor in the grant of a blank check to the Bush administration to go to war in Iraq.

Pertinent Questions about the Iraq Resolution

Three pertinent questions arise from the resolution: How did Congress determine that Iraq posed a "continuing threat" to the United States? Did the president of the United States have the legal authority to "enforce all relevant United Nations Security Council resolutions regarding Iraq" without the specific authorization of the United Nations Security Council to do so? Were there any echoes and lessons of the Gulf of Tonkin Resolution and its aftermath that Congress should have carefully pondered before adopting the October 2002 Iraq Resolution?

The First Question

Regarding the first question, it is clear that Congress did not independently determine that, in fact, Iraq constituted a "continuing threat" to the United States. It deferred to the executive branch and merely accepted and rubber-stamped the conclusions of the Bush administration. There was every reason, constitutionally and otherwise, for Congress not to accept and rubber-stamp those conclusions. There was enough evidence that the refusal of the president's father, President George H. W. Bush, to go all the way to Baghdad to remove Saddam Hussein from power during the first Gulf War in 1991 had left the neoconservatives—especially Donald Rumsfeld, Paul Wolfowitz, and Richard Perle—in the George W. Bush administration with a bad taste and the conviction of a need to overthrow the hated dictator of Iraq. In an open letter to President Clinton on 26 January 1996, they and other members of their group, the Project for a New American Century, had warned that the policy of containing Iraq was "dangerously inadequate." They advocated,

> The only acceptable strategy is one that eliminates the possibility that Iraq will be able to use or threaten to use weapons of mass destruction. In the near term this means a willingness to undertake military action as diplomacy is clearly failing. In the long term, it means removing Saddam Hussein and his regime from power. That now needs to become the aim of American foreign policy.[392]

President Clinton ignored their prescription. But those of the group who became members of the George W. Bush administration persisted in this belief. Well before the events of 11 September 2001, they adroitly succeeded to convince President Bush of the necessity to preemptively strike at Saddam in order to bring about regime change in Iraq and to promote democracy in the greater Middle East. The terrorist attacks of 11 September became a crucial justification for the policy they had convinced Bush to pursue. For example, "barely five hours after American Airlines Flight 77 plowed into the Pentagon, Defense Secretary Donald H. Rumsfeld was telling his aides to come up with plans for striking Iraq.... Go massive.... Sweep it all up. Things related and not."[393] Thus, after the events of 11 September 2001, the call for a policy of an aggressive unilateral preemptive action against Iraq became the cause of a fierce internal, but open, debate within the Bush administration between its advocates—Vice President Cheney, Defense Secretary Rumsfeld, and his Deputy Paul Wolfowitz—and Secretary of State Colin Powell, who favored diplomacy and containment.

There was also sufficient evidence that, in order to implement their policy of a more aggressive action against Saddam, the offices of both the Defense Secretary Donald Rumsfeld and Vice President Dick Cheney were exerting enormous political pressure on the Central Intelligence Agency (CIA) and the entire Intelligence Community to coax from them intelligence that would fit their policy on Iraq.[394] Critics of the process argued that Cheney and the neoconservatives at the Pentagon started with the conclusion they earlier had reached and then, through political pressure, "massaged and manipulated the intelligence [community] to back up their [reasoning and conclusion]."[395] Thus, from 11 September 2001 through the start of the Iraq War on 19 March 2003, "the neoconservative nexus in the administration, led by Vice President Dick Cheney, leaned heavily on the CIA to come up with intelligence to support the White House's preordained determination to go to war against Iraq."[396] Their intense pressure was directed at Tenet, McLaughlin, and scores of other CIA managers, analysts, and field officers. Rumsfeld and other administration officials asked so many repetitive questions generated by the Office of Special Plans and discredited fabricators, such as Ahmed Chalabi of the Iraqi National Congress (see below), that some analysts felt that they were being pushed beyond the evidence they had. The analysts therefore had to reach back to old data, relied on several sources of questionable veracity, and made assumptions about available data that were unwarranted. Dissent within the CIA and the anger of its analysts about being manipulated by the Bush administration were palpable, just as were the complaints about the agency emanating from other neoconservatives and supporters of war in Iraq, such as David Brooks of the *New York Times* and the syndicated columnist Robert Novack.[397]

Michael Isikoff and David Corn have written that there was no obvious pressure by Vice President Cheney and Defense Secretary Rumsfeld on CIA analysts to alter their conclusion on Iraq. But they observe that the barrage of questions they asked during their frequent visits to the CIA headquarters at Langley created a subtle environment that unmistakably influenced the agency's work, as the analysts became "overly eager to please." Cheney, they believed, did not pose the sort of questions a policy maker would need answered in order to determine whether Iraq posed a threat to the United States. "He was not seeking information *whether* [sic] Saddam was dangerous because he possessed weapons of mass destruction. He was not soliciting material that would help him decide if an invasion of Iraq was absolutely necessary. His queries were all pegged to the assumption that Iraq would be invaded. And he was not happy with what he was hearing for the analysts were unable to provide concrete answers to his queries about the invasion to come."[398]

During its first two years, the Bush administration made several but futile efforts to unify fractious Iraqi opposition groups that it hoped could establish an Iraqi government in exile. In addition, its most hawkish offices, those of Defense Secretary Rumsfeld and Vice President Cheney, relied heavily for their insight into Iraq on intelligence from sources with vested interest in regime change in Iraq. The significant leading sources included Ahmed Chalabi,[399] the exile group—the Iraqi National Congress—that Chalabi headed, and defectors from Iraq with a track record of creating and manipulating information designed to avenge ill treatment they believed they had suffered at the hands of Iraqi rulers. As it turned out, these sources obliged the hawks in the Bush administration with highly exaggerated or fabricated information about Iraq's chemical and biological weapons. Investigations into prewar US intelligence failures revealed that some of the most erroneous information about Saddam's weapons of mass destruction programs had come from sources provided by Chalabi. One of the informants, a hard-drinking relative of a Chalabi aide, code-named Curveball, affirmed, albeit falsely, that Iraq had mobile weapons labs. Curveball's German handlers said in November 2005 that the Bush administration and the CIA had repeatedly exaggerated and mischaracterized the Iraqi informant's claims during the run-up to the war in Iraq, even though the officials had been warned that his information "was not proven." The German intelligence officials added that they had made it clear that they could not verify the things Curveball had said and were shocked when President Bush and Colin Powell used the unproven information in key prewar speeches.[400]

Another Iraqi informant, Khidar Hamza, a nuclear scientist who had defected to the United States in 1994, was discredited by information UN weapons inspectors obtained from General Hussein Kamel, Saddam's ill-fated son-in-law who himself had defected to Jordan in 1995 and was subsequently murdered by Saddam.[401] Vice President Cheney himself became a strong advocate for Chalabi and the Iraqi National Congress to the extent that, in the fall of 2002, he intervened in a feud between the Departments of State and Defense over more funding for Chalabi's Iraqi National Congress. "We're getting ready to go to war [in Iraq], and we're nickel-and-diming the INC at a time they're providing us with unique intelligence on Iraqi WMD," Cheney said in a rare burst.[402] It is significant to note that this rare burst occurred well before Congress passed the Iraq Resolution in October 2002.

Before 11 September 2001, Cheney, who was distrustful of the national Intelligence Community, was known to have given his staff clear instructions to collect intelligence by going "beyond the typical information channels in the official bureaucracy," a practice of "outsourcing" he had perfected when he was the chief executive officer of Halliburton. He did not want to rely solely on official intelligence reports and State Department cables and Department of Defense memos.[403] Similarly, at the Pentagon, where Defense Secretary Rumsfeld and his colleagues believed that the CIA was unable to perceive the reality of the situation in Iraq, Douglas Feith, under instructions from Deputy Defense Secretary Wolfowitz, set up the Office of Special Plans in September 2001. The specific purpose of the office was "to find evidence that Saddam

Hussein had close ties to al-Qaeda as well as enormous arsenal of biological, chemical, and nuclear weapons that threatened his neighbors and potentially the United States."[404] In that way it would serve as a shadow intelligence agency to produce "evidence" to bolster the Bush administration's case against Saddam Hussein's ties to terrorists and threat to Iraq's neighbors and the United States and to shape public opinion.

The influence of the Office of Special Plans immediately brought about a crucial change of direction in the American Intelligence Community: The government's customary procedures for vetting intelligence were bypassed, and the influence of both the CIA and the Defense Intelligence Agency declined. By the fall of 2002, the Office of Special Plans rivaled both agencies as the Bush administration's main source of intelligence regarding Iraq's alleged possession of chemical and biological weapons and connection with al-Qaeda.[405] Karl Rove, President Bush's chief strategist, put a stamp of approval on this when he told *USA Today* that the terrorist attacks of 11 September 2001 proved that officials should "be contesting, not simply receiving, information from security analysts."[406] It was in this manner that the Defense Department and the Office of Vice President Dick Cheney wrote their own pieces of intelligence based on their own ideology and preferred information generated by the Defense Department's Office of Special Plans. It was not until November 2005, when House and Senate Democrats criticized the administration's prewar claims that Iraq had banned weapons and ties to al-Qaeda and other terrorist groups, that the Defense Department's Inspector General's Office said it was going to investigate the Office of Special Plans used by the administration to build its case against Saddam Hussein and to plan the war in Iraq.[407]

Eventually an investigation by the Pentagon's Acting Inspector General, Thomas F. Gimble, into the handling of prewar intelligence documented unusual efforts by Pentagon's policymakers, using the Office of Special Plans identified above, to bypass regular intelligence channels and influence officials at the highest levels of the Bush administration. According to the inspector's report the Office of Special Plans produced and disseminated to senior decision-makers alternative assessments on Iraq and Al Qaeda relationships. Including conclusions that were inconsistent with the consensus of the Intelligence Community, the assessments affirmed that there were links between Saddam Hussein and Al Qaeda; that Mohammed Atta, the presumed ringleader of the 11 September 2001 hijackers that attacked U.S. territory, had met with an Iraqi agent at Prague before the attacks that killed 3000 Americans. Form this it is apparent that although the Bush administration's primary rationale for war in Iraq was to disarm the country of its alleged weapon's of mass destruction, a more important argument that resonated with many Americans in the lead-up to the war in Iraq was the claimed link between Iraq and Al Qaeda.[408]

Prewar practices, such as these, designed to make intelligence suit policy goals apparently failed to raise an alarm in Congress as its distinguished members deliberated on the Bush administration's draft resolution. Only a few of its members, such as Senator Robert Byrd and Representative Dennis Kucinich, braved the confidence to tell the Bush administration that it was off base. However, the intelligence was so shaky that it did alert Secretary of State Colin Powell to spend four days and three nights at the CIA headquarters at Langley trying to vet the material he was given by the Office of Vice President Cheney to present to the UN Security Council on Iraq's possession of nuclear arsenal. Powell eliminated aspects of the information he had deduced were questionable but still learned, to the hurt of his reputation, a year or so after his Security Council presentation on 5 February 2003, that he had been given wrong information about Iraq's arsenal.[409]

Unlike Powell, Congress, including its intelligence committees, totally failed to ascertain whether the intelligence the Bush administration shared with it was shaded or was being used selectively to make the administration's case for war in Iraq. This was the case even when some of its members believed that some of the intelligence shared with them was either ambiguous or had been contradicted. This notwithstanding, Congress still failed to reject boldly the administration's claim in October 2002, repeated in the State of the Union address in January 2003, that the British government had learned that Saddam Hussein had sought to obtain uranium from Africa, as part of its case for war in Iraq. The October 2002 National Intelligence Estimate that the administration shared with Congress (at its request) as it deliberated the draft resolution to authorize war in Iraq included many qualifiers and a Department of State's caveat that claims of Iraqi pursuit of uranium in Africa were highly dubious. But only seventeen members of Congress read the document.[410] Similarly, based on its conclusions, after its authorized fact-finding mission to Niger, West Africa, by former ambassador Joseph Wilson, the CIA had provided the administration an assessment that the evidence that Iraq sought uranium in Africa was weak and overblown. Knowledge of these things did not cause Congress to pause and not to rush to pass the Iraq Resolution.

Worse still, Congress failed, as a deliberative body, to scrutinize President Bush's doctrine of preemption, as well as his motives and justification for war in Iraq, in order to ensure that these were indeed in accord with US national security interests as a global power, broadly, not narrowly, defined. It failed to question the administration on whether Iraq, dwarfed to insignificance by the

United States in both latent and actual power, posed an imminent and sufficient threat to the national security of the United States to warrant preventive war. The evidence of such a threat was not there. Furthermore, Congress failed to question the administration on whether a preemptive war in Iraq was in accord with the nation's hallowed advocacy of respect for the rule of law and the rights of other nations. It also failed to ask enough hard questions about the administration's exit strategy, including plans to reconstruct a defeated and occupied Iraq and what it would require to turn the occupied nation around and point it in a better direction. These questions should have been raised, because President Bush, although commander in chief of US armed forces, had no constitutional authority to decide on war, except in response to sudden attacks or in hot pursuits. He had "no constitutional authority to make military and financial commitments of tens of billions of dollars."[411]

It is also significant to observe that the US Congress had been far more reluctant to support the first Gulf War (1990–1991) than the UN Security Council. The Security Council had voted unanimously for a resolution authorizing that war to liberate Kuwait from Iraqi occupation, while members of the US Congress vigorously debated President George H. W. Bush's request for authority to commit US armed forces to the war. Members of the House voted 250 to 183 on the resolution, while the Senate voted fifty-two to forty-seven. Remembering America's experience in Vietnam and Southeast Asia, Congressional opponents of US participation in the Security Council-authorized war in Iraq demanded that the George H. W. Bush administration should abide by the provisions of the 1973 War Powers Resolution.

In the case of the George W. Bush administration's approach to the same Iraqi regime of Saddam Hussein, Congress acted differently. It totally refused to appreciate and vigorously support the advocacy of Secretary of State Powell for diplomacy and containment through the UN Security Council. It failed, early in 2002, to scrupulously scrutinize the $48 billion increase in defense spending the administration had requested for fiscal year 2003. Ten billion dollars of the requested amount was designated as an unspecified contingency fund for further operations in the war on terrorism. It is surmised that that amount was most probably the initial funding for the war in Iraq.[412] This meant that Congress was irresponsibly funding a war it had not declared or authorized.

Congress also failed to wait on the impending UN Security Council decision regarding authorization of the use of force in Iraq and voted to authorize Bush to decide at his own discretion to go to war in Iraq. In allowing Bush to exercise such authority, Congress again acted irresponsibly. Furthermore, not only did it abdicate its constitutional responsibility, but its members also failed to uphold their oath to defend the Constitution of the Federal Republic of the United States. Collectively, their actions were indeed a colossal failure to perform their solemn duties. The Constitution requires congressional judicious deliberation at all times but especially whenever a president's means of conducting foreign policy indicates any use of force, an approach to a national commitment to war, and a probable cost that would disproportionately consume national resources. Such rigorous deliberation by Congress was designed by the framers of the US Constitution to prevent error and to uncover blind spots and critical foreign policy details ignored by the executive branch. Such critical congressional participation in foreign policy forces the president and his subordinates, including the Intelligence Community, especially the Central Intelligence Agency, to exercise greater judiciousness in their advice and the analysis of strategic information they provide the president and the ultimate policy he chooses. In this case, Congress failed to induce them to do so.

This congressional behavior, juxtaposed with the findings of the Chicago Council on Foreign Relations surveys, raised the question as to how it was possible that Congress was so out of step with the preferences of the public and the elite on such a range of foreign policy issues as those delineated above, including waging war on Iraq. The authors of the Chicago Council on Foreign Relations surveys cited above opined that one of the facts that may explain the congressional behavior was that "Americans in all types of leadership position, including the Congress and high level members of the executive branch, misread the attitudes of the general American public," especially in regard to participating in multilateral efforts. Furthermore, they suggest that Congress may not feel that the public supports such positions to the extent "that it is politically risky to pursue them."[413] Perhaps, this is best explained by the trend in recent American politics: Politicians have come to rely more on corporate America and their political parties' machines for their election or reelection than on their voting constituents.

Another factor may be pressure exerted by the executive branch on members of Congress in a variety of ways. The circumstances of the 11 September 2001 horrific terrorist attacks enhanced Bush's pressure. On that occasion, it was relatively easy for President Bush to effectively capitalize on the trauma and fears engendered by the terrorist attacks and deploy a moralistic rhetoric of good and evil, very consistent with America's conception of itself as an exceptional nation, to persuade Congress and the nation to rally around the flag. Accordingly, Bush adeptly used such moralistic language and exaggerated claims of Saddam Hussein's possession of weapons of mass destruction to solicit from Congress a green light to invade Iraq in order to eliminate Hussein's dictatorship and alleged threat to the United States.

Part of the administration's pressure on Congress was exerted through the following examples. First, as the Senate was considering the administration's draft resolution, Director of Central Intelligence George Tenet and Secretary of State Colin Powell respectively testified before the Senate Foreign Relations Committee that Iraq had sought uranium from Niger to advance its nuclear weapons program. This information was fabricated but it helped to mollify the opposition of some members of Congress to the resolution and eventually contributed to its passage. Later, President Bush included the information in his State of the Union address on 28 January 2003. The perceived threat posed by Iraq had indeed become more important than the integrity of the US intelligence-vetting process, as well as the credibility of the US government!

The second example was the release on 2 October 2002 by the director of the CIA, George Tenet, of a new National Intelligence Estimate affirming that Iraq had an atomic bomb. The new estimate was released nine days before the Senate voted on the war resolution and as American troops and aircraft carriers were already taking up positions for battle in Iraq. Later, though, in the summer of 2004, the Senate Intelligence Committee issued a scathing report that "most of the major key judgments" in the October 2002 National Intelligence Estimate on Iraq's illicit weapons "were overstated, or were not supported by the underlying intelligence reporting."[414]

On the same day, 2 October 2002, that the National Intelligence Estimate on Iraq's weapons of mass destruction was released, President Bush met at the Rose Garden with the House and Senate leadership (except Senate Majority Leader Tom Daschle, who was absent) on the resolution.[415] Bush used the august occasion to rehearse his charges against Saddam Hussein, whom he described "as a student of Stalin," and to reiterate the need for regime change in Iraq. He insisted that "America's leadership and willingness to use force" was "the best way to ensure" Saddam's compliance with the demands to disarm, to defend the United States, to shape a peaceful world, and to serve the interests of the Iraqi people. Indecision and inaction, he avowed, "could lead to a massive and sudden horror."[416]

The congressional leaders expressed their agreement with the president's analysis of the Iraqi situation and their acceptance of his demand for a resolution to authorize the use of force to disarm Saddam Hussein and eliminate his regime. Speaker Hastert assured him that the redrafted and pending resolution "does not tie the President's hand, it gives him flexibility he needs to get the job done. The resolution does not require the President to get United

Nations approval before proceeding. It supports the President's effort to work with the United Nations, but it doesn't require him to seek U.N. approval first. If the President determines that he has to act unilaterally to protect American people, he can, and he has the ability to do that."[417] Senator Warner affirmed, adding: "Mr. President, we delivered for your father. We will deliver for you. And I predict, while the vote was a margin of five in 1991, it will be a stronger bipartisan margin this time." Note, Congress was delivering to Bush as it did to his father, not to the US national security interest!

For his part, Senator Joseph Lieberman asserted that "the moment of truth" had arrived for Saddam Hussein and that the redrafted resolution was "the last chance for the international community to come together behind the rule of law, and to show that the resolutions of the United Nations are worth more than the paper on which they are written."[418] It must be added that Senator Lieberman was one of the cosponsors of the 1998 Iraq Liberation Act by which Congress authorized the expenditure of $97 million in aid to organizations dedicated to the overthrow of Saddam Hussein. Senator McCain thanked the president "for his leadership" and conferred on him a constitutional authority he did not have when he asserted, "at the end of the day, the final, most serious responsibility of sending young American men and women into harm's way rests with the President of the United States."[419]

In light of President Bush's strategic pressures, Congress chose to defer the issue of war in Iraq to the executive branch and abdicated its constitutional responsibility as a coequal manager of American foreign policy. Perhaps, Congress may have been motivated to do so by an assumption that presenting a united front to the world was essential to succeed, while a scrupulous analysis of the situation and consequent debate might undercut the nation's ability to do so. Such motivation was most likely a function of the fact that some members of Congress had come to see their role in foreign policy as legitimizing rather than criticizing presidential decisions.

Above all, that choice may have been influenced by partisan politics as well. Republicans had a political need to support the policies of a Republican president. Bush submitted to Congress his draft resolution for authorization to go to war in Iraq barely two months before the November congressional elections, thus coloring the vote and the political calculations. His administration demanded that lawmakers should complete action on an authorizing resolution before they adjourned for those November midterm elections. Demanding the authorization in the months just before the November elections increased partisan exploitation of the war issue. Several Republican nominees in the congressional contests made a political weapon out of the Bush policy on Iraq. Bush himself, with an eye on the need for his reelection in November 2004, accused Senate Democrats of being interested in special interests in Washington and not in the security of the American people. In his 7 October 2002 speech to the nation on Iraq, just two days before the House voted on the resolution, Bush declared that, in light of the devastating attacks of 11 September 2001 and facing "clear evidence of peril," America was "unwilling to wait for the final proof, the smoking gun, that could come in the form of a mushroom cloud.... Having every reason to assume the worst and...an urgent duty to prevent the worst from occurring, it simply cannot and will not resume the old approach to inspections, and applying diplomatic and economic pressure."[420] He was thus able to manipulate members of Congress through this strategy of fear to pass his draft resolution under partisan pressures, without their knowing fully well the decision the Security Council would adopt on the use of force against Iraq and Iraq's response to such decision.

For their part, the Democrats had a political interest in challenging Bush in the 2004 presidential election. While the Republicans wanted Bush to win that election, as he eventually did, to ensure their party's continued control of the executive branch of the US national government, as well as the perquisites of that office, the Democrats, in their desire to win congressional seats and the presidency, did not want to be seen as unpatriotic by the electorate amidst a national emergency. They failed woefully to provide a vigorous opposition to the resolution in light of a lack of credible evidence to support the Bush administration's case for war. Indeed, only two of the Democratic Party members of Congress, Senator Bob Graham and Representative Dennis Kucinich who cherished presidential ambition in the 2004 election, voted against the resolution. Senator Graham asserted that President Bush and ranking officials of his administration had manipulated and hyped the intelligence. He believed that it was a serious error for Congress to pass the resolution. The other democratic contenders for the presidency—the House Minority Leader Dick Gephardt, the Senate Majority Leader Tom Daschle, and Senators John Kerry, John Edwards, and Joseph Lieberman—supported the redrafted resolution. In announcing his support for it, Gephardt explained that he had done so in order to foster a consensus that would lead the country in the right direction.[421] Senate Majority Leader Daschle said that it was essential to support President Bush and give him the benefit of the doubt. Accordingly, he worked closely with the president on the resolution.[422] Senator Kerry, who became the Democratic Party's presidential candidate in the 2004 elections, earlier argued against war with Iraq, but, with an eye on the presidential elections, he eventually supported the resolution. Curiously, he asserted, "We are affirming a president's right and responsibility to keep the American people safe [through war against Iraq?] and the president must take that grant of responsibility seriously."[423]

The lone strident Democratic Party voice in the Senate was that of Robert Byrd, who insisted that the resolution amounted to a "blank check" to the Bush administration and was the Gulf of Tonkin Resolution all over again. Senator Byrd urged his colleagues to remember the Constitution and not give the president unchecked power. He attempted to mount a filibuster but was cut off by a vote of seventy-five to twenty-five.

In this typical behavior by members of the two political parties lies the tragedy of America's political party system: Parochial interests and partisan politics and ideology tend to take precedence over relatively more important vital national security interests and thus promote indifference to public opinion. In this manner, Congress frequently defers to the president and avoids a rational discussion and debate of foreign policy issues. This accounts for the abject failure of both Republicans and Democrats in Congress to ask the Bush administration hard questions on its Iraqi policy prior to the war. In the end, the administration's commitment to a war of choice in Iraq was not a Republican Party commitment. It was an American commitment requiring American sacrifice.

Another factor in the congressional behavior in passing the resolution was that service in the American professional military had become voluntary. The public and members of Congress were not as agitated by President Bush's war of choice as they would have been if their children were being drafted to fight the war. Protests around the nation, as in the case of Vietnam, would have been much more extensive, strident, and enduring, inducing Congress to pay closer attention than it did in authorizing Bush to decide at his own discretion to wage a preemptive war even when the threat was not, by all credible accounts, imminent.

The Second Question
Regarding the second question, as to whether the president of the United States, George W. Bush, had the legal authority to enforce all relevant United Nations Security Council resolutions regarding Iraq as stipulated by the resolution passed by Congress, most legal experts insist that he did not have such legal authority. The Security Council Resolution 1441, adopted unanimously in November 2002, sent UN weapons inspectors back to Iraq after a four-years hiatus to verify Iraq's disarmament in compliance with earlier resolutions. The resolution stipulated that there would be "serious consequences" if there was a "material breach," including denial of unrestricted access to the weapons

inspectors, of the resolution. However, the resolution did not specifically identify the serious consequences but reserved the authority to determine them for the Security Council. The resolution further stated that a finding of a "material breach" required both omissions or lies in Iraq's arms declaration and noncompliance with the weapons inspectors. The resolution provided no authorization for war. In seeking a second resolution, which it eventually withdrew for lack of support and threat of veto, the Bush administration implicitly acknowledged this fact. It is clear, therefore, that under Resolution 1441 or with no prior, explicit authorization of the UN Security Council, the Bush administration had no legal authority to launch an attack on Iraq. But it did so anyway, even without allowing the weapons inspectors to complete their work.

Under Article 2 of the UN Charter, member states of the organization, including the United States, pledge to "refrain in their international relations from the threat or use of force against the territorial integrity or political independence of any state." Chapter VII of the UN Charter allows the Security Council to approve necessary coercive action, including military action, against a state when it deems doing so necessary in order "to maintain or restore international peace and security." Article 51 of the UN Charter stipulates, "Nothing in the present Charter shall impair the inherent right of individual or collective self-defense if an armed attack occurs against a member of the United Nations, until the Security Council has taken measures to maintain international peace and security." The Security Council had not found it necessary to specifically authorize any military action by any member state against Iraq. Realizing that the Security Council would deny a resolution it had demanded to that effect, the Bush administration withdrew the request and proceeded to invade Iraq. The UN Secretary General Kofi Annan described the US invasion as illegal. His characterization of the war as such aroused the ire of some conservative members of US Congress against him and the organization. A report commissioned by Annan after the unilateral preemptive war in Iraq insisted,

> in a world full of potential perceived threats, the risk to the global order and the norm of nonintervention on which it continues to be based is simply too great for the legality of unilateral preventive action, as distinct from collectively endorsed action, to be accepted. Allowing one to so act is to allow all. We do not favour the rewriting or reinterpretation of Article 51.[424]

The end result of rewriting Article 51 would be insecurity for all, including the most powerful.

The report further emphasized that, in the world of the twenty-first century, "the international community does have to be concerned about nightmare scenarios combining terrorists, weapons of mass destruction and irresponsible States...which may conceivably justify the use of force, not just reactively but preventively and before a latent threat becomes imminent. The question is not whether such action can be taken: it can, by the Security Council as the international community's collective security voice, at any time it deems that there is a threat to international peace and security." But, before the Security Council does so, the report went on, it would take into account

> issues of prudence and legitimacy...whether such preventive action *should* be taken. Crucial among such issues is whether there is credible evidence of the reality of the threat in question (taking into account both capability and specific intent) and whether the military response is the only reasonable one in the circumstances.[425]

The Third Question

Regarding the third question, as to whether there were any echoes or lessons of the Gulf of Tonkin Resolution and its aftermath that members of Congress should have seriously considered before adopting the Iraq Resolution, the answer is definitely yes, even though the two situations were different in a number of respects. There were echoes regarding the use of force to achieve foreign policy goals. One of the lessons of Vietnam, which many regarded as a case of governmental folly and deceit, was that US citizens, especially their representatives in Congress, should view the presidency with extreme skepticism; they should trust, but they have the obligation to verify.[426] In passing the Iraq Resolution, members of Congress failed to verify but simply trusted and deferred to President Bush.

The Vietnam experience very clearly demonstrated that the use of force may not always achieve desired foreign policy goals and that, in certain situations, a militarily inferior but determined foe could stymie US forces. Thus, as powerful as it is, the United States cannot do everything everywhere. It also demonstrated the limits of doctrine—the domino theory—which was a significant justification for the intervention. At that time, the American public was specifically told, and it believed, that the purpose of the intervention was to protect Vietnam, Southeast Asia, and, by extension, the United States and the so-called free world from the embrace of evil—Communist and totalitarian regimes as represented by the Soviet Union and its allies. Initially that cause for intervention—that the fall of South Vietnam to the Communist bloc would have a domino effect on its neighbors and the so-called free world, including the United States—had appeared to be righteous and was portrayed by US officials as such. But, over the course of a decade of catastrophe, the case for it gradually disintegrated to the point that it was very difficult to argue that the United States was on the side of right and that North Vietnam was evil. The result was national frustration and a syndrome that, for years, would haunt the US role in world affairs, reminding the nation that violent intrusions into other people's history have unforeseen negative consequences.

Another echo of the Gulf of Tonkin Resolution is the probability of escalation and expansion of the resultant war into neighboring countries as happened in the Vietnam war. President Lyndon B. Johnson incrementally increased the number of American forces in that war as initial efforts were failing to produce the desired result. President Richard M. Nixon, who inherited the war from him, expanded it to Cambodia at considerable cost in human and natural resources without congressional authorization. There is a potential danger that President George W. Bush may prolong US involvement in Iraq with similar consequences as the level of insurgency and instability in the country increases. In fact, in 2006, Bush vowed to "stay the course" in Iraq until the mission is accomplished, leaving the withdrawal of American forces from Iraq, he affirmed, to his successor and future Iraqi governments.

Other echoes of the Gulf of Tonkin Resolution and its aftermath include the polarization of the nation by the Vietnam War as that war slowly and incrementally sucked the nation into a quagmire totally not envisaged or contemplated by its leaders and the high incidence of posttraumatic disorder and addiction to drugs that afflicted the nation after the war. There was also widespread condemnation of the war by the international community, including some US allies, such as Britain, that flatly refused to assist President Johnson in his military intervention in Southeast Asia. Finally, there were the political effects of two incidents. The first was the Tet Offensive launched in January 1968 by North Vietnam to force the withdrawal of US forces from South Vietnam.[427] Even though the Communist forces suffered more casualties in the attack, the political effects of the Tet Offensive ranked as a defeat for the United States and a victory for North Vietnam and its Vietcong allies in South Vietnam. The second incident was the embarrassing episode at My Lai in March 1968, when the massacre of more than three hundred Vietnamese civilians by US soldiers was covered up for eighteen months by US army officials.[428] The political effects of these incidents were replicated in the Iraq War by the torture of detainees at Abu Ghraib and Guantanamo Bay prisons and in secret prisons maintained by the CIA overseas. Apparently, members of Congress did not factor these lessons into their debates and votes on the resolution. Their failure to do so worked together with the status of the United States as the lone superpower to leave President Bush freer to launch a preventive war than he would have otherwise. Not only did it contribute to his rush to war, but it also contributed to his failure to prepare adequately for it and for peace and reconstruction.

Consequences of the Iraq Resolution

When the 107th Congress granted President George W. Bush the authority to decide at his own discretion on a war against Iraq, it departed unnecessarily from a major tradition of American foreign policy: War is to be waged as a last resort after diplomacy, moral suasion, and other means of conflict resolution had been exhausted. In doing so, it allowed itself to be entrapped by a president who had already made up his mind to go to war without exhausting diplomacy and other means of conflict resolution. Bush was therefore emboldened by the 107th Congress to give lip service to multilateral diplomacy at the United Nations and to rush to war in defiance of the United Nations Security Council. He did so when there was no imminent threat from Iraq to the security of the United States. His rush to war was ideologically driven: to implement his doctrine of preemptive war and to acquire capital for domestic political advantage. Bush rushed to such war without adequately calculating and preparing for its economic and political consequences, including the credibility of the US Congress and government. Nor did he seriously contemplate or plan an exit strategy. His doctrine of preemptive, actually preventive, war itself was denounced by most members of the international community. In the case of Iraq the doctrine of preemptive war was inappropriate, for Iraq obviously had posed no imminent danger to the security of the United States. Rather, in that case, the Bush administration was seeking authority from the 107th Congress to wage an unlawful preventive war.

It is clear that, by authorizing the Bush administration to initiate a preventive war that is so radical a departure from American tradition and one that was condemned by most members of the international community, the 107th Congress allowed itself to become a collaborator with it in exchanging the US "long-established reputation as the principal *stabilizer* of the international system for one that serves as its chief *destabilizer*."[429] The US Congress's reputation as a seasoned deliberative body was severely damaged at home and abroad by the rush to pass the Bush administration's draft resolution authorizing a preventive war in Iraq.

Obviously, the Iraq Resolution of October 2002 was a major failing of the US Congress, because its esteemed members failed to show an administration that was apparently eager to degrade the rule of law and to resort to violence an alternative strategy of protecting US national security. Those members had solid constitutional authority to do so but abdicated their responsibility. Their authorization of the administration to wage war in Iraq fostered its attempts to resuscitate the imperial presidency, reminiscent of that of the Richard M. Nixon administration and the Watergate scandal. The policy to go to war was conceived in secrecy and deception, out of exaggerated propaganda, fear mongering, and manipulation of intelligence to suit policy and neoconservative ideology rather than the security interests of the United States. For partisan interests and political advantage, Congress tolerated the policy and gave it a great fillip.

George Galloway, a British legislator, accused of illegal payments in the United Nations' Iraq Oil-for-Food Program by the Senate Permanent Subcommittee on Investigations looking into scandals in the program, lambasted the US Senate on its own grounds in Washington, D.C., on the probe. The British legislator told the subcommittee members that their probe was "the mother of all smoke screens" to divert attention from the "real scandal": US policy in Iraq. He described the subcommittee chairman, Senator Norm Coleman, as a "pro-war neocon hawk and the lickspittle of George W. Bush," who, he said, sought revenge against anyone who did not support his invasion of Iraq. He went further to proclaim,

> Now, I know that standards have slipped in the last few years in Washington, but for a lawyer, you are remarkably cavalier with any idea of justice.... Most people think the villains of the piece in Iraq are not the [UN Secretary General] Kofi Annan and the [French President Jacques] Chirac but here in Washington and in the White House and in the Republican majority."[430]

The Iraq Resolution and the consequent war it authorized brewed a perfect stormy confrontation not only between the United States and its Western European allies but also between it and the United Nations. The pity of it all is that the United States had cooperated actively with the major powers of Western Europe, including its carefully built North Atlantic Treaty Organization, during the cold war to keep the Soviet Union at bay. Perhaps, more importantly, it had played the leading role to establish the United Nations, among other reasons, to promote international cooperation, peace, and security through peaceful settlement of disputes and to save humanity from the scourge of wars. The Bush administration's defiance of the world organization not only humiliated and marginalized the organization and devastated any prestige it had but also demonstrated that "absolute power corrupts absolutely."

The Bush administration's humiliation of the organization contradicted sharply with the praises his father, George H. W. Bush, as president of the United States, had heaped upon it during the first Gulf War. At that time, President George H. W. Bush commended the United Nations for performing "as envisioned by its founders." The organization, he said, was backing up its words with actions and had taken decisive steps to ensure compliance with its resolutions.[431] Thus, the UN is honored when it performs as envisioned by its founders but humiliated and vilified when it refuses to be the lap dog of a US administration. This vilification and humiliation of the United Nations resulted in a perfect storm of global rejection of US leadership that had been taken for granted since the end of World War II. Furthermore, because of the fallout from the Iraq war, the Bush administration lost a good measure of diplomatic leverage to pursue its foreign policy goals through the United Nations. Its decision to sidestep the organization in the Iraq war intensified resistance to using the threat of multinational sanctions and military force as a tool of diplomacy in the nuclear weapons disputes with Iran and North Korea. It also contributed to the opposition of the Sudanese government to a proposed UN peacekeeping mission to Darfur, Sudan, because that government feared that the mission might result in another Iraq.

Apart from the antipathy it provoked between the United States and the United Nations, the war in Iraq authorized by Congress precipitated a collapse of support for the United States abroad and dissipated the near universal sympathy generated earlier for the nation by the 11 September 2001 terrorist bombings on its territory. It generated worldwide anti-America resentment, as most of the world, including Europe, complained that the Bush administration was wielding great power without great responsibility and saw President Bush as a greater threat to world security than Saddam Hussein. President Jacques Chirac of France asserted that the world had become less safe after the US conquest and occupation of Iraq. Other overseas critics charged that, under George W. Bush, the United States had become an imperial power that was using its military power to build a global empire, impose its values, and assure access to oil and other resources. After he spoke with eloquence in his second inaugural address about expanding freedom, the leading Green newspaper in Germany responded with the headline: "Bush Threatens More Freedom."[432] Here is how one observer portrayed the expression of an anti-Bush sentiment in Europe:

> When I saw Bush booed and whistled (whistling being the European boo) at the Pope John Paul II's funeral, and realized that people devout and grief-stricken enough to brave those crowds to attend their religious leader's last rites felt moved even in that

solemn context to tell the international cameras what they thought about the American president, it occurred to me—not for the first time, but more strikingly than ever—that most of the world would not buy a used car or a Bill of Rights from this man.

A president who was respected around the world would make a far more effective pitchman for our values. Bush does not have the world's respect, and it's very hard to imagine he'll gain it by the time he leaves office. This isn't just some woolly-eyed plaint. It's a ground-level real-world problem…. The world's despots have a handy straw man at their disposal as long as Bush is president.[433]

The ramifications and consequences of the Bush administration's rush to war in Iraq for Iraq, the entire Middle East, the United States, and the international community generally are discussed in chapter 10. Here, it suffices to identify a few of those consequences. According to Swedish Foreign Minister Jan Eliasson, president of the UN General Assembly (2005–2006), postwar Iraq had become a "bleeding wound in world Politics" for which "everyone is paying a price."[434] UN Secretary General Kofi Annan himself asserted that most of the leaders of the Middle East believe that the US-led invasion of Iraq has been a real disaster that has destabilized the entire region.[435] Although the authorized war was, as expected, easily won, and the country tenuously occupied, it stirred profound passions at home and abroad as the administration could not impose peace and political stability on the occupied territory. Large-scale breakdown in public order occurred in Iraq following the collapse of Saddam's regime. Failure by an insufficient number of deployed American troops to secure the ammunition dumps and to control looting and civil disobedience in Baghdad created a climate of impunity and encouraged criminal violence and street crime unknown under the Saddam regime. The level of terrorism, later surpassed by sectarian violence, has not been reduced; instead, it has increased.[436] This situation, in turn, seriously undermined support for the coalition authorities and the willingness of the Iraqis to cooperate with them, as indigenous insurgents, driven by their own ideology and supported by outsiders, dug in, spreading death and violence through roadside and suicide bombings.

Studies by the Saudi government and an Israeli think tank found that foreign fighters in Iraq were not terrorists before the war but were radicalized by the war itself.[437] The International Institute for Strategic Studies (London) said the occupation of Iraq has provided a "potent global recruitment pretext" for al-Qaeda and probably has increased worldwide terrorism.[438] The CIA corroborated these findings. In May 2005, it reported that Iraq had become a magnet for Islamic militants and a terrorist training ground. This was so to the extent that the agency said that it believed that the Iraqi insurgency "poses an international threat and may produce better trained Islamic terrorists than the 1980s Afghanistan war that gave rise to Osama bin Laden and al-Qaeda. Once the insurgency ends," the agency said, "the Islamic militants are likely to disperse battle-hardened combatants capable of operating throughout the Arab[ic] speaking world and in other regions including Europe."[439] This conclusion was echoed by the Royal Institute of International Affairs (London). The Institute reported (after the 7 July 2005 terrorist bombings that killed fifty-five people in London and wounded many more) that the Iraq War had boosted recruitment and fund-raising for al-Qaeda. The war, it added, had proved costly in terms of US and British military lives, Iraqi lives, military expenditure, and the damage caused by the counterterrorism campaign.[440]

Capping these findings was a US National Intelligence Estimate completed in April 2006, portions of which concluded that the Iraq war had diffused a new generation of Islamic fundamentalism and Jihad ideology and had worsened the overall terrorism problem since the 11 September 2001 terrorist attacks. It had fanned Islamic radicalism and was providing a training ground for lethal methods that were increasingly being exported to other countries.[441]

The authorized war allowed autocrats in the Middle East to use post-Saddam chaos in Iraq as a justification for denying their people more freedom. "With us," the autocrats say, "life is stable and predictable. Without us, we will reap the whirlwind. Without us, radical fundamentalists will take our place."[442] The hopeful movement for democracy in Iran went into remission after the authorized invasion of Iraq. According to some experts, "Some Middle Eastern countries may be provoking a degree of instability in Iraq because they do not want a democracy on their doorsteps...and may not want to see Washington succeed in its experiment to remake the Middle East to its liking."[443] Saudi rulers, close friends of the Bush administration, are alarmed by the impact of developments in Iraq on their kingdom. They make no secret of their concerns that, after the Iraq War, large numbers of their citizens began to receive a free and highly practical education in revolutionary insurgency in Iraq.

The invasion of Iraq was supposed to send a message to Iran and North Korea that there would be severe consequences if they continued their nuclear weapons program. The two of the three countries President Bush identified as comprising an axis of evil, whose weapons of mass destruction capability surpassed that of Iraq, continue their nuclear weapons programs. While the two nations accelerated their programs during and after the Iraq War, the United States, which had warned them of severe consequences if they did so, became so bogged down in Iraq that it is either cautious or unable to issue a credible threat militarily against them.

Fuller details of the legacy of the war in Iraq authorized by the 107th Congress of the United States will be provided by future historians and political analysts. Presently, the following conclusions are reasonably warranted. Throughout the world, outside the United States, confidence in the propriety and purposes of US power dropped precipitously as a consequence of the war. So far, it has shown little sign of recovery. In waging the war without an internationally accepted legal basis or the backing of the traditional allies of the United States, the Bush administration, with the nod of the 107th Congress, "undermined Washington's long-held commitment to international law, its acceptance of consensual decision-making, its reputation for moderation, and its identification with the preservation of peace. The road back will be a long and hard one."[444]

The resentment of Americans as occupiers instead of the expected bouquets of flowers that were to greet them as liberators has persisted, even beyond Iraq, to the rest of the Muslim world. The enormous effort the Bush administration has devoted to public diplomacy in the Islamic world—increasing educational and cultural exchanges, putting US officials on media that reach the Arab world, and building working relations with Arab and Muslim advocates for democracy—has not appreciably improved the American image in Muslim societies. Perhaps, this is largely because the US invasion, conquest, and occupation of Iraq alienated Muslim societies and turned the country into a deeply alluring target for anti-American rage among Islamic fundamentalists, if not the entire Muslim world. Ironically, a review by the *Washington Post* of Internet postings paying tribute to the suicide "martyrs" in Iraq showed that most of the foreign terrorists wreaking mayhem there came from Saudi Arabia. This is the nation the United States protected from Saddam Hussein's army in the first Gulf War.[445] It is also the homeland of Osama bin Laden and fifteen of the nineteen terrorist bombers of 11 September 2001, a country that, according to Senator Bob Graham's account, had actively supported the activities of the bombers.[446] Finally,

> If the consequences [of the Bush administration's rush to war in Iraq] in the years to come will not be as disastrous as they were for Southeast Asia, it will be because of good fortune, not because President Bush articulated persuasive reasons for war, and not, because Congress fulfilled its constitutional duties. [It certainly did not.] The political process followed in 2003 did great harm to a "republic." The experience left us with a question: Do we still have an interest in living in—and fighting for—representative democracy? If not, how can we pretend to advise other countries on how to establish democratic regimes?[447]

Chapter 10
The War in Iraq and
Its Consequences

The story of the Iraq War is a story of ideas about the role of the United States in the world, and of the individuals who conceived and acted on them.... The manner in which the country argued with itself seemed wholly inadequate to the scale of what [it got] into.

The Bush administration took on the largest foreign policy project in a generation with little planning or forethought. It occupied a foreign country of 25 million people in the heart of the Middle East pretty much on the fly.... Swaddled in abstract ideas...indifferent to accountability, those in positions of highest responsibility for Iraq turned a difficult undertaking into a needlessly deadly one. When things went wrong they found other people to blame.[448]

Across the last 60 years, wars have been waged to no purpose. Millions of civilians have been killed. Enemies have been empowered, not defeated. That history is denied with every national budget drawn to give primacy to weapons, at the expense of humane investments that attack structures of violence at the source. The only justification for these terrible wars today will be if they lead to new thinking tomorrow.[449]

President Bush contemplated and, in fact, publicly articulated the idea of a unilateral preemptive war to enforce UN Security Council resolutions requiring Iraq to destroy its weapons of mass destruction. He was particularly determined to bring about "regime change" in the Persian Gulf state. By the summer of 2002, he had made up his mind to do so. A secret Downing Street Memo leaked to the *Times of London* during the British parliamentary elections in May 2005 affirms this. "Bush," the memo revealed, "wanted to remove Saddam, through military action, justified by the conjunction of terrorism and WMD. But," adds the memo,

the intelligence and facts were being fixed around the policy. The NSC had no patience with the UN route, and no enthusiasm for publishing material on the Iraqi regime's record.... The US had already begun "spikes of activity" to put pressure on the regime. There was little discussion in Washington of the aftermath after military action.[450]

Secretary of State Colin Powell persuaded Bush, against the advice of Vice President Dick Cheney and Defense Secretary Donald Rumsfeld, to approach diplomatically the issue of disarming Iraq of its weapons of mass destruction through the UN Security Council. In the meantime, the international community, including America's European allies, France and Germany, in addition to Russia and the People's Republic of China, refused to endorse Bush's pronouncements and intentions on Iraq because of their own specific interests and the danger and precedent the Bush policy would establish. It was under this atmosphere that the issue was submitted to and debated within the UN Security Council.

To emphasize its resolve to carry out its intentions on Iraq and to assure the world that the nation was united on the issue, the administration drafted a resolution that it submitted to Congress to pass to authorize it to pursue its intentions on Iraq. After a time-constrained and unscrupulous debate in the midst of an impending political election, and after modification of the draft resolution, Congress resolved to give the president the authority to decide to go to war in Iraq. However, as international opposition and internal division within the administration persisted, the Security Council continued its debate on disarming Iraq of its assumed weapons of mass destruction. Before the UN organ, US Secretary of State Colin Powell, with Director of Central Intelligence George Tenet sitting beside him, made an eloquent and impassioned presentation, "documenting" Iraq's deceptions, and continued possession and production of weapons of mass destruction.[451] Eventually, the UN Security Council Resolution 1441 was unanimously adopted, fifteen to zero, calling upon Iraq to comply with UN demands and to allow UN inspectors into its territory in order to resolve the issues raised by the Bush administration diplomatically.

For three months, the inspectors did their work meticulously. They ordered the destruction of some missiles but were unable to find any weapons of mass destruction. Impatient with the inspection process and what it resolutely insisted was Iraq's noncompliance with UN Security Council resolutions requiring it to disarm, the Bush administration ultimately decided on a policy of war with its so-called "coalition of the willing," the most militarily significant of which was Britain, to enforce UN sanctions and to disarm Iraq. At the persistence of its most ardent supporter, British Prime Minister Tony Blair, who was intent on saving his political neck in London for supporting the Bush administration, it reluctantly sought a second resolution to authorize the disarming of Iraq by force. Unable to muster the required nine votes in the Security Council to adopt such a resolution and faced with a veto threat from France and Russia, the Bush administration withdrew the resolution. On 19 March 2003, Bush launched a war on Iraq amidst great division at home and even greater resistance abroad.

In launching the war in defiance of the UN, President Bush acted against the cautionary exhortation that President Harry S. Truman had delivered to the nation at the conclusion of the 1945 San Francisco Conference that established the United Nations. On that occasion, President Truman exhorted his fellow Americans "to recognize, no matter how great our strength, that we must deny ourselves the license to do always as we please. This is the price," he added, "which each nation will have to pay for world peace. Unless we pay that price, no organization for world peace can accomplish its purpose. And what a reasonable price that is."[452] Thus, Truman understood from the birth of the UN what the Bush administration, fifty-eight years later, was unwilling to concede: "that the benefits of international cooperation are well worth the cost."[453]

The Bush Administration's Policy Approach to the War in Iraq

The premise of the Bush administration's foreign policy in general was that, as the only remaining superpower, the United States no longer needed cumbersome alliances and international institutions to pursue its foreign policy goals. It could act unilaterally to reshape world politics. Instead of waiting for enemies to attack the homeland, it would preemptively strike them overseas. Instead of negotiating with hostile regimes, it could just replace them. Democracy would produce transforming effects in the greater Middle East "not seen since the days of Aladdin."[454]

The buildup to the war in Iraq provides copious evidence of the George W. Bush administration's approach to foreign policy. A review of the administration's National Security Strategy (2002), as well as several publications on the administration and the war in Iraq by the *New York Times*, summarizes significant elements of that approach. This text relies heavily here on that review and similar sources, such as the piece in *Foreign Affairs* (March–April 2006) by a former CIA officer, Paul R. Pillar.[455]

The buildup to the war in Iraq reflects the administration's penchant for out-of-channels policy making, as well as its subordination of policy to political consideration. It also symbolized Bush's yearning to leave a lasting mark on US foreign policy by being an "event-making leader who by himself changed the course of history." His grand strategy after the terrorist attacks of 11 September 2001, his reduction of US reliance on permanent alliances and international institutions, his expansion of the traditional right of preemption into a new doctrine of preventive war, and his emphasis on spreading democracy and reshaping the Middle East by bringing about a regime change by military force in Iraq are all a manifestation of this longing.[456] Thus, Bush and his foreign policy principals "held almost constant crisis-atmosphere meetings, making decisions on the fly" after the terrorist attacks on US territory on 11 September 2001. "Instead of proposals gradually rising up through the normal layers of government, they were introduced and imposed from above. Debate was short-circuited."[457]

The usual channels for intelligence assessment were sidelined too, contributing to prewar assertions that Saddam Hussein possessed weapons of mass destruction. Because the Bush White House preferred intelligence acolytes to analysts and saw ulterior motives in any policy criticism, an intelligence unit—the Office of Special Plans—was set up in the Pentagon as an alternative to the CIA. The major purpose of the unit was to find evidence of what Vice President Dick Cheney, Defense Secretary Rumsfeld, and his Deputy Paul Wolfowitz believed to be true—Saddam Hussein had close ties to al-Qaeda, and Iraq had an enormous arsenal of chemical, biological, and possibly even nuclear weapons. "Much of what the unit reviewed was raw data, unvetted by intelligence professionals; it was cherry-picked for its usefulness in supporting the hawks' ideé fixés about Iraq…and then stovepiped to the President."[458]

The result was that before the invasion the administration inadvertently or deliberately failed to provide the American people the true state of Iraq's program for the development of weapons of mass destruction. Incredibly, it also ignored the need to obtain for itself a clear picture of Iraqi public opinion as well as a history of the country —critically, a realization of the depth of the fault lines in Iraqi society between Kurds and Arabs, Sunnis and Shiites, and members of other ethnic and religious groups—it was about to conquer and occupy, before it embarked on the United States' most ambitious nation-building experiment since the end of World War II.

As a consequence of a number of factors, including Vice President Cheney's enormous power and the influence he exerted on President Bush, bureaucratic fighting between the Defense and State Departments, and the reluctance of Bush's national security adviser, Condoleezza Rice, "to knock heads, " the role of the National Security Council in advising the president and forging interagency consensus was diminished in the days before the war was launched. Essential decision making and planning for the war did not take place in "the statutory process of the NSC but in the parallel process run by Vice President Cheney, who had assembled his own national security staff of 14 and had maintained direct ties to his old friend Donald Rumsfeld at the Pentagon."[459]

For the war, a "decision was not made—a decision happened, and you can't say when or how." The top leaders were often at odds among themselves. Thus, a real weighing of pros and cons about the war never took place. "It was an accretion, a tipping point."[460] According to Bob Woodward's *Plan of Attack*, Condoleezza Rice was the only member of the administration's national security team that President Bush said he asked whether she thought he should go to war in Iraq. "He knew what Cheney thought, he said, and he decided not to ask Colin Powell or Donald Rumsfeld because he could tell what they thought."[461]

It is plausible that President Bush did not ask such question because he and his top advisers had deliberately reinforced each other on the decision for war in Iraq. The neocon advisers had insisted even before Bush became president that removing Saddam Hussein from power had become the aim of American foreign policy. Bush's immediate predecessor, President Clinton, had rejected such advice from them in 1998. As president, Bush readily embraced the objective. He gave its authors a green light to start war preparations when he signaled them to do so, even before he said in his State of the Union address in January 2002 that the United States was prepared to deal preemptively with nations he considered part of an "axis of evil." The publication (later in the year) of his administration's National Security Strategy of the United States of America, prepared by the same advisers, delighted the neoconservatives, who consequently increased their pressure on the president to launch a war for regime change in Iraq. The result was a massive military buildup in the Persian Gulf from which President Bush could not easily retreat.

What is even more striking is that the administration, upon all its elaborate and sustained case for war, had not requested the CIA to prepare a National Intelligence Estimate on the rationale for its case for war against Iraq, including the military and post-invasion occupation expectations. Rather, it only asked the agency for a document that could be used to make a public case for the invasion of the country.[462] The Senate Intelligence Committee, which requested such an estimate in September 2002, was stunned that the administration was about to plunge the nation into a war without the best, unvarnished, and unbiased information by which to judge the war's necessity and ramifications. From this, Senator Bob Graham, who was the chair of the Committee at the time, wrote that it seemed clear to him that Bush and his national security advisers "had made up their minds to go to war and didn't want to take the chance that additional facts might show that decision to be flawed, raise questions about the credibility of their claims, or otherwise put their agenda in doubt."[463]

By many accounts, preparations for the occupation of Iraq were even more cavalier and disorganized than the decision for the war. The administration did not understand, and made no deliberate effort to understand, the scope of the problem that would confront Iraq once Saddam was removed from power. Initially, little thought was given to the aftermath of the war. Planning efforts for the occupation, when they began, were undertaken in several different parts of the executive bureaucracy with little or no coordination. Defense Secretary Rumsfeld was known to be disengaged from the nuts and bolts of occupying and reconstructing Iraq.[464] President Bush himself was described as being aloof and distant from the postwar planning. The administration cavalierly assumed that Iraq would be transformed without any extraordinary US efforts. Instead of mobilizing the entire US government to ensure that the hard questions regarding the invasion were asked and answered, the administration's principal neocon advisers deliberately ignored available expertise, including that from the CIA and the Department of State. Furthermore, the Bush White House apparently paid little or no attention to prewar assessments by the CIA that warned of major cultural and political obstacles to stability in postwar Iraq. This it did because its senior officials "simply weren't ready to pay attention to analysis that didn't conform to their own optimistic scenarios."[465]

Colin Powell's former chief of staff, Col. Lawrence Wilkerson, wrote that, in dealing with Iraq, President Bush was "too aloof, too distant from the details of postwar planning," making it easy for underlings to exploit his detachment.[466] Besides, he failed to manage well the intelligence-gathering process before the war. He never sought second and third opinions or took unwelcome advice into account. Rather, his administration sought opinion mainly from people chosen on narrow grounds, including Iraqi exiles, who often were quite ignorant or were acting out of self-interest and so told the administration officials what they wanted or expected to hear in the hope of gaining political power after regime change in Iraq. Its rush to war, without preparing for a post-Saddam Iraq, was accompanied by a divisive diplomacy that tarnished the invasion's legitimacy and, consequently, international support for an extended occupation.

Hardliners within the administration frequently shrugged off arguments that dissented from their position and rosy postwar story lines that they envisaged. Similarly, expert advice, such as that by Army Chief of Staff General Eric K. Shinseki, General Anthony C. Zinni, and Economic Adviser Lawrence Lindsey, was ignored or rebuffed. General Shinseki testified before the Senate Armed Services Committee that postwar Iraq would require several hundred thousand soldiers but was rapidly shot down by Deputy Defense Secretary Wolfowitz, who asserted that the estimate was "wildly off the mark." General Shinseki was eventually sidelined.[467] General Zinni's contingency plan for Iraq should Saddam Hussein fall from power was dismissed by the civilian leaders of Pentagon as "too negative." And Lawrence Lindsey, who predicted that the war would cost as much as $200 billion, was quickly reprimanded and eventually dismissed from his position as Bush's economic adviser.

The administration's overly optimistic picture during the planning of the invasion is reflected in the prewar slide show by General Tommy Franks and his top officers on 15 August 2002. The slide show that reviewed the invasion plan cast Iraq in rosy hues. The slides projected a stable pro-American and democratic Iraq and presented a decidedly upbeat vision of what the country would look like after the ouster of Saddam Hussein from power: "A broadly representative Iraqi government would be in place. The Iraqi Army would be working to keep the peace. And the United States would have as few as 5,000 troops in the country."[468] The reality on the ground, prompting President Bush's decision to augment the 140,000 US troops deployed to the country with 21,500 more troops almost four years after the invasion, belied the projections and the general optimism portrayed by the prewar slide show as well as the Bush administration's assumptions that had laid the basis for an exercise in "preemptive" war.

In planning for the first Gulf War, as a last resort and a multilateral effort, President George H. W. Bush effectively used the United Nations to build a worldwide coalition against Iraq's conquest and annexation of Kuwait. Saddam Hussein was diplomatically isolated. Most of the world supported UN-imposed economic sanctions against Iraq, as well as the demand for the withdrawal of its forces from Kuwait. The conflict was not viewed as one between the United States and Iraq. It was seen mainly as Iraq against the world. Furthermore, Bush the elder's secretary of state, James Baker; National Security Adviser Brent Scowcroft; and Secretary Treasurer Nicholas Brady took into account the steep potential material cost of US leadership in the process of the conflict. To manage and minimize that cost, including the energy-related cost from lost Iraqi and Kuwaiti oil output and the cost of purely humanitarian effort, they met with many world leaders to underscore that the burden of that impending collective effort should be shared. That was indeed subsequently and magnificently done, so that the United States paid only a fraction of the total cost of the effort. Critical in producing these results, as in the success of the Cuban Missile Crisis, was the kind of diverse group, rather than a group of ideologues and cheerleaders, that President George H. W. Bush, just as President John F. Kennedy before him, had assembled to advise him.

The George W. Bush administration ignored this approach in the second Gulf War. His group of advisers were too preoccupied with their neoconservative conception of America's role in the twenty-first century to think through the critical aspects of the war. From the start, the administration antagonized most of the world by its unilateral and imperial approach. It underestimated the cost of the war, as well as the strength of the troops to prosecute it. As a consequence, the US military became overstretched by deployments in Iraq and elsewhere. This development and the difficulty in attracting recruits forced the Pentagon to keep thousands of soldiers and reservists in uniform beyond their release dates, with dangerous effects on the morale and psyche of several of them. Belatedly in January 2007, almost four years into the war, President Bush admitted the error and decided to commit 21,500 more troops to Iraq to pacify Baghdad and reverse what he described as an "unacceptable situation" in the country.[469]

Obviously, the administration did not adequately calculate the risks of launching the war and its aftermath. According to Bob Woodward's *Plan of Attack*, "As the war planning had progressed over nearly...16 months, [Colin] Powell had felt that the easier the war looked, the less Rumsfeld, the Pentagon and General [Tommy] Franks [the combatant commander for the Persian Gulf] had worried about the aftermath. They seemed to think that Iraq was a crystal goblet and that all they had to do was to tap it and it would crack."[470] Thus, the Bush administration avoided a more thorough discussion of the cost and risks of reconstructing Iraq after the war. Overly optimistic about such a task, the top officials asserted that Iraq had enough resources to fund its own reconstruction. The administration had no thorough counterinsurgency plan in the belief that US soldiers would be welcomed as liberators. As we now know, that was a miscalculation. In spite of the excessive burden of federal debt due largely to the administration's tax cuts, Congress has been called upon repeatedly to appropriate funds at the expense of taxpayers and domestic needs for the reconstruction of Iraq. A pertinent criticism was that the George W. Bush administration had rushed to war without a plan to win the peace.

After the fall of Baghdad, the administration adopted three parallel tracks for politics, economics, and security that it hoped would ensure victory in Iraq. The political and economic tracks sought to use democratic reforms and economic reconstruction to persuade the Iraqis to support the government in Baghdad and to oppose the insurgents. The third track, staying the course in Iraq, focused on creating Iraqi armed forces—military and police—that would assume the burden of counterinsurgency, so that, as Iraqi security forces stood up, the coalition forces could stand down.

Just as expert advice was ignored or shrugged off, ultimately, the media, in spite of their support for the administration's case for the war, not the administration's miscalculations in the war and the realities in Iraq, were considered by the Bush White House to be at fault for poisoning Americans' view of the war and for the sagging US national support for it. Thus, only the consequent   lack   of   fortitude   among   the   American   people,   in   the administration's view, could defeat America's awe-inspiring military in Iraq! Part of the blame game.

The administration resisted requests for information on its secret operations in the process of the war in Iraq and on terrorism that raised serious issues of civil liberties or human rights. Examples of such operations include the National Security Agency's compilation, for more than four years, of a massive database of phone calls by hundreds of millions of Americans, the agency's warrantless surveillance of phone calls between the United States and foreign countries, and the CIA's creation and operation of secret prisons overseas, where suspected terrorists were held without charge, due process of the law, or access to the International Red Cross. To such requests for information, President Bush invariably asserted curtly, and even imperiously, that such operations were legal, even as his administration moved quickly to head off any intervention by Congress. The administration countenanced a public debate on such secret operations only to the extent that it could be "put to partisan use, as a means of casting Democratic critics as weak on national security."[471]

The Bush policy on the war in Iraq sidelined America's major European allies and shifted the strategic focus of US concerns from Europe to the Middle East and East Asia. At the same time, the invasion, conquest, and occupation of Iraq seemed to have convinced the leaders of North Korea and Iran of the urgent necessity to have their own nuclear capability as a means of deterring US invasion. Their possession of such a capability would constitute a failure of the Bush administration's larger strategy of combating the spread of weapons of mass destruction.

Finally, in planning for the war, the Bush administration failed totally to take into account the legacy of Western colonialism in the Middle East and elsewhere. It ignored the deep suspicion about US motives and the deep resentment in the Arab world of US support for Israel in the latter's conflict with Palestinians. This pattern of behavior, in conjunction with events in Iraq and the Bush administration's policy elsewhere in the Middle East, produced a fertile environment breeding a variety of species of anti-Americanism from European condescension to Latin American historical resentment and murderous jihadist impulses in the Middle East. This is so in spite of President Bush's appointment of Karen Hughes to the newly created office of assistant secretary of state for public diplomacy and public affairs to reshape foreign perception of the United States. Unfortunately, "foreigners now blame not just the US government but the American people for the policies they dislike.... A majority of Europeans think that the world would be better off if a second great power, like the European Union, were to challenge American primacy."[472]

Perhaps, by more careful and meticulous planning, the Bush administration might have created a playing field different from the one which produced this perception and desire and the one in which not only sectarian violence has surged but also Jihadists have increased in both number and geographic dispersion.

US Conquest and Occupation of Iraq

The war, launched by the Bush administration on 19 March 2003, was a one-sided affair. Iraq had been severely weakened and exhausted by its eight-year war with Iran (1980–1988), its humiliating defeat in Kuwait three years later, and thirteen long years of UN sanctions. Furthermore, Saddam Hussein had not been fully convinced that the Bush administration would mount a war against his country. Thousands of documents captured during the war and interviews with dozens of senior Iraqi officials, including Deputy Prime Minister Tariq Aziz, revealed that Hussein had been very confident that the Bush administration would not dare to invade Iraq.[473] He believed that Russia and France, each of which had veto power in the UN Security Council and had secured millions of dollars worth of trade and service contracts in Iraq, would prevent US invasion. Furthermore, Saddam was convinced that, even if the Bush administration did invade Iraq, he and his regime would survive. Fed a stream of lies by his frightened underlings, Saddam focused mainly on internal, rather than external, security. Such a behavior made the outcome of the US invasion a foregone conclusion.

Thus, within a few weeks of the invasion, US forces captured Baghdad in April 2003. The Saddam regime was history. Saddam's sons were killed, and he himself was captured and imprisoned later in December 2003. Three years later, he was executed on 30 December 2006 after trial and conviction. Many Iraqis hailed his capture and ouster from power. Aboard a US aircraft carrier, President Bush proclaimed to the American people and the world generally that the mission had been accomplished.

Developments on the ground and the reality in Iraq belied the proclamation. The American "mission" in Iraq as conceived by President Bush, had not been accomplished. Rather, the war to accomplish it was, in fact, just beginning. There was widespread looting, civil disruption, economic chaos, and instability in Iraq. More than one hundred sites of weapons of mass destruction that had been identified by UN weapons inspectors were left unguarded and consequently were systematically looted by the Iraqis. Iraqi police officers abandoned their posts by the tens of thousands. In the resulting security vacuum, mobs looted government ministries and burned police stations and government ministries. American troops stood by, having received no orders to stop the looting.[474]

This chaotic situation was accompanied by a strong Iraqi resistance movement to the US occupation The Sunnis and jihadists who descended upon Iraq from other Muslim countries in the region embarked upon a large-scale insurgency and lawlessness, contrary to the certainty with which Vice President Cheney and Deputy Defense Secretary Wolfowitz had claimed that US troops would be welcomed by the Iraqis as "liberators." Above all, embarrassingly, the Bush administration and its coalition of the willing failed to find any weapons of mass destruction in Iraq, their major rationale for the war. Many experts believe that it was unlikely that the type of weapons of mass destruction that agitated the Bush administration ever existed, or, if they did, they had been destroyed by UN weapons inspectors. The administration immediately adjusted its rationale for the war: It was part of the global war against terrorism and was to promote representative government, democracy, and human rights in the greater Middle East. The White House had concluded that arguing about why the United States invaded Iraq was a political loser.

Critics of the administration were not convinced by its adjusted rationale for the war. Terrorism, to which the administration linked its war on Iraq, has political roots. It is a politically motivated violence committed against a nation's civilian or noncombatant targets, including its economic infrastructure, by clandestine agents or disaffected subnational groups. Its solution requires more than reciprocal violence but should include change or a modification of the policies that comprise its underlying political roots. There was no evidence or intention of this in the Bush administration's policy. Nor was there any credible evidence linking Iraq to terrorist attacks on US territory or security interest overseas. Therefore, if the Iraq War was part of the global war on terrorism, as President Bush proclaimed, then his administration had committed a fundamental error when it defied the UN Security Council and launched a war against Iraq. In doing so, it failed to recognize the international dimension of terrorism and that, ultimately, most progress against terrorists depends on the perspectives and behavior of other governments, groups, publics, and individuals.

Responsibility for postwar reconstruction was entrusted to the Department of Defense rather than, traditionally, at least since the end of World War II, the Department of State. Neoconservatives in Donald Rumsfeld's Department of Defense rejected the Department of State's exhaustive postwar planning, just as they had rejected top army officials' prewar estimates of the number of troops needed to establish stability in Iraq after the war. The Pentagon hoped to transfer power swiftly to its favorite leader of the Iraqi National Resistance, Ahmed Chalabi, who had fed it with false information about Iraq's alleged weapons of mass destruction. However, it soon found out that Chalabi was not at all popular among the Iraqis. Subsequently, the lead function of writing a new Constitution and building a democratic government was allocated to the coalition led by the United States, christened the Coalition Provisional Authority. The authority was placed under an American proconsul, Paul Bremer, a senior Department of State official. An Iraqi Governing Council was appointed to work at the direction of Bremer.

Bremer's policies, among them to disband the Iraqi army and to exclude the Sunnis from political offices, albeit approved by Defense Secretary Rumsfeld, fueled the insurgency.[475] High-ranking US military officers had warned that dissolving the Iraqi army would be a disaster and also had questioned the wisdom of his de-Baathification policy. As warned, his de-Baathification not only left most institutions in Iraq shorn of expertise and leadership, also it left many mid-level Sunni civilian and military officials unemployed, humiliated, and attracted to the ranks of the insurgents. The vacuum his de-Baathification and dissolution of the security forces created immediately elevated the most reactionary conservative forces—clerics and ethnic leaders—to political influence in Iraqi society. By June 2004, as US casualties in the occupied country increased, the Iraqi Governing Council was disbanded. It was replaced by an interim Iraqi government with a prime minister, a Shiite, Iyad Allawi, selected by the US administration, while general elections were planned for, and subsequently held in, January 2005. In the meantime, most elements of real sovereignty in the country remained in American hands.

US troops, to date (January 2007), have been mainly responsible for maintaining security in Iraq. Confronting increasing political difficulty in keeping their forces in an unpopular war in Iraq, the European members of Bush's coalition of the willing informed him late in 2004 of their decision to withdraw their troops completely from Iraq. In view of this, and as the insurgency in Iraq grew in intensity, President Bush began to shift his strategy away from pressing his European allies to "join or remain in the American-led force in Iraq."[476] Instead, he decided to seek to work more closely with them in other initiatives in the entire Middle East and Persian Gulf. Such cooperation focused on planting the seeds of reform across much of the Muslim world, providing economic support for Iraq, providing political backing and legitimacy for whatever government emerged from Iraq's first competitive national elections in more than four decades, and diminishing terrorist threats common to the United States and Europe.

The administration's policy persistently remained to stay the course and train more Iraqi forces, so that, as they stand up and progressively take control over more and more territory in their country, US troops will stand down. This central premise, that as Iraqi armed forces are trained and equipped to secure their own country American troops will be withdrawn, is President Bush's attempt to replicate the Richard M. Nixon administration's policy of Vietnamization of the Vietnam War. However, how long it will take the Iraqis to stand up is yet unknown.[477] Some, especially the police, within 260,000 trained security forces, suffered from corruption and the influence of militias.[478] The Bush administration had not put enough focus on the police. What attempts there were to train the police were marred by poor coordination. Some of the other forces trained by American armed forces to work for the Interior Ministry actually did the bidding of Shiite political and religious leaders. They harassed, kidnapped, and murdered people who espoused different religious practices or supported competing politicians. They did so often with weapons and equipment provided by the forces of the American-led coalition of the willing that had very different objectives in mind. For their part, "Sunni forces, working for the Ministry of Defense, who were supposed to be guarding Iraq's oil pipeline were instead freelancing as death squads, assassinating people who cooperated with the same government that paid the gunmen's salaries."[479]

The result was increased sectarian violence in the country, causing, by UN estimate, the deaths of at least one hundred Iraqi civilians every day, the overwhelming majority of them in Baghdad. From all indications—the evidence of brutal and lawless elements within the military and civilian police forces, numerous private militias, redoubtable insurgents and jihadists, for example—the country appears to some observers to be in a civil war among the armed groups competing to impose order on their own terms.[480] Testifying before the Senate Armed Services Committee on 3 August 2006, senior American military commanders pointedly warned that Iraq was heading towards civil war. Their testimony undercut the Bush administration's strategy of Iraqification of the war. Thus, in August 2006, to stop the slide towards civil war, the administration decided to double the number of American troops in Baghdad to about 14,200 from about 7,200.[481] Later in the month, the marine corps recalled 2,500 of its forces to beef up security in the country. This deployment of more US troops failed to resolve the problem of sectarian violence, especially in Baghdad.

Since January 2005, two elections, the first for a provisional government, have been held. The Sunnis boycotted the first. The second, held in December 2005, followed the approval of a new Constitution. After a protracted period of about four months, it led to the formation of a government in May 2006. In effect, both elections, heralded by the Bush administration as milestones, advanced Iraq closer to a Shiite-led fundamentalist theory and apparent cooperation with the American arch antagonist Iran. The open question remained: How long will it take for the constitutional government to provide all its citizens with basic order and security? President Bush insisted he would stay the course in Iraq and said that he expected that his successor in office and the future governments of Iraq would determine how long American forces would remain in the country.[482] Such an expectation may be regarded as tantamount to an abdication of a responsibility President Bush had assumed by launching the war. But Bush insisted that, so long as he is the president, American troops will not withdraw from Iraq until the job is done.

While the majority of American forces in Iraq have performed their military duties honorably, a few brought agony and obloquy to American prestige in Iraq and around the world. The American people and the world with it were appalled by photographs showing American service men and women torturing Iraqi captives held at the Abu Ghraib prison. Less than two years later, a platoon of American marines in Haditha went berserk in November 2004 when one of its own was killed by a roadside improvised electronic device. The small group of American marines allegedly went on a rampage, searching, shooting, and killing at least two dozen Iraqis, including men, women, and children, in retaliation for the fatality.

Critics of the administration accused it of mishandling the occupation of Iraq. From the beginning, they argued, the occupation differed dramatically and consciously from other post–cold war nation-building efforts. For example,

> In Bosnia and Kosovo, the US military…quickly handed authority over most civilian matters to the United Nations, the State Department, and non-governmental organizations (NGOs) such as the Red Cross. But rather than follow [proven] previous experience and use experienced personnel, the Bush administration decided to do things differently. It chose to invade Iraq with a fraction of the troops that many senior military leaders thought necessary. It kept the United Nations, the State Department and the NGOs on the periphery, both in the planning process and in the administration of the country. In their place, it created the Coalition Provisional Authority CPA)…. It staffed the CPA with personnel drawn from the ranks of D.C. think tanks, law firms, and political appointees, many with more loyalty to the president than experience in the field…. During previous occupations, the UN headquarters in New York and the State Department's D.C. offices had served as the clearinghouses for plans and personnel. For Iraq, however, the nerve centers were Donald Rumsfeld's Pentagon and the politically connected law firms and lobbyists on K Street.[483]

The role of Secretary of Defense Donald Rumsfeld in the conduct and management of the war, including the occupation, was criticized by a number of members of Congress and military generals. Senators Edward Kennedy and Hillary Clinton, for example, repeatedly asked for his resignation. In an unprecedented manner in the United States, where the military is under civilian control, retired army and marine generals and many of their silent allies still in active service criticized Rumsfeld's planning and conduct of the war. They insisted that, in planning the war, Rumsfeld had "endangered the lives of his troops and [had] lost the trust of his officers by ignoring longstanding principles of warfare (for instance, how many are needed not just to fight battles but also to impose order afterwards) and by dismissing the advice of his commanders and shunning those that criticized his war plan."[484] The war itself, they continued, was unnecessary and a diversion from the main conflict with al-Qaeda. Retired Army Major General, Paul Eaton, who had been in charge of the program to train the Iraqi military, described the defense secretary as "incompetent strategically, operationally" and as a man who has "put the Pentagon at the mercy of his ego, his Cold Warrior's view of the world, and his unrealistic confidence in technology to replace manpower."[485]

In an opinion editorial in the *New York Times* (23 May 2005), Bob Herbert attributed the problems of US forces in Iraq to Rumsfeld:

> Much of what has happened to the military on [Rumsfeld's] watch has been catastrophic.... The generals are telling us now that the US is likely to be bogged down in Iraq for years, and there are whispers circulating about the possibility of "defeat.".... Parents from coast to coast are going out of their way to dissuade their children from joining the military. Recruiters, desperate, and in many cases emotionally distraught after repeatedly missing their monthly goals, began abandoning admission standards and signing up individuals who were physically, mentally or morally unfit for service.... The military spent decades rebuilding its reputation and regaining the respect of the vast majority of the American people after the debacle in Vietnam. Under...Rumsfeld, that hard-won achievement is being reversed. He invaded Iraq with few troops, and too many of them were poorly trained and inadequately equipped. The stories about American troops dying in the battlefield because of a lack of a protective armor have now been widely told.[486]

Judging by Rumsfeld's own statement that the "measure of success in this global war is whether the number our side is killing or deterring and dissuading every day is larger than the number the [terrorists] and the radical clerics are recruiting, training and deploying against us,"[487] the United States is doing poorly. In November 2003, the official number of terrorists was five thousand. By August 2006, the number had quadrupled to twenty thousand. Compounding this situation, in the view of critics, is the administration's lack of an exit strategy beyond staying the course. Its original justification for the war—the charge that Saddam Hussein possessed stockpiles of weapons of mass destruction that he might provide to terrorist enemies of the United States and its allies—evaporated, instead of confirming the charge and yielding the administration's expected international consensus that its diplomacy had failed to produce. And Congress had allotted hundreds of millions of dollars for the hunt of the alleged weapons of mass destruction that so far have not been found. Largely because of these failings and the administration's foreign policy and war in Iraq, forty-one US newspapers that had editorially endorsed Bush in the 2000 presidential election refused to do so in 2004. An editorial in the *Los Angeles Times* (1 November 2004) suggested,

> If elections were solely a job performance review, President George W. Bush [would] lose in a landslide. He has been a reckless steward of the nation's finances and its environment, a divisive figure at home and abroad. It's fair to say that Bush has devalued the American brand in the global marketplace.[488]

President Bush himself, after his reelection and a prolonged and persistent refusal to admit any personal mistake in the war in Iraq, eventually acknowledged major misjudgments in its execution. He admitted that he had spent on Iraq most of the political capital he claimed he had won in the 2004 presidential election.[489] In the spring of 2006, eighteen months after that reelection, Bush had become "the most powerless president of all time."[490] At a press conference in May 2006, he publicly acknowledged his administration's failure to plan sufficiently for the occupation and rebuilding of Iraq. These admissions were made after his public support had declined dramatically and he and his most ardent supporter in the war, British Prime Minister Tony Blair, politically were badly damaged at home and abroad by the war and the continuing violence in Iraq. The decision to invade Iraq proved to be a political albatross for both leaders, indeed, a misjudgment that had not only adversely affected their job approval ratings, but perhaps their legacies as well. The British news magazine, the *Economist*, pictured the two leaders on its cover page under the headline "Axis of Feeble."[491]

President Bush's current secretary of state and, formerly, his adviser on national security, Condoleezza Rice, also admitted that the administration made "thousands of tactical errors" in the Iraq War. The apparent weakening of public support for his administration forced President Bush and key members of his administration to make a series of speeches, perceived by some analysts as "political spin" to stabilize the president's job approval ratings, to convince the American people on the need "to stay the course" in Iraq.

Part of the political spin was the glowing commendation President Bush bestowed on Rumsfeld, in his opinion, for doing a commendable job in Iraq and for transforming the military. This was done in spite of contrary views.[492] Close to the 7 November 2006 mid-term elections, Bush announced that Rumsfeld would continue to serve as his secretary of defense until the end of his administration. In reality, by the time of the announcement, he had already decided to replace him. After the electorate, in effect, cast a vote of no confidence on the administration's performance in Iraq by transferring control of both chambers of Congress from the Republican to the Democratic party, Bush accepted Rumsfeld's resignation on 8 November, a day after the elections. At the same time he announced his nomination of former CIA director, Robert M. Gates, to replace him.[493]

Consequences of the War

Before the war began, Bush administration officials made the following predictions:

- We will find weapons of mass destruction
- Our armed forces shall be greeted as liberators
- A capable democratic government would quickly emerge in Iraq and spread to its neighbors
- US military presence would be modest and temporary
- Iraqi oil revenues would pay for Iraq's reconstruction
- The insurgency, initially denied, later, was said by Vice President Cheney to be in it's last throes

But in an opinion editorial in *Los Angeles Times* (11 February 2007), as the occupation of Iraq continued, former adviser on national security to former President Jimmy Carter, Zbigniew Brzezinski offered the following assessment:

THE WAR IN IRAQ is a historic strategic and moral calamity undertaken under false assumptions. It is undermining America's global legitimacy. Its collateral civilian casualties, as well as some abuses, are tarnishing America's moral credentials. Driven by Manichean impulses and imperial hubris, it is intensifying regional instability [The United States is now bogged down in a protracted and potentially expanding war] Initially justified by false claims about weapons of mass destruction in Iraq, the war is now being redefined as the decisive ideological struggle of our time, reminiscent of the earlier collisions with Nazism and Stalinism. In that context, Islamic extremism and Al Qaeda are presented as the equivalent of the threat posed by Nazi Germany and Soviet Russia, and 9/11 as the equivalent of the Pearl Harbor attack that precipitated U.S. involvement in World War II.[494]

In 2005, news of millions of Iraqis voting freely for a Constitution and a new national government shared leading television broadcasts and the front pages of major newspapers with stories describing the near-daily loss of

American and Iraqi lives. There also was evidence of stability and widespread unrest, economic recovery and ruin, political progress and alienation in the country. Almost everything said and written about the Persian Gulf country then and a year later in 2006 was true.[495] Truly, the invasion made a few positive achievements: the overthrow of the Saddam Hussein regime, although at great cost and without replacing its core institutions with stable new ones; the adoption of a new Constitution; the emergence of a stronger civil society and new political parties, leading to successful elections in January and December 2005; the installation of a new national government; the recruitment and training of new security forces; the stimulation of the growth of local self-government; and the establishment of a less dogmatic educational system.

But these do not presently outweigh the negatives of the war. The security forces trained and commanded by Americans are not yet able to operate independently without US forces. The police forces are largely controlled by local governments and have few, if any, viable links to the central government in Baghdad. Rather than diminish in influence and ferocity, the insurgency is on the increase, although it has been surpassed by sectarian violence as a menace to security. When the situation in the country appears to be improving, a spectacular act of violence brings the country to the edge of abyss, leaving it in a perpetual state of uncertainty. Thus, in spite of the presence in the country of 140,000 American troops as well as those from the other states that comprised the coalition of the willing, Iraq may be viewed as a failed state. Its government has so far failed to fulfil the fundamental functions of a state: insurance of law and order, provision of basic security for its citizens, as well as effective control of its territory and its inhabitants. Whatever real freedom the people had under Saddam Hussein has evaporated as Islamic fundamentalists, sponsored by political parties the American conquest and occupation brought to power, curtailed the rights of women and Christians. Hence, Kenneth Pollack, a former Persian Gulf analyst at the CIA, asserted that the US-led invasion of Iraq "created a failed state that has absolutely no capacity."[496] A report by the Saban Center for Middle East Policy at the Brookings Institution added: "The only thing standing between Iraq and descent into Lebanon-or Bosnian-style maelstrom is 140,000 American troops, and even they are merely slowing the fall at this point.[497]

As a spokesperson of the radical Shiite cleric Moqtada al-Sadr assessed the post-invasion situation, Iraq was better off under Saddam Hussein. According to the spokesperson Baha Al-Araji:

Saddam Hussein killed my father and my elder brother and jailed one of my brothers and my mother for a long time. Some of my family escaped Iraq and lived in exile, while others remained in the country. Now we are able to see, unfortunately, that the situation during Saddam's reign was better than today because then, the oppression was targeted and predictable. Today the danger and oppression overwhelm all Iraqi people without exception.[498]

This is after the George W. Bush administration had embarked upon the war in Iraq on the thesis of its hawkish neocon advisers that American military power could resolve most foreign policy problems. The Iraq War has demonstrated both the potency and the impotency of US military power[499] and that Bush and his neocon team had a totally unrealistic view of what they could accomplish with military force and threats of force. True, as the administration's Secretary of Defense Donald Rumsfeld had projected, Iraq was "shocked and awed," easily and swiftly overwhelmed. It was conquered and occupied. But it was not pacified. More than three years after the conquest and occupation, Iraq remains politically, economically, and socially unstable and seriously menaced by a major insurgency that the administration failed to anticipate and initially denied existed. Indeed, the stark reality was that, for the Iraqi people, tyranny was replaced by terrorism as many of them experienced a series of suicide bombings, roadside explosions, and attacks on mosques.[500] Under Saddam Hussein, they had lived in a police state with virtually no street crime for twenty-five years. They were therefore dismayed as murder, kidnapping, and rape soared after his removal. Obviously, the planners of the war had seriously underestimated the role the United States would play in the occupation and postwar reconstruction of the country. The neocon hawks, who started the war without the kind of broad international consensus that the United States had obtained during the first Gulf War, failed to appreciate the limited utility of hard power. Eventually, the swiftness of the US military victory contrasted vividly with the very slow pace of the administration's pacification, stabilization, and reconstruction of the conquered and occupied country.

This experience confirmed the view of military generals who considered the war militarily unwinnable. Other critics of the war argued that the United States was in Iraq because of the delusions of the Bush administration that "raw military power can resolve even the most complex transnational issues"; that the administration "is incapable of grasping the importance of real moral legitimacy in modern warfare; that without that legitimacy that can win over the hearts and minds of a world that has grown skeptical of the great powers' intervention in the developing world, even the most powerful military force in the world is likely to [become] dragged in a quagmire and, when it does, the public's weariness is entirely predictable. [This is] another error in post-war planning"[501] by the Bush administration.

The following is an excerpt from an e-mail to journalist Paul Reickhoff by a disgruntled American soldier describing the situation:

> The bottom line is, the overwhelming majority of people live in fear. We can do NOTHING [*sic*] to help them. We don't have anywhere near the manpower, and our actions are too severely restricted. Good thing 2500 people died for this. What are the good news? I would love to hear them. Spare me the heart warming tales of a single family or school or neighborhood that was helped. Operation Iraqi Freedom is, at this point, an abject failure. This is the most dangerous place on earth and it's getting worse, not better.[502]

In an interview he granted to the *Los Angeles Times* (6 March 2006), the Bush administration's ambassador to Iraq, Zalmay Khalilzad, candidly corroborated the postwar Iraqi situation as explained by the excerpt from the disgruntled soldier's e-mail. He described the situation in the country as a Pandora's box that the United States had opened when it removed Saddam Hussein from power. The removal of Saddam Hussein from power, the ambassador affirmed, created "the potential for widespread sectarian violence to lead to a civil war between the Sunnis and the Shiites."[503] The ambassador warned that "it would be disastrous for the United States to abandon Iraq the way it disengaged from civil wars in Lebanon and Somalia."

By April 2006, sectarian violence was killing more people and destabilizing Iraq more than the antigovernment insurgency ever did. The insurgency itself kept mutating, finding new recruits and even new weapons. It is no wonder that the British medical journal the *Lancet* calculated that 655,000 Iraqis had died by September 2006 as a result of the invasion and its ensuing chaos.[504] In a press conference on 12 September 2006 President Bush, who had revised his administration's estimate of the Iraqi fatalities from thirty thousand to fifty thousand, dismissed the *Lancet* figure as "not credible." But in January 2007 the United Nations said that 134,000 Iraqis had died from the war in 2006 alone.[505]

From the perspective of many an Iraqi national, the rate and texture of sectarian violence in the country has so destroyed postwar Iraq as a national community that, in the words of Ms. Shirouq Abayachi, a distraught resident of the mixed neighborhood of Zayuna, "there is no core left to rebuild it.... Now the Iraq I wish to have cannot come back.... Maybe I see the end more clearly now: The end of Iraq." "But what is coming after the end of Iraq?" Abayachi asked. "I don't know what it will be," she concluded.[506] Indeed, by the end of December 2006 the war had generated about two million refugees, including an estimated 40 percent of Iraq's professional classes.[507] All levels of education in the country have suffered a similarly devastating toll.[508]

An American soldier, Lt. Col. Patrick Donahoe, found himself in a similar quandary about Iraq after an Iraqi police officer told him in a meeting that he just wished the United States could put his country back the way it had found it. The American soldier said he was unsure whether that could be done. "How will it end?" he asked. "I don't know," he answered. "I think it will come down to an attrition of spirit. Either they will get tired of fighting and quit. Or we will."[509]

For the United States, although the jury is still out, observers believe so far that the war is "a strategic blunder of immeasurable consequences."[510] Strategically, it has not benefited the United States or Israel, its major ally in the Middle East, but Iran on several fronts. It eliminated for now and the foreseeable future Iran's most formidable enemy, Iraq, and reduced the danger the Taliban presented to Iran. It enthroned in Iraq the Shiites, who are the allies of Iran, and caused Iran to become even more determined to develop its own nuclear weapons in order to avoid a fate similar to that which befell Iraq. At the same time, the administration's preoccupation with Iraq diminished its capacity to deal with such determination by Iran. Also, the war diverted US close attention from the perception that China was a potential global competitor. The more the Bush administration focused attention and resources on Iraq, the more the People's Republic of China devoted more of its own resources to extending its global influence and strengthening itself in the Middle East. The journalist and fellow at the New America Foundation, Nir Rosen, predicts decades of hostility between the West and the Middle East as a result of the war.[511] He forecasts the probability of very well-trained and experienced fighters in Iraq going to Europe and elsewhere in the world to menace the interests of the United States and those of its Western allies.

Nowhere else in the world, since the invasion, has the surge in terrorism been more evident than in Iraq. A camp of CIA officers, and, indeed, several others among the foreign policy elite, believed that the Bush administration's venture into Iraq had dangerously diverted US counterterrorism policy. Among the CIA officers was Mary O. McCarthy, the agency's deputy inspector general who was dismissed from office on 20 April 2006 for allegedly sharing classified information with journalists. An independent-minded analyst who had worked for the CIA for two decades, McCarthy became disenchanted with the Bush administration's war in Iraq "after seeing—in e-mails, cable traffic, interview transcripts and field reports—some secret fruits of the Iraq intervention."[512]

The war in Iraq and documented accusations of abuse and brutalities at Abu Ghraib prison and Guantanamo Bay did a lot of damage to the image of the United States. They fostered the conclusion by many an observer that the United States had changed fundamentally after the 11 September terrorist attacks but not for the better. After those events, it had, under the Bush administration, steadily drifted away dangerously from the ideals that had identified it in the post–World War II era as a moral beacon.[513] Thus, consequent political backlash at home and abroad certainly contributed to the downward spiraling of President Bush's job approval rating.

The invasion was counterproductive to critical clusters of US foreign policy objectives—regional stability and the steady flow of Persian Gulf oil to the United States and its allies at reasonable price. Arguments about the brutalities of Saddam Hussein to his people notwithstanding, the conquest and occupation led to more instability in Iraq than what had existed there under his regime.[514] The occupation strengthened sectarian ties among the Kurds, Sunnis, and Shiites but weakened Iraqi national identity, such as when seats on the interim Iraqi Governing Council were apportioned according to the factions identified above. Inside and outside Iraq, the war strengthened political Islam. In addition to the electoral strength shown by the Shiites in Iraq, Hamas won elections in Palestine, and the Muslim Brotherhood gained strength in Egypt.

More than three years after the invasion, Iraq's oil output is below what it was before the war, contributing to postwar increases in oil prices. Electricity production in the country is 10 percent below prewar levels. The war turned the country into a haven and training ground for terrorists. It squandered the global goodwill that flowed naturally to the United States from the terrorist attacks of 11 September 2001. The Bush administration's fixation with the terrorist threat (made part of its rationale for the war in Iraq), to the extent that it rejected America's fundamental values and sense of fair play, alarmed allies and "led people everywhere to brand the United States—however unfairly—as a hegemonic power intent on exercising its muscle without restraint."[515] The war in Iraq itself galvanized the view of many non-Americans that the United States was arrogantly using its military and economic levers to accentuate its global influence.

By the end of December 2006 the war had cost the lives of 3,000 American soldiers, not including those of the United Kingdom and other members of the coalition of the willing, and for Iraqis only estimates are available. In addition, more than twenty-two thousand Americans had been severely wounded in the conflict. The war is regarded as "the deadliest conflict for reporters in modern times."[516] From its start in March 2003 to 30 May 2006, seventy-one journalists, not including two dozen media support staff that also had been killed, had lost their lives as casualties to the war.[517] The steady drumbeat of American casualties evoked a sense of consternation among the American people and adversely affected President Bush's job approval rating.

It is significant to observe that most of the US casualties in the war occurred during roadside and suicide bombings and battles against the insurgency that emerged after the April 2003 collapse of the Saddam Hussein regime and for which the Bush administration had neither anticipated nor planned. Apart from the fatalities and casualties of the war, about 12 percent of its veterans developed posttraumatic stress disorder, which produced flashbacks, nightmares, and intrusive thoughts that disrupted work and home life. According to a comprehensive report by US army experts, veterans of the war consistently reported more psychic distress than those who returned from Afghanistan and other conflicts, such as those in Bosnia and Kosovo.[518]

Furthermore, the war soured the relations between the United States and its major European allies. The European Union's ambition, dating to 1998, to have a common foreign and security policy broke on the shoals of the Iraqi conflict. The Bush administration exploited the Iraqi situation to foster that breakdown. Along with British Prime Minister Tony Blair, it launched an offensive, divisive of the EU, in obtaining the signature of a statement supporting the United States by some old members and by leaders of most of the future East European members—the "new" Europe. The administration went further to marginalize NATO, the mutual defense organization that the United States had created in 1949. Because some members of NATO were not sufficiently docile to its preferred strategy in Iraq, the administration resorted to recruiting a "coalition of the willing" which, with exception of Britain, was essentially symbolic. Furthermore, NATO was paralyzed for several weeks by the confrontation between the United States and three dissident members of the organization—Germany, France, and Belgium—over the issue of preparations that had to be made to facilitate the defense of Turkey in the event of a war with Iraq. The American historian Gunter Bischof writes that the manner in which the administration embarked upon the conquest and occupation of Iraq "managed to do more damage to transatlantic relations in three years than [its] predecessors had done in the aggregate over more than half a century as they tried to build a relatively harmonious relationship."[519]

Increasingly, the Bush administration has been seen as weakened both at home and abroad by its invasion and occupation of Iraq. At home, public support for the war eroded rapidly, as the main rationale for the war, Saddam Hussein's pursuit of weapons of mass destruction, proved hollow and the occupation of Iraq became a longer and costly endeavor. Criticisms and debates continued to rage over whether the war was necessary or wise and over whether the costs were outweighing the benefits.[520]

As public support for the war declined rapidly, there were calls, initiated by a seasoned veteran of the Vietnam War, Congressman John Murtha, a Pennsylvania Democrat, for an early withdrawal of American forces from Iraq. He asserted that the presence of US troops in Iraq was fueling the urgency and hatred of US soldiers. The future of the country, he said, was at risk. Hence the United States could not continue the Bush administration's course in the country, which he described as a failed policy wrapped in illusion. Some Americans demanded an immediate withdrawal of US forces, because they believed that the United States had already lost the hearts and minds of Iraqi communities. The nation should therefore reduce its losses earlier than it had done in the Vietnam War. Senator John Kerry and others suggested that American combat forces should be withdrawn by the end of 2006, leaving only troops essential to finishing the job of training Iraqi forces.

Specifically, in an article in *Foreign Policy* (May–June 2006), Lt. General William E. Odom argued for immediate withdrawal of US troops. First, invading Iraq, he wrote, was not in the national security interest of the United States. Secondly, the invasion and consequent occupation of the country had effectively paralyzed the United States diplomatically and strategically. Rapid withdrawal would enable the United States to regain diplomatic and military mobility and allow it to "attract the diplomatic and military cooperation necessary to win the real battle against terror." Furthermore, immediate withdrawal of US troops, Lt. General Odom explained, would be the United States' "only chance to set things right in Iraq.... European politicians would be more likely to cooperate in a strategy for stabilizing the greater Middle East. Following a withdrawal, all the countries bordering Iraq would likely respond favorably to an effort to help stabilize the situation."[521] The Lt. General insisted that only by withdrawing from Iraq can the United States regain the leadership role it lost by invading the country. Staying there, he affirmed, costs American lives and postpones an effective policy that could achieve much of what is in US national interest in the greater Middle East.

Senator Joseph Biden and Leslie Gelb, former president of the Council on Foreign Relations, put out a plan to withdraw US troops by 2008, leaving a "small but effective residual force to combat terrorists and keep the neighbors honest."[522] In an opinion editorial in the *Washington Post* (24 August 2006), Senator Biden maintained that no number of troops could successfully deal with "the new central reality in Iraq"—the violence between Shiites and

Sunnis—which he insisted had surpassed the ongoing insurgency and foreign terrorists as the main security threat. "The only way to hold Iraq together and create the conditions for [US] armed forces to responsibly withdraw," he said, "is to give Shiites, Sunnis and Kurds incentives to pursue their interests peacefully and forge a sustainable political settlement." To achieve this goal, the senator and Leslie Gelb offered a five-point plan that would

1. Maintain a unified Iraq by decentralizing it and giving Kurds, Shiites and Sunnis their own regions. The central government would be left in charge of common interests, such as border security and the distribution of oil revenues.
2. Bind the Sunnis to the deal by guaranteeing them a proportionate share of oil revenue, which would become the glue that binds the country together.
3. Create a massive jobs program while increasing reconstruction aid— especially from the oil-rich Gulf states—but tying it to the protection of minority rights.
4. Convene an international conference that would produce a regional nonaggression pact and create a Contact Group to enforce regional commitments.
5. Begin the phased redeployment of US forces by the end of 2006 and withdraw most of them by the end of 2007; and maintain a small follow-on force to keep the neighbors honest and to strike any concentration of terrorists.[523]

Anthony Cordesman of the Center for Strategic and International Studies argued against any precipitate withdrawal of American troops that could "convey the message that America has been defeated and abandoned a nation and a people.... Having broken Iraq," he claimed, "the United States has a responsibility for its people and cannot leave a power vacuum in an already dangerous region."[524]

Articulating a perspective similar to that of Anthony Cordesman, Stephen Biddle argued that the United States could not in good conscience withdraw abruptly from Iraq, because doing so would remove the last significant barrier to a total conflagration. Even more significantly, it would not be in the national interest of the United States to do so. Biddle saw the escalating violence in Iraq as a "communal civil war" rather than a nationalist insurgency. Turning over responsibility for counterinsurgency to Iraqi army and police forces, as President Bush's stay-the-course policy insisted, he wrote, would risk inflaming the ongoing communal conflict either by empowering the Shiites and the Kurds to slaughter the Sunnis or enabling select Sunni insurgents to penetrate the multiethnic security forces and undermine them. Biddle suggested that the Bush administration should "stop shifting the responsibility for the country's security to others and instead threaten to manipulate the military balance of power among Sunnis, Shiites, and Kurds in order to force them to come to a durable compromise. Only once an agreement is reached should [the administration] consider devolving significant military power and authority to local forces."[525]

The added rationale for the war after the failure to find the weapons of mass destruction in Iraq—democratization of the Middle East slowed down after elections in Iraq, Egypt, and the Palestinian areas. Additional steps in the process were apparently blocked by legal maneuvers and official changes of heart throughout the region. Those who believe the added rationale and objective of the war was doomed from the start insist that "only the politically naive and the historically illiterate could have contemplated constructing a working democracy out of the ruins of Saddam Hussein's tyranny." "No region," they stressed, "offered a more forbidding setting for experimentation with democratization than the Middle East, with all its ethnic and cultural divisions, and no country within the region held less promise than Iraq, brutalized as it was by decades of oppression, wars, and sanctions."[526] Other analysts and officials attribute this apparent failure of the experimentation with democratization to "the political rise of Islamists, the chaos in Iraq, the new found Shiite power in Iraq with its implications for growing Iranian influence, and the sense among rulers that they can wait out the end of the Bush administration."[527] These collectively, they say, have put the brakes on the democratization process.

Thus, after allowing a contested presidential election in Egypt in 2005, President Hosni Mubarak delayed municipal elections by two years. He did so because the Muslim Brotherhood had made big gains in parliamentary elections in 2005 despite his government's violent efforts to stop the group's supporters. In Jordan, King Abdullah II weakened the hands of proponents of political change and democratization by putting the document advocating change on a back burner. The rulers of Qatar postponed parliamentary elections in their country for the second time to 2007 and stymied the emergence of nongovernmental organizations through legal regulation. The government of Yemen cracked down on the news media, ahead of presidential elections in 2006. In Saudi Arabia, King Abdullah flatly rejected calls for the election of members of the country's consultative council. Syria followed promises for political reform with a harsh crackdown on the opposition.[528] The Bush administration's response to the setbacks in the promotion of democracy in the

Middle East is that they do not discredit its approach, that democracy is not always linear. Rather, it takes time, is evolutionary, and requires consistent support.

When Secretary of State Condoleezza Rice visited Egypt in January 2007, she ignored the concerns of Egyptian nationalists with such issues as torture and political repression but spoke softly and avoided pushing democracy. With the Egyptian Foreign Minister Ahmed Aboul Ghent by her side, Rice expressed her appreciation for Egypt's support in the region. It was apparently not politic to pressure Egypt as in a previous occasion on the need to respect the rule of law and the independence of the judiciary and to minimize emergency decrees and arbitrary justice. But facing unpopularity in the region, chaos in Iraq, rising Iranian influence, and the destabilizing Israeli-Palestinian conflict, the Bush administration had changed course (see chapter 2) and decided that stability, not democracy, was its priority in the Greater Middle East.[529] Critics of the administration's policy, however, assert that continuing American support for autocratic regimes, such as those in Saudi Arabia, Egypt, and elsewhere in the region, leaves the nation open to charges of hypocrisy.

Richard N. Haass, president of the Council on Foreign Relations and head of policy planning at the US Department of State during the outbreak of the war, offers the following perspectives on its impact and consequences.[530] Although it is too soon to do its complete accounting, so far, on the balance, the war, he says, has had a negative impact on US foreign policy. He affirms that it "has absorbed a tremendous amount of US military capacity." The result is that "the United States has far less spare or available capacity, not just to use in the active sense, but to exploit in the diplomatic sense. It has therefore weakened the [nation's] position against both North Korea and Iran." The American homeland experienced a similar result. Because the army was already too stretched by the war, Defense Secretary Rumsfeld was unwilling to allow the dispatch of army troops to New Orleans during the Hurricane Katrina to fill the vacuum in the number of first responders—firefighters, police officers, and other members of the national guard—created by the deployment of civilians to Iraq.

Economically, according to Haass, the war also has clearly "exacerbated the US fiscal situation, which," he believes, "obviously has all sorts of economic repercussions." Before the war started, the Bush administration never told Congress specifically how much it would cost. On the eve of the war, the administration rebuked Lawrence B. Lindsey, its chief economic adviser, for claiming that the war would cost as little as $2 billion. White House officials claimed that that estimate was too high. But, more than three years later, the actual tally is four times more than that amount and counting. Worse still, while the administration has poured resources into Iraq, it has fallen behind in measures needed to protect the homeland.

Diplomatically, Haass believes that the war "has contributed to the world's alienation from the United States…. It has made it somewhat more difficult for the United States to galvanize its national interest or galvanize international partners in dealing with problems related to weapons of mass destruction." Clearly, in that area, Haass asserts, the war delivered a major blow to US credibility. The impact, he surmises, might become even more severe if suddenly Iraq imploded or became the venue for not just civil war but a regional armed conflict. In such a circumstance, "the implications for US foreign policy would be both greater and more negative," given the enormous investments the United States has already made in Iraq. Furthermore, such an eventuality, Haass adds, would clearly energize forces and movements opposed to the United States and "would raise large questions of doubt and confidence with those who are inclined to work with a [US government]." Similarly, oil and gas production that powers the world economy would be gravely disrupted by a regional war in the oil-rich Persian Gulf.

In March 2005, Anthony Cordesman of the Center for Strategic and International Studies and a leading Middle East and intelligence expert, offered from his own vantage point a pessimistic three-year review of the Bush administration's war effort in Iraq.[531] Cordesman stressed that, if one looks back on why the Bush administration went to war and what its objectives were, "a number of things are painfully obvious": The administration

> did not really prepare to liberate Iraq. Essentially, it went in a bull to liberate a china shop. As a result, the legacy in many ways is very destructive. Security for the average Iraqi [after more than three years of the war] is worse than it was under Saddam Hussein, who focused really on political dissidents. The living standards of the average Iraqi are far worse. There's far more unemployment [about 50 to 60 percent] in the nation. The distribution of income is terrible. And though [one] can make a paper case that some microeconomic measures have improved, in the real world, Iraqis are worse off, on average, as individuals, than they were before [the Bush administration] invaded [their country].

Worse still, Cordesman added, the risks of an intense civil war are very serious. Equally serious, he insisted, the Bush administration did not provide added security to Iraq's oil sector. Iraq exported less oil after the invasion and occupation than it did before those events. What the administration projected to be major increases in Iraqi production not only have not occurred, but also cannot occur for several years. It certainly has not made Iraq an example of a democracy that can transform the Middle East, as the administration argued in making its case for the war. Furthermore, the administration found that there was no real terrorist linkage between the Iraqi regime and the extremists the United States was fighting. After the invasion, the administration found it had an insurgency in the occupied country that is dominated by three neo-Salafist extremist groups posing a major new threat. Therefore, once again, it redefined the central justification for continued US involvement in Iraq: defeating terrorism within the country.

Cordesman concluded that the invasion of Iraq has not so far provided regional stability. It created far more problems for Turkey. It gave Iran considerable leverage and a potential option to interfere in Iraq. Iran appears to be exploiting that option. More than three years after the invasion and occupation, the United States has major problems in the region in terms of attitudes of Arabs, and of virtually all Persian Gulf states that allow it to base and support forces, towards it as a result the invasion and occupation.

One can reasonably surmise from this Cordesman review and other evidence of the situation in Iraq that, although the Bush administration linked removing Saddam Hussein from power with liberation of the Iraqi people, there was really no demonstrable connection between the two. Emancipation of Iraq was not the reason the administration went to war in the country or invoked international law to justify doing so. For its architects, Vice President Dick Cheney and Defense Secretary Ronald Rumsfeld, "the war was about solving the Saddam problem" and promoting the interests of business and corporate supporters of the Bush administration rather than the Iraqi problem, "about [promoting] security rather than justice, about toppling a regime rather than building one. After all, the Bush administration [itself] had proudly said that it was not in the business of nation building and would happily leave [that] to others."[532]

After providing the Bush administration with its political and ideological ammunition to invade Iraq, the hawkish neoconservatives in Washington are burned out and have no credible plan for victory. Iraq is a long way from the model democracy that, under their influence, the Bush administration set out to create by force. And, furthermore, they have no answers to what is happening in Iran or, closer to home, in Latin America, where a succession of leftist governments are being elected to office.

No wonder, in January 2006, President Bush reached beyond his inner circle of neoconservative advisers and deep into the past as he sought the views of about twelve former secretaries of state and defense on his postwar strategy in Iraq.[533] After their meeting at the White House, Bush publicly acknowledged that not everyone of the former secretaries had agreed with his invasion of Iraq and his postwar policy in the country, but he urged the need for a consensus on a strategy to succeed after the fact of the invasion and promised to "take to heart" suggestions on Iraq by the former secretaries. However, in spite of his promise, and unlike Robert S. McNamara, defense secretary under the John F. Kennedy and Lyndon B. Johnson administrations, who helped to shape the American strategy in Vietnam but eventually became disillusioned with it, President Bush and the neocons in the inner circle of his administration inflexibly insisted on continuing his stalemated strategy for victory in Iraq. They will stay the course by relying on a political process involving all Iraqis, training Iraqi armed forces, and helping them to quell the violence within their country. The administration remained adamantly opposed to calls for withdrawal of US forces or the setting of a timetable for doing so. It argued that setting a timetable for US troop withdrawal would encourage the terrorists to wreak more havoc and damage the morale of the troops. It added that withdrawal of American forces would promote civil war in Iraq and would undermine US credibility in the world.

This inflexibility and reluctance to make course corrections was praised by Bush's admirers as an asset and a sign of strong leadership. But critics saw the behavior differently: as dangerous when it slows course correction and as smacking of arrogance, stubbornness, and hubris and indicating a disregard for both history and long-term consequences. In *Against All Enemies*, Richard A. Clarke argues that Bush looks for "the simple solution, the bumper sticker description of the problem." But on such issues like terrorism and Iraq that require substantive analysis, he and his inner circle of advisers had no real interest. "On the issues that they cared about they already know the answers."[534]

US intelligence agencies were acutely blemished by events leading up to the war. The hobnobbing of the director of central intelligence with the Bush administration violated the intent of the 1947 National Security Act that created the CIA as an independent agency. Apparently, Director George Tenet cooperated with the administration in politicizing prewar intelligence on Iraq even though he had personal reservations about invading Iraq.[535] His erroneous, perhaps subtly induced, conclusion and assurance to President Bush that Iraq possessed stockpiles of biological and chemical weapons threatening the United States and its allies damaged the credibility of the US Intelligence Community. Political analysts, including the Commission on the Intelligence Capabilities of the United States Regarding Weapons of Mass Destruction, appointed by President Bush himself, concluded that the damage would take years to undo. The Iraq War also provided a particularly stark illustration of the problems in the relationship between the US Intelligence Community and policy makers.

That relationship is broken. In the wake of the war, it became quite clear that official intelligence analysis was not relied on in making even the most significant US national security decisions, that intelligence was aggressively manipulated and misused publicly to justify decisions already made, that the Intelligence Community's own work was politicized, and that damaging ill will developed between policy makers and intelligence officers. That "ill will may not be reparable, and the perception of the intelligence community on the part of some policymakers—that Langley is enemy territory—is unlikely to change."[536]

George W. Bush wants to be remembered as a president who left a lasting mark on US foreign policy, especially by spreading democracy and reshaping the greater Middle East. So far, the results of his policy choices and management style, especially the invasion and occupation of Iraq, may have already denied him that legacy. Rather, because of his policy in Iraq and elsewhere in the Middle East and his approach to global problems generally, the rest of the world, foes and allies alike, are seeing US primacy as increasingly troubling. Increasingly alarmed by the ways his administration chose to use America's unparalleled power, some are now preoccupied with devising ways to tame, contain, or reduce it. Others seek to harness and exploit it.

So far (in January 2007), the Iraq gamble's cost in lives, money, prestige, and US strategic focus and position is enormous. The adventure increased the level of partisanship in the United States and polarized the American people as well. Furthermore, it has "fueled a precipitous decline in America's prestige abroad, and Bush's pugnacious style during his first term and his tin ear for foreign opinion made a bad situation worse. This is more than just a public relations problem. National prestige is diplomatic capital; the more unpopular America becomes, the higher the price of foreign policy support."[537] Although as president of the United States Bush remained the leader on the global stage, yet by the time it was two years to the end of his administration he had lost stature and credibility both at home and overseas mainly as a consequence of his administration's war in Iraq.

Thus, in conclusion, a "foreign policy that was supposed to demonstrate America's might has become an ongoing source of weakness. The war that was supposed to prevent a rogue state from obtaining nuclear weapons has led two others, Iran and North Korea, to spur their development. And by empowering the Shia in Iraq while tying up US forces there, the Bush strategy has strengthened Iran."[538] This is in part how the "transformational" presidency of George W. Bush, whose ambition was to reinvigorate America's global leadership and enhance its ability to project power throughout the world, appears to be reversing that ambition. Debilitated by the quagmire in Iraq under his administration, America is increasingly disrespected by its adversaries and mistrusted by its allies. And it has become the object of widespread ill-will around the world.[539]

Towards a Review of the Iraq Policy

The negative consequences of the war called for a review of the Iraq policy as well as a necessary course correction. President Bush flatly refused to undertake such a review and course corrections. Instead, he insisted that his administration's policy was working. He cited the successful representative democratic elections in Iraq, and urged patience as he stayed the course while Maliki's government matured in time. Democratic party critics were accused of defeatism and described as individuals who would cut and run rather than support US forces in Iraq.

However, five specific developments, among others, occurring in the summer and fall of 2006 eventually convinced President Bush of the need to undertake a review of his policy. The first development was the failure of the administration's fundamental belief for more than three years that once a representative democratic government was installed in Baghdad, the Sunni insurgency and sectarian violence would subside. This did not happen, and in the summer of 2006 the second of two military operations designed to quell surging violence in Baghdad collapsed. The administration became convinced from this that the political process would not lead to security in Iraq but, rather, security, it opined, would come by increasing the number of US troops in the country.

The second development was the findings of the national security adviser Stephen J. Hadley during his 25 October to 5 November 2006 mission to Iraq. Hadley reported that he was "profoundly disturbed by the Maliki government, uncertain whether the prime minister was capable of doing what was necessary to rein Shiite militias."[540] On 8 November 2006 he sent President Bush a five-page classified memo that proposed to bolster Maliki's political and security capacities and thus raised the prospects of deploying more U.S. troops to Iraq.

The third development was the conclusions and grim picture of a National Intelligence Estimate (NIE) about the situation in Iraq and its probable adverse consequences presented to President Bush in the fall of 2006.[541] A declassified summary of the document was made public almost two months after the November 2006 midterm congressional elections. Among other conclusions the intelligence report warned that rising violence in Iraq could permanently tear the country apart and, in the worst case, create a state of anarchy with no legitimate authority that combines "extreme ethnosectarian violence with debilitating intragroup classes."

The fourth development was the verdict of the 7 November 2006 midterm congressional elections in which the electorate clearly repudiated the administration's Iraq policy. From this development the administration fully realized that it would have to deal with the Democratic-controlled Congress not the Republican-controlled one that had allowed it free rein.

The fifth development was the report of the bipartisan group—the Iraq Study Group—of ten members, co-chaired by former Secretary of State James Baker and former Congressman Lee H. Hamilton. Congress had commissioned the group to study the deteriorating situation in Iraq and to recommend ways to remedy it and protect American interests. Bush had been persuaded by Secretary of State Rice to accept and cooperate with the group notwithstanding the opposition of Vice President Cheney to the commissioning of the group. The Iraq Study Group delayed issuing its report until after the November 2006 midterm elections. In December it presented its very comprehensive unanimous report to President Bush. Among sixty-six others, the group made three key recommendations—open diplomatic talks with Iraq's neighbors Iran and Syria, initiate a plan to withdraw US combat forces by early 2008, and condition US assistance to Iraq on the Maliki government meeting specific benchmarks. However, upon receiving the much-awaited report, the Bush administration quickly make it clear that the key recommendations were unacceptable. It would not talk to America's enemies.

The result of these developments was that President Bush concluded a policy review, the outcome of which was to push for victory by sending 21,500 more troops to Iraq despite doubts and opposition along the way from his own military commanders, lawmakers, and the public at large. Bush never seriously considered the withdrawal or redeployment of US troops as urged by the newly Democratic congressional leaders and the bipartisan Iraq Study Group. But on 10 January 2007, he told the nation in his televised address the major decisions of the policy review. He had decided to commit 21,500 more combat forces to Iraq. This, in effect, was a decision that would make US soldiers responsible for keeping the Iraqi people safe. Also, he had warned the Iraqi prime minister that the US commitment was not "open-ended." Maliki, he added, had to meet definite benchmarks.[542] President Bush did not, however, inform the nation the specifics of the benchmarks Prime Minister Maliki was required to meet. His administration stone-walled a request by the Chairman of the Senate Armed Services Committee, Carl Levin, to see a list of security and political benchmarks the government of Maliki was required to meet.

Congressional and public reaction to the decision to deploy additional troops to Iraq was immediate. About 61 percent of the public did not favor the plan. Congressional Democrats and a few leading Republicans opposed it. Opponents asserted that the decision would place American troops in the middle of an Iraqi civil war. American forces, they urged, should quickly transition from a combat role to one focused on training Iraqi forces, counterterrorism, and controlling Iraq's borders. While Senator Edward M. Kennedy asserted that what the situation in Iraq needed was not a troop surge but a diplomatic surge, working closely with other countries in the region, other lawmakers talked of cutting off funds. The Chairman of the Senate Foreign Relations Committee Joseph Biden and others began to craft a non-binding congressional resolution opposing the administration's so-called new approach to commit more American forces to Iraq put protecting funding for the troops. Senator Biden suggested that the October 2002 congressional resolution that authorized the war could be repealed since its rationale—the presence of stockpiles of weapons of mass destruction in Iraq—turned out to be nonexistent and the target—Saddam Hussein—was dead. In addition, he said he would propose a substitute legislation that would narrow the mission of the troops deployed to Iraq and begin to bring some of them home.

Early in February 2007, the Senate Democrats sought to debate a non-binding resolution, worked out by Republican Senator John Warner and Senate Democrat Ben Nelson, opposing the Bush administration's decision. However, Senate Republican supporters of the president, employing procedural maneuvers, blocked the debate. They insisted on offering their own alternative favoring the president's decision instead of exerting influence on the president to pursue a less divisive partisan policy on the Iraq war.

Disappointed at the Senate's failure to show leadership on the issue, House Democrats, joined by seventeen Republicans, adopted a non-binding resolution (246–182), disapproving of Bush's decision to deploy 21,500 more troops to Iraq while affirming Congress's support for "the members of the United States Armed Forces who are serving or who have served bravely and honorably in Iraq." The resolution, adopted after almost four days debate, was characterized by many lawmakers as a first step towards a more concrete Democratic push to change the Bush administration's course in Iraq. Indeed, after the vote Representative John P. Murtha, chair of the House Defense Appropriations subcommittee, proposed a measure that he hoped would limit in several ways the Bush administration's options to obtain funding for the additional troops: Iraqi veterans would be guaranteed a year between tours, combat tours could no longer be extended, officers could no longer be prohibited from leaving the military when their tour of duty was completed, special training in urban warfare and counterinsurgency as well as safety equipment would be provided to the forces before their deployment.[543]

On 17 February, three days after the House action, Senate Democrats, joined by seven Republicans, convened a rare Saturday session as they sought to build on the momentum from the vote in the House of Representatives to debate a similar resolution. Again, Senate Republican supporters of President Bush prevented a debate even though many had significant reservations about the conduct of the war and concerns for its political repercussions. They accused the democrats of engaging in dangerous political posturing in advance of the 2008 presidential and congressional elections and of undermining US forces in Iraq as well as the Bush administration. Thus for ideological and partisan purposes the Bush administration and its Republican supporters defied the expressed will of the American people regarding the war in Iraq. As a consequence two of the most fundamental presidential prerogatives—the power to prosecute wars and to initiate foreign policy—were challenged by the 110th Congress.

The answer to the tragedy in Iraq as well as the deteriorating broader strategic position of the United States in the Middle East is not such a challenge and a probable constitutional crisis. Congress and the Bush administration should honestly accept the truth in Colin Powell's warning to President Bush as the president was eagerly preparing to plunge the nation into a war in Iraq later authorized by the 107th Congress at his request: "You break it, you own it." The United States under the Bush administration, has broken Iraq and owns it. It has caused Iraq's turmoil and cannot escape the consequences. Therefore, President Bush and the legislators have an obligation to realistically and conscientiously work out a political strategy to extricate both the nation and Iraq from the consequences of embarking on a war of choice in the Persian Gulf country. "Nothing"

wholly good can come out of a war that resulted from a mix of self-deception and a deliberate deception, waged in a part of the world in which alien control has for a long time fostered turmoil and tragedy. The presence of terrorism is not an invitation to empire, but an incentive for finding policies that reduce its appeal, and pursuing the terrorists in ways that do not help them to multiply. In the case of the Middle East, an exit from Iraq, combined with a new effort by the U.S., the U.N., the EU, and Russia to end Israeli occupation of Palestinian lands and to create a livable Palestinian state, would mark a return to reality, to good sense, and to morality.[544]

Chapter 11
Consequences of Deference by
Congress to the Executive Branch
on Foreign Policy

Although the Constitution designates the president and Congress as coequal managers of America's foreign relations, the practical realities of the responsibility made the executive branch the more dominant partner in the making and conduct of American foreign policy. This is as it should be. For most of the time, it has been so, given customary international practice—foreign policy is a government-to-government affair—and the nature and composition of both branches of the US government, the dictates of national security interest, and the state of the world. The state of the world, including external threats and challenges to national security, may demand secrecy and swift measures that a cumbersome and deliberative body such as the US Congress is ill equipped to handle appropriately in partnership with the presidency. In such instances, the Louisiana Purchase, for example, the chief executive who is in continuous session acts swiftly and appropriately and duly informs the Congress. But that, in view of the provisions of the Constitution, is the exception rather than the rule or a matter of routine. In such instances, it would be normal for the lawmakers, in the national security interest, to defer to the chief executive. And the chief executive, fully aware that Congress is an important instrument of popular control over the government and a vital forum for debate and compromise, would prudently seek the benefit of the wisdom and mature experience of the lawmakers through timely consultation as he deals with extraordinary emergencies.

The national security interest may be jeopardized, and the people may suffer unnecessarily, when the chief executive adopts imperial and unilateral approaches to foreign policy or Congress routinely defers to it on foreign policy matters. The Bay of Pigs invasion of April 1961; the series of plots in the late 1950s, the 1960s, and early 1970s to assassinate leaders of foreign governments; the Johnson and Nixon administrations' imperial policies in Vietnam and Cambodia; and the Reagan administration policy in Lebanon and its Iran-Contra maneuvers were instances when presidents ignored the need for consultation with Congress. Each of these occasions turned out to be a fiasco that among other things damaged the image of the United States. The George W. Bush administration's war in Iraq is apparently breaking that record in damaging the image and credibility of the Republic.

Clearly then, imperial foreign policies and routine deference by Congress to the executive branch on foreign policy do not serve the national interest. Both are a departure from the provisions of the constitutional framework established by the framers of the American political system. In their wisdom, the framers of the American Constitution (see Article 3 of the US Constitution) ordained limited presidential authority and a robust role for lawmakers in the making of the nation's foreign policy. Imperial foreign policies, abetted by routine deference by Congress, defies that wisdom. They prevent Congress and the executive branch from working together in a foreign policy compact that taps into the combined experience and wisdom of America's political institutions to address global challenges and promote American interests.

Recent Historical Record

In spite of the fact that imperial foreign policies and routine deference by Congress to the executive branch on foreign policy tend not to serve the national security interest, in the critical war powers area, Congress historically has tended to defer routinely to presidents, declaring only five of the numerous wars the United States has waged since the Peace of Paris in 1783. It acquiesced in the rest to presidential war making, only fighting unsuccessfully, in some cases, rearguard battles to minimize the erosion of its constitutional war powers by the executive branch. The Eisenhower Doctrine or Middle East Resolution, the Formosa Resolution, the war in Vietnam (1964–1975), and the repeal of the Clark Amendment in 1985 illustrate how, since the end of World War II, US lawmakers have tended to defer foreign policy matters, such as war making, to the executive branch. To cap it all, in October 2002, the 107th Congress of the United States demonstrated that it had lost its will to lead and to make hard decisions on foreign affairs when it precipitately passed a resolution authorizing President George W. Bush to make war in Iraq at his own discretion. Therefore, it is not too much to say that, by doing so, it substantially ceded Congress's fundamental constitutional role in foreign policy to the presidency.

On his watch and in waging the authorized war in Iraq at his own discretion, President George W. Bush and his top foreign policy team committed several errors in foreign policy and in the planning, execution, and aftermath of the war in Iraq. Above all, he and his team antagonized the international community in their unilateralist policies. They thus brought the nation to a position that observers described as a military quagmire. Furthermore, the administration persisted in a policy that was demonstrated by the realities and facts on the ground in Iraq to be counterproductive to the goals the administration sought. It rejected calls by experienced lawmakers and elder statesmen to make a course correction but insisted on staying the course regardless of the human, material, and political consequences of staying the course. President Bush went further to describe opponents of his policy of staying the course in Iraq as individuals prescribing a "cut and run" policy and to assert that he would persist in his Iraq policy even if his wife and dogs were his only supporters. It was only as an act of political desperation as he faced public dismay over the war and pressure from Republican party candidates for the November 2006 midterm election that he abandoned the phrase "stay the course in Iraq" and promised flexibility in setting milestones and adapting his policy to realities in Iraq.

The apparent ceding of its role in foreign policy to the presidency, as it is the case in the war in Iraq, is frequently a function of the lawmakers' preoccupation with reelection pressures, such as endless fund-raising and campaigning, and political partisanship. At times, it is the result of political pressure by the executive branch, as well as the frequency at which many lawmakers equivocate on foreign policy decisions. They tend to place the blame on the executive branch should things go wrong overseas rather than bear the responsibility themselves. "They do not want to be part of any crash landings, so they avoid the takeoffs too."[545]

Evidently, it is clear that, after the end of the cold war, when the United States became the sole superpower, US lawmakers—Democrats, Republicans, liberals, and conservatives alike—could not agree on the purpose their nation's unprecedented power and primacy in the world should serve. Political partisanship and considerations of financial contributions from political action committees and other powerful interest groups to fund their periodic reelection campaigns preoccupied their time and clouded their judgment regarding the future US role in world affairs. They failed to consider the implications of the US position as the world's most powerful nation at the end of the cold war. Nor did they bother to consider that how they, as co-determinants (with the president) of American foreign policy, responded to the complex problems that confronted the world at the start of the twenty-first century might very likely dictate the course of the rest of the century for the United States and world politics generally.

Lawmakers display much more initiative and leadership on domestic issues or on those issues that impact their constituencies or impose on their ideology than they tend do in foreign affairs.[546] Convinced that they have no constituency in foreign affairs, several lawmakers do not accord foreign policy a high priority. Since the 1990s both the Senate Foreign Relations Committee and the House International Relations Committee have had difficulty recruiting members because they are not particularly strong committees from which to raise campaign funds. Several lawmakers have the perception that preoccupation with foreign affairs might easily lead to a defeat at the polls. Few of those who are members of subcommittees or committees on foreign affairs show up during committee hearings or read relevant documents thoroughly in their entirety. Fewer still undertake sustained or extended foreign travels to strengthen their capacity on foreign policy.

A manifestation of deference by Congress to the executive branch in war making is the extent to which American lawmakers have placed an excessive emphasis on military budget and the use of force. Since the end of the Second World War, they readily have been willing to appropriate an ever increasing annual budget on defense. Richard N. Gardner wrote that, in 2000, US lawmakers allocated 16 percent of the annual budget to defense, while the percentage they earmarked for international diplomacy plummeted from 4 percent in the 1960s to 1 percent in that year.[547] During the second term of President Bush, Congress was authorizing the expenditure of $68 billion on weapons research alone, a figure that is greater than the entire defense budget of any other country in the world. At the same time that it appropriated $444 billion for the Pentagon, not including supplemental appropriations, to finance the wars in Afghanistan and Iraq, it appropriated a budget for the Department of State that was merely a pittance compared to the lavish funding enjoyed by the Department of Defense.[548]

Sometimes, huge expenditures on the military—speaking softly but carrying a big stick—can assist diplomacy, since a show of force might induce an adversary to negotiate differences rather than fight. But there are other forces accounting for US lawmakers' excessive emphasis on military budget and their tolerance of the overt or covert use of force by the US chief executive to resolve foreign policy disputes. The most prominent of these is the role of the "iron triangle"—the military, industrial, and congressional complex—in search of profits from weapons manufacturing and exercising an unwarranted influence in foreign policy. President Dwight Eisenhower had warned against such influence as he was leaving office in 1961. In 2006, Loch K. Johnson wrote, "America's profligate spending on the military is fueled by the sophisticated lobbying of generals and veteran groups, joined by savvy bureaucrats in search of expanded programs, strategists in the White House, pork-minded lawmakers, munitions-makers like Boeing and Lockheed-Martin, and the national laboratories where many of the weapons are designed."[549] It is also noteworthy that every one of about five hundred congressional districts in the nation has a defense industry, creating jobs for constituents and fostering arms buildup and sales. This readily turns war into a matter of jobs and profiteering, not of security.[550]

The result of all this is the availability of an unparalleled military arsenal to ideological or ill-advised presidents who resort to it to intervene overseas to resolve disputes without exhausting diplomatic or other means. The George W. Bush administration, for example, was so determined to "shock and awe" the Iraqis and the rest of the world with US military might that it would not allow the UN Security Council process to work its will in Iraq. And, for their part, the US lawmakers acquiesced in its doing so.

The executive branch tends to grow too strong and arrogant at the expense of national security when it operates without adequate checks from Congress. Inadequate checks from lawmakers tend to facilitate resort to unilateral actions by the executive branch on international issues that require negotiation and compromise with other nations. Furthermore, they encourage the executive branch to resort with undue haste to the use of US armed forces and secret intelligence agencies to deal covertly with problems overseas.[551] Frequently, the nation and its people suffer unduly because the lawmakers fail to exercise their war powers and to perform their constitutional duty of oversight of the executive branch in foreign affairs. Sometimes this is a function of the lawmakers' preoccupation with electoral politics and the apprehension of being castigated as weak on defense. At other times, it is a manifestation of their lack of courage to vote their conscience and to bow to pressure from the executive branch and its parochial supporters.

Years ago, in 1972, a member of the Senate Foreign Relations Committee, Frank Church of Idaho, sought to remedy this tendency. He urged,

> The sooner we learn to impose some reasonable restraint on our tendency to intervene too much in other people's affairs the happier land we will have and the less burden we will place upon our own people to undertake sacrifices that are not really related to their own good or the good of their country.[552]

In October 2002, as indicated above, US lawmakers totally ignored this counsel when, precipitately, without a deliberate and sustained debate or independent inquiry, they passed overwhelmingly the Iraq Resolution authorizing President George W. Bush to wage war in Iraq at his own discretion. They did so even though the Bush administration's casus belli was thought by many to have been manufactured to promote the administration's ideological goals. The consequent US invasion and occupation of Iraq in 2003 under the administration "has become the worst US foreign policy mistake in living memory."[553] The war and, thus, the mistake would have been averted had the US Congress dutifully performed its constitutional duties on American foreign policy at that time and not simply deferred to President Bush on that role. The lawmakers never consulted former President George H. W. Bush and members of his national security team as to why they deliberately refused to extend the first Gulf War to Baghdad. Factoring the information obtained through such consultation into their deliberations would have assisted them in their decision on the George W. Bush administration's draft resolution asking for authority to wage war in Iraq.

In fact, such information was available at the time George W. Bush submitted the draft resolution to the lawmakers. It had been consistently articulated by James Baker and Brent Scowcroft, former President George H. W. Bush's secretary of state and national security adviser, respectively, and by Colin Powell, the chairman of the Joint Chiefs of Staff during the first Gulf War. The lawmakers also knew that, as George W. Bush's secretary of state, Powell advocated a multilateral diplomatic approach and strengthened UN Security Council sanctions as a means of fostering regime change in Iraq. Furthermore, they were fully aware that Brent Scowcroft had publicly supported such an approach. However, they ignored the facts and the call for a multilateral approach through the UN Security Council to the Iraqi problem. Displaying an incapacity to analyze President Bush's rationale and proposal for war, as well as protecting their own institutional powers, they chose to act on the basis of the steady stream of unreliable and unproven information that the Bush administration had supplied them over a period of one year.

Because of the high level of partisanship that had bedeviled so much other work in Washington, the intelligence oversight committees in Congress failed to carry out their very important role. Political partisanship prevented any effort to monitor the relationship between the Intelligence Community and policy makers. It also prevented efforts to investigate the Bush administration's prewar use and politicization of intelligence on Iraq. Very few members read beyond the executive summary of the National Intelligence Estimate on Iraq that had been provided them at the request of the relevant committee.

The lawmakers made no attempt to consider objectively and to understand the perspectives of other members of the UN Security Council on Iraq. Rather, they displayed the same unwillingness as the Bush administration to work with America's European allies to resolve the conflict under UN Security Council auspices. They became critical and disparaging of France and

Germany—labeled "old Europe" by Defense Secretary Rumsfeld—for opposing a precipitate war in Iraq. To snub the French, the popular American fast food, French fries, was rechristened "freedom fries." The original nomenclature was restored in the summer of 2006.

A meticulous and sustained effort by Congress to obtain a realistic estimate of the requirements and cost of the war would have slowed the rush to the passage of the Iraq Resolution. Without undertaking its own independent efforts to obtain a realistic estimate of the requirements and costs of the war, as well as a clear exit strategy, Congress simply accepted the prewar pattern of underestimating and covering up of troop requirements and the costs of the war by its proponents. The proponents argued, and the lawmakers accepted their assurances, that invading Iraq would be cheap and easy and that Iraq had adequate resources to fund its own reconstruction. It would leave plenty of resources for other purposes as well. The lawmakers even failed to defend or protect from dismissal from their jobs by the administration such courageous individuals as General Shinseki and Lawrence Lindsey who, while testifying before its committees, offered moderately realistic estimates of the troop requirements and material costs of the war.

Moreover, the lawmakers failed to obtain concrete answers from the Bush administration's witnesses, such as Defense Secretary Rumsfeld and his deputy, Wolfowitz, about the planning and the cost of the war, especially after these witnesses dismissed the evidence of Army Chief of Staff Shinseki, who had testified that the impending war could require four hundred thousand military occupation troops for ten years at a cost of almost $1 trillion. Soon after the fall of Baghdad, it became abundantly clear to the nation and the world, from the chaos, looting, and insurgency, that the United States did not have enough troops to occupy and pacify the conquered country. Now, four years into the war, it is estimated that, when all is said and done, the war will cost $1.27 trillion—the equivalent of a million dollars a day for a million years.[554]

Had Congress played its role, and still the United States waged a war in Iraq, the consequences for the nation, Iraq, and the global community generally would be far different from those that resulted from the war of choice based on shaky ideological grounds launched by the George W. Bush administration. The rationale, the preparation, and the strategy for the war would have been more transparent and the cost more modest as a result of congressional investigation, deliberation, and oversight of the entire process. Thus, the lesson of the Bush administration's war in Iraq is clear: US lawmakers served the nation and world security and stability poorly when they overwhelmingly passed the Iraq Resolution in October 2002.

US interests, broadly defined, are best served when Congress and the chief executive truly perform their coequal role in the making and management of American foreign policy. The nation loses, and the American constitutional system is impaired, when Congress abdicates its constitutional duties in deference to an imperial and ideological presidency. This will become even more devastating to the peace and security of the world, because, after the collapse of the Soviet Union in 1991, the United States became too powerful to fear attack from other states. Given that reality, a US president allowed by lawmakers to pursue an imperial and ideological foreign policy, as happened in Iraq in 2003, might succumb to the temptation of fighting wars of choice based on shaky ideological grounds that are open to debate rather than a response to a clear and present danger. In that case, Iraq would not be America's last drawn-out adventure in the global south. The nation would then "shed blood on the soil of far-off little countries that most Americans can't find on a map, the media [would] hype other tin-pot dictators as the next coming of Hitler, and the defense industry [would] have other opportunities to shake some silver out of the treasury. And [Americans would] wake up in a decade or so facing another quagmire and realize it's Groundhog Day all over again."[555]

Persistence of a Culture of Deference in Congress

Although a major contributor to the culture of deference in Congress to the presidency on foreign affairs, the cold war, ultimately ended in 1989, the culture persists. The persistence is essentially a function of several forces. First is the complexity, instability, and insecurity of the post–cold war world. The end of the cold war left the United States without a single great power or coalition of powers as a clear and present danger to its national security. But it did not bring peace to the world. Instead, the world became less stable and more violent. Terrorism became a global menace at the same time that global migration increased. Thus, the condition of instability and insecurity in the post–cold war world was perceived as requiring urgent action, which Congress as a large and deliberative body is not very well equipped to handle.

Secondly, and perhaps more importantly, the persistence of the culture of deference in Congress is a function of the custom and tradition in Congress that nurtured it. Lawmakers, as well as the executive branch, accept the axiom of presidential superiority in foreign affairs. Accordingly, presidents tend to arrogate to themselves maximum and unfettered authority over such affairs, and lawmakers tend to leave the making and day-to-day management of foreign policy to the executive branch, which is considered to be best equipped to formulate and manage it.

Thirdly, political partisanship is a factor promoting the persistence of a culture of deference to the presidency on foreign policy. This is especially so when the presidency and Congress are controlled by the same political party. The desire to hold on to political power and to the perquisites of office promotes a culture of deference to the presidency. This is frequently done at the expense of national security. In that case, loyalty to the political party and its leader as represented by the president becomes the "national interest." It thus supersedes the interest of the nation. The overwhelming support of Republican lawmakers for the Bush administration's war in Iraq provides strong evidence of this tendency. President Bush's shifting rationale for the war and his administration's conduct of it cannot explain that support.

Stephen R. Weissman has identified the following key postulates of continuing congressional deference to the presidency in foreign policy:[556]

1. *Congress gives the president leeway to unilaterally undertake new and urgent initiatives, which imply a future commitment of legislative support.*
   Many presidential foreign policy decisions, such as those that transfer military aid to a friendly government waging a civil war, launch a secret paramilitary campaign against an unfriendly government, or deploy US troops on a humanitarian mission to another state, touch directly upon the constitutional powers of Congress to make laws and appropriate funds. In such cases, presidents tend to invoke national security, urgency, or secrecy to justify their unilateral action. Invariably, Congress enacts legislation to legitimate and appropriate funds for such actions regardless of the party affiliation of the president. Congress has, to date, continued to fund the war in Iraq even though some of its members and 61 percent of the American public are now strongly against it.

2. *Congress declines to wield its weapons against executive branch deceptions.*
   Very seldom does Congress unmask executive branch deception through persistent demand of relevant information, reports, and cables, often classified, or by swearing in official witnesses during committee hearings on foreign policy. This is in spite of the executive branch's well-known capacity to deceive the Congress and the public at large. This practice "sacrifices a potential legal sanction—felony prosecution—against the most extreme form of deception, clear-cut lying."[557]

3. *Congress does not deploy its resources to ensure that it develops an independent perspective on international events.*

    Very few members of Congress spend time on foreign policy issues for a variety reasons, including electoral politics and constituency pressures. For most of the time, they rely on their staff, who are numerically and technically ill-equipped to investigate and master the issues that would most enable lawmakers to be competent partners in foreign policy making. Therefore, they rely on information from the presidency and a compliant media as the bases of their foreign policy decisions.

4. *Congress has a weak commitment to making and upholding clear and binding law.*

    Lawmakers tend to enact laws that are vague or ambiguous and are often ineffective to oversee their implementation by the executive branch. The Clark Amendment illustrates both tendencies. It forbade covert assistance to any of the factions involved in the Angolan war of political succession. Its meaning was subsequently disputed while it was violated by the Ronald Reagan and George H. W. Bush administration. It was eventually repealed in 1985 at the behest of a defiant President Reagan. The vagueness and lack of will to oversee the implementation of law by the executive branch is often a function of political compromise and realistic recognition of the need for executive branch flexibility in the midst of changing international circumstances.

5. *Congress is sometimes driven by relatively narrowly based special interests, with access to a few key legislators.*

    This aspect of the culture is due to the lawmakers' increased electoral insecurity, campaign contributions, and lobbying by narrowly interested and well-organized groups. The paucity of broad-based constituencies for foreign policy also contributes to foster the culture. However, by exerting strong leadership, Congress could effectively address the problem of weak political constituency for foreign affairs,

6. *Congress views some major executive branch policies in almost total secrecy, further narrowing its access to critical information and limiting its choices.*

    Most of the reviews of major executive branch policies are carried out by the intelligence committees of Congress. The reviews involve information furnished to the committees in secret by the Intelligence Community on covert actions of the US government, which, by law, are not to be apparent or acknowledged publicly. Committee members have no way of counterbalancing that information with additional information.

Consequently, they support the administration's policy on the bases of the information provided to them.

What Is to Be Done

To reverse or, more realistically, to dilute the culture of deference in Congress to the presidency on foreign policy matters, such as war making, a number of specific steps should be adopted. Many more American citizens than is presently the case should shed their ignorance about the rest of the world, as well as their lack of knowledge of the constitutional provisions for the management of the nation's foreign relations. This is an opportune time for many more Americans to develop more and stronger interest in American foreign policy. Doing so is even more critical given the blurring of the line between foreign and domestic issues, how one affects the other, and the significant range of contemporary developments that transcend national boundaries. The terrorist attacks of 11 September 2001, the promulgation of the Bush doctrine of preemption, the US invasion and occupation of Iraq in 2003, and the Bush administration's rejection of global instruments, such as the Kyoto Protocol and the International Criminal Court, all call for scrutiny and analytic clarity by both scholars and US lawmakers. Similarly, many more American citizens should become more fully aware about how faithfully their lawmakers fulfill their constitutionally designated foreign policy responsibility. It is not enough to shed ignorance about such matters. It is critical to hold members of Congress accountable constantly for the performance of their constitutionally stipulated foreign policy role and during periodic elections.

American citizens who are experts in the historical experience and political developments in various regions of the world, and there are several, should share their knowledge and make their voices heard by the general public, especially when occasions call for doing so, even if they are the one voice crying in the wilderness. Silence on their part "is part of a larger problem, of why public discourse in the United States about foreign affairs is so often driven by the lowest common denominator, by ill-informed pundits rather than by people who are actually knowledgeable about the rest of the world."[558]

Furthermore, American people in general should also ask more questions of their rulers and representatives on such a critical foreign policy issue as war making. They should demand openness and public debate as the nation shapes its foreign policies, especially the decision to go to war. American experience at war, at least since Vietnam, demonstrates that the brutalities of war do not discriminate against any of its belligerents, although the range of the war's fatalities, psychological traumas, and other costs may differ. Therefore,

American people should be wary of those who never served in the military and never were within a thousand miles of combat but who vociferously call for the most bellicose foreign policy. They should clearly reject relying on the ideology and instincts of a president or vice president or on the schemes of unelected bureaucrats, as was the case in the Bush administration's war in Iraq, for a decision to go to war. Since they would be providing the human and material sinews and making other sacrifices of any war embarked upon by the nation, they should impel lawmakers to reject the rush to military options, such as the chief executives have so frequently adopted, to resolve complicated international disputes that require patient diplomacy.

There is also a need for US administrators to reduce the causes of anti-Americanism around the world by putting transparent fairness and pragmatism in American foreign policy. To achieve this, Julia E. Sweig, a senior fellow at the Council on Foreign Relations suggests the following:

> [A]nti-Americanism will begin to ebb if the new watchwords of US policy and conduct are pragmatism, generosity, modesty, discretion, cooperation, empathy, fairness, manners and lawfulness. This softer lexicon should not be construed as a refutation of the use of force against hostile states or terrorist groups. Rather, a foreign policy that deploys US power with some consideration for how the US is perceived will gradually make legitimate US military action more acceptable abroad.... Recovering [America's] global standing will come not only from how [the nation] fights or prevents the next war, or manages an increasingly chaotic world. Domestic policy must change as well. Steering the body politic out of its insular mood, reducing social and economic inequalities, and decreasing its dependence on fossil fuels will help improve its moral standing and its security.[559]

The presidency, however, cannot imperially or unilaterally address all the causes of anti-Americanism as well as the other problems confronting the nation. Congress was designed to be a deliberate and effective evaluator and actor, not a rubber-stamp of the presidency, in addressing the nation's problems. Therefore, for its part, Congress should not abandon its critical role in the making and conduct of foreign policy. Doing so negates the national security interest and casts aside the wisdom of the framers of the American political system. The lawmakers should work with the president to control the executive branch through regular oversight and tethering the president and the bureaucrats to the will of the people in the conduct of the nation's foreign affairs.

Congress has the tools, if it exerts leadership, to play a much more significant and thoughtful role in foreign policy making. American diplomatic history confirms that major foreign policy transformations fail without congressional support. William McKinley's vogue for colonialism after the 1898 war with Spain did not last long because popular and congressional opinion shifted against it after the beginning of a costly insurgency in the Philippines in 1899. Woodrow Wilson's grandiose plan to reform the international system was rejected by the Senate, and the United States never became a member of an international organization—the League of Nations—that was the brainchild of its chief executive. Harry Truman's policy of containing the Soviet Union was not firmly established until congressional support for it was organized by Republican Senator Arthur Vandenberg. Attempts at a unilateral and imperial foreign policy at the expense of the American Republic and constitutional system will fail if Congress shows strong and genuine leadership and exerts its constitutional powers in foreign policy.

America's national security interest and special position in the world require that Congress should play such a leadership role as well as exert greater devotion to its oversight of all executive branch bureaucracies and agencies involved in the conduct and management of foreign affairs. It should demand peak performance from the president and his national security team. Given recent experience, it should ensure that the quality of intelligence used to send US armed forces to war and to enact treaties, for example, are of the highest caliber. In accordance with the US Constitution and political system, the American people want neither an imperial president free of legislative restraints nor an imperiled president dominated by an overbearing Congress. Institutional flaws in both the legislative and executive branches of government require the active involvement of both of them in the making of foreign policy to help ensure the pursuit of the national interest rather than the ambition of individuals. There is therefore a critical need for an infusion of men and women committed to the legislative body as a national institution, men and women who will engage each other "seriously enough to search out and find areas of agreement, and join hands with each other to insist on the rights and prerogatives of the national legislature, not make it simply an echo chamber of presidential politics."[560]

Notes

Chapter 1

1. Robert C. Tucker and David Hendrickson, "The Sources of American Legitimacy," *Foreign Affairs* 83, no. 6 (November–December 2004): 32. See also Zoltan Grossman, "A Century of US Military Interventions: From Wounded Knee to Afghanistan," *ZNet*, September 20, 2001, http://www.zmag.org/CrisesCurEvts/interventions.htm.
2. Leslie H. Gelb and Anne Marie Slaughter, "Declare War: It's Time to Stop Slipping into Armed Conflict," *Atlantic Monthly* 296, no. 4 (November 2005): 56.
3. Stephen M. Walt, "Who Will Be Blamed for Iraq? It's Easy for Politicians to Point Fingers at Each Other. But Ultimately, the Buck Stops at the Oval Office," *Foreign Policy* (November–December 2005): 46.
4. For more details see: Norman Ornstein and Frank E. Mann, "When Congress Checks Out," *Foreign Affairs*, Volume 85, Number 6 (November/ December 2006), pp. 67–82.
5. See Anatol Lieven, "Depose and Conquer," review of *Overthrow: America's Century of Regime Change from Hawaii to Iraq*, by Stephen Kinzer, *New York Times*, April 16, 2006, http://www.nytimes.com/2006/04/16/books/review/16lievan.html. See also Robert Sherrill, "America's 100 Years of Overthrow," *AlterNet* (20 July 2006), http://www.alternet.org/story/ 39416.
6. Louis Fisher, "The Way We Go to War: The Iraq Resolution," in *Considering the Bush Presidency*, ed. Gary L. Gregg II and Mark J. Rozell (New York: Oxford University, 2004), 118.
7. *Congressional Record* (1964): 18462.
8. The destroyer, USS *Maddox*, was patrolling the Gulf of Tonkin, twenty-five miles off the coast of North Vietnam, on 2 August 1964 when it was allegedly attacked by three North Vietnamese torpedo boats. Two days later the destroyer was joined by the USS *Turner Joy*, which, amidst confusion and hysteria, reported that it was under attack. The alleged attacks led to the Gulf of Tonkin Resolution.
9. David E. Sanger, "New Tapes Indicate Johnson Doubted Attack in Tonkin Gulf," *New York Times*, November 6, 2001, http://www.nytimes.com/2001/1/06/politics/06TAPE.html.
10. Norman Solomon, "War-Loving Pundits," *AlterNet*, March 16, 2006, http://www.alternet.org/story/33661/.

11. Russ Baker, "The Sins of Judith Miller," *AlterNet*, http://www.alternet. org/story/22301/.
12. Joseph C. Wilson IV, "What I Didn't Find in Africa," *New York Times*, July 6, 2003.
13. Joseph C. Wilson, "What I Didn't Find in Africa," *The New York Times* (6 July 2003), http://www.nytimes.com/ 2003/07/06/opinion/o6WILS.html.
14. Tim Rutten, "Regarding Media: Woodward Joins a Decadent Dance," *Los Angeles Times*, November 19, 2005, http://www.latimes.com/.
15. F. Ugboaja Ohaegbulam, *A Concise Introduction to American Foreign Policy* (New York: Peter Lang, 1999), 98–99.
16. Examples include the following: Bob Woodward, *Bush at War* (New York: Simon and Schuster, 2002) and *Plan of Attack* (New York: Simon and Schuster, 2004); Richard Clarke, *Against All Enemies* (New York: Free Press, 2004); Stanley Hoffmann with Frederic Bozo, *Gulliver Unbound: America's Imperial Temptation and Iraq War* (Lanham, MD: Rowman and Littlefield, 2004); John Dean, *Worse Than Watergate* (New York: Warner Books, 2004); Tariq Ali, *Bush in Babylon: The Recolonization of Iraq* (London: Verso, 2003); James Bamford, *A Pretext for War* (New York: Anchor Books, 2005); Benjamin Barber, *Fear's Empire: War, Terrorism and Democracy* (New York: W. W. Norton and Co., Inc., 2004); Seymour Hersh, *Chain of Command* (New York: HarperCollins, 2005); David Harvey, *The New Imperialism* (Oxford: Oxford University Press, 2005); and John Newhouse, *Imperial America: The Bush Assault on World Order* (New York: Vintage Books, 2004).

Chapter 2

17. David J. Rothkopf, "Inside the Committee That Runs the World," *Foreign Policy* (March–April 2005): 38–9.
18. Ivo H. Daalder and James M. Lindsey, *America Unbound: The Bush Revolution in Foreign Policy* (Washington, DC: Brookings Institution, 2003), 80.
19. Patrick E. Tyler, "US Strategy Plan Calls for Insuring No Rivals Develop a One-Superpower World: Pentagon's Document Outlines Ways to Thwart Challenges to Primacy of America," *New York Times*, March 8, 1992, http://work.column.edu/-amilar/wofowitz1992.htm; David Armstrong, "Dick Cheney's Song of America," *Harper's Magazine*, 305, no. 1829 (October 2002), http://www.informationclearinghouse. info/article1544.htm; Stanley Hoffmann with Frederic Bozo, *Gulliver*

Unbound: America's Imperial Temptation and the War in Iraq (Lanham, MD: Rowman and Littlefield, 2004), 21.

20. Quoted in Bob Woodward, *Plan of Attack* (New York: Simon and Schuster, 2004), 91; Robert Jervis, "Understanding the Bush Doctrine," in *American Foreign Policy: Theoretical Essays*, 5th ed., ed. G. John Ikenberry (New York: Pearson/Longman, 2005), 578.

21. President George W. Bush, "Address to a Joint Session of Congress and the American People" (September 20, 2001), http://www.whitehouse.gov/.

22. Specific examples of the multipronged global approach included UN resolutions, intelligence sharing with other governments, obtaining military support and overflight rights for American aircraft, international sanctions against the Taliban government of Afghanistan, Osama bin Laden, and al-Qaeda, and a conscious effort to assure the Islamic world that impending US military actions against the Taliban were just that and not against Islam.

23. The final USA PATRIOT Act introduced sweeping threatening changes to civil liberties under US law, including the Wiretap Statute (Title III), Electronic Communications Privacy Act, Computer Fraud and Abuse Act, Foreign Intelligence Surveillance Act, Family Education Rights and Privacy Act, Pen Register and Trap and Trace Statute, Money Laundering Act, Immigration and Nationality Act, Money Laundering Control Act, Bank Secrecy Act, Right to Financial Privacy Act, and Fair Credit Reporting Act.

24. Electronic Private Information Center (EPIC),"The USA PATRIOT Act," http://www.epic.org/privacy/terrorism/usapatriot.

25. American Civil Liberties Union (ACLU), "Keep America Safe and Free: USA PATRIOT Act," http://www.aclu.org/safefree/index.html.

26. See ACLU, "Keeping America Safe and Free: USA PATRIOT Act"; EPIC, "The USA PATRIOT Act."

27. Editorial, "Signs of Life at State," *New York Times*, July 4, 2005, http://www.nytimes.com/2005/07/04/opinion/04mon1.html.

28. Evan Thomas, "'Running the World': In the War Room," *New York Times*, June 26, 2005, http://www.nytime.com/2005/06/26/books/review/THOMASL.html.

29. See Seymour M. Hersh, *Chain of Command: The Road From 9/11 to Abu Ghraib* (New York: Harper Collins, 2005), 177–8; Glenn Kessler and Peter Slevin, "Rice Fails to Repair Rifts, Officials Say; Cabinet Rivalries Complicate Her Role," *Washington Post*, October 12, 2003, http://www.mtholyoke.edu/acad/intrel/bush/role. htm.

30. Bob Woodward, *Plan of Attack* (New York: Simon & Schuster, 2004), 414–5.

31. Thomas, "'Running the World': In the War Room."

32. G. John Ikenberry, "America's Imperial Ambition," *Foreign Affairs* 81 no. 5 (September–October 2002): 46.

33. Woodward, *Plan of Attack*, 19.

34. Richard Perle, "The War Behind Closed Doors: Interviews: Richard Perle," *Frontline*, PBS, January 25, 2003, http://www.pbs.org/wgbh/pages/frontline/shows/iraq/interviews/perle.html.

35. Perle.

36. James P. Rubin, "Stumbling into War," *Foreign Affairs* 82, no. 5 (September–October 2003): 59–60; Bob Woodward, *State of Denial: Bush at War, Part III* (New York: Simon and Schuster, 2006), 75–77, 87.

37. Helen Cooper and Steven Erlangen, "No Progress in Middle East Talks," The *New York Times* (19 February 2007), http://www.nytiumes.com/2007/02/19/world/middleeast/19end-mideast.html?; Ken Ellingwood, "Rice Calls Mideast Meeting 'Productive,'" *Los Angeles Times* (20 February 2007).

38. Daalder and Lindsey, *America Unbound*, 81. The administration shared intelligence with other countries. It initiated an international effort to foil al-Qaeda's use of banks and other international financial institutions to finance terrorist activities and provided antiterrorist training and assistance around the world.

39. *National Security Strategy of the United States of America*, September 20, 2002, http://www.whitehouse.gov/nsc/nss/2002/ index.html.

40. Benjamin R. Barber, *Fear's Empire: War, Terrorism, and Democracy* (New York: W. W. Norton and Co., Inc., 2004), 110.

41. Michael Hirsh, "Bush and the World," Foreign Affairs, 81, no. 5 (September–October 2002): 18–43. Note especially page 36.

42. *National Security Strategy of the United States of America.*

43. "Star Wars' Political Bull's-Eye," *New York Times*, June 24, 2005, http://www.nytimes.com/2005/06/24/opinion/24fri3.html.

44. Ibid.

45. Princeton N. Lyman and J. Stephen Morrison, "Africa: The New Front in the War on Terror," *Foreign Affairs* 83, no. 1 (January–February 2004): 75–86.

46. Bryan Bender, "Pentagon Plans New Command to Cover Africa," *Boston Globe* (21 December 2006).

47. Steven W. Hook, *US Foreign Policy: The Paradox of World Power* (Washington, DC: Congressional Quarterly, 2005), 7.

48. Quoted in John B. Judas, "The Author of Liberty: Religion and U.S. Foreign Policy," *Annual Editions: American Foreign Policy 07/08*, Glenn P. Hastedt, editor, (Dubuque, IA: McGraw Hill,2007), 77–82.
49. Ibid 81.
50. Ibid 82.
51. John Lewis Gaddis, "Grand Strategy in the Second Term," *Foreign Affairs* 84, no. 1 (January–February 2005): 7.
52. *National Security Strategy of the United States of America*.
53. It is important to observe that preemptive wars have been rare in modern history. The closest examples are the start of World War I in 1914, China's 1950 intervention in the Korean War, and Israel's attack on Egypt in 1967.
54. President George W. Bush (address at West Point, New York, June 1, 2002), http://www.whitehouse.gov/news/releases/2002/06/20020601-3.html.
55. Juan A. Alsace, "In Search of Monsters to Destroy: American Empire in the New Millennium," *Parameters*, Autumn 2003, 123.
56. President George W. Bush (address at West Point, New York, June 1, 2002); *National Security Strategy of the United States of America*.
57. *New York Times*, October 20, 2002, in Robert Jervis, "Understanding the Bush Doctrine," in *American Foreign Policy: Theoretical Essays*, ed. G. John Ikenberry, 5th ed. (New York: Pearson/Longman, 2005), 581.
58. *National Security Strategy of the United States of America*.
59. Michael Howard, "The Bush Doctrine: It's a Brutal World, So Act Brutally," *Sunday Times*, March 23, 2003, 21. Quoted in Rashid Khalidi, *Resurrecting Empire: Western Footprints and America's Perilous Path in the Middle East* (Boston: Beacon Press, 2005), 21.
60. Benjamin R. Barber, *Fear's Empire: War, Terrorism, and Democracy*, 118.
61. John Lewis Gaddis, *Surprise, Security, and the American Experience* (Cambridge, MA: Harvard University, 2004), 42–43.
62. Amos A. Jordan, William J. Taylor, and Michael J. Mazarr, *American National Security*, 5th ed. (Baltimore, MD.: Johns Hopkins University, 1999), 57.
63. Steven W. Hook, *US Foreign Policy: The Paradox of World Power* (Washington, DC: Congressional Quarterly, 2005), 311.
64. See Council on Foreign Relations, "Q & A: Max Boot on President Bush's Agenda," *New York Times*, January 12, 2005, http://www.nytimes.com/cfr/international/slot1_011205.html.
65. See "Special Report United States of America: Spot the Differences," *Guardian Unlimited*, February 18, 2005, http://www.guardian.co.uk/usa/story/0,12271,1417433,00.html; William Pfaff, "Why Bush Will Fail in

Europe," *Observer*, February 20, 2005, http://www.guardian.co.uk/usa/story/0,12271,1418548,00.html.

66. Amitabh Pal, "Blanket Immunity: Bush Twists Arms to Evade Court," *The Progressive* 71, No. 1 (January 2007): 26–28.

67. President George W. Bush, "The National Security Strategy of the United States of America" (March 2006), http://www.whitehouse.gov/nsc/nss/2006/print/index.html.

68. Ivo H. Daalder, "Statement on the 2006 National Security Strategy," *Foreign Policy Studies* (The Brookings Institution, 16 March 2006).

69. Editorial, "Bush and the World Bank," *Le Monde*, March 19, 2005, http://www.lemonde.fr/web/article/0,1-0@2-3222,36-631775,0.html.

70. Mary Crane, "Q & A: EU-US Relations and the War on Terror," *New York Times*, December 7, 2005, http://www.nytimes.com/cfr/international/slot/2_120705.html.

Chapter 3

71. Robert W. Tucker and David C. Hendrickson, "Thomas Jefferson and American Foreign Policy," *Foreign Affairs* 69, no. 2 (Spring 1990): 135–56. Note that this quotation appears on page 139.

72. Quoted in Richard B. Bilder, "The Role of States and Cities in Foreign Relations," in *Foreign Affairs and the US Constitution*, ed. Louis Henkin et al. (New York: Transnational, 1990), 115.

73. Louis Henkin, *Foreign Affairs and the US Constitution*, 2nd ed. (New York: Oxford University, 1996), 127.

74. See Earl H. Fry, *The Expanding Role of State and Local Governments in US Foreign Affairs* (New York: Council on Foreign Relations, 1998); Michael N. Shuman, "Dateline Main Street: Local Foreign Policies," *Foreign Policy* 65 (Winter 1986–1987): 154–74; Spiro, "Taking Foreign Policy Away from the Feds," *Washington Quarterly* 1 (1988): 191–203.

75. Shuman, "Dateline Main Street," 154–69; Raymond Rogers, *American Journal of International Law* (October 1967); Kenneth E. Boulding, "The City as an Element in the International System," *Daedalus* 97, no. 4 (Fall 1968): 1123.

76. James O. Goldsborough, "California's Foreign Policy," *Foreign Affairs* 72, no. 2 (Spring 1993): 88–96. Note this quotation appears on page 90.

77. Louis Henkin, "Foreign Affairs and the Constitution," *Foreign Affairs* 66, no. 2 (Winter 1987–1988): 284–310; Cecil V. Crabb, Jr., and Pat M. Holt, *Invitation to Struggle: Congress, the President and Foreign Policy*, 4th ed. (Washington, DC: Congressional Quarterly Press, 1992).

78. Arthur Bestor, "'Advice' from the Very Beginning, 'Consent' When the End Is Achieved," in *Foreign Affairs and the US Constitution*, ed. Louis Henkin et al. (New York: Transnational, 1990), 15.
79. Quoted in Henkin, *Foreign Affairs*, 292.
80. Donald M. Snow and Eugene Brown, *Puzzle Palaces and Foggy Bottom: US Foreign and Defense Policy-Making in the 1990s* (New York: St. Martin's, 1994), 33.
81. Snow and Brown, *Puzzle Palaces*, 37–40.
82. "Barry Goldwater v. Carter," in *Foreign Affairs and the US Constitution,* ed. Louis Henkin et al. (New York: Transnational, 1990), 271–78. Note this quotation appears on page 277.
83. Shuman, "Dateline Main Street," 162.
84. Bestor, "'Advice'" 9–10.
85. Ibid., 12.
86. Ibid.
87. Ibid., 13.
88. Dexter Perkins, *The American Approach to Foreign Policy* (New York: Athenaeum, 1968), 191; Crabb and Holt, *Invitation to Struggle*, 43; Snow and Brown, *Puzzle Palaces*, 125.
89. Alexander Hamilton, "Federalist No. 75," in *The Federalist*, George Stade, editor (New York: Barnes and Noble, 2006), 413–15.
90. Peter Grier, "Why 48 Treaties Languish in Senate," *Christian Science Monitor*, March 26, 1997, 3.
91. Bestor, "'Advice,'" 13.
92. Ibid., 14–5.
93. Crabb and Holt, *Invitation to Struggle*, 43.
94. There are two types of executive agreements. The vast majority, those entered into with prior congressional approval, are statutory. Tariff reductions and agreements based on prior treaties approved by the Senate fall within this category. Statutory executive agreements are the more controversial type, because, often, Congress is not fully aware of the extent of its authorization or of that of the contemplated agreement. The second type is the pure executive agreement. These are made by the president or his representative orally or in writing without prior congressional authorization. Roosevelt's Yalta Agreements with Stalin and other arrangements made by presidents, as commander in chief, for military or naval facilities are typical examples. See: *Department of State Bulletin* 28 (February 1972): 279–84; Loch Johnson and James M. McCormick, "The Making of International Agreements: A Reappraisal of Congressional Involvement," *Journal of Politics* 40

(May 1978): 468–78.
95. James M. McCormack, *American Foreign Policy and Process*, 4th ed. (Belmont, CA: Thomson/Wadsworth, 2005), 261–63.
96. Ibid., 262. See Table 7.2.
97. Harold W. Stanley and Richard G. Niemi, *Vital Statistics in American Politics* (Washington, DC: Congressional Quarterly, 1992), 278; James M. Lindsay, *Congress and the Politics of US Foreign Policy* (Baltimore, MD: Johns Hopkins University, 1994), 30.
98. McCormack, *American Foreign Policy*, 262. See Table 7.2.
99. Loch Johnson and James M. McCormick, "Foreign Policy Executive Fiat," *Foreign Policy* 28 (Fall 1977): 117–38.
100. For details see Stephen A. Garrett, "Foreign Policy and the American Constitution: The Bricker Amendment in Comparative Perspective," *International Studies Quarterly* 16 (June 1972): 187–220.
101. Johnson and McCormick, "Foreign Policy Executive Fiat," 118–24.
102. Bestor, "'Advice,'" 11.
103. Crabb and Holt, *Invitation to Struggle*, 43.
104. Cited in Louis Fisher, "How Tightly Can Congress Draw the Purse Strings?" in *Foreign Affairs and the US Constitution,* ed. Louis Henkin et al. (New York: Transnational, 1990), 50.
105. Glenn P. Hastedt, *American Foreign Policy: Past, Present, Future*, 3rd ed. (Upper Saddle River, NJ: Prentice Hall, 1997), 161.
106. See David Scheffer, "Nouveau Law and Foreign Policy," *Foreign Policy* 76 (Fall 1989): 44–65.
107. "Court Jettisons Line-Item Veto," *Christian Science Monitor*, June 26, 1998, 1, 14; "No to the Line-Item Veto," *Washington Post*, June 26, 1998, A26.
108. For details, see "Controversy over the Presidential Impoundment of Appropriated Funds," *Congressional Digest* 52 (April 1973): 65–96; Lawrence C. Dodd and Bruce Oppenheimer, ed., *Congress Reconsidered* (New York: Praeger, 1977), 163–92.
109. Thomas M. Franck, "Rethinking War Powers: By Law or by 'Thaumaturgic Invocation'?" in *Foreign Affairs and the US Constitution*, ed. Louis Henkin et al. (New York: Transnational, 1990), 57.
110. Loch K. Johnson, *America as a World Power*, 2nd ed. (New York: McGraw-Hill, 1995), 287.
111. See Johnson, *America as a World Power*, 162–3.
112. Elliot L. Richardson, "Checks and Balances in Foreign Relations," in *Foreign Affairs and the US Constitution*, ed. Louis Henkin et al. (New York: Transnational, 1990), 25.

Chapter 4

113. Paul Krugman, "The War President," *New York Times*, June 24, 2005, http://www.nytimes.com/2005/06/24/opinion/24krugman.htm.
114. Charles A. Lofgren, "War-Making Under the Constitution: The Original Understanding," *Yale Law Review* (March 1972): 685. Quoted in Bruce W. Jentleson, *American Foreign Policy: The Dynamics of Choice in the 21st Century*, 2nd ed. (New York: W. W. Norton & Co., 2004), 219–20.
115. Arthur M. Schlesinger, Jr., "The President and Congress: What the Founding Fathers Intended," in *American Foreign Policy: The Dynamics of Choice in the 21st Century*, ed. Bruce W. Jentleson, 2nd ed. (New York: W. W. Norton & Co., 2004), 220.
116. James Madison to Thomas Jefferson (2 April 1798), James Madison, *Writings*, ed. Gaillard Hunt (New York, 1906), both quoted in Arthur M. Schlesinger, Jr., "The President and Congress: What the Founding Fathers Intended," in *American Foreign Policy: The Dynamics of Choice in the 21st Century*, ed. Bruce W. Jentleson, 2nd ed. (New York: W. W. Norton & Co., 2004), 220.
117. James M. Lindsay, *Congress and the Politics of US Foreign Policy* (Baltimore, MD: Johns Hopkins University, 1994), 13.
118. Alexander Hamilton, "Federalist No. 69," *The Federalist*, with an Introduction and Notes by Robert A. Ferguson, George Stade, editor (New York: Barnes and Noble, 2006), 382; Also quoted in Schlesinger, Jr., "The President and Congress," 221.
119. W. Michael Riesman, "War Powers: The Operational Code of Competence," in *Foreign Affairs and the US Constitution*, ed. Louis Henkin et al. (New York: Transnational Publishers, Inc., 1990), 69.
120. Arthur Schlesinger, Jr., "Back to the Womb? Isolationism's Renewed Threat," *Foreign Affairs* 74, no. 4 (July–August 1995): 5.
121. Louis Henkin, "Foreign Affairs and the Constitution," *Foreign Affairs* 66, no. 2 (Winter 1987–1988): 289.
122. David Gray Adler, "The Constitution and Presidential War Making: The Enduring Debate," *Political Science Quarterly* 193, no. 1 (Spring 1988): 1–36.
123. Dean Acheson, *Present at the Creation: My Years in the State Department* (New York: Norton, 1987), 413–4; Lindsay, *Congress and the Politics of US Foreign Policy*, 19.
124. Alexis de Tocqueville, *Democracy in America* (New York: Anchor Books, 1969), 126; Also quoted in James M. Lindsay, *Congress and the Politics of US Foreign Policy* (Baltimore, MD: The Johns Hopkins University, 1994), 18.

125. Thomas M. Franck, "Rethinking War Powers: By Law or by 'Thaumaturgic Invocation'?" in *Foreign Affairs and the US Constitution*, ed. Louis Henkin et al. (New York: Transnational, 1990), 57.

126. Arthur M. Schlesinger, Jr., *The Imperial Presidency* (Boston: Houghton Mifflin, 1973), 138.

127. Lindsay, *Congress and the Politics of US Foreign Policy*, 22.

128. The War Powers Resolution: Relevant Documents, Correspondence, Reports, Subcommittee on International Security and Scientific Affairs, House Committee on Foreign Affairs (December 1973), 1–6; Also see Text of the Resolution in *The New York Times* (8 November 1973), 20.

129. See Text of the Resolution in *The New York Times* (8 November 1973), 20.

130. Senator Spark Matsunaga, "War Powers Legislation: Practical and Constitutional Problems," *Department of State Bulletin* 28 (June 1971): 834.

131. *Department of State Bulletin* 26 (November 1973): 662.

132. Franck, "Rethinking War Powers," 59.

133. Eugene R. Wittkopf et al., *American Foreign Policy: Pattern and Process*, 6th ed. (Belmont, CA: Thomson/Wadsworth, 2003), 418.

134. Arthur Schlesinger, Jr., "Back to the Womb?" *Foreign Affairs* 74, no. 4 (July–August 1995): 6.

Chapter 5

135. Stephen R. Weissman, *A Culture of Deference: Congress's Failure of Leadership in Foreign Policy* (New York: Basic Books, 1995), 3.

136. James Madison, "Federalist 51," *The Federalist*, with an introduction and notes by Robert A. Ferguson (New York: Barnes and Noble Classics, 2006), 288; see also Gary Hart and Joyce Appleby, "Facing Down a Constitutional Crisis," *AlterNet*, March 29, 2006, http://www.alternet.org/story/ 34084/.

137. Alexander Hamilton, "Federalist 75," *The Federalist* (New York: Barnes and Noble Classics, 2006), 415; see also Gene Healy, "Arrogance of Power Reborn: The Imperial Presidency and Foreign Policy in the Clinton Years," *Policy Analysis*, December 13, 2000, http://www.cato.org/pubs/pas/ pa389.pdf.

138. After the end of World War II, the bulk of US foreign commitments, about 95 percent, took the form of executive agreements, oral and written. See James M. McCormick, *American Foreign Policy and Process*, 4th ed. (Belmont, CA: Thomson/Wadswoth, 2005), 260–3; Bruce W. Jentleson and Thomas G. Paterson, ed., *Encyclopedia of US Foreign Relations*

(New York: Oxford University, 1997), 318.

139. Past and more recent examples of judicial rulings that strengthened the role of the presidency in foreign affairs include the following: *US v. Curtiss-Wright Export Corporation et al.* (1936) in which the Supreme Court, among other things, held that the president alone had the power to speak or listen as the representative of the nation; *US v. Belmont* (1937) and *US v. Pink* (1942) in which the Supreme Court accorded legal standing to executive agreements; and *Edward v. Carter* (1978) and *Goldwater et al. v. Carter* (1979)— by the former, the Supreme Court upheld President Carter's decision to return the Panama Canal to Panama, and, by the latter, it similarly upheld the Carter administration's decision to abrogate the defense treaty with Taiwan without the approval of Congress in order to reestablish diplomatic relations with the People's Republic of China.

140. Senator Robert C. Byrd, quoted in Jon Western, *Selling Intervention and War: The Presidency, the Media, and the American Public* (Baltimore, MD: Johns Hopkins University, 2005), 175.

141. Daniel S. Papp et al., *American Foreign Policy: History, Politics, and Policy* (New York: Pearson/Longman, 2005), 239.

142. Arthur M. Schlesinger, Jr., *The Imperial Presidency, with a New Introduction* (Boston: Houghton Mifflin Company, 2004), xv.

143. Stuart Taylor, Jr., "Comment: The Man Who Would Be King," *Atlantic Monthly* 297, no. 3 (April 2006): 26.

144. Editorial, "The Imperial Presidency," *Nation*, September 16, 2002, http://www.thenation.com/doc/20020916/editors. See also Helen Thomas, "[George W.] Bush Acting as Imperial President," *Seattle Post-Intelligencer*, July 3, 2002.

145. Senator J. William Fulbright, *The Arrogance of Power* (New York: Random House, 1966); Schlesinger, Jr., *The Imperial Presidency*.

146. Quoted in Steven W. Hook, *US Foreign Policy: The Paradox of World Power* (Washington, DC: Congressional Quarterly, 2005), 125.

147. Schlesinger, Jr., *The Imperial Presidency*, 9, 298.

148. Papp et al., *American Foreign Policy*, 240.

149. Mark Danner, "The Secret Way to War," *New York Review of Books* 52, no. 10 (June 2005): 8.

150. Lawrence B. Wilkerson, "The White House Cabal," *Los Angeles Times*, October 25, 2005, http://www.latimes.com/; Brian Knowlton, "Former Powell Aide Says Bush Policy Is Run by 'Cabal,'" *New York Times*, October 21, 2005.

151. Stephen K. Bailey, *Congress in the Seventies*, quoted in Loch K. Johnson, *America as a World Power: Foreign Policy in a Constitutional*

Framework , 2nd ed. (New York: McGraw-Hill, Inc., 1995), 203.

152. Lee H. Hamilton with Jordan Tama, *A Creative Tension: The Foreign Policy Roles of the President and Congress* (Washington, DC: Woodrow Wilson Center, 2002), 2–3.

153. As senator, J. F. Kennedy was critical of Eisenhower's foreign policy. But the criticism tended to advance his presidential candidacy, as he did not depart radically from Eisenhower's foreign policy after he succeeded him in 1961.

154. The Yalta Agreement required, among other things, free elections and constitutional safeguards of freedom in Eastern Europe immediately after World War II. The Soviet Union violated the agreement by installing in the countries governments friendly to its political system and thereby precipitated the cold war.

155. James Risen and Eric Lichtblau, "Bush Lets US Spy on Callers without Courts," *New York Times*, December 16, 2005, http://www.nytimes.com/ 2005/12/16/politics/16program.html; James Risen and Eric Lichtblau, "Spying Program Snared US Calls," *New York Times*, December 21, 2005, http://www.nytimes.com/2005/12/21/ politics/21nsa.html; Warren Richey, "Did Bush Exceed His Powers?" *Christian Science Monitor*, December 22, 2005, also in *AlterNet*, December 22, 2005, http://www. alternet.org/story/ 29950/.

156. Schlesinger, Jr., *The Imperial Presidency*, x.

157. J. William Fulbright, *The Arrogance of Power* (New York: Random House, 1966), 45.

158. George W. Bush, *National Security Strategy of the United States of America*, (20 September 2002), http://www.whitehouse.gov/nsc/nssa/ index.html.

159. Bush, *National Security Strategy of the United States of America* (20 September 2002)

160. Quoted in Janet Hook, "Opposition Tests Bush's Hold on GOP," *Tampa Tribune*, February 26, 2006, 5.

161. Weissman, *A Culture of Deference*, x.

162. Mary McGrory, quoted in Johnson, *America as a World Power*, 203.

163. Later, on 30 November 2005, in a PBS broadcast with Jim Lehrer, Senator Warner regretted that he had made a mistake in not probing the administration's case for war deeper.

164. Several of his fellow Senate Democrats criticized him for working very closely with the Bush administration on the Iraq Resolution without obtaining anything in return.

165. Louis Fisher, "Deciding on War against Iraq: Institutional Failures," *Political Science Quarterly* 118, no. 3 (Fall 2003): 390.

166. Gary Hart, "Intelligence Abuse Déjà Vu," *Los Angeles Times*, December 21, 2005, http://www.latimes.com/.

167. Jason Leopold, "CIA Leak Scandal Goes to the Top," *AlterNet*, http://www.alternet.org/story/32073/; Tom Hamburger and Sonni Efron, "A CIA Cover Blown, a White House Exposed," *Los Angeles Times*, August 25, 2005, http://www.latimes.com/; Later, in August 2006, it was reported in both print and electronic media that Undersecretary of State Armitage was the first to leak the name to Robert Novack. However, there was evidence that the Bush administration had independently leaked the name for its own political purposes.

168. Quoted in Daniel S. Papp et al., *American Foreign Policy: History, Politics, and Policy* (New York: Pearson/Longman, 2005), 21.

169. The Byrd Amendment to the Military Appropriations Act of 1969–1970 violated US obligations to enforce UN Security Council sanctions on Rhodesia by requiring that the United States could not be prevented from importing any commodities from a non-Communist country, which it was at that time, importing from a Communist nation. The Clark Amendment to the Arms Export Act of 1976 prohibited American assistance to any of the groups in the Angolan civil war.

170. For more details, see James M. McCormick, *American Foreign Policy and Process,* 4th ed. (Belmont, CA: Thomson Wadsworth, 2005), 312–7.

171. For examples of these measures, see F. Ugboaja Ohaegbulam, *A Concise Introduction to American Foreign Policy* (New York: Peter Lang, 1999), 188–90.

172. The cover-up included false and misleading statements to lawfully authorized investigative officers and employees of the US national government; attempts to misuse the CIA; political use of the CIA, the IRS, the Secret Service, the Justice Department, and the FBI; wire tapping and surveillance against those in the Nixon administration's "enemy list"; and refusal to honor congressional subpoenas for tapes secretly recorded by President Nixon relevant to the Watergate investigation.

173. Center for American Progress, "Bush Legacy on Iraq: Misinformation and False Pretense," January 12, 2004, http://www.americanprogress.org/.

174. George Tenet (speech at Georgetown University, February 5, 2004), http://www.americanprogress.org/.

Chapter 6

175. Robin Cook, former British foreign secretary to the British House of Commons (March 2003), upon resigning from Prime Minister Tony Blair's government in protest against the George W. Bush/Tony Blair-

led war in Iraq. Quoted in Alan Cowell, "Robin Cook, Former British Foreign Secretary, Dead at 59," *New York Times*, August 7, 2005, http://www.nytimes. com/.

176. Angelo M. Cordevilla, "The Sorcerer's Apprentices," *American Spectator* November 2003, 24. Reproduced in Glenn P. Hastedt, ed., *Annual Editions: American Foreign Policy*, 11th ed. (Dubuque, IA: McGraw-Hill/Dushkin, 2005), 191.

177. Baghdad severed diplomatic relations with Washington in June 1967 as a consequence of the Arab-Israeli War of that year, even though it had not been one of the belligerents in that war.

178. Sabrina Tavernise, "Iraqi Government, in Statement with Iran, Admits Fault for 1980s War," *New York Times*, May 20, 2005, http://www.nytimes. com/.

179. National Security Archive, "Shaking Hands with Saddam Hussein: The US Tilts toward Iraq, 1980–1984," *National Security Archive Electronic Briefing Book*, no. 82, February 25, 2003, 2.

180. Michael Dobbs, "US Had Key Role in Iraq Buildup," *Washington Post*, December 30, 2002, A01.

181. Ibid.

182. Ibid.

183. Ibid.

184. National Security Archive, "Shaking Hands with Saddam Hussein," 6.

185. Thomas M. Magstadt, *An Empire if You Can Keep It: Power and Principle in American Foreign Policy* (Washington, DC: Congressional Quarterly, 2004), 171; Phyllis Bennis, "Understanding the US-Iraq Crisis, Part IV: The History of US-Iraq Relations," Institute for Policy Studies, http://www.ips-dc.org/iraq/primer4.htm; *Frontline*/PBS, "The Long Road to War: Transcripts—The Arming of Iraq," http://www.pbs.org/wgbh/pages/frontline/shows/long road/etc/arming.html; Michael Dobbs, "US Had Key Role in Iraq Buildup," A01.

186. *Frontline*/PBS, "The Long Road to War: Chronology," http://www.pbs.org/wgbh/pages/frontline/shows/longroad/etc/cron.html.

187. Cordevilla, "The Sorcerer's Apprentices," in Hastedt, *Annual Editions*, 192.

188. *Frontline*/PBS, "The Gulf War: Oral History: Brent Scowcroft," http://www.pbs.org/wgbh/pages/frontline/gulf/oral/scowcroft/1.html.

189. *Frontline*/PBS, "The Long Road to War: Transcript—The Arming of Iraq."

190. Ibid.

191. *Frontline*/PBS, "The Long Road to War: Chronology."

192. Michael Dobbs, "US Had Key Role in Iraq Buildup," A02.

193. Ted Thornton, "The Gulf Wars, 1990–1991," *History of the Middle East Database*, http://www.nmhschool.org/thornton/mehistorydatabase/gulf_war.htm.

194. Thomas B. Allen et al., *War In the Gulf* (Atlanta, GA: Turner Publishers, 1991), 65.

195. Ayad Al-Qazzar, review of *War in the Gulf, 1990–1991: The Iraqi-Kuwait Conflict and Its Implications: Views from the Other Side*, by Majid Khadduri and Edmund Ghareeb, *Arab Studies Quarterly*, Summer 1998, http://www.findarticles.com/p/articles/mi_m2501/is_3_20/ai_53286322.

196. President George H. W. Bush, "Remarks by the President to the Joint Session of Congress" (September 11, 1990), http://www.cryan.com/war/speech.

197. H.J RES 77 (12 January 1991) to Authorize the United States Armed Forces to enforce UNSC Res. 678 on Iraq.

198. James Baker, "Gunning for Saddam: Interviews: James Baker," *Frontline*, PBS, http://www.pbs.org/wgbh/pages/frontline/shows/gunning/interviews/baker.html.

199. Quoted in Michael Tomasky, "Better Late Than Never," *The New York Review of Books* 54, No. 1 (11 January 2007).

200. PBS/*Frontline*, "The Gulf War: Oral History: Brent Scowcroft."

201. Charles Pope, "Cheney Changed his view on Iraq," *Seattle Post-Intelligence,* (29 September 2004).

202. Brent Scowcroft, President George H. W. Bush's national security adviser, denied that Bush incited Iraqis to revolt. He quoted the president as really saying, "Who governs Iraq is a problem for the Iraqi people, not a problem for the United States to determine. Our problem is Iraqi aggression in Kuwait." See Brent Scowcroft, "Gunning for Saddam: Interviews: Brent Scowcroft," *Frontline*, PBS, http://www.pbs.org/wgbh/pages/frontline/shows/gunning/interviews/scowcroft.html.

203. PBS/Frontline: "The Gulf War: Oral History: Brent Scowcroft."

204. Bob Woodward, *Plan of Attack* (New York: Simon and Schuster, 2004), 70.

Chapter 7

205. George W. Bush, "Remarks on Iraq to Congressional Leaders" (Rose Garden, September 26, 2002).

206. Paul Krugman, "The War President," *New York Times*, June 24, 2005, http://www.nytimes.com2005/06/24/opinion/24krugman.htm.

207. Helen Thomas, White House correspondent, quoted in Paul Krugman, "The War President," *New York Times*, June 24, 2005.
208. Scott Ritter, Former UN Weapons Inspector, quoted in Condoleezza Rice, "Interview with Condoleezza Rice Conducted by Wolf Blitzer," *CNN Late Edition*, CNN, September 8, 2002, http://www.mtholyoke.edu/acad/intel/bush/wolf.htm.
209. Bob Woodward, *Plan of Attack* (New York: Simon and Schuster, 2004), 27–28.
210. Condoleezza Rice was the chair of the Vulcans; she became Bush's national security adviser. Paul Wolfowitz was the deputy chair; he became deputy secretary of defense. Richard Perle became chair of the Defense Policy Board, Richard Armitage became deputy secretary of state, Stephen Hadley became deputy national security adviser, and Robert Zoellick became US trade representative. The other members of the group were Robert Blackwell and Dov Zackheim.
211. Bob Herbert, Opinion, "Spoils of War," *New York Times*, April 10, 2003.
212. For details on the emergence of neoconservatives in the United States, see the following: Francis Fukuyama, *America at the Crossroads: Democracy, Power, and the Conservative Legacy* (New Haven: Yale University, 2005); Tod Lindberg, "Neoconservatism's Liberal Legacy," *Policy Review*, no. 127 (2004): 3–22; *Wikipedia: The Free Encyclopedia*, s.vv. "Neoconservatism in the United States," http://en.wikipedia.org/wiki/Neoconservatism_in_the_United_States (accessed July 2, 2005); Michael Lind, "A Tragedy of Errors," *Nation,* February 23, 2004, http://www.thenation.com/doc.mhtml?i=20040223&s=lind; Irving Kristol, "The Neoconservative Persuasion: What It Was, and What It Is," *Weekly Standard* 8, no. 47 (August 2003).
213. For how they achieved influence in the George W. Bush administration, see the following: Michael Lind, "How Neoconservatives Conquered Washington—and Launched a War," April 10, 2003, http://www.Antiwar.com; Jim Lobe, "Neoconservatives Consolidate Control over US Mideast Policy," *Foreign Policy in Focus*, December 6, 2002.
214. Stanley Hoffmann, "The High and the Mighty: Bush's National Security Strategy and the New American Hubris," *American Prospect* 13, no. 24 (January 2003): 2.
215. See G. John Ikenberry, "America's Imperial Ambition," *Foreign Affairs* 81, no. 5 (September–October 2002): 44–60.
216. Most neoconservatives believe that the United States should emulate Great Britain, which reached the peak of its world power largely as a result of its imperial ruthlessness and Victorian values.

217. Robert W. Tucker and David C. Hendrickson, "The Sources of American Legitimacy," *Foreign Affairs* 83, no. 6 (November–December 2004): 20.

218. Hoffmann, "The High and the Mighty," 2.

219. Ibid., 3.

220. Tucker and Hendrickson, "The Sources of American Legitimacy," 23.

221. Hoffmann, "The High and the Mighty," 4.

222. Ibid.

223. Richard Perle, "The War Behind Closed Doors: Interviews: Richard Perle," *Frontline*, PBS, January 25, 2003.

224. John Mearsheimer and Stephen Walt, "The Israel Lobby," *London Review of Books* 28, no. 6 (March 2005): 23.

225. Robert Scheer, "Before the Invasion, There Was Feith," *AlterNet* (14 February 2007), http:''www.alternet.org/story/48053.

226. Michael Lind, "How Neoconservatives Conquered Washington—and Launched a War."

227. "Bush Says Iraq War Is Good for Israel: View Clashes with Opinion of Israeli Aides" *Forward*, December 16, 2005.

228. President George W. Bush, "President [George W. Bush] Discusses the Future of Iraq" (Washington, DC, February 26, 2003), http://www.whitehouse.gov/news/releases/2003/02/20030226-11.html.

229. Tucker and Hendrickson, "The Sources of American Legitimacy," 21.

230. Robert Scheer, "Bush Is Serving up the Cold War Warmed over," *Los Angeles Times*, July 5, 2005, http://www.latimes.com/.

231. Michael Lind, "A Tragedy of Errors," *Nation*, February 23, 2004, 5, http://www.thenation.com/doc.mhtml?i=20040223&s=lind.

232. Lind, "A Tragedy of Errors," 6.

233. Quoted in *The Constitution in Crisis: The Downing Street Minutes and Deception, Manipulation, Torture, and Cover-ups in Iraq* (Washington, DC: Investigative Status Report of the House Judiciary Committee Democratic Staff, n.d. [2005]),18–19. Also available at http://www.gnn.tv/articles/article.php?id=761.

234. Franklin Foer and Spencer Ackerman, "What Dick Cheney Really Believes," *New Republic*, December 2003, http://www.masnet.org/articleinterest.asp?id=715.

235. Richard A. Clarke, *Against All Enemies: Inside America's War on Terror* (New York: Free Press, 2004), 237–8.

236. Clarke, *Against All Enemies*, 30.

237. *The Constitution in Crisis*, 19. The letter is available at http://www.newamericancentury.org/iraqclintonletter.htm; Zalmay Khalilzad and Paul Wolfowitz, "Overthrow Him," *Weekly Standard*, December 1, 1997, 14; Glenn Kessler, "US Decision on Iraq Has Puzzling Past: Opponents of War Wonder When, How Policy Was Set," *Washington Post*, January 12,

2003, A1.

238. Clarke, *Against All Enemies*, 32.

239. Greg Thielmann, "Truth, War and Consequences: Interviews: Greg Thielmann," *Frontline*, PBS, http://www.pbs.org/wgbh/pages/frontline/shows/truth/interviews/thielmann.html.

240. Joseph C. Wilson, "What I Didn't Find in Africa," *New York Times*, July 6, 2003, http://www.nytimes.com/2003/07/06/opinion/ 06WILS.html; J. C. Wilson, "Truth, War and Consequences: Interviews: J. C. Wilson," *Frontline*, PBS, http://www.pbs.org/wbgh/pages/frontline/shows/truth/interviews/Wilson.html.

241. PBS/*Frontline*, "Truth, War and Consequences: Why Did We Go to War," http://www.pbs.org/wgbh/pages/frontline/shows/truth/interviews/perle.html.

242. Woodward, *Plan of Attack*, 2–3.

243. Ibid., 3.

244. Ibid., 4.

245. Steven R. Weisman, "Preemption: Idea with a Lineage Whose Time Has Come," *New York Times*, March 23, 2003.

246. Paul R. Pillar, "Intelligence, Policy, and the War in Iraq," *Foreign Affairs* 85, no. 2 (March–April 2006): 15, 19.

247. James Risen, *State of War: The Secret History of the CIA and the Bush Administration*, quoted in Jan Frel, "The Scoop From 'State of War,'" *AlterNet*, January 5, 2006, http://www.alternet.org/story/30404. See also Sidney Blumenthal, "How Bush Destroyed the CIA," *AlterNet*, May 19, 2006, http://www.alternet.org/story/36343/.

248. Seymour Hersh, *Chain of Command: The Road From 9/11 to Abu Ghraib* (New York: HarperCollins, 2005), 228.

249. See Seymour M. Hersh, "Selective Intelligence," *New Yorker*, May 12, 2003, http://www.newyorker.com/fact/content/?030512fa_fact.

250. Hersh, *Chain of Command*, 207–8.

251. Editorial, "Playing Hardball with Secrets," *New York Times*, April 7, 2006, http://www.nytimes.com/.

252. Stanley Hoffmann with Frederic Bozo, *Gulliver Unbound: America's Imperial Temptation and the War in Iraq* (New York: Rowman and Littlefield, 2004), 65.

253. For more details, see Louis Fisher, "How We Go to War: The Iraq Resolution," in *Considering the Bush Presidency*, ed. Gary L. Gregg II and Mark J. Rozell (New York: Oxford University, 2004), 114–6.

254. PBS/*Frontline*, "The War Behind Closed Doors: Chronology—The Evolution of the Bush Doctrine," http://www.pbs.org/wgbh/pages/frontline/shows/iraq/etc/cron.html.

255. Press Release, "President G.W. Bush, Speech to Joint Session of Congress and the American People," (20 September 2001), Office of the Press Secretary (20 September 2001).

256. President G.W. Bush, "State of the Union Address," (29 January 2002), Office of the Press Secretary (29 January 2002).

257. President George W. Bush (address, 2002), http://www.american progress.org/.

258. Press Release, "President G.W. Bush's Remarks at the United Nations General Assembly," (Office of the Press Secretary, 12 September 2002).

259. Two weeks later, the International Atomic Energy Agency (IAEA) told the UN General Assembly that it had concluded, with the concurrence of outside experts, that the documents on which the Bush administration had relied for its accusation were fakes and not authentic. This was later confirmed by the report of former Ambassador Joseph Wilson's investigation of the accusation in Niger.

260. Hersh, *Chain of Command*, 238.

261. See PBS/*Frontline*, "Blair's War: Introduction," http://www.pbs.org/wgbh/pages/frontline/shows/blair/etc/synopsis.html; Tony Blair (speech to the House of Commons, March 18, 2003), http://www.guardian.co.uk/.

262. A critical moral justification the administration advanced was that inaction was morally unacceptable in the face of the perceived evil, unrepresentative, repressive, and murderous regime of Saddam Hussein.

263. President George W. Bush, "Remarks by the President at the Cincinnati Museum Center" (October 8, 2002), cited in *New York Times*, October 9, 2002. See also Benjamin A. Barber, *Fear's Empire: War, Terrorism, and Democracy* (New York: W.W. Norton & Co., Inc., 2004), 104.

264. President George W. Bush (address to the United Nations September 12, 2002).

265. President George W. Bush, "State of the Union Address" (January 28, 2003), http://www.mtholyoke.ecu/acad/intrel/bush/iraqjust.htm.

266. President G.W. Bush, Speech on the Future of Iraq Before the American Enterprise Institute (26 February 2003).

267. For numbers 26 through 27, see President George W. Bush, "President [George W. Bush] Discusses the Future of Iraq" (Washington, DC, February 26, 2003).

268. President George W. Bush (address to the nation announcing the beginning of military operations against Iraq, March 19, 2003).

269. President George W. Bush, "President [Bush] Says Saddam Hussein Must Leave Iraq within 48 Hours" (address to the nation, March 17, 2003), http://www.whitehouse.gov/news/releases/2003/03/20030317-7.html.

270. Ivo Daalder, who for five years had run a Brookings Institution-University of Maryland Study Project on the National Security Council.

Cited in Glenn Kessler and Peter Slevin, "Rice Fails to Repair Rifts, Officials Say: Cabinet Rivalries Complicate Her Role," *World Politics*, October 12, 2003, http://www.mtholyoke.edu/acad/intrel/bush/role.htm; Foer and Ackerman, "What Dick Cheney Really Believes;" John W. Dean, *Worse Than Watergate: The Secret Presidency of George W. Bush* (New York: Warner Books, 2004), 95–7.

271. "Tough Guy: How Dick Cheney's View of the World Is Driving US Policy," *US News & World Report*, January 23, 2006, 40–8.

272. Dean, *Worse Than Watergate*, 96.

273. President Bush on Dick Cheney, quoted in Woodward, *Plan of Attack*, 420.

274. Woodward, *Plan of Attack*, 292.

275. Lawrence D. Freeman, review of *The Assassins' Gate: America in Iraq* by George Packer, *Foreign Affairs* 85, no. 1 (January–February 2006): 132.

276. Warren Hoge, "Ex-UN Inspector Has Harsh Words for Bush," *New York Times*, March 16, 2004, http://www.nytimes.com/2004/03/16/interna tional/middleeast/16BLIX.html.

277. Woodward, *Plan of Attack,* 30.

278. Foer and Ackerman, "What Dick Cheney Really Believes."

279. Hersh, *Chain of Command,* 230

280. Ibid.

281. Ibid.

282. Vice President Dick Cheney (speech to veterans of foreign wars, Nashville, TN, August 26, 2002), http://www.mtholyoke.edu/acad/intrel/ bush/cheneyvfw.htm; PBS/*Frontline*, "The War Behind Closed Doors: Chronology: The Evolution of the Bush Doctrine," http://www.pbs.org/ wgbh/pages/frontline/shows/iraq/etc/cron.html.

283. Cheney (speech to veterans of foreign wars, Nashville, TN, August 26, 2002).

284. Dick Cheney, Meet the Press with Tim Russert (14 March 2003).

285. Dean, *Worse Than Watergate*, 96; Glenn Kessler and Peter Slevin, "Rice Fails to Repair Rifts Officials Say: Cabinet Rivalries Complicate Her Role."

286. I.M. Dexter, "The Power Brokers: An Uneven History of the National Security Council," *Foreign Affairs* 84, no. 5 (September–October 2005): 158.

287. Donald Rumsfeld, interview by Larry King, CNN, April 12, 2002.

288. Donald Rumsfeld (press conference, Kuwait City, June 11, 2002), PBS/*Frontline*, "In Their Own Words: Who Said What When," http://www.pbs.org/wgbh/pages/frontline/shows/truth/why/said.html.

289. Secretary of Defense Donald Rumsfeld (September 18, 2002; September 19, 2002), Center for American Progress, "In their Own Words: Iraq's 'Imminent' Threat," http://www.americanprogress.org/.

290. Donald Rumsfeld, interview, Infinity CBS Radio, November 14, 2002, http://www.mtholyoke.edu/acad/intrel/bush/infinity.htm.

291. Secretary of Defense Donald Rumsfeld (January 3, 2003), Center for American Progress, "In Their Own Words: Iraq's 'Imminent' Threat," http://www.americanprogress.org/.

292. Secretary of Defense Donald Rumsfeld (January 20, 2003), Center for American Progress, "Then and Now: Heeding and Ignoring Intel on Weak WMD Evidence," http://www.americanprogress.org/.

293. Woodward, *Plan of Attack*, 21.

294. Ibid., 22.

295. Ibid., 21.

296. Jim Vallette, "The Wolfowitz Chronology: Introduction," Institute for Policy Studies, http://www.ips-dc.org/wolfowitz/tl_intro.htm.

297. Ivo H. Daalder and James M. Lindsay, *America Unbound: The Bush Revolution in Foreign Policy* (Washington, DC: Brookings Institution, 2003), 46.

298. Woodward, *Plan of Attack,* 426.

299. Ibid.

300. Seymour M. Hersh, *Chain of Command: The Road From 9/11 to Abu Ghraib* (New York: HarperCollins, 2005), 193.

301. Ibid.

302. Quoted in Seymour Hersh, "Selective Intelligence," *New Yorker*, May 12, 2003.

303. Perle, "The War Behind Closed Doors: Interviews: Richard Perle."

304. Quoted in Hersh, *Chain of Command*, 169; Seymour M. Hersh, "Fact: Annals of National Security: The Stovepipe—How Conflicts between the Bush Administration and the Intelligence Community Marred the Reporting on Iraq's Weapons," *New Yorker*, October 27, 2003, 1–13, http://www. newyorker. com/.

305. Nicholas Lemann, "The Next World Order," *New Yorker Magazine*, April 1, 2002, 7.

306. Phyllis Bennis, "Understanding the US-Iraq Crisis: A Primer," Institute of Policy Studies, http://www.ips-dc-.org/iraq/primer1.htm.

307. David Manning, memorandum, March 14, 2002, http://www.downing streetmemo/.

308. Woodward, *Plan of Attack*, 436.

309. Jim Abrams, "Senate: Saddam Saw Al-Qaida as Threat," *Miami Herald*, September 8, 2006.

310. Woodward, *Plan of Attack*, 251.
311. Lemann, "The Next World Order," *New Yorker Magazine*, April 1, 2002, 4.
312. Ibid., 9.
313. Condoleezza Rice. "Rice on Iraq, War and Politics," *NewsHour with Jim Lehrer*, PBS, September 25, 2002, http://www.pbs.org/newshour/bb/international/july-dec02/rice_9-25.html.
314. Woodward, *Plan of Attack*, 94–5.
315. Ibid., 308.
316. BBC News, "Moral Case For Deposing Saddam," August 15, 2002, http://www.mtholyoke.edu/acad/intrel/bush/moralcase.htm; Yossef Bodansky, *The Secret History of the Iraq War* (New York: HarperCollins, 2005), 39.
317. Condoleezza Rice, interview conducted by Wolf Blitzer, *CNN Late Edition*, CNN, September 8, 2002, http://www.mtholyoke.edu/acad/intel/bush/wolf.htm.
318. Hersh, *Chain of Command*, 85.
319. Woodward, *Plan of Attack*, 67.
320. Ibid., 139–40.
321. Ibid., 71–4.
322. Robert Dreyfuss, "The Yes-Man: President Bush Sent Porter Goss to the CIA to Keep the Agency in Line. What He's Really Doing Is Wrecking It," *American Prospect* 16, no. 11 (November 2005): 18–24; Tom Hamburger and Sonni Efron, "A CIA Cover Blown, a White House Exposed," *Los Angeles Times*, August 25, 2005, http://www.latimes.com/; Council on Foreign Relations, "Q and A: Tenet Resigned to Protect CIA from 'Barrage of Criticism,'" *New York Times*, June 3, 2004, http://www.nytimes.com/cfr/international/slot1_060304.html; Center For American Progress, "Neglecting Intelligence, Ignoring Warnings: A Chronology of How the Bush Administration Repeatedly and Deliberately Refused to Listen to Intelligence Agencies That Said Case for War Was Weak," http://www.american progress. org/.
323. Woodward, *Plan of Attack*, 295.
324. Secretary of State Colin L. Powell, "The Administration's Position with Regard to Iraq" (testimony before the Senate Foreign Relations Committee, September 26, 2002).
325. Woodward, *Plan of Attack*, 22.
326. Secretary of State Colin L. Powell (speech at the World Economic Forum in Davos, Switzerland, January 23, 2003), *New York Times*, January 26, 2003, http://www.mtholyoke.edu/.

327. Powell, Statement at the World Economic Forum at Davos, Switzerland, *The New York Times* (26 January 2003).
328. Powell, "Iraq, Denial and Deception," Presentation before the UN Security Council (5 February 2003), http://www.whitehouse.gov/news/releases/2003/02/20030205-1.html-llk.
329. Ibid.
330. Secretary of State Colin L. Powell, "Remarks at UN Security Council Meeting" (March 7, 2003), http://www.whitehouse.gov/news/releases/2003/03/20030307-10.html.
331. Woodward, *Plan of Attack*, 433–4.
332. Ibid., 436.
333. Steven Weisman, "Powell Calls His U.N. Speech a Lasting Blot on His Record," *New York Times*, September 9, 2005, http://www.nytimes.com/2005/09/09/politics/09powell.html; Associated Press, "Powell Calls Pre-Iraq U.N. Speech a 'Blot' on His Record," *USA Today*, September 8, 2005, http://www.usatoday.com/news/ washington/2005-09-08-powell-iraq_x.htm.
334. "President G.W. Bush Addresses Nation, Discusses Iraq, War on Terror," http://www.whitehouse.gov/news/releases/2005/06/print/2005/0628-7.html.

Chapter 8

335. James R. Rubin, "Stumbling into War," *Foreign Affairs* 82, no. 5 (September–October 2003): 65.
336. Louis Fisher, "Deciding on War against Iraq: Institutional Failures," *Political Science Quarterly* 18 (2003): 389, quoted in Loch K. Johnson, *Seven Sins of American Foreign Policy* (New York: Pearson-Longman, 2006), 137.
337. Michael Dobbs, "US Had Key Role in Iraq Buildup," *Washington Post*, December 30, 2002, A01.
338. R. Jeffrey Smith, "Bush Authorized Secrets' Release, Libby Testified," *Washington Post*, April 7, 2006, A01.
339. David Kay, "Claims vs. Fact: Pre-War Assertions Compared to David Kay's Report," Center for American Progress, http://www.americanprogress.org/.
340. US Senate, *Report of the Select Committee on Intelligence on Postwar Findings about Iraq's WMD Programs and Links to Terrorism and How They Compare with Prewar Assessments Together with Additional Views*, September 8, 2006, http://intelligence.senate.gov/; Senate Intelligence Committee, *Report of the Select Committee on the Use by Intelligence Community of Information Provided by the Iraqi National Congress*

Together with Additional Views, September 8, 2006, http://intelligence. senate.gov/. See also Jim Abrams, "Senate: No Prewar Saddam-al-Qaida Ties," *Miami Herald*, September 8, 2006.

341. *CNN.com*, "Transcript David Kay at Senate Hearing (28 January 2004), http://www.cnn.com/2004/US/01/28/kay.transcript.

342. John B. Judis, "The Author of Liberty: Religion and U.S. Foreign Policy," in *Annual Editions: American Foreign Policy, 07/08*, Glenn P. Hastedt, editor (Dubuque, IA: McGraw Hill, 2007), 81.

343. Stanley Hoffmann, "The Foreign Policy the US Needs," *New York Review of Books* 53, no. 13 (August 2006): 4, http://www.nybooks.com/articles/19217; Brady Keisling, "Iraq: A Letter of Resignation," *New York Review of Books*, April 10, 2003.

344. Paul R. Pillar, "Intelligence, Policy and the War in Iraq," *Foreign Affairs* 85, no. 2 (March–April 2006): 24.

345. Steven W. Hook, *US Foreign Policy: The Paradox of World Power* (Washington, DC: Congressional Quarterly, 2005), 80.

346. David Gergen, "Getting out of the Bunker," *US News and World Report*, November 28, 2005, 84; Tim Rutten, "Cheney's History Needs a Revise," *Los Angeles Times*, November 26, 2005, http://www.calendarlive. com/.

347. Cathy Young, "A Silver Lining in Iraq," *Boston Globe*, October 31, 2005, http://www.boston.com/news/globe/editorial_opinion/oped/articles/2005/10/31/a_silver_lining_in_iraq; PIPA, "Iraq: The Separate Realities of Republicans and Democrats," http://www.worldpublicopinion.org/pipa/articles/brunitedstatescanadara/186.php?nid=&id=&pnt=186.

348. Daniel Yankelovich, "The Tipping Point," *Foreign Affairs* 85, no. 3 (May–June 2006): 119, 122.

349. Robert Kuttner, "Bush Imploding Presidency," *Boston Globe*, October 29, 2005.

350. Bob Woodward, "Ford Disagreed with Bush about Invading Iraq," *The Washington Post* (28 December 2006), A01.

351. Brent Scowcroft, "Don't Attack Saddam: It Would Undermine Our Anti-terror Efforts," *Wall Street Journal*, August 15, 2002, http://www. opinion journal.com/editorial/feature.html?id=110002133.

352. Zbigniew Brzezinski, "Time for Course Corrections in US Foreign Policy" (address to the Middle East Institute, November 7, 2005), (Washington, DC: National Press Club, 2005).

353. The WorldPublicOpinion.Org/Knowledge Networks, Americans On Iraq: Three Years On (PIPA, March 15, 2006).

354. Http://www.worldpublicopinion.org/incl/printable_version.php?

355. House Judiciary Committee Democratic Staff, *Investigative Status Report, The Constitution in Crisis: The Downing Street Minutes and Deception,*

Manipulation, Torture, Retribution, and Cover-ups in the Iraq War, 2005, 28.

356. Quoted in Mark Danner, "The Secret Way to War," *New York Review of Books* 52, no. 10 (June 2005): 6.

357. James P. Rubin, "Stumbling into War," *Foreign Affairs* 82, no. 5 (September–October 2003): 47.

358. Quoted in Robert W. Tucker and David C. Hendrickson, "The Sources of American Legitimacy," *Foreign Affairs* 83, no. 6 (November–December 2004): 20.

359. Charter of the United Nations, Article 2 Paragraph 4.

360. Tucker and Hendrickson, "The Sources of American Legitimacy," 24.

361. Charles J. Hanley, "Piecing Together the Story of the Weapons That Weren't," *USA Today*, September 9, 2005, http://www.usatoday.com/.

362. Jonathan Clarke, "New Balance: What Other Countries Can Do about American Power," *Washington Monthly* 37, no. 12 (December 2005): 38.

363. Michael Lind, "A Tragedy of Errors," *Nation*, February 23, 2004, 9, http://www.thenation.com/doc.mhtml?i=20040223&s=lind.

364. Rashid Khalidi, *Resurrecting Empire: Western Footprints and America's Perilous Path* (Boston, MA: Beacon Press, 2005), x.

365. Comment, "Plan for Quagmire," *The Progressive* 70, no. 1 (January 2005): 8.

366. G. John Ikenberry, "America's Imperial Ambition," *Foreign Affairs* 81, no. 5 (September–October 2002): 44–5.

367. Ikenberry, "America's Imperial Ambition," 49.

Chapter 9

368. Irving Kristol, "The Fettered Presidency," quoted in Michael Lind, "A Tragedy of Errors," *Nation*, February 23, 2004, 8, http://www.thenation.com/ doc.mhtml?i=20040223&s=lind.

369. CCFR with PIPA, "The Hall of Mirrors: Perceptions and Misperceptions in the Congressional Foreign Policy Process," (Fall 2003), 3.

370. Payne and Scott, in Ralph G. Carter, ed., *Contemporary Cases in US Foreign Policy*, 2nd ed. (Washington, DC: CQ Press, 2005), 355–6. Also see James M. McCormack, *American Foreign Policy and Process*, 4th ed. (Belmont, CA: Thomson/Wadsworth, 2005), 362.

371. Arthur Schlesinger, Jr., "Bush's Thousand Days," *Washington Post*, April 24, 2006, A17, http://www.washingtonpost.com/.

372. President G.W. Bush, State of the Union Address (29 January 2002), http://whitehouse.gov/news/releases/2002/01/20020129-ll.html.

373. Ibid.

374. Douglas Jeil, "British Memo on US Plans for Iraq War Fuels Critics," *New York Times*, May 20, 2005, http://www.nytimes.com/.
375. This is as repeated by Richard Haass in an interview with PBS (September 12, 2003). See Richard Haass, "Truth, War and Consequences: Interviews: Richard Haass," *Frontline*, PBS, http://www.pbs.org/wgbh/pages/frontline/shows/truth/interviews/haass.html.
376. John Daniszewski, "New Memos Detail Early Plans for Invading Iraq: British Officials Believed the US Favored Military Force a Year before the War, Documents Show," *Los Angeles Times*, June 15, 2005, http://www. latimes.com/.
377. Charles J. Hanley, "Piecing Together the Story of the Weapons That Weren't," *USA Today*, September 9, 2005, http://www.usatoday.com/.
378. Mark Danner, "The Secret Way to War," *New York Review of Books* 52, no. 10 (June 2005); The Downing Street Memo(s), "Text of the Downing Street Memo," http://www.downingstreetmemo.com/memos.html; Douglas Jeil, "British Memo on US Plans for Iraq War Fuels Critics," *New York Times*, May 20, 2005, http://www.nytimes.com/2005/05/20/politics/20weapons. html? page; Paul Krugman, "Staying What Course?" *New York Times*, May 16, 2005, http://www.nytimes.com/.
379. See The Downing Street Memo(s), "Text of Downing Street Memo," http://www.downingstreetmemo.com/memos.html.
380. Danner, "The Secret Way to War."
381. Richard A. Clarke, *Against All Enemies: Inside America's War on Terror* (New York: Free Press, 2004); Ron Suskind, *The Price of Loyalty: The Bush Files* (New York: Simon & Schuster, 2004), http://thepriceof loyalty.ronsuskind.com/ thebushfiles/.
382. President G.W. Bush, "Remarks at the United Nations General Assembly" (12 September 2002), http://www.whitehouse.gov/news/releases/2002/09/200209/12-l.html.
383. Agence France-Press, "In Bush's Words: 'Use All Means' on Iraq, Text of the Resolution that President Bush Sent to Congress, Seeking Approval for Action Against Iraq," *New York Times*, September 20, 2002), http://www.mtholyoke.edu/acad/intrel/bush/congressres.htm.
384. Louis Fisher, "The Way We Go to War: The Iraq Resolution," in *Considering the Bush Presidency*, ed. Gary L. Gregg II and Mark J. Rozell (New York: Oxford University, 2004), 111.
385. 107th Congress, 2nd Session, H.R. Joint RES 114 (10 October 2002), "Joint Resolution to Authorize the Use of United States Armed Forces Against Iraq," http://www.whitehouse.gov/news/releases/2002/10/20021 002-2.html; US Congress Joint Resolution to Authorize the Use of United States Armed Forces Against Iraq," *The New York Times* (11 October

2002).

386. The six Republican members of the House were Ron Paul of Texas, Connie Morella of Maryland, Jim Leach of Iowa, Amo Houghton of New York, John Hostettler of Indiana, and John Duncan of Tennessee.

387. 107th Congress, 2nd Session, House of Representatives. *House of Representatives Report*, 2002, H. Rep. 107–721.

388. CNN, "Senate Approves War Resolution: Administration Applauds Vote," http://archives.cnn.com/2002/ALLPOLITICS/10/11/iraq.us/.

389. As summarized in Danner, "The Secret Way to War."

390. Fisher, "The Way We Go to War: The Iraq Resolution," in Gregg and Rozell, *Considering the Bush Presidency*, 107.

391. Jonathan Rield, "Broad Resolution Allows Bush to Set Terms of War without Review," *Congressional Quarterly Report*, October 12, 2002, 2679.

392. *Frontline*/PBS, "The War behind Closed Doors: Chronology—The Evolution of the Bush Doctrine," http://www.pbs.org/wgbh/pages/frontline/shows/iraq/etc/cron.html. Signatories to the letter who became members of the George W. Bush administration included Donald Rumsfeld, Paul Wolfowitz, Richard Perle, Richard Armitage, and John R. Bolton. Another was William Kristol of the Project for a New American Century.

393. CBS Broadcast, "Plans For Iraq Attack Began On 9/11," CBS, September 4, 2002.

394. F. Ugboaja Ohaegbulam, *US Policy in Postcolonial Africa: Four Case Studies in Conflict Resolution* (New York: Peter Lang, 2004), 5; Franklin Foer and Spencer Ackerman, "What Dick Cheney Really Believes," *New Republic*, December 2003, http://www.masnet.org/article interest. asp?id =715; Pat M. Holt, "US Intelligence: Seeing What It Wants to See in Iraq," *Christian Science Monitor*, November 7, 2002, http://www.csmonitor.com/.

395. Maureen Dawd, "I Spy a Screw-Up," *New York Times*, March 31, 2005, http://www.nytimes.com/2005/03/31/opinion/31dowd.html.

396. Robert Dreyfuss, "The Yes-Man: President Bush and Porter Sent Goss to the CIA to Keep the Agency in Line, What He's Really Doing is Wrecking It," *American Prospect* 16, no. 11 (November 2005): 18–24. The quotation is from page 18.

397. Dreyfuss, "The Yes-Man," 21.

398. Michael Isikoff and David Corn, *Hubris: The Inside Story of Spin, Scandal, and the Selling of the Iraq War* (New York: Crown Publishers, 2006), 5 and 11.

399. Paul Wolfowitz and Richard Perle had a close personal bond with Ahmed Chalabi dating back many years. That relationship deepened after Bush became president in January 2001. The ties with Chalabi extended to others in the administration, including Douglas Feith and I. Lewis Libby, Vice President Cheney's chief of staff. Chalabi also had the support of the American Enterprise Institute and other conservatives.

400. Bob Drogin and John Goetz, "The Curveball Saga: How US Fell under the Spell of 'Curveball,'" *Los Angeles Times*, November 20, 2005, http://www.latimes.com/.

401. Seymour M. Hersh, "Annals of National Security: Selected Intelligence," *New Yorker*, May 12, 2003, http://www.newyorker.com/fact/content/?030512fa_fact.

402. Seymour Hersh, *Chain of Command: The Road From 9/11 to Abu Ghraib* (New York: HarperCollins, 2005), 215; Foer and Ackerman, "What Dick Cheney Really Believes," *The New Republic* (December 2003).

403. Foer and Ackerman, "What Dick Cheney Really Believes."

404. Foer and Ackerman, "What Dick Cheney Really Believes," *The New Republic* (December 2003).

405. *Atlantic Monthly* (January 2004), *The New York Times* (October 20, 2003), and *New Yorker* (May 12, 2003), as summarized by Center for American Progress, "Neglecting Intelligence, Ignoring Warnings," http://www.americanprogress.org/; Seymour M. Hersh, "Fact: Annals of National Security: The Stovepipe—How Conflicts between the Bush Administration and the Intelligence Community Marred the Reporting on Iraq's Weapons," *New Yorker*, October 27, 2003, 1–13, http://www.newyorker.com/print ables/fact/ 031027fa_fact.

406. Maureen Dawd, "U.N. Leash Woolly Bully Bolton," *New York Times*, April 27, 2005, http://www.nytimes.com/.

407. Greg Miller and Mark Mazzetti, "Pentagon Team's War Plan Probed: An Intelligence Unit Helped Make the Case for Invading Iraq, Saying the CIA Overlooked Links to Al-Qaeda—Claims Now Discredited," *Los Angeles Times*, November 19, 2005, http://www.latimes.com/.

408. Gregg Miller and Julian E. Barnes, "CIA Doubts Didn't Deter Feith's Team," *Los Angeles Times* (10 February 2007); David S. Cloud and Mark Mazzetti, "Prewar Intelligence Unit at Pentagon Is Criticized," *The New York Times* (9 February 2007).

409. Steven R. Weisman, "Powell Calls His U.N. Speech a Lasting Blot on His Record," *New York Times*, September 9, 2005, http://www.nytimes.com/ 2005/ 09/ 09/politics/ 09powel. html; Associated Press, "Powell Calls Pre-Iraq U.N. Speech a 'Blot' on His Record," *USA Today*, September 8,

2005, http://www.usatoday.com/news/washington/2005-09-08-powell-iraq_x.htm.

410. Hanley, "Piecing Together the Story."
411. Fisher, "The Way We Go to War," in Gregg and. Rozell, *Considering the Bush Presidency*, 107.
412. Nicholas Lemann, "The Next World Order," *New Yorker Magazine*, April 1, 2002, 10.
413. CCFR with PIPA, "The Hall of Mirrors," 1.
414. Todd S. Purdum, "A Peephole to the War Room: British Documents Shed Light on Bush Team's State of Mind," *New York Times*, June 14, 2005, http://www.nytimes.com.
415. President George W. Bush, "President, House Leadership Agree on Iraqi Resolution" (White House, October 2, 2002), http://www.whitehouse. gov/news/releases/2002/10/print/20021002-7.html.
416. Ibid.
417. Ibid.
418. Ibid.
419. Ibid.
420. President George W. Bush, "President Bush Outlines Iraqi Threat: Remarks by the President on Iraq at Cincinnati Museum Center" (White House, October 7, 2002), http://www.whitehouse.gov/news/releases/ 2002/10/print/20021007-8.html. Also cited in Benjamin R. Barber, *Fear's Empire: War, Terrorism, and Democracy* (New York: W. W. Norton and Co., Inc., 2004), 104.
421. "For Gephardt, Risks and a Crucial Role," *Washington Post*, October 3, 2003, A15.
422. John H. Cushman, "Daschle Predicts Broad Support for Military Action against Iraq," *New York Times*, October 7, 2002, 10.
423. Helen Dewar and Juliet Eilperin, "Iraq Resolution Passes Test, Gains Support," *Washington Post*, October 10, 2002, A16.
424. From UN Report Commission by Secretary General Kofi Annan, in "U.N. Report Urges Big Changes; Security Council Would Expand," *New York Times*, December 1, 2004, http://www.nytimes.com/2004/12/01/ international/01nations. html.
425. "A More Secure World: Our Shared Responsibility: A Report to the Secretary General of the United Nations" (December 2, 2004), in John T. Rourke, ed., *Taking Sides: Clashing Views on Controversial Issues in World Politics,* 12th ed. (Dubuque, IA: McGraw Hill, 2006), 21–213.
426. Bob Herbert, "Truth and Deceit," *New York Times*, June 2, 2005, http://www.nytimes.com/2005/06/02/opinion/02herbert.html?pagew.

427. For more details, see Bruce W. Jentleson and Thomas G. Paterson, ed., *Encyclopedia of US Foreign Relations*, vol. 4 (New York: Oxford University, 1997), 191–2.

428. Ibid., 186.

429. Gaddis, *Surprise, Security, and the American Experience*, 101.

430. Maggie Farley and Johanna Neuman, "Accused British Official Slams the US on Iraq," *Los Angeles Times*, May 18, 2005, http://www.latimes.com/.

431. President George H. W. Bush, "Remarks to the Joint Session of Congress" (September 11, 1990).

432. Senator Biden, "Credit Bush's Rhetoric, Not His Actions," *Washington Monthly* 37, no. 5 (May 2005): 21.

433. Michael Tomasky, "Praise the Message, Blame the Messenger," *Washington Monthly* 37, no. 5 (May 2005): 31.

434. Bill Varner, "Bush Finds Iraq War Undermines Threat of Force as Tool at UN," *Bloomberg.com* (18 September 2006), http://www.bloomberg.com/apps/news?pid=20670001&refer=home&sid=adO0gufo14Cs.

435. Nick Wadhams, "'Mideast Sees Iraq 'Disaster,' Annan Says," *Washington Post*, September 13, 2006, http://www.washingtonpost.com/.

436. David Cloud and Eric Schmitt, "US General Sees No Ebb in Fight," *New York Times*, June 24, 2005, http://www.nytimes.com/; Carol J. Williams, "The World: Suicide Attacks Rising Rapidly [in Iraq]," *Los Angeles Times*, June 2, 2005, http://www.latimes.com/; John F. Burns, "Violence Surges across Iraq with 30 New Deaths Reported," *New York Times*, May 29, 2005, http://www.nytimes.com/; Council on Foreign Relations, "Q&A: What Is Driving the Iraqi Insurgency," *New York Times*, May 20, 2005, http://www.nytimes.com/cfr/international/slot1_052005.html; Editorial, "This Is Winning?" *Los Angeles Times*, April 29, 2005.

437. Tom Regan, "Studies: War Radicalized Most Foreign Fighters in Iraq," *Christian Science Monitor*, July 18, 2005, http://www.csmonitor.com/.

438. Richard Norton-Taylor, "Occupation Has Boosted Al-Qaida, Says Think Tank," *Guardian*, May 26, 2006, http://www.guardian.co.uk/.

439. Reuters, "CIA Says Iraq Is Now a Terrorist Training Ground," *New York Times*, June 22, 2005, http://www.nytimes.com/.

440. Reuters, "Blair Contests Idea Iraq War Made London a Target," *New York Times*, July 18, 2005, http://www.nytimes.com/.

441. Mark Mazzatte, "Spy Agencies Say Iraq War Worsens Terror Threat," *The New York Times* (24 September 2006), http://www.nytimes.com/206/09/24/world/middleeast/24terror.html.

442. Senator Joseph Biden, "Credit Bush's Rhetoric, Not His Actions," *Washington Monthly* 37, no. 3 (May 2005): 21

443. Council on Foreign Relations, "Q & A: What is Driving the Iraqi Insurgency?"

444. Robert W. Tucker and David C. Hendrickson, "The Sources of American Legitimacy," *Foreign Affairs* 83, no. 6 (November–December 2004): 18.

445. Robert Scheer, "The US Is Its Own Worst Enemy in Iraq," *Los Angeles Times*, May 17, 2005.

446. Senator Bob Graham with Jeff Nussbaum *Intelligence Matters: The CIA, the FBI, Saudi Arabia and the Failure of America's War on Terror* (New York: Random House, 2004), 166–169, 223–233.

447. Fisher, "How We Go to War," in Gregg and Rozell, *Considering the Bush Presidency*, 121.

Chapter 10

448. Fareed Zakaria, review of *The Assassins' Gate*, by George Packer, *New York Times*, November 30, 2005.

449. James Carroll, "War's Reckoning," *Boston Globe*, August 28, 2006, http://www.boston.com/news/globe/editorial_opinion/oped/articles/200 6/08/28/wars_reckoning.

450. The memo was the minutes of the British Prime Minister Tony Blair's meeting on 23 July 2002 with his cabinet colleagues to discuss Iraq. See The Downing Street Memo(s),"Text of the Downing Street Memo," http://www. downing street memo.com/memos. html; Paul Krugman, "Staying What Course?" *New York Times*, May 16, 2005, http://www. nytimes.com/2005/ 05/16/ opinion/ 16krug man.html?page.

451. Months later, the presentation proved to be an embarrassment, as it had been based on false intelligence. No weapons of mass destruction were found after the overthrow of Saddam Hussein and the conquest of Iraq. Anticipating this fact, President Bush expanded his rationale for the war beyond disarming Iraq: to liberate Iraqis from a brutal dictator who had used biological weapons against his own people, to extend freedom and democracy to the entire Middle East, and to deny terrorists a safe haven.

452. Quoted in Stephen Schlesinger, "An Annoying Necessary Friend: In Most Cases the United Nations Has Helped to Further US Objectives," *Los Angeles Times*, January 31, 2005, http://www.latimes.com/.

453. Schlesinger, "Commentary," *Los Angeles Times*, January 31, 2005.

454. Paul Starr, "A Rendezvous with Failure," *American Prospect*, September 2006, 3.

455. Michiko Kakutani, "All the President's Books," *New York Times*, May 11, 2006, http://www.nytimes.com/; Paul R. Pillar, "Intelligence, Policy, and War in Iraq," *Foreign Affairs* 85, no. 2 (March–April 2006): 15–27.

456. Joseph S. Nye, Jr., "Transformational Leadership and US Grand Strategy," *Foreign Affairs* 85, no. 4 (July–August 2006): 139–48.

457. Kakutani, "All the President's Books."

458. Ibid.

459. Ibid.

460. Ibid.

461. Bob Woodward, *Plan of Attack*, 4, 437.

462. Senator Bob Graham with Jeff Nussbaum, *Intelligence Matters* (New York: Random House, 2004), 182.

463. Ibid.

464. David E. Singer, "Book Says Bush Ignored Urgent Warnings on Iraq," The *New York Times* (29 September 2006), http://www.nytimes.com. 2006/09/29/washington/29account.html.

465. Nye, Jr., "Transformational Leadership and US Grand Strategy," 148.

466. Ibid.

467. Thom Shanker, "Bush's [10 January 2007] Speech is Vindication for a General," The *New York Times* (11 January 2007), http://www.nytimes. com/2007/01/11/world/middleeast/11cnd-shinseki.html.

468. Michael R. Gordon, "A Prewar Slide Show Cast Iraq in Rosy Hues," *The New York Times* (15 February 2007); http://www.gwu.edu/nsarch/ NSAEBB/NSAEBB214/index.htm.

469. See: "Transcript of President Bush's Address to the Nation on US Policy in Iraq," The *New York Times* (11 January 2007), http://www.nytimes. com/ 2007/01/11/us/ptext.html.

470. Bob Woodward, *Plan of Attack* (New York: Simon & Schuster, 2004), 414.

471. "A Pattern of Excess," *Washington Post*, May 14, 2006, B06, http:// www.wahingtonpost.com/.

472. Suzanne Nossel, "Why Don't They Like Us?" *American Prospect*, July–August 2006, 54.

473. Kevin Woods et al., "Saddam's Delusions: The View from the Inside," *Foreign Affairs* 85, no. 3 (May–June 2006): 2–26.

474. Michael Moss and David Rohde, "Law and Order: Misjudgments Marred Plans for Iraqi Police," *New York Times*, May 21, 2006, http://www. nytimes.com/2006/05/21/world/middleeast/21security.html.

475. Rajiv Chandrasekaran, "Who Killed Iraq?" *Foreign Policy*, September–October 2006, 36–43.

476. Tyler Marshall, "The Conflict in Iraq: The US Reportedly Shifts on Involving Europeans," *Los Angeles Times*, January 4, 2005, http://www.

latimes.com/.

477. In May 2006, Iraq's new prime minister, Nuri Kamal al-Maliki, predicted that Iraqi forces could control security in all of the country's provinces within eighteen months.

478. David E. Sanger and Jim Rutenberg, "Bush and Blair Concede Errors, but Defend War," *New York Times*, May 26, 2006, http://www.nytimes.com/2006/05/26/world/middleeast/26prexy.html.

479. Editorial, "The Price of Iraq," *New York Times*, May 28, 2006, http://www.nytimes.com/2006/05/28/opinion/ 28sun1. html.

480. Thom Shanker, "US General Says Iraq Could Slide into a Civil War," *New York Times*, August 4, 2006, http://www.nytimes.com/2006/08/04/world/middleeast/04rumsfeld.html; Julian E. Barnes, "The Conflict in Iraq: Generals Give Grim Report on Iraqi Strife," *Los Angeles Times*, August 4, 2006, http://www.latimes.com/.

481. Dexter Filkins, "Baghdad's Chaos Undercuts Tack Pursued by U.S," *New York Times*, August 6, 2006, http://www.nytimes.com/ 2006/08/06/world/middleeast/ 06baghdad.html. Jim Rutenberg, "Washington Memo: 'Civil War' Is Uttered, and White House's Iraq Strategy Is Dealt a Blow," *New York Times*, August 6, 2006, http://www.nytimes.com/2006/08/06/washington/06memo.html; Editorial, "A Reality Check on Iraq," *Los Angeles Times*, August 6, 2006, http://www. latimes.com/. See also Daniel L. Byman and Kenneth M. Pollack, "What Next?" *Washington Post*, August 20, 2006, B01, http://www.washingtonpost.com/.

482. Elisabeth Bumiller, "Bush Concedes Iraq War Erodes Political Status," *New York Times*, March 22, 2006, http://www.nytimes.com/2006/03/22/politics/22prexy.html; Susan Milligan, "Bush Says Iraq Pullout up to Future Presidents, Warns Leaving Too Soon Would Boost Al-Qaeda," *Boston Globe*, March 22, 2006, http://www.boston.com/.

483. Aram Roston, "The Unquiet American: US-Iraqi Policy and the Murder of a Whistle-Blowing Contractor," *Washington Monthly* 37, no. 6 (June 2005): 30.

484. Fred Kaplan, "Defending Rumsfeld from the Generals," *Slate*, April 21, 2006, http://www.slate.com/toolbar.aspx?action=print&id=2140318.

485. Fred Kaplan, "The Revolt against Rumsfeld," *Slate*, April 12, 2006, http://www.slate.com/toolbar.aspx?action=print&id=2139777.

486. Bob Herbert, "The Rumsfeld Stain," *New York Times*, May 23, 2005, http://www.nytimes.com/2005/05/23/opinion/23herbert.html.

487. Donald Rumsfeld, "Rumsfeld's War-on-Terror Memo to General Dick Myers et al.," *USA Today*, October 16, 2003, http://www.usatoday.com/news/washington/executive/rumsfeld-memo.htm; J. S. Nye, Jr., "In Mideast, the Goal Is 'Smart Power' *Boston Globe*, August 19, 2006,

http://www.boston.com/.

488. Editorial, "A Failed Presidency," *Los Angeles Times*, November 1, 2004, http://www.latimes.com/.

489. Bumiller, "Bush Concedes Iraq."

490. Claus Christian Malzahn, "The Most Powerless Man in the World," *New York Times*, May 8, 2006, http://www.nytimes.com/2006/05/08/world/europe/08spiegel.html.

491. Sanger and Rutenberg, "Bush and Blair Concede."

492. Thomas L. McNaugher, "The Real Meaning of Military Transformation: Rethinking the Revolution," *Foreign Affairs*, Volume 86, Number 1 (January/ February 2007), 140–147.

493. Michael Abramowitz and Peter Baker, "Embattled, Bush Held to Plan to Salvage Iraq," The *Washington Post* (21 January 2007), A01.

494. Zbigniew Brzezinski, "A Road Map Out of Iraq." *Lost Angeles Times* (11 February 2007).

495. Richard N. Haass, "Op-ed: Iraq and the Fortunes of War," Council on Foreign Relations, *Los Angeles Times*, December 27, 2005, http://www.cfr.org/publication/9478/iraq_and_the_fortunes_ofr_war.ht ml; Max Boot, "Up Close, Iraq Gets Blurry: There Are No Pat Answers Where Setbacks and Successes Exist Side by Side," *Los Angeles Times*, March 1, 2006, http://www.latimes.com/.

496. Kevin Whitelaw and Anna Mulrine, "What Is Plan C?" *U.S. News and World Report*, Volume 142, Number 6 (19 February 2007), 22.

497. *U.S. News and World Report* (19 February 2007), 23.

498. "Why American Will Fail in Iraq" *Foreign Policy* (November/December 2006), 20.

499. Fraser Cameron, *US Foreign Policy after the Cold War: Global Hegemon or Reluctant Sheriff?* 2nd ed. (London: Routledge, 2005), 33.

500. See Howard Kurtz, "A Turning Point on Iraq," *Washington Post*, March 27, 2006, http://www.washingtonpost.com/.

501. Joshua Holland, "Groundhog Day in Iraq," *AlterNet*, May 16, 2006, http://www.alternet.org/story/36032/.

502. Quoted in Kurtz, "A Turning Point in Iraq." Read also the view of Lt. Col. Patrick Donahoe as expressed in Jeffrey Gettleman, "Iraqi Divide, Echoes of Bosnia for US Troops," *New York Times*, April 16, 2006, http://www.nytimes.com/2006/04/16/world/middleeast/16peace keeping.html.

503. Editorial, "Now He Tells Us," *Los Angeles Times*, March 8, 2006, http://www.latimes.com/.

504. Eugene Robinson, "Counting the Iraqi Dead," The *Washington Post* (13 October 2006), A29.

505. Jon Wiener, "Iraqi Death Toll: Why the UN Can't Count," *AlterNet* (17 January 2007), http://www.alternet.org/story/46872.

506. Sabrina Tavernise, "Mixed Section of Iraqis Sees Hope Dashed," *New York Times*, March 1, 2006, http://www.nytimes.com/2006/03/01/international/middleeast/01neighborhood.html. See also Gettleman, "Iraqi Divide."

507. The *Los Angeles Times*, Editorial: "Shunning Iraq's Refugees," The *Los Angeles Times* (17 January 2007); Christian Caryl, "What About the Iraqis?" The *New York Review of Books* 54, No. 1 (11 January 2007).

508. Christian Caryl, "The Next Jihadists: Iraqis Lost Children," MSNBC. COM: *Newsweek* (22 January 2007), msnbc.msn.com/id/16610767/site/newsweek/print/1/displamode/1098.

509. Gettleman, "Iraqi Divide."

510. Loch K. Johnson, *Seven Sins of American Foreign Policy* (New York: Pearson-Longman, 2006), 307.

511. See "Seven Questions: What Next for Iraq?" *Foreign Policy*, March 10, 2006, http://www.foreignpolicy.com/story/cms.php?story_id=3412&print=1.

512. R. Jeffrey Smith, "Fired Officer Believed CIA Lied to Congress," *Washington Post*, May 14, 2006, A01, http://www.washingtonpost.com/.

513. Johnson, *Seven Sins of American Foreign Policy*, 250.

514. Joshua Holland, "Chaos Accomplished," *AlterNet*, March 20, 2006, http://www.alternet.org/story/33768/.

515. Johnson, *Seven Sins of American Foreign Policy*, 250.

516. Marc Santora and Bill Carter, "Iraq Becomes the Deadliest of Modern Wars for Journalists," *New York Times*, May 30, 2006, http://www.nytimes.com/2006/05/30/world/middleeast/30embed.html.

517. Ibid.

518. Shanker Vedantam, "Veterans Report Mental Distress," *Washington Post*, March 1, 2006, A01; Sally Satel, "For Some, the War Won't End," *New York Times*, March 1, 2006, http://www.nytimes.com/2006/03/01/opinion/01satel.html.

519. Quoted in Johnson, *Seven Sins of American Foreign Policy*, 307.

520. Jim VandeHei, "Old Forecasts Come to Haunt Bush: Erosion in Confidence Will Be Hard to Reverse, Say Pollsters, Strategists," *Washington Post*, March 21, 2006, A14.

521. Lt. Gen. William E. Odom, "Cut and Run? You Bet: Why America Must Get out of Iraq Now," *Foreign Policy*, May–June 2006, 61.

522. H.D.S. Greenway, "Iraq May Already Be Lost to Us," *Boston Globe*, May 16, 2006, http://www.boston.com/.

523. Joseph R. Biden, "A Plan to Hold Iraq Together," *Washington Post*, August 24, 2006; Senator Biden, e-mail to the author, August 24, 2006.
524. Greenway, "Iraq May Already Be Lost to Us."
525. Stephen Biddle, "Seeing Baghdad, Thinking Saigon," *Foreign Affairs* 85, no. 2 (March–April 2006): 2–3.
526. Lawrence D. Freedman, "Writing of Wrongs: Was the War in Iraq Doomed from the Start?" *Foreign Affairs* 85, no. 1 (January–February 2006): 129.
527. Hassan M. Fattah, "Democracy in the Arab World, a US Goal, Falters," *New York Times*, April 10, 2006, http://www.nytimes.com/2006/04/10/world/middleeast/10democracy.html/.
528. Fattah, "Democracy in the Arab World."
529. Michael Slackman, "Rice Speaks Softly in Egypt, Avoiding Democracy Push," The *New York Times* (16 January 2007).
530. Richard N. Haass, "Haass: On Balance, Iraq War's Impact on US Foreign Policy Clearly Negative,'" interview by Bernard Gwertzman, March 14, 2006, http://www.cfr.org/publication/10132/.
531. Anthony Cordesman, "Iraq: After Three Years of War, Results Are Disastrous," interview by Bernard Gwertzman, *New York Times*, March 24, 2006, http://www.nytimes.com/cfr/international/slot2_032406.html.
532. Lawrence D. Freedman, "Writing of Wrongs," 134.
533. David Stout, "Bush and Former Cabinet Members Discuss Topic No. 1," *New York Times*, January 5, 2006, http://www.nytimes.com/2006/01/05/politics/05cnd-prexy.html.
534. Richard A. Clarke, *Against All Enemies* (New York: Free Press, 2004), 243.
535. Graham with Nussbaum, *Intelligence Matters*, 183. David E. Sanger, "Book Says Bush Ignored Urgent Warnings on Iraq," The *New York Times* (29 September 2006).
536. Pillar, "Intelligence, Policy, and the War in Iraq," 25.
537. Jonathan Rauch, "Comment: Unwinding Bush, How Long Will It Take to Fix His Mistakes?" *Atlantic* 298, no. 3 (October 2006): 28. See also James P. Rubin, "'Stumbling into War," *Foreign Affairs* 82, no. 5 (September– October 2003): 46–66.
538. Starr, "A Rendezvous with Failure," 3.
539. Nikolas Gvosdev and Ray Taketh, "America's Shrinking Global Prestige," The *Boston Globe*, Editorial (30 November 2006).
540. Abramowitz and Baker, "Embattled, Bush Held to Plan to Salvage Iraq," The *Washington Post* (21 January 2007), A01.
541. Office of the Press Secretary, "Press Briefing by Stephen Hadley" (2 February 2007).

542. For details see: "Transcript of President Bush's Address to the Nation of US Policy in Iraq," The *New York Times* (11 January 2007).

543. E.J. Dionne, "The Antiwar Rallying Point," *The Washington Post* (20 February 2007), A13; Jonathan Weisman and Shailagh Murray, "Pelosi Backs War Funds Only With Conditions," *The Washington Post* (16 February 2007), A01.

544. Stanley Hoffmann with Frederic Bozo, *Gulliver Unbound: America's Imperial Temptation and the War in Iraq* (Lanham, MD: Rowan & Littlefield, 2004), 114-115.

Chapter 11

545. Loch K. Johnson, *Seven Sins of American Foreign Policy* (New York: Pearso–Longman, 2006), 280.

546. Senator Jesse Helms opposed the Jimmy Carter policy on Rhodesia (now Zimbabwe) in the 1970s on ideological grounds and held up trade bills offering concessions to Caribbean countries until he secured greater protection for North Carolina textiles. Because of the opposition of Democrats beholden to labor unions, the Bill Clinton administration failed to obtain fast-track legislation to negotiate trade agreement with Latin American and Caribbean states.

547. Richard N. Gardner, "The One Percent Solution: Shirking the Cost of World Leadership," *Foreign Affairs* 79, no. 4 (July–August 2000): 3.

548. Johnson, *Seven Sins of American Foreign Policy*, 121–3.

549. Johnson, *Seven Sins of American Foreign Policy*, 121.

550. Edward Said, "Who's In Charge? A Tiny, Unelected Group, Backed by Powerful Unrepresentative Interests," *CounterPunch*, March 8, 2003, http:// www.counterpunch.org/said03082003.html.

551. Johnson, *Seven Sins of American Foreign Policy*, 281.

552. Quoted in Johnson, *Seven Sins of American Foreign Policy*, 7.

553. H.D.S. Greenway, "Iraq May Already Be Lost to Us," *Boston Globe,* May 16, 2006, http://www.boston.com/.

554. Matthew Yglesias, "$1.27 Trillion: The Price Is Wrong," *American Prospect*, July–August 2006, 28–32.

555. Joshua Holland, "Groundhog Day in Iraq," *AlterNet*, May 15, 2006, http://www.alternet.org/story/36032/.

556. Stephen R. Weissman, *A Culture of Deference: Congress's Failure of Leadership in Foreign Policy* (New York: Basic Books, 1995), 17–32.

557. Ibid., 18.

558. Rashid Khalidi, *Resurrecting Empire: Western Footprints and America's Perilous Path in the Middle East* (Boston: Beacon Press, 2005), vii.

559. Julia E. Sweig, "Why They Hate Us," *Los Angeles Times*, August 15, 2006, http://www.latimes.com/.
560. David S. Broder, "Fixing a Broken Congress," *Washington Post*, September 3, 2006, B07, http://www.washingtonpost.com/.

Index